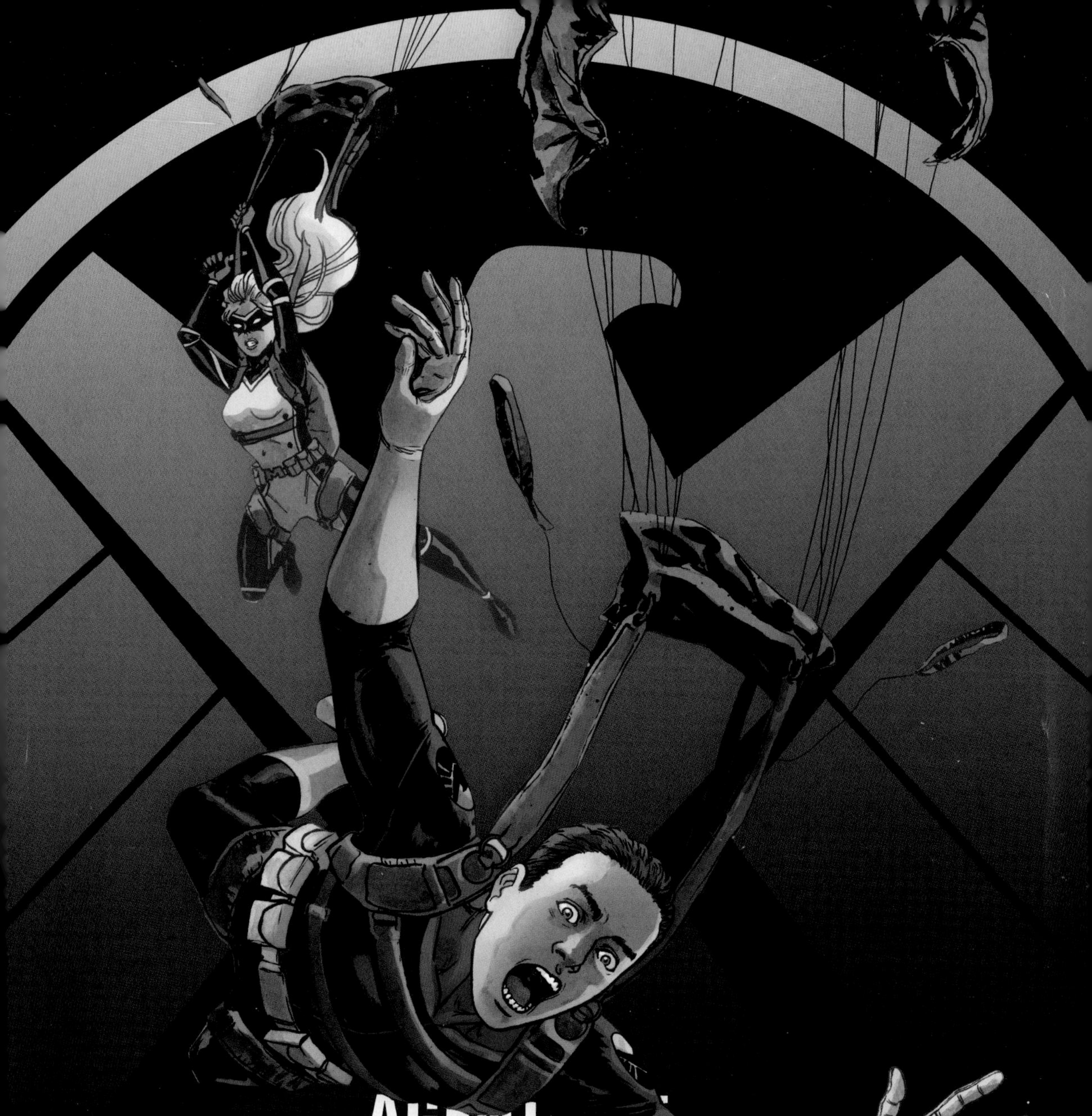

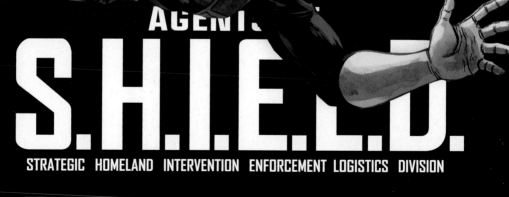

AGENTS OF S.H.I.E.L.D.

STRATEGIC HOMELAND INTERVENTION ENFORCEMENT LOGISTICS DIVISION

THE COULSON PROTOCOLS

AGENTS OF S.H.I.E.L.D. VOL. 1: THE COULSON PROTOCOLS. Contains material originally published in magazine form as AGENTS OF S.H.I.E.L.D. #1-6 and ALL-NEW, ALL-DIFFERENT POINT ONE #1. First printing 2016. ISBN# 978-0-7851-9628-0. Published by MARVEL WORLDWIDE, INC., a subsidiary of MARVEL ENTERTAINMENT, LLC. OFFICE OF PUBLICATION: 135 West 50th Street, New York, NY 10020. Copyright © 2016 MARVEL No similarity between any of the names, characters, persons, and/or institutions in this magazine with those of any living or dead person or institution is intended, and any such similarity which may exist is purely coincidental. Printed in the U.S.A. ALAN FINE, President, Marvel Entertainment; DAN BUCKLEY, President, TV, Publishing & Brand Management; JOE QUESADA, Chief Creative Officer; TOM BREVOORT, SVP of Publishing; DAVID BOGART, SVP of Business Affairs & Operations, Publishing & Partnership; C.B. CEBULSKI, VP of Brand Management & Development, Asia; DAVID GABRIEL, SVP of Sales & Marketing, Publishing; JEFF YOUNGQUIST, VP of Production & Special Projects; DAN CARR, Executive Director of Publishing Technology; ALEX MORALES, Director of Publishing Operations; SUSAN CRESPI, Production Manager; STAN LEE, Chairman Emeritus. For information regarding advertising in Marvel Comics or on Marvel.com, please contact Vit DeBellis, Integrated Sales Manager, at vdebellis@marvel.com. For Marvel subscription inquiries, please call 888-511-5480. Manufactured between 5/27/2016 and 7/4/2016 by R.R. DONNELLEY, INC., SALEM, VA, USA.

10 9 8 7 6 5 4 3 2 1

AGENTS OF
S.H.I.E.L.D.

STRATEGIC HOMELAND INTERVENTION ENFORCEMENT LOGISTICS DIVISION

THE COULSON PROTOCOLS

WRITER
MARC GUGGENHEIM

ARTIST
GERMÁN PERALTA

COLOR ARTISTS
RACHELLE ROSENBERG
WITH **CHRIS SOTOMAYOR**
(ALL-NEW, ALL-DIFFERENT POINT 1)

LETTERER
VC's JOE CARAMAGNA

COVER ART
MIKE NORTON & F.C.O. PLASCENCIA

ASSISTANT EDITORS
ALANNA SMITH &
CHRISTINA HARRINGTON

EDITORS
KATIE KUBERT &
JON MOISAN

EXECUTIVE EDITOR
TOM BREVOORT

SPECIAL THANKS TO JEPH LOEB
AND MEGAN THOMAS BRADNER

S.H.I.E.L.D. CREATED BY
STAN LEE & JACK KIRBY

COLLECTION EDITOR
SARAH BRUNSTAD

ASSOCIATE MANAGING EDITOR
ALEX STARBUCK

EDITORS, SPECIAL PROJECTS
MARK D. BEAZLEY &
JENNIFER GRÜNWALD

VP, PRODUCTION & SPECIAL PROJECTS
JEFF YOUNGQUIST

SVP PRINT, SALES & MARKETING
DAVID GABRIEL

BOOK DESIGNER
ADAM DEL RE

EDITOR IN CHIEF
AXEL ALONSO

CHIEF CREATIVE OFFICER
JOE QUESADA

PUBLISHER
DAN BUCKLEY

EXECUTIVE PRODUCER
ALAN FINE

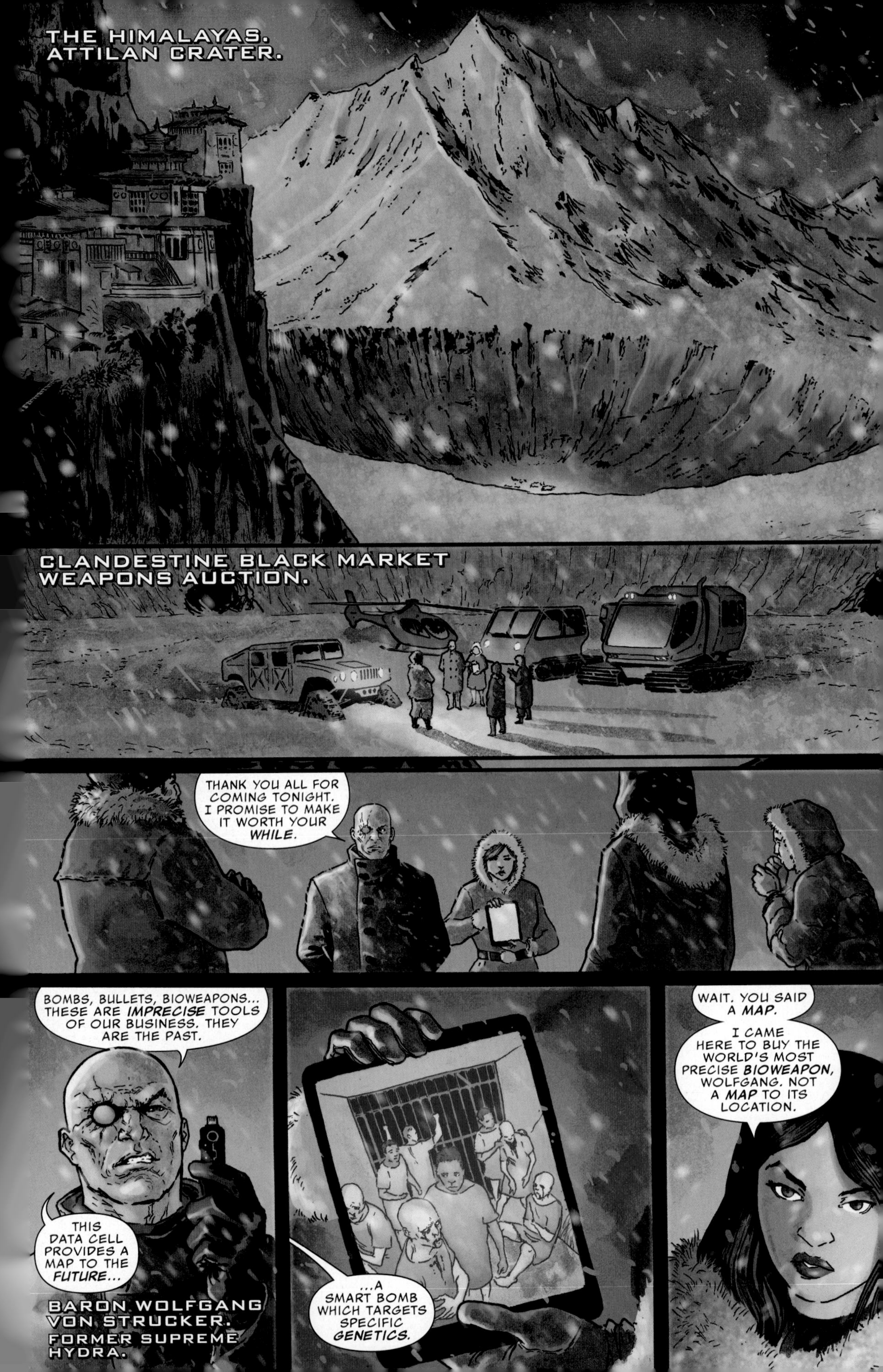
THE HIMALAYAS. ATTILAN CRATER.
CLANDESTINE BLACK MARKET WEAPONS AUCTION.
THANK YOU ALL FOR COMING TONIGHT. I PROMISE TO MAKE IT WORTH YOUR WHILE.
BOMBS, BULLETS, BIOWEAPONS... THESE ARE IMPRECISE TOOLS OF OUR BUSINESS. THEY ARE THE PAST.
THIS DATA CELL PROVIDES A MAP TO THE FUTURE...
BARON WOLFGANG VON STRUCKER.
FORMER SUPREME HYDRA.
...A SMART BOMB WHICH TARGETS SPECIFIC GENETICS.
WAIT. YOU SAID A MAP.
I CAME HERE TO BUY THE WORLD'S MOST PRECISE BIOWEAPON, WOLFGANG. NOT A MAP TO ITS LOCATION.

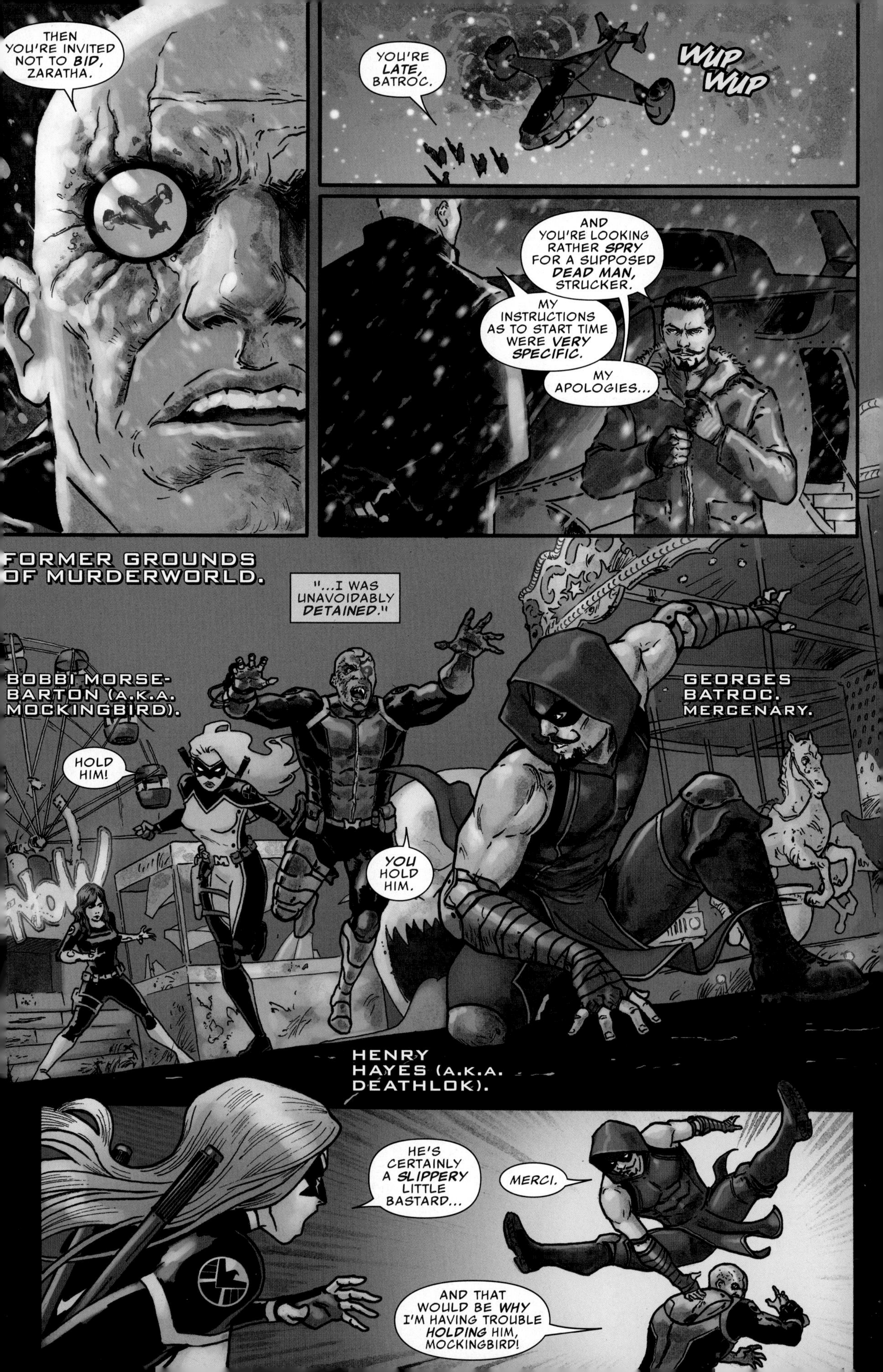
THEN YOU'RE INVITED NOT TO BID, ZARATHA.
YOU'RE LATE, BATROC.
WUP WUP
AND YOU'RE LOOKING RATHER SPRY FOR A SUPPOSED DEAD MAN, STRUCKER.
MY INSTRUCTIONS AS TO START TIME WERE VERY SPECIFIC.
MY APOLOGIES...
FORMER GROUNDS OF MURDERWORLD.
"...I WAS UNAVOIDABLY DETAINED."
BOBBI MORSE-BARTON (A.K.A. MOCKINGBIRD).
GEORGES BATROC. MERCENARY.
HOLD HIM!
YOU HOLD HIM.
HENRY HAYES (A.K.A. DEATHLOK).
HE'S CERTAINLY A SLIPPERY LITTLE BASTARD...
MERCI.
AND THAT WOULD BE WHY I'M HAVING TROUBLE HOLDING HIM, MOCKINGBIRD!

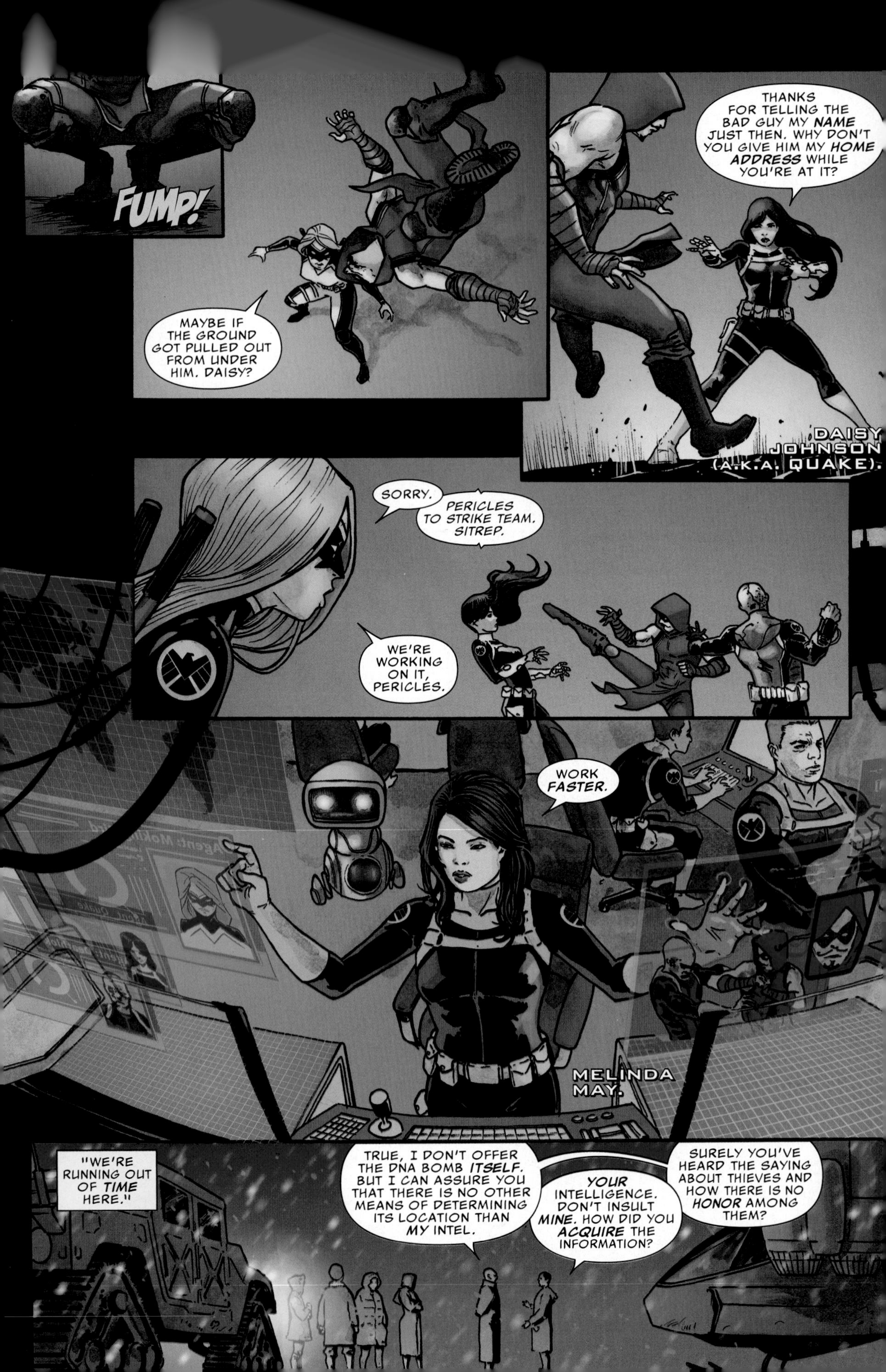
FUMP!
MAYBE IF THE GROUND GOT PULLED OUT FROM UNDER HIM. DAISY?
THANKS FOR TELLING THE BAD GUY MY NAME JUST THEN. WHY DON'T YOU GIVE HIM MY HOME ADDRESS WHILE YOU'RE AT IT?
DAISY JOHNSON (A.K.A. QUAKE).
SORRY.
PERICLES TO STRIKE TEAM. SITREP.
WE'RE WORKING ON IT, PERICLES.
WORK FASTER.
MELINDA MAY.
"WE'RE RUNNING OUT OF TIME HERE."
TRUE, I DON'T OFFER THE DNA BOMB ITSELF. BUT I CAN ASSURE YOU THAT THERE IS NO OTHER MEANS OF DETERMINING ITS LOCATION THAN MY INTEL.
YOUR INTELLIGENCE. DON'T INSULT MINE. HOW DID YOU ACQUIRE THE INFORMATION?
SURELY YOU'VE HEARD THE SAYING ABOUT THIEVES AND HOW THERE IS NO HONOR AMONG THEM?

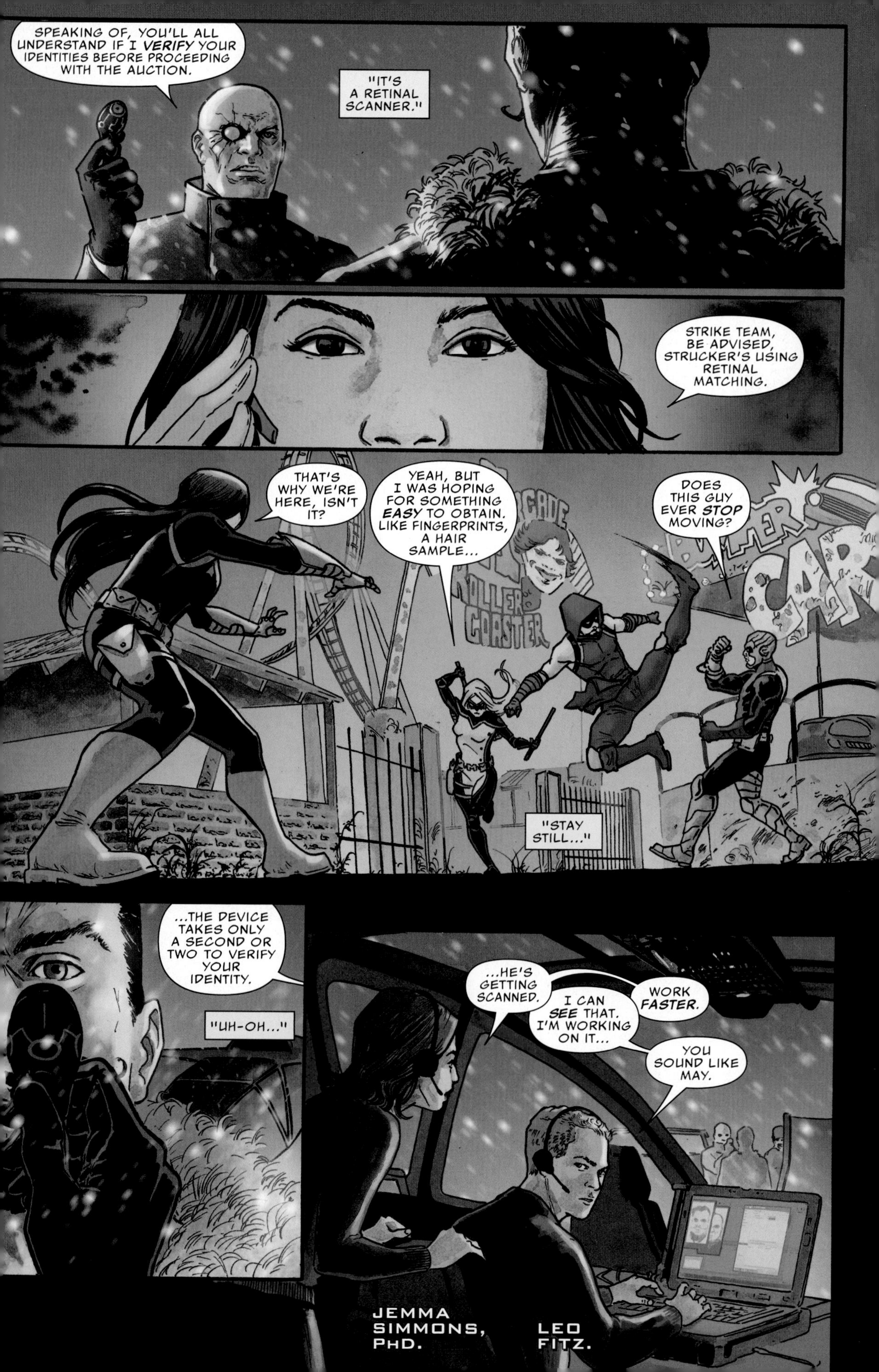
SPEAKING OF, YOU'LL ALL UNDERSTAND IF I VERIFY YOUR IDENTITIES BEFORE PROCEEDING WITH THE AUCTION.
"IT'S A RETINAL SCANNER."
STRIKE TEAM, BE ADVISED, STRUCKER'S USING RETINAL MATCHING.
THAT'S WHY WE'RE HERE, ISN'T IT?
YEAH, BUT I WAS HOPING FOR SOMETHING EASY TO OBTAIN. LIKE FINGERPRINTS, A HAIR SAMPLE...
DOES THIS GUY EVER STOP MOVING?
ROLLER COASTER
"STAY STILL..."
...THE DEVICE TAKES ONLY A SECOND OR TWO TO VERIFY YOUR IDENTITY.
"UH-OH..."
...HE'S GETTING SCANNED.
WORK FASTER.
I CAN SEE THAT. I'M WORKING ON IT...
YOU SOUND LIKE MAY.
JEMMA SIMMONS, PHD.
LEO FITZ.

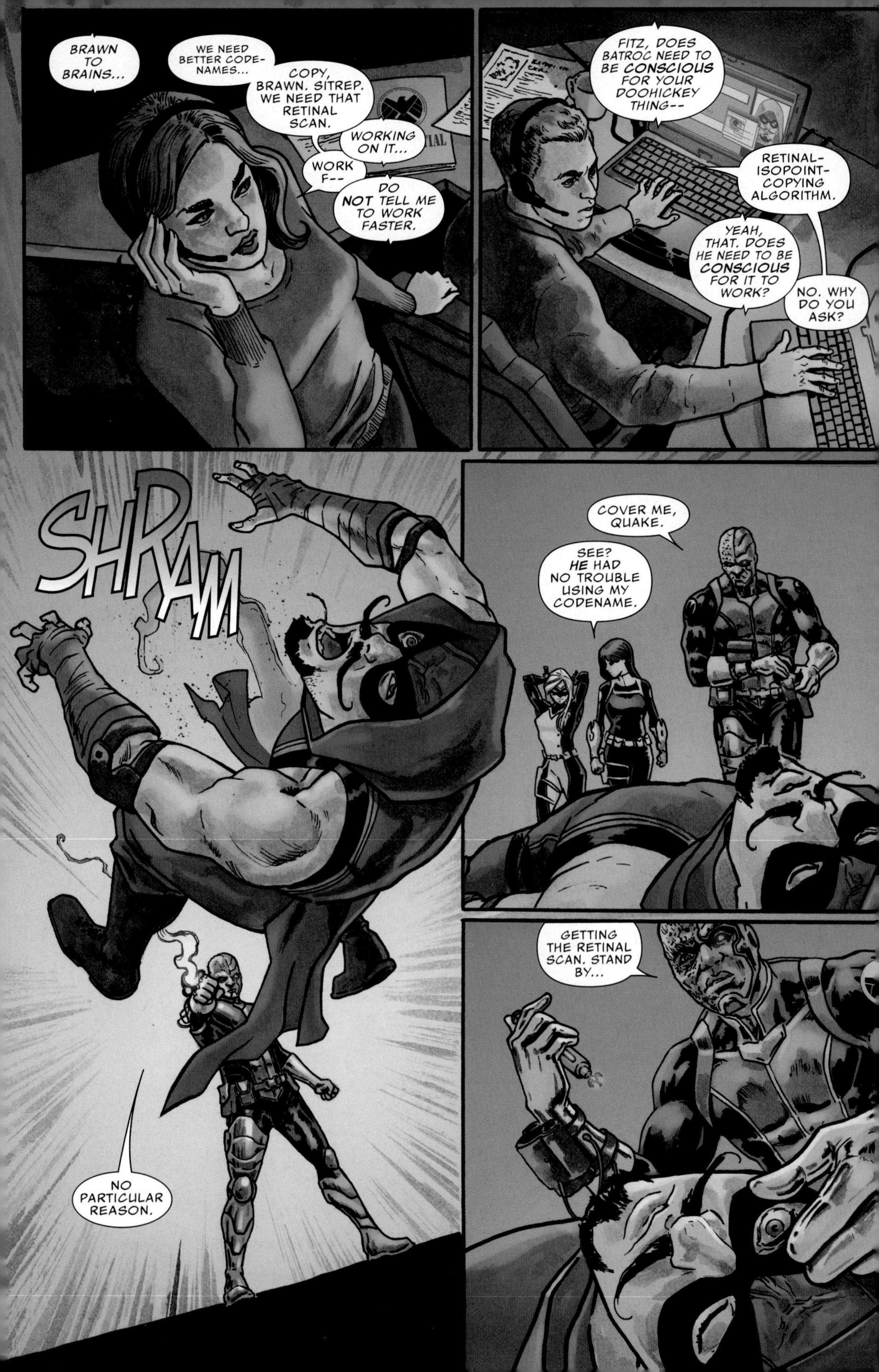
BRAWN TO BRAINS...
WE NEED BETTER CODE-NAMES...
COPY, BRAWN. SITREP. WE NEED THAT RETINAL SCAN.
WORKING ON IT...
WORK F--
DO NOT TELL ME TO WORK FASTER.
FITZ, DOES BATROC NEED TO BE CONSCIOUS FOR YOUR DOOHICKEY THING--
RETINAL-ISOPOINT-COPYING ALGORITHM.
YEAH, THAT. DOES HE NEED TO BE CONSCIOUS FOR IT TO WORK?
NO. WHY DO YOU ASK?
SHRAM
NO PARTICULAR REASON.
COVER ME, QUAKE.
SEE? HE HAD NO TROUBLE USING MY CODENAME.
GETTING THE RETINAL SCAN. STAND BY...

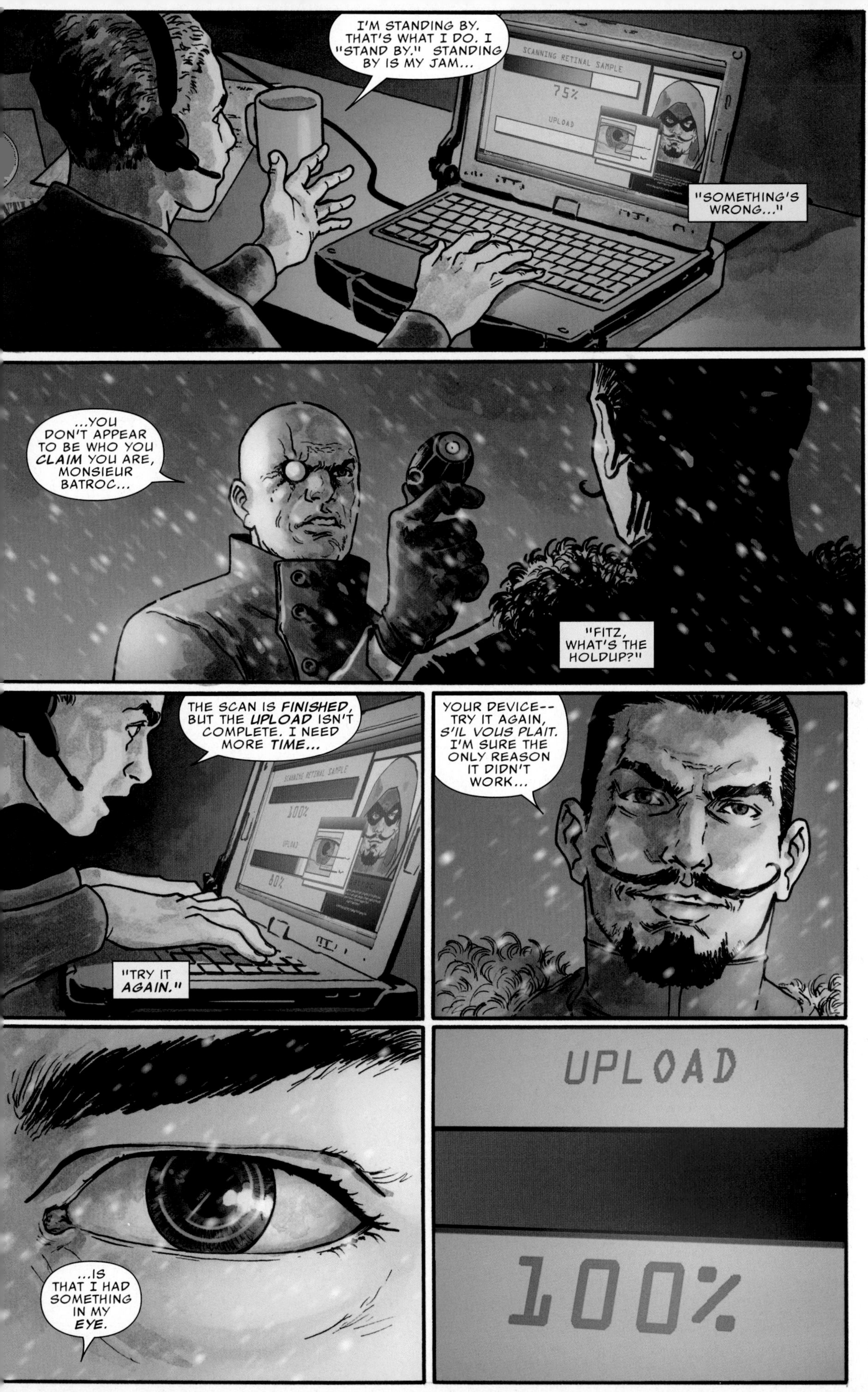

SCANNING RETINAL SAMPLE
75%
UPLOAD
I'M STANDING BY. THAT'S WHAT I DO. I "STAND BY." STANDING BY IS MY JAM...
"SOMETHING'S WRONG..."
...YOU DON'T APPEAR TO BE WHO YOU *CLAIM* YOU ARE, MONSIEUR BATROC...
"FITZ, WHAT'S THE HOLDUP?"
THE SCAN IS ***FINISHED***, BUT THE ***UPLOAD*** ISN'T COMPLETE. I NEED MORE ***TIME***...
"TRY IT ***AGAIN***."
YOUR DEVICE--TRY IT AGAIN, *S'IL VOUS PLAIT*. I'M SURE THE ONLY REASON IT DIDN'T WORK...
...IS THAT I HAD SOMETHING IN MY ***EYE***.
UPLOAD
100%

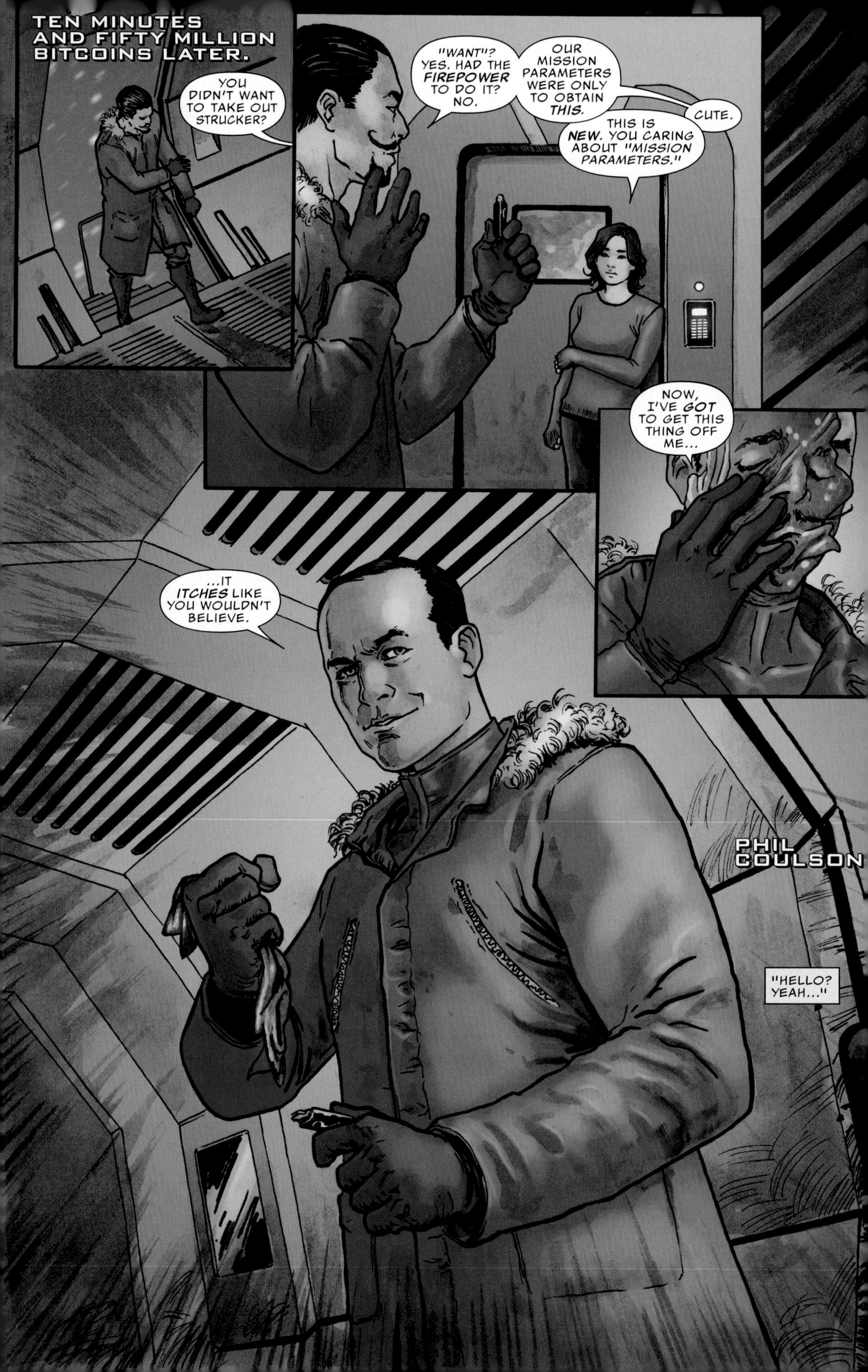

TEN MINUTES AND FIFTY MILLION BITCOINS LATER.
YOU DIDN'T WANT TO TAKE OUT STRUCKER?
"WANT"? YES. HAD THE FIREPOWER TO DO IT? NO.
OUR MISSION PARAMETERS WERE ONLY TO OBTAIN THIS.
CUTE.
THIS IS NEW. YOU CARING ABOUT "MISSION PARAMETERS."
NOW, I'VE GOT TO GET THIS THING OFF ME...
...IT ITCHES LIKE YOU WOULDN'T BELIEVE.
PHIL COULSON
"HELLO? YEAH..."

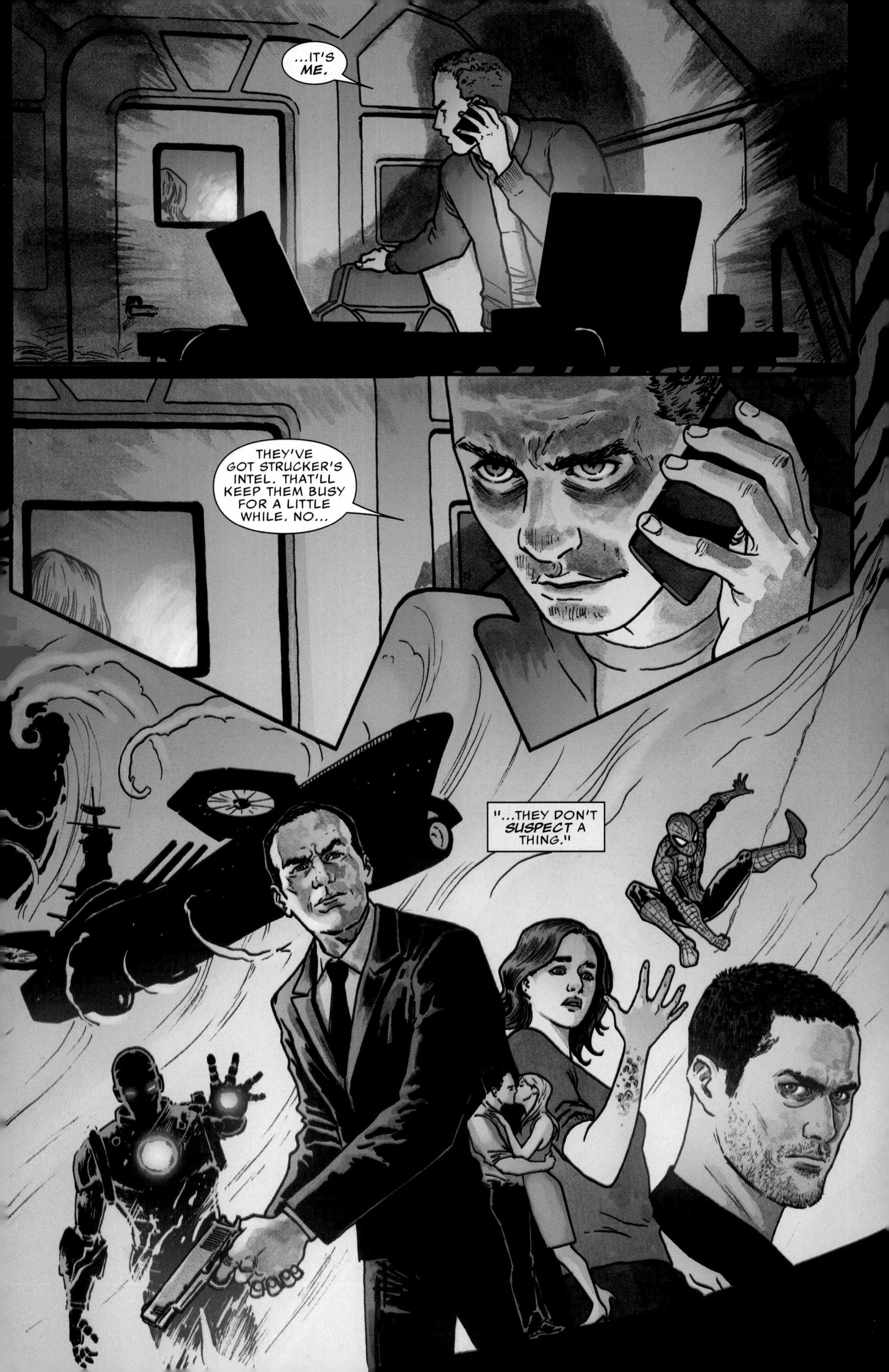
...IT'S ME.
THEY'VE GOT STRUCKER'S INTEL. THAT'LL KEEP THEM BUSY FOR A LITTLE WHILE. NO...
"...THEY DON'T SUSPECT A THING."

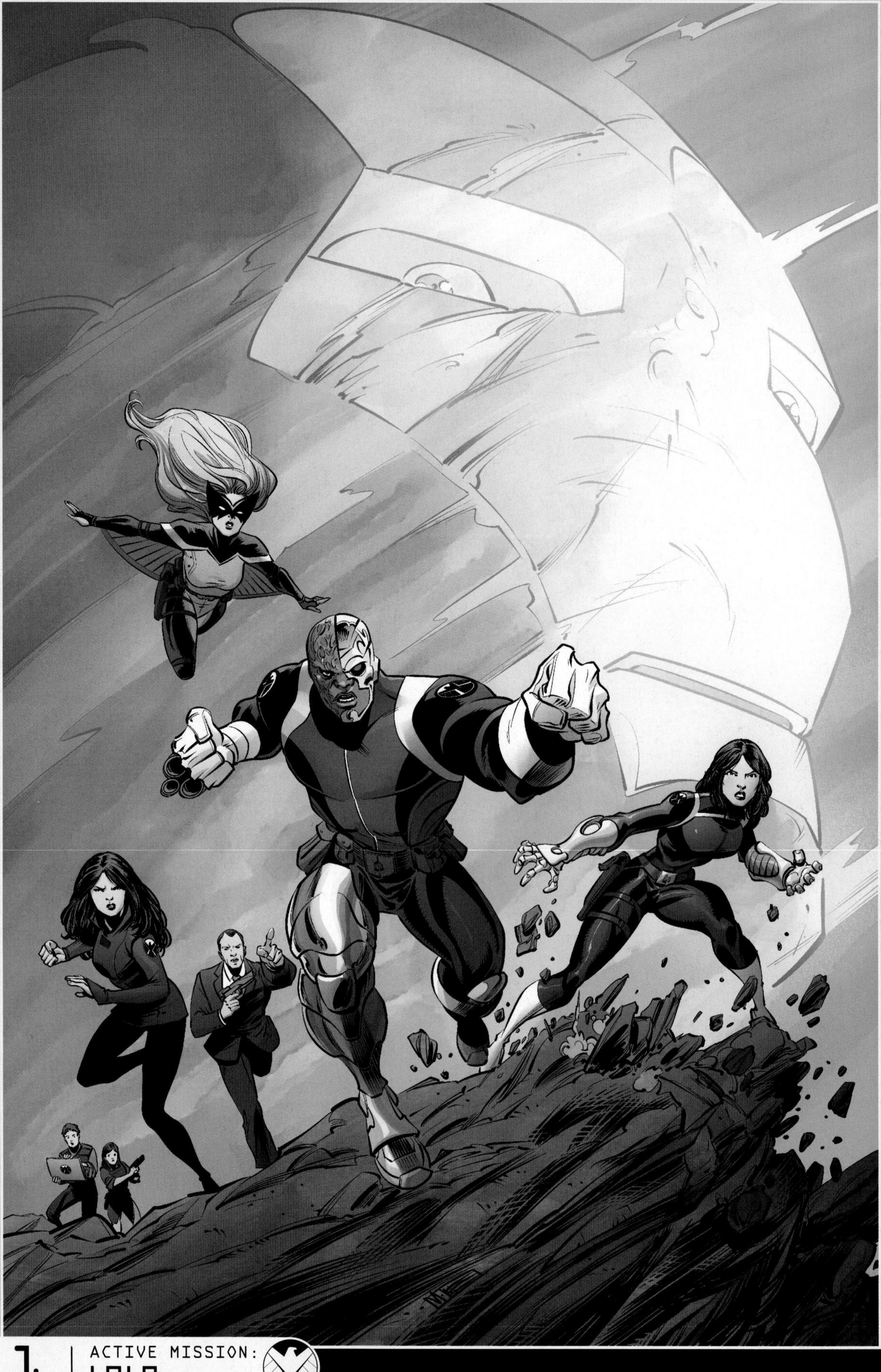

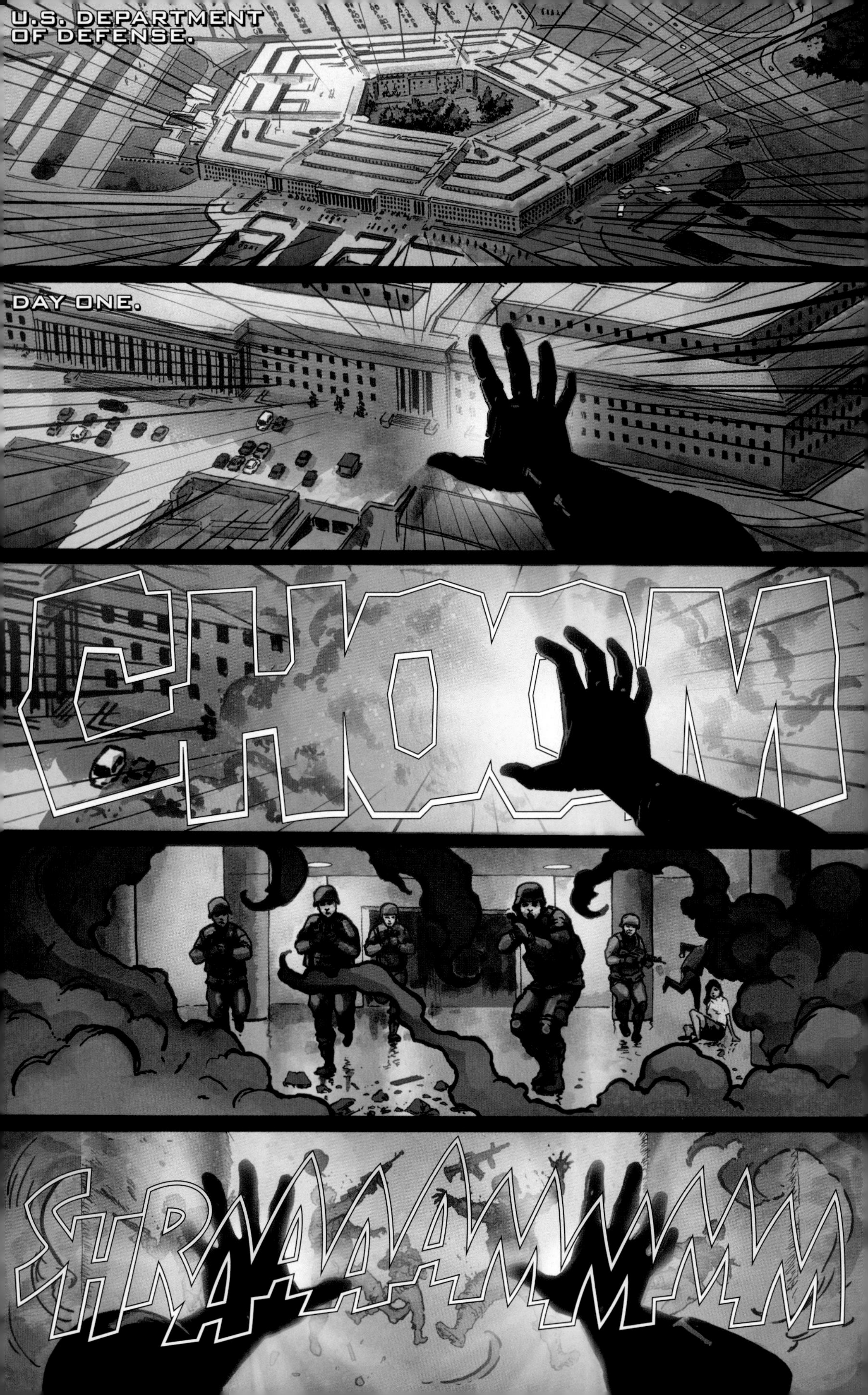
U.S. DEPARTMENT OF DEFENSE.
DAY ONE.
CHOOM
SHRAAAAMMMMM

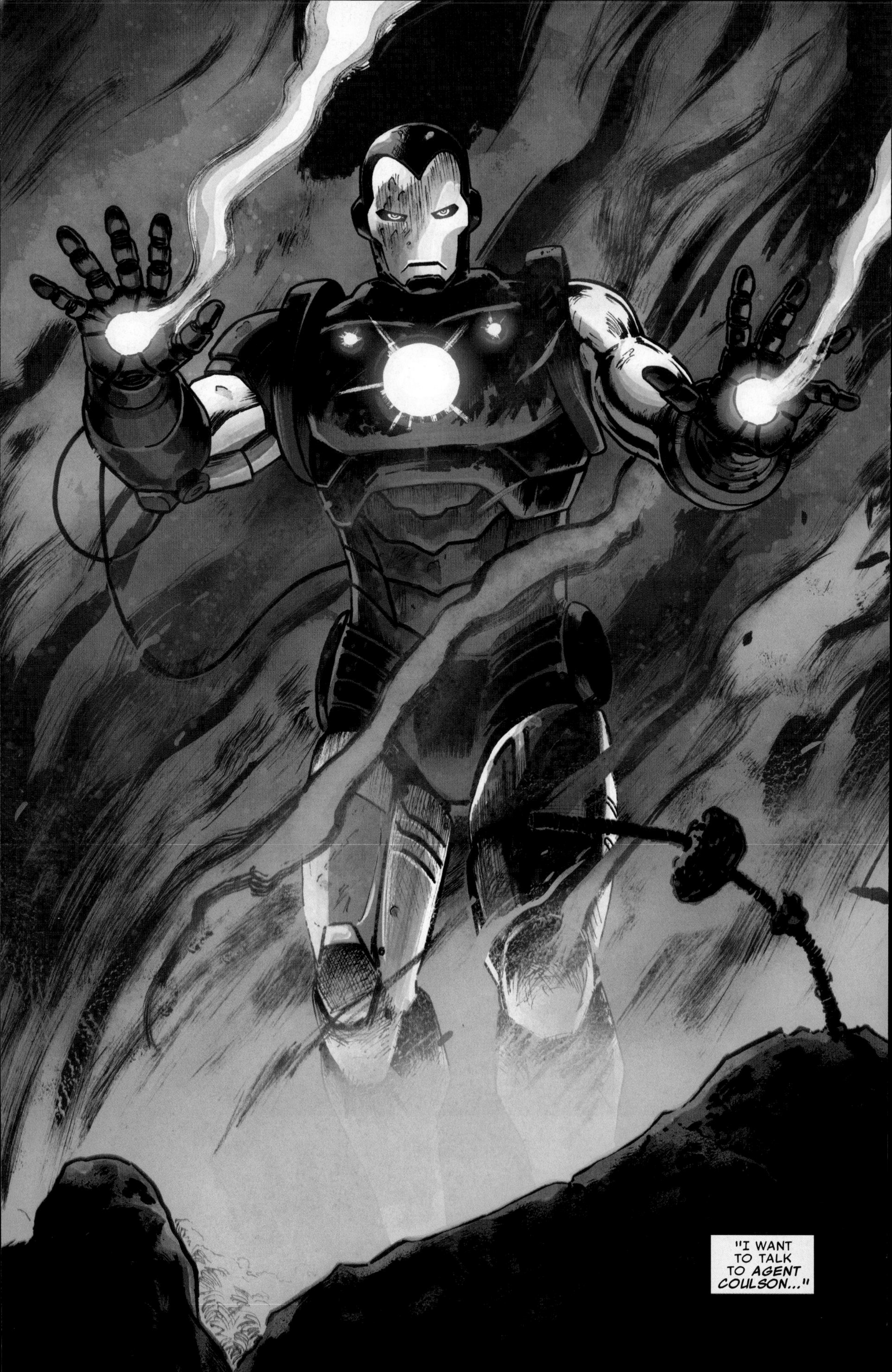
"I WANT TO TALK TO AGENT COULSON..."

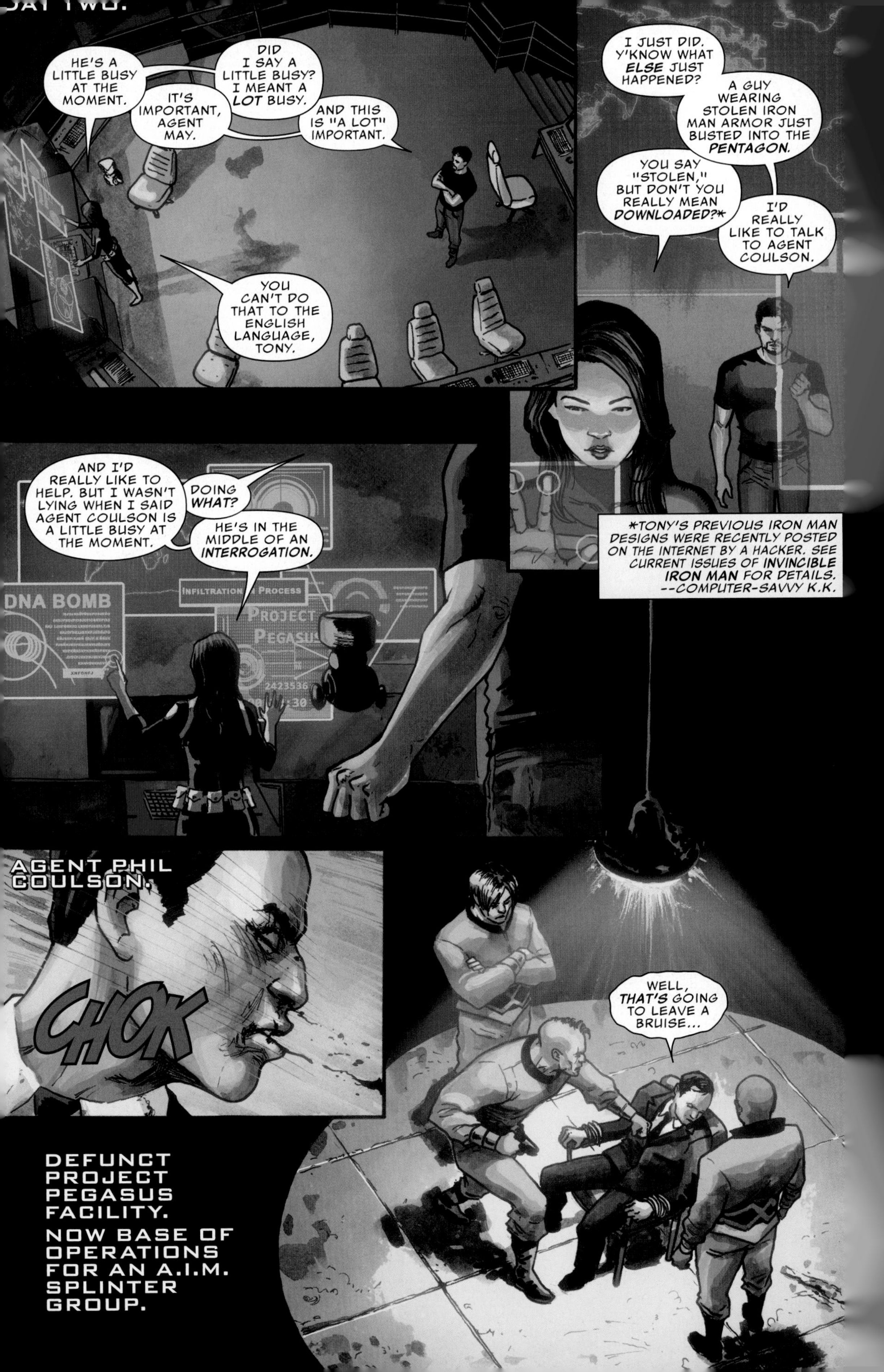
DAY TWO.
HE'S A LITTLE BUSY AT THE MOMENT.
DID I SAY A LITTLE BUSY? I MEANT A LOT BUSY.
IT'S IMPORTANT, AGENT MAY.
AND THIS IS "A LOT" IMPORTANT.
YOU CAN'T DO THAT TO THE ENGLISH LANGUAGE, TONY.
I JUST DID. Y'KNOW WHAT ELSE JUST HAPPENED?
A GUY WEARING STOLEN IRON MAN ARMOR JUST BUSTED INTO THE PENTAGON.
YOU SAY "STOLEN," BUT DON'T YOU REALLY MEAN DOWNLOADED?*
I'D REALLY LIKE TO TALK TO AGENT COULSON.
*TONY'S PREVIOUS IRON MAN DESIGNS WERE RECENTLY POSTED ON THE INTERNET BY A HACKER. SEE CURRENT ISSUES OF INVINCIBLE IRON MAN FOR DETAILS. --COMPUTER-SAVVY K.K.
AND I'D REALLY LIKE TO HELP. BUT I WASN'T LYING WHEN I SAID AGENT COULSON IS A LITTLE BUSY AT THE MOMENT.
DOING WHAT?
HE'S IN THE MIDDLE OF AN INTERROGATION.
DNA BOMB
INFILTRATION IN PROCESS
PROJECT PEGASUS
2423536
AGENT PHIL COULSON.
CHOK
WELL, THAT'S GOING TO LEAVE A BRUISE...
DEFUNCT PROJECT PEGASUS FACILITY.
NOW BASE OF OPERATIONS FOR AN A.I.M. SPLINTER GROUP.

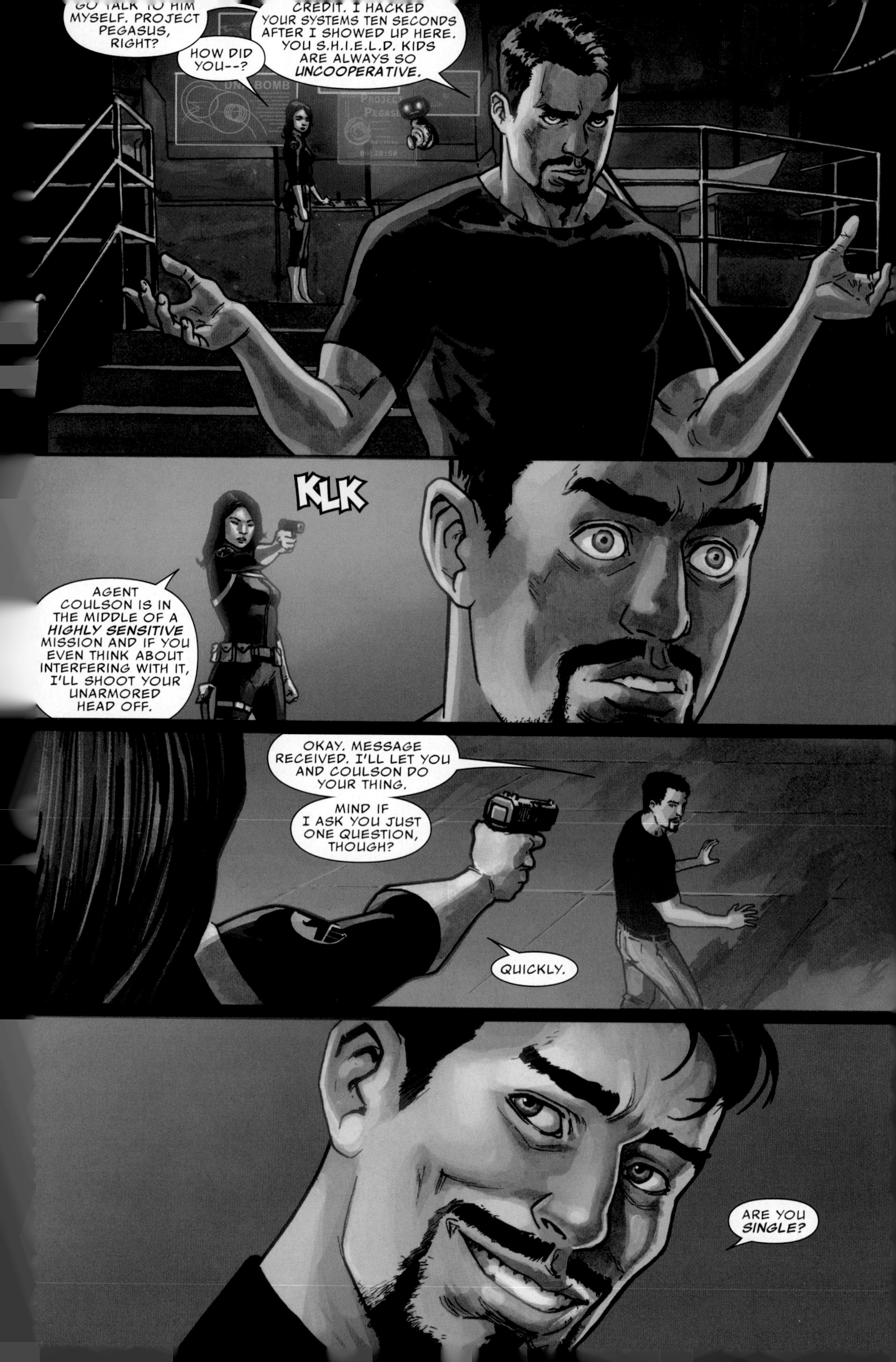
GO TALK TO HIM MYSELF. PROJECT PEGASUS, RIGHT?
HOW DID YOU--?
CREDIT. I HACKED YOUR SYSTEMS TEN SECONDS AFTER I SHOWED UP HERE. YOU S.H.I.E.L.D. KIDS ARE ALWAYS SO UNCOOPERATIVE.
KLK
AGENT COULSON IS IN THE MIDDLE OF A HIGHLY SENSITIVE MISSION AND IF YOU EVEN THINK ABOUT INTERFERING WITH IT, I'LL SHOOT YOUR UNARMORED HEAD OFF.
OKAY. MESSAGE RECEIVED. I'LL LET YOU AND COULSON DO YOUR THING.
MIND IF I ASK YOU JUST ONE QUESTION, THOUGH?
QUICKLY.
ARE YOU SINGLE?

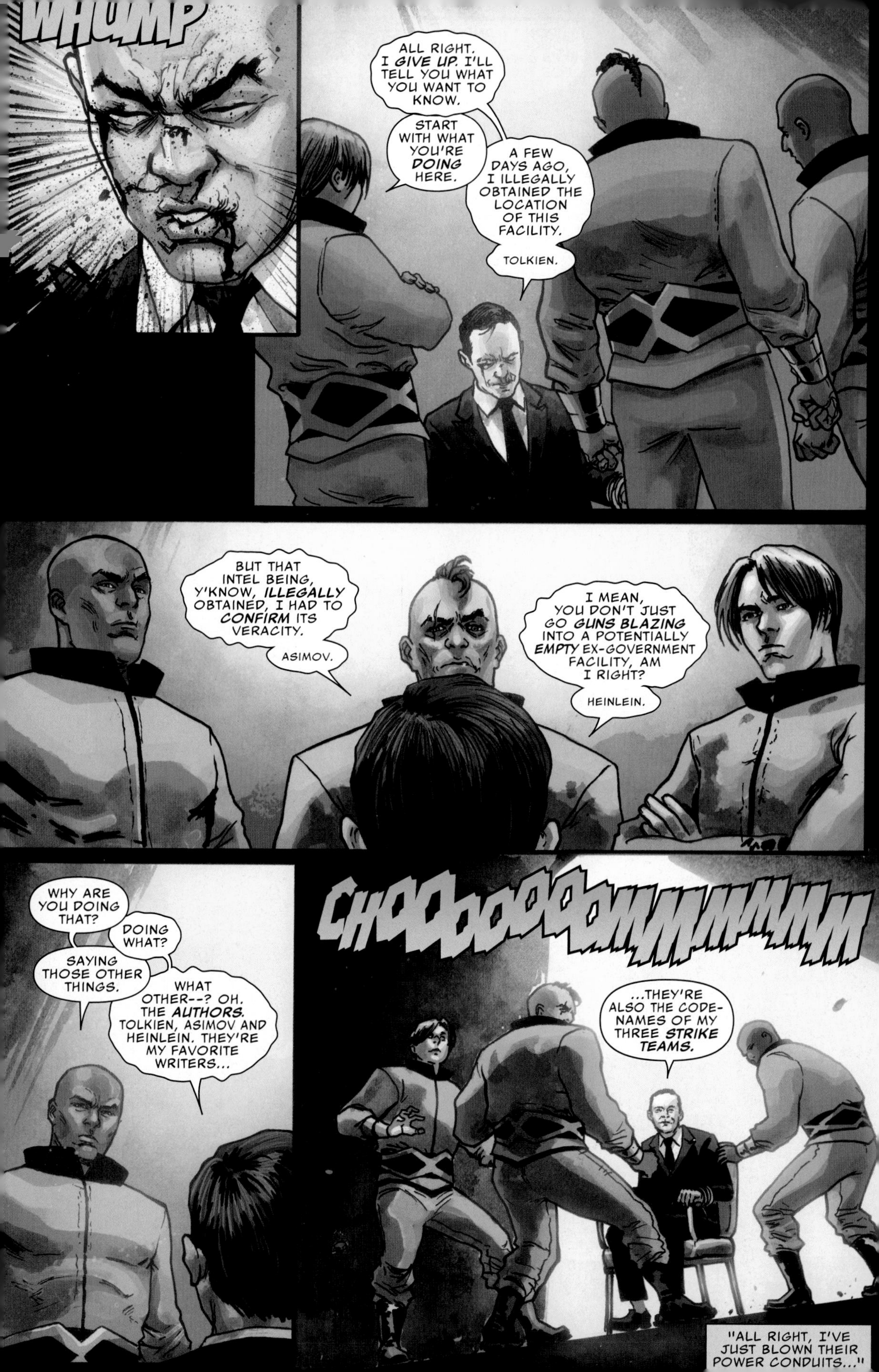
WHUMP
ALL RIGHT. I GIVE UP. I'LL TELL YOU WHAT YOU WANT TO KNOW.
START WITH WHAT YOU'RE DOING HERE.
A FEW DAYS AGO, I ILLEGALLY OBTAINED THE LOCATION OF THIS FACILITY.
TOLKIEN.
BUT THAT INTEL BEING, Y'KNOW, ILLEGALLY OBTAINED, I HAD TO CONFIRM ITS VERACITY.
ASIMOV.
I MEAN, YOU DON'T JUST GO GUNS BLAZING INTO A POTENTIALLY EMPTY EX-GOVERNMENT FACILITY, AM I RIGHT?
HEINLEIN.
WHY ARE YOU DOING THAT?
DOING WHAT?
SAYING THOSE OTHER THINGS.
WHAT OTHER--? OH. THE AUTHORS. TOLKIEN, ASIMOV AND HEINLEIN. THEY'RE MY FAVORITE WRITERS...
CHOOOOOOOMMMMMMMM
...THEY'RE ALSO THE CODE-NAMES OF MY THREE STRIKE TEAMS.
"ALL RIGHT, I'VE JUST BLOWN THEIR POWER CONDUITS..."

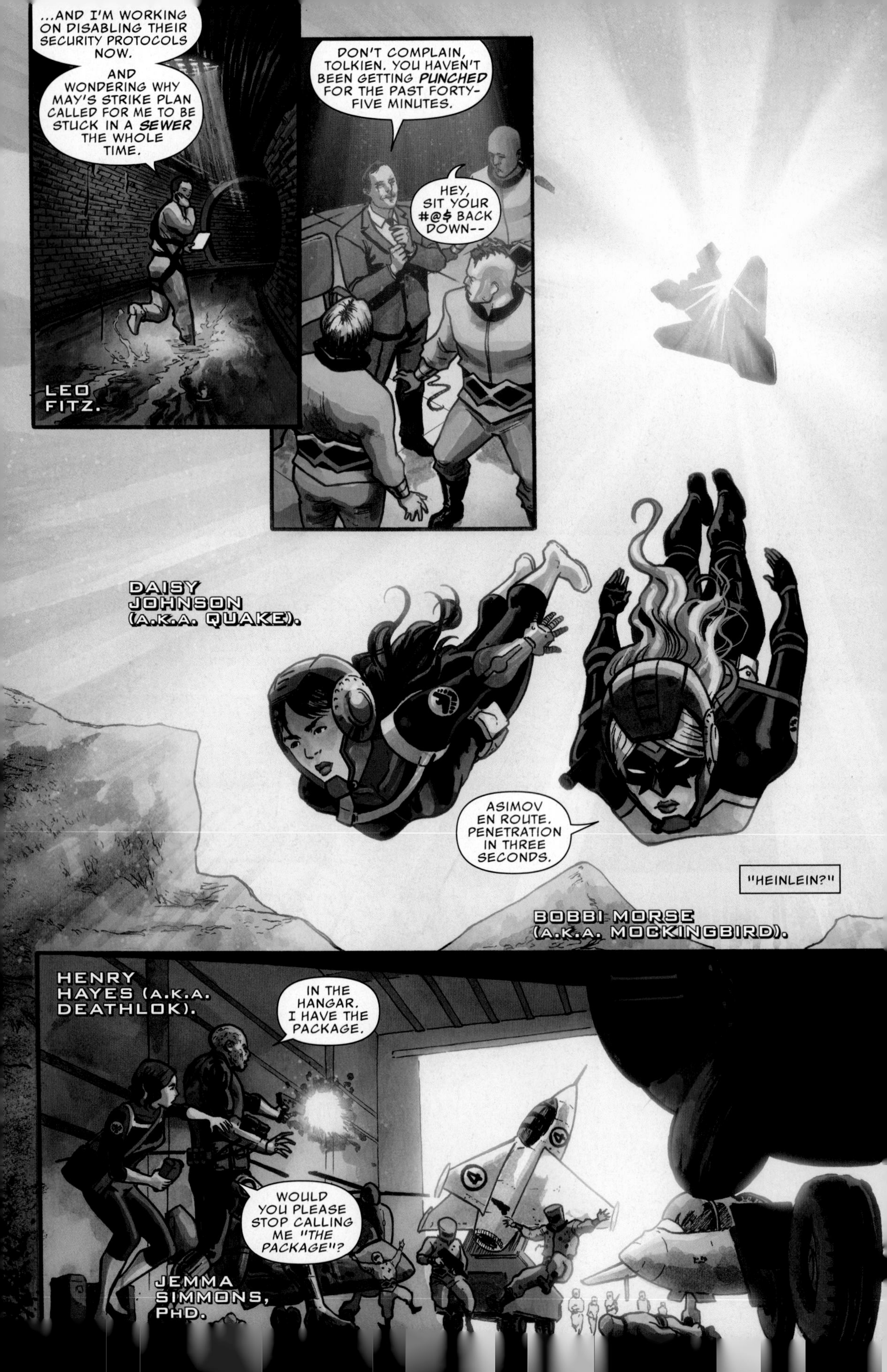
...AND I'M WORKING ON DISABLING THEIR SECURITY PROTOCOLS NOW.
AND WONDERING WHY MAY'S STRIKE PLAN CALLED FOR ME TO BE STUCK IN A SEWER THE WHOLE TIME.
LEO FITZ.
DON'T COMPLAIN, TOLKIEN. YOU HAVEN'T BEEN GETTING PUNCHED FOR THE PAST FORTY-FIVE MINUTES.
HEY, SIT YOUR #@$ BACK DOWN--
DAISY JOHNSON (A.K.A. QUAKE).
ASIMOV EN ROUTE. PENETRATION IN THREE SECONDS.
"HEINLEIN?"
BOBBI MORSE (A.K.A. MOCKINGBIRD).
HENRY HAYES (A.K.A. DEATHLOK).
IN THE HANGAR. I HAVE THE PACKAGE.
WOULD YOU PLEASE STOP CALLING ME "THE PACKAGE"?
JEMMA SIMMONS, PhD.

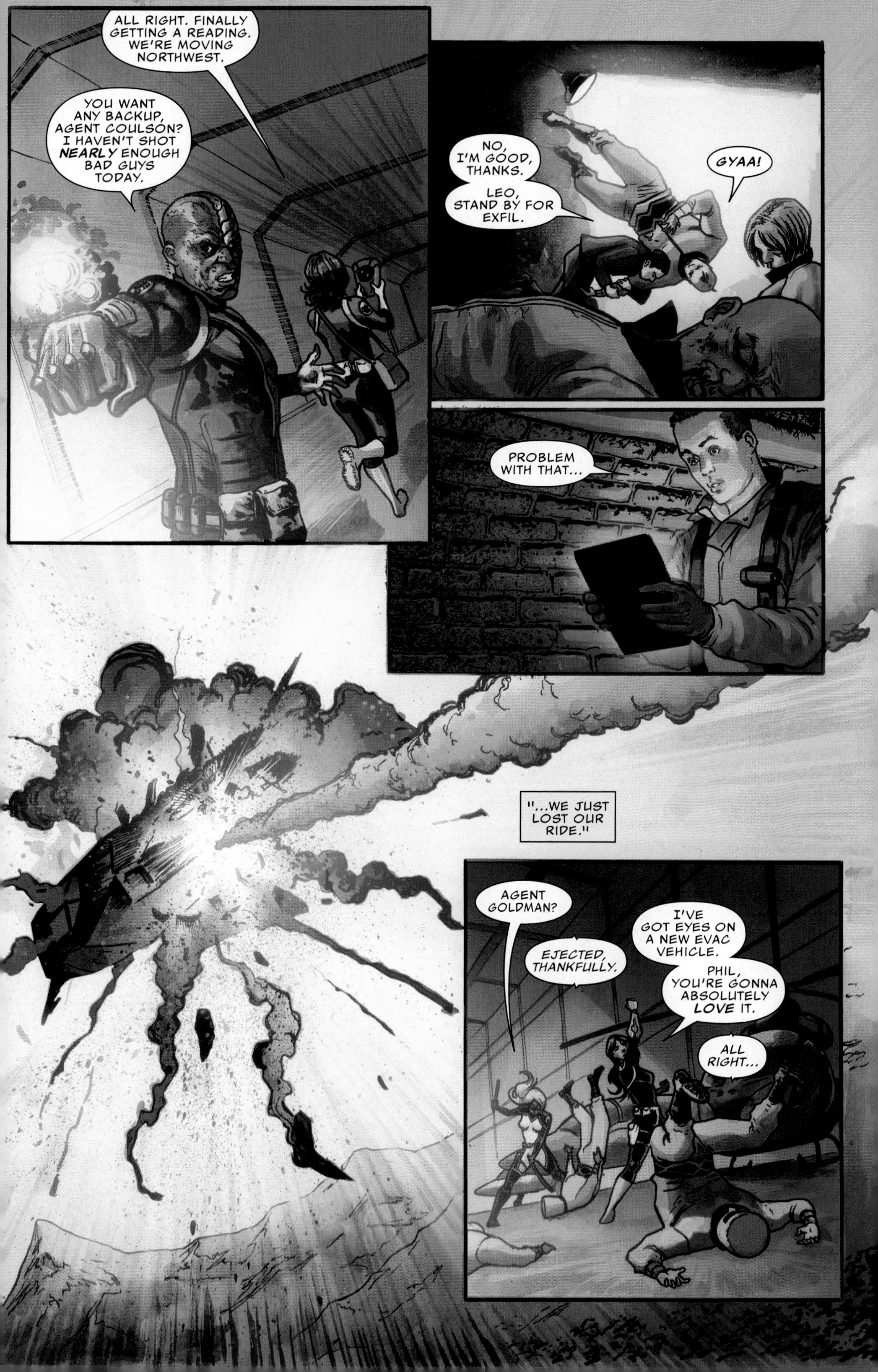
ALL RIGHT. FINALLY GETTING A READING. WE'RE MOVING NORTHWEST.
YOU WANT ANY BACKUP, AGENT COULSON? I HAVEN'T SHOT NEARLY ENOUGH BAD GUYS TODAY.
NO, I'M GOOD, THANKS.
LEO, STAND BY FOR EXFIL.
GYAA!
PROBLEM WITH THAT...
"...WE JUST LOST OUR RIDE."
AGENT GOLDMAN?
EJECTED, THANKFULLY.
I'VE GOT EYES ON A NEW EVAC VEHICLE.
PHIL, YOU'RE GONNA ABSOLUTELY LOVE IT.
ALL RIGHT...

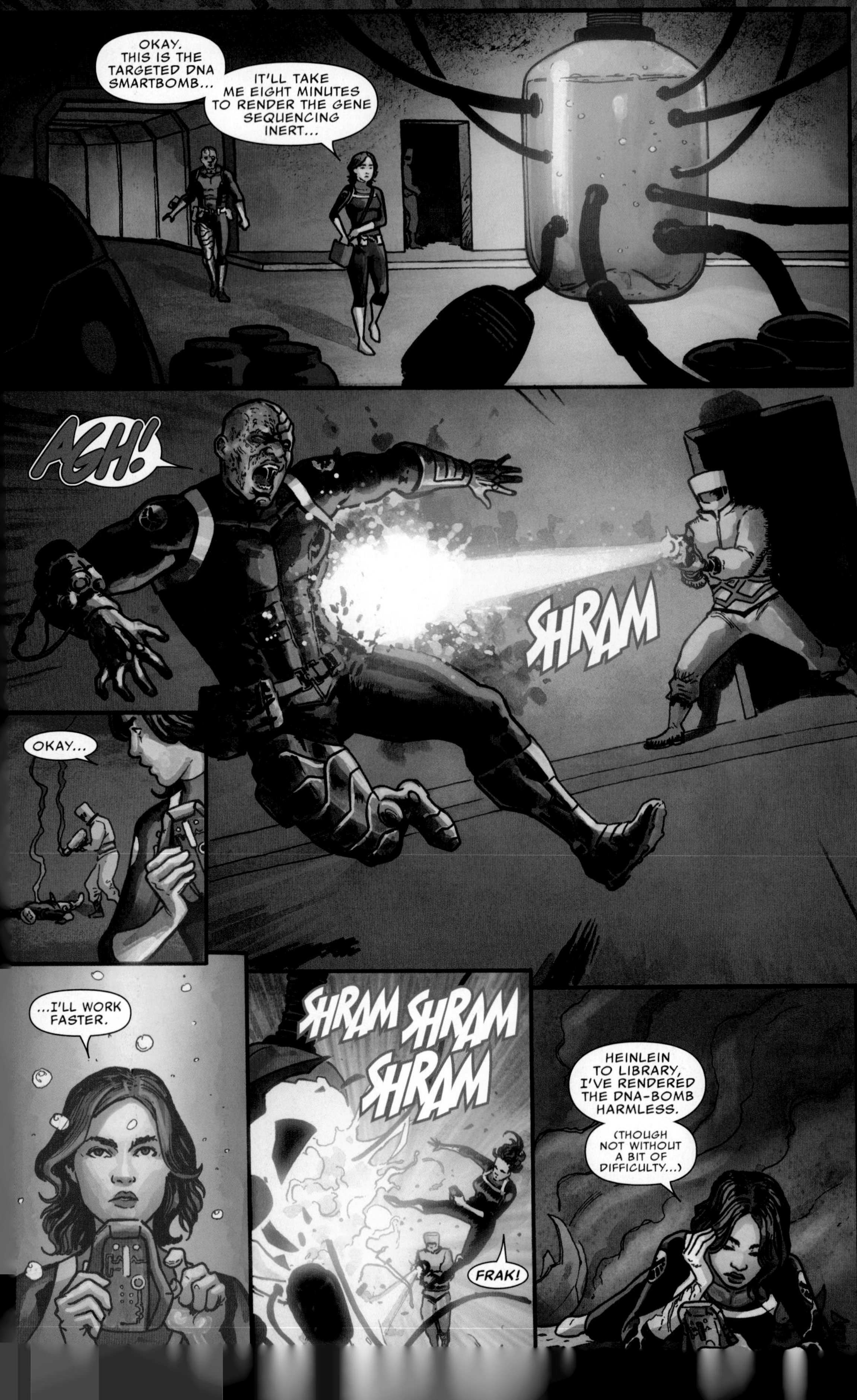

OKAY. THIS IS THE TARGETED DNA SMARTBOMB...
IT'LL TAKE ME EIGHT MINUTES TO RENDER THE GENE SEQUENCING INERT...
AGH!
SHRAM
OKAY...
...I'LL WORK FASTER.
SHRAM SHRAM SHRAM
FRAK!
HEINLEIN TO LIBRARY, I'VE RENDERED THE DNA-BOMB HARMLESS.
(THOUGH NOT WITHOUT A BIT OF DIFFICULTY...)

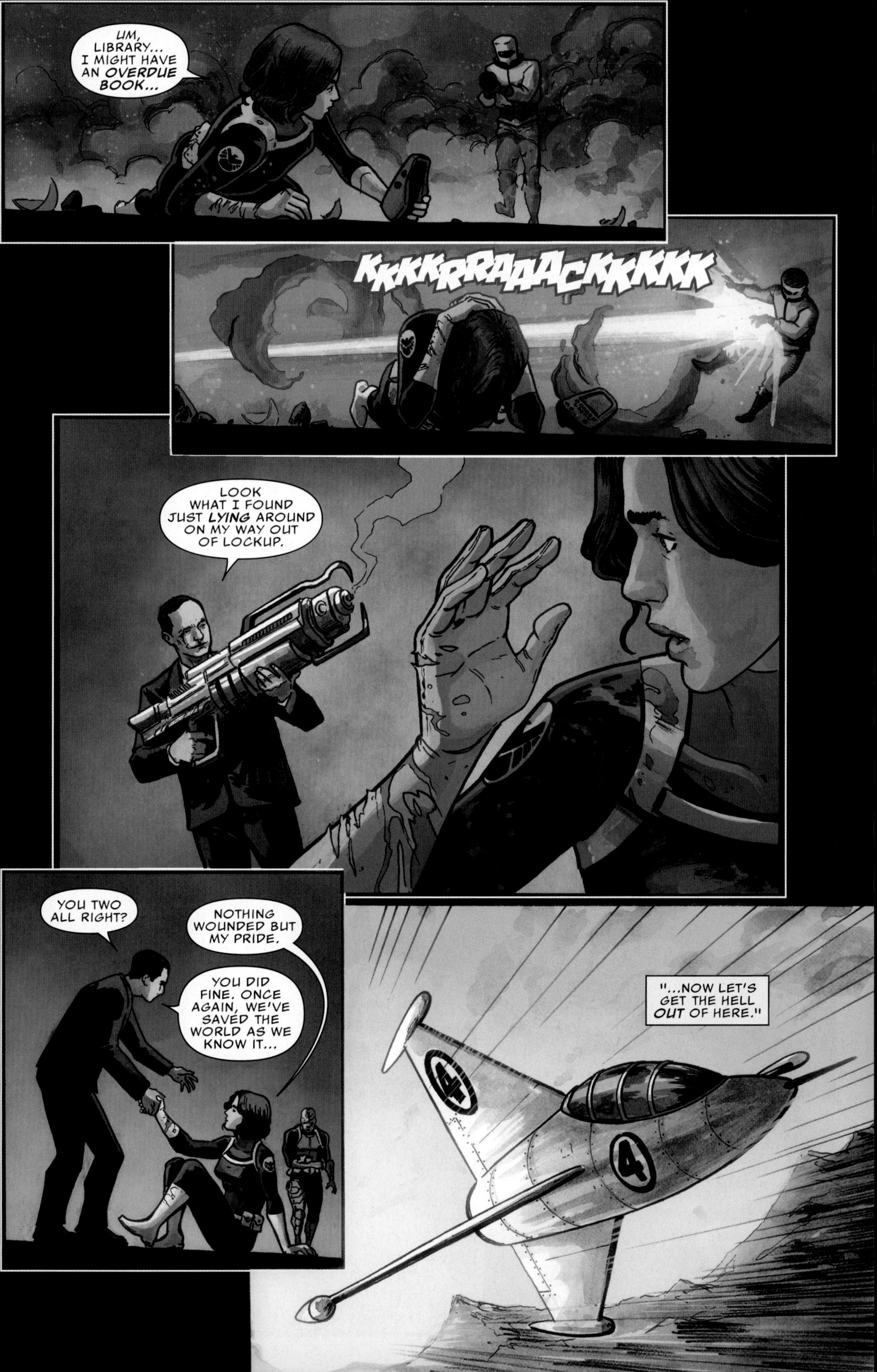
UM, LIBRARY... I MIGHT HAVE AN OVERDUE BOOK...
KKKKRRAAACKKKKK
LOOK WHAT I FOUND JUST LYING AROUND ON MY WAY OUT OF LOCKUP.
YOU TWO ALL RIGHT?
NOTHING WOUNDED BUT MY PRIDE.
YOU DID FINE. ONCE AGAIN, WE'VE SAVED THE WORLD AS WE KNOW IT...
"...NOW LET'S GET THE HELL OUT OF HERE."

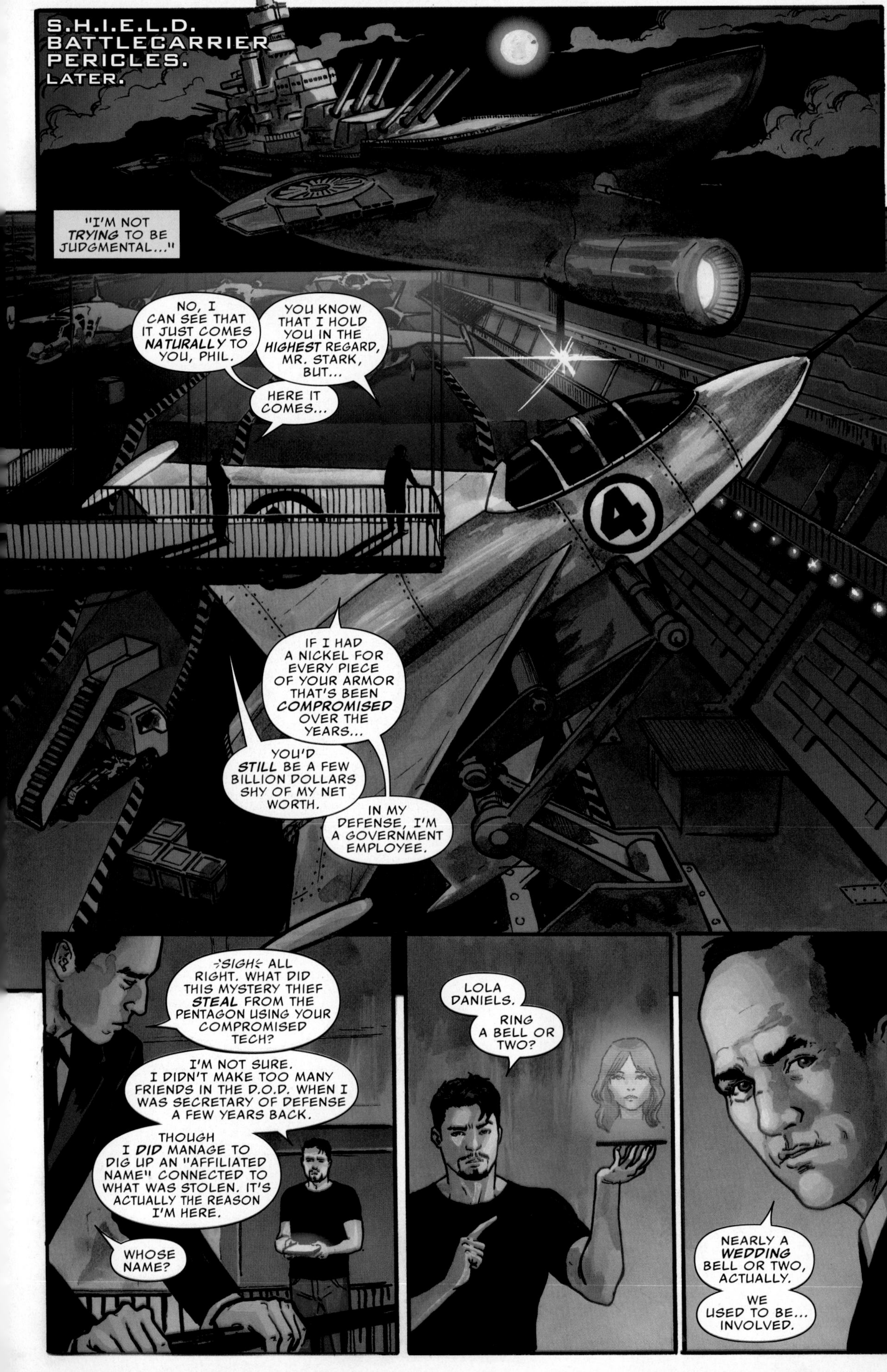
S.H.I.E.L.D. BATTLECARRIER PERICLES. LATER.
"I'M NOT TRYING TO BE JUDGMENTAL..."
NO, I CAN SEE THAT IT JUST COMES NATURALLY TO YOU, PHIL.
YOU KNOW THAT I HOLD YOU IN THE HIGHEST REGARD, MR. STARK, BUT...
HERE IT COMES...
IF I HAD A NICKEL FOR EVERY PIECE OF YOUR ARMOR THAT'S BEEN COMPROMISED OVER THE YEARS...
YOU'D STILL BE A FEW BILLION DOLLARS SHY OF MY NET WORTH.
IN MY DEFENSE, I'M A GOVERNMENT EMPLOYEE.
SIGH ALL RIGHT. WHAT DID THIS MYSTERY THIEF STEAL FROM THE PENTAGON USING YOUR COMPROMISED TECH?
I'M NOT SURE. I DIDN'T MAKE TOO MANY FRIENDS IN THE D.O.D. WHEN I WAS SECRETARY OF DEFENSE A FEW YEARS BACK.
THOUGH I DID MANAGE TO DIG UP AN "AFFILIATED NAME" CONNECTED TO WHAT WAS STOLEN. IT'S ACTUALLY THE REASON I'M HERE.
WHOSE NAME?
LOLA DANIELS.
RING A BELL OR TWO?
NEARLY A WEDDING BELL OR TWO, ACTUALLY.
WE USED TO BE... INVOLVED.

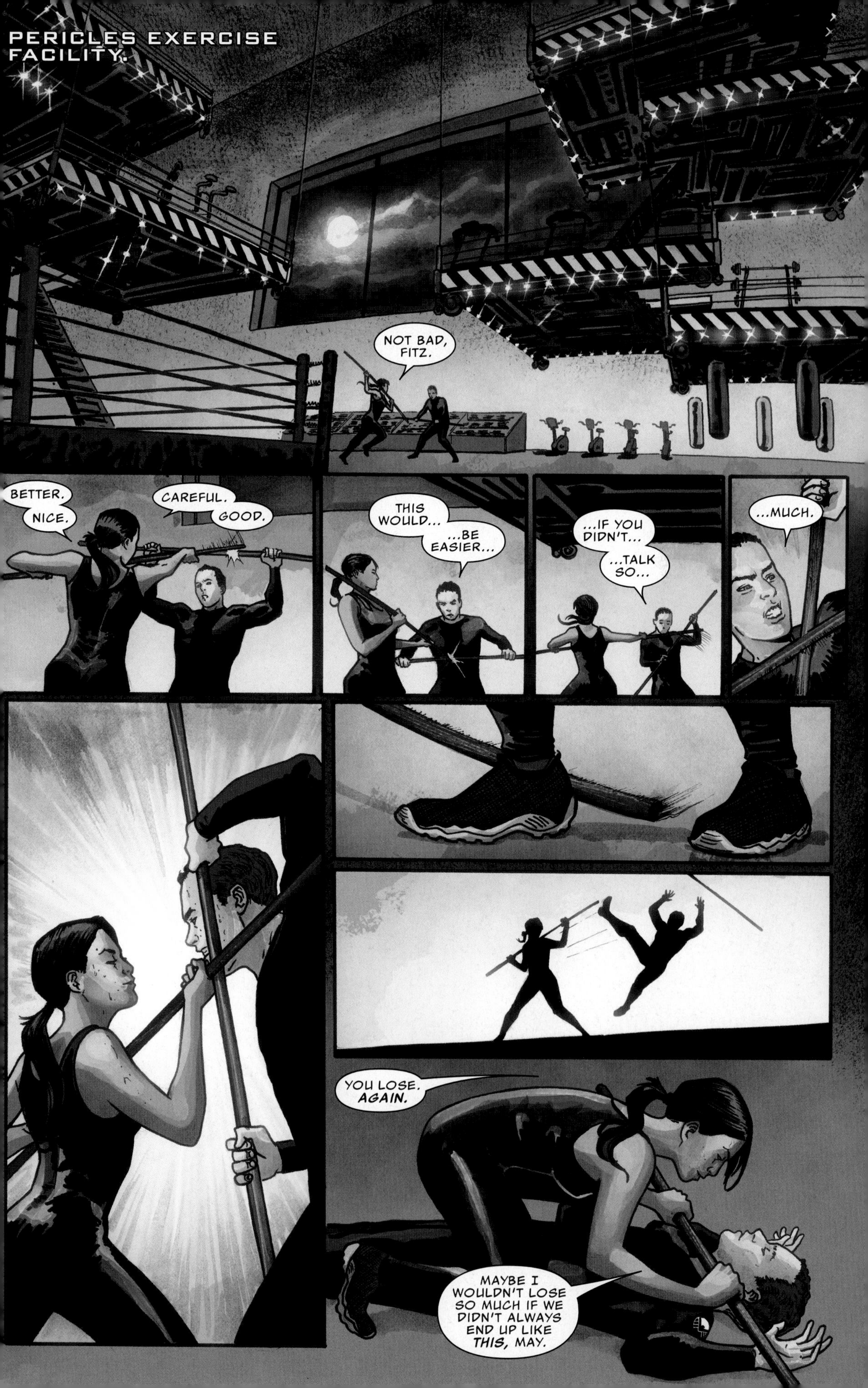
PERICLES EXERCISE FACILITY.
NOT BAD, FITZ.
BETTER.
NICE.
CAREFUL.
GOOD.
THIS WOULD...
...BE EASIER...
...IF YOU DIDN'T...
...TALK SO...
...MUCH.
YOU LOSE. AGAIN.
MAYBE I WOULDN'T LOSE SO MUCH IF WE DIDN'T ALWAYS END UP LIKE THIS, MAY.

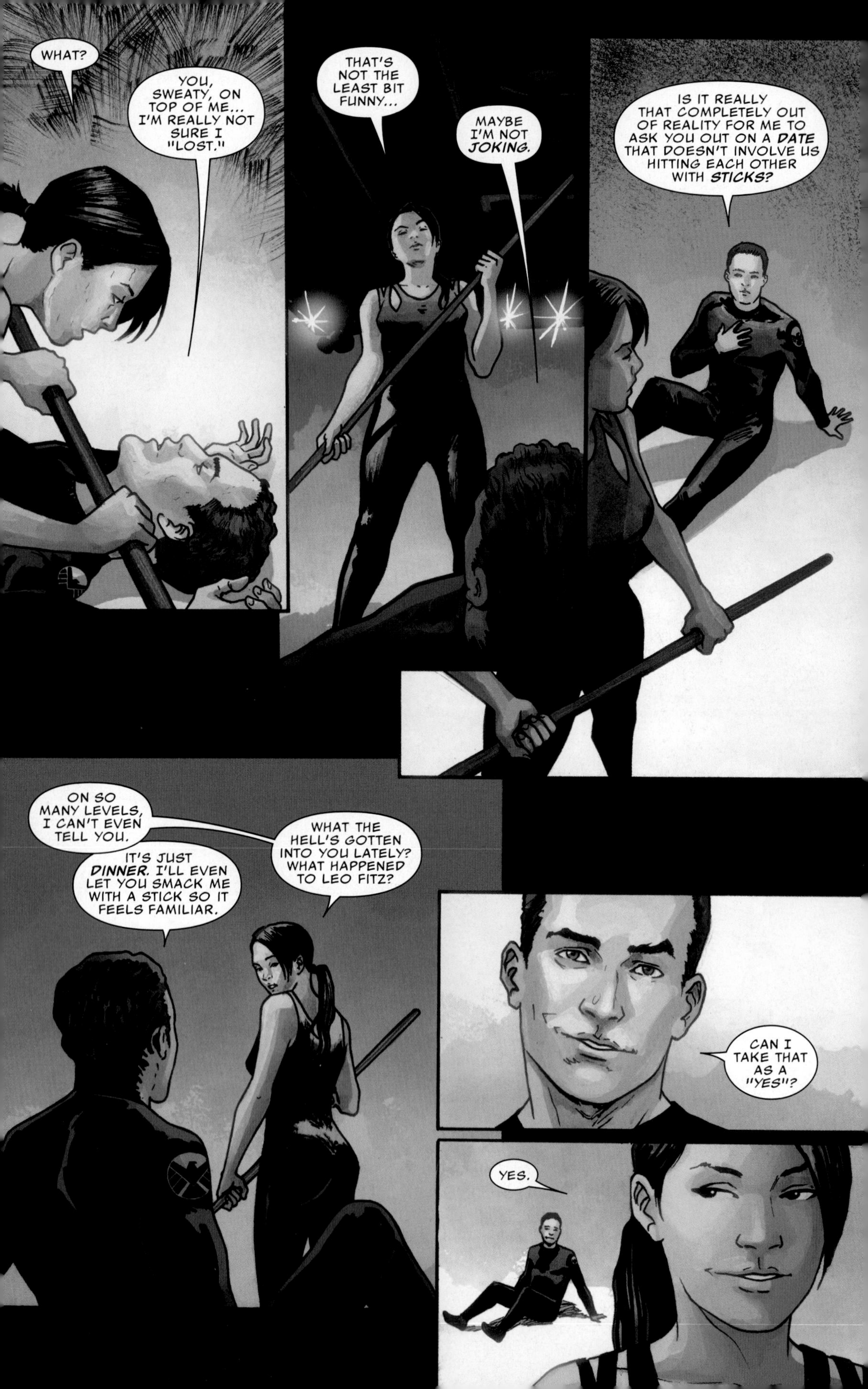
WHAT?
YOU, SWEATY, ON TOP OF ME... I'M REALLY NOT SURE I "LOST."
THAT'S NOT THE LEAST BIT FUNNY...
MAYBE I'M NOT JOKING.
IS IT REALLY THAT COMPLETELY OUT OF REALITY FOR ME TO ASK YOU OUT ON A DATE THAT DOESN'T INVOLVE US HITTING EACH OTHER WITH STICKS?
WHAT THE HELL'S GOTTEN INTO YOU LATELY? WHAT HAPPENED TO LEO FITZ?
ON SO MANY LEVELS, I CAN'T EVEN TELL YOU.
IT'S JUST DINNER. I'LL EVEN LET YOU SMACK ME WITH A STICK SO IT FEELS FAMILIAR.
CAN I TAKE THAT AS A "YES"?
YES.

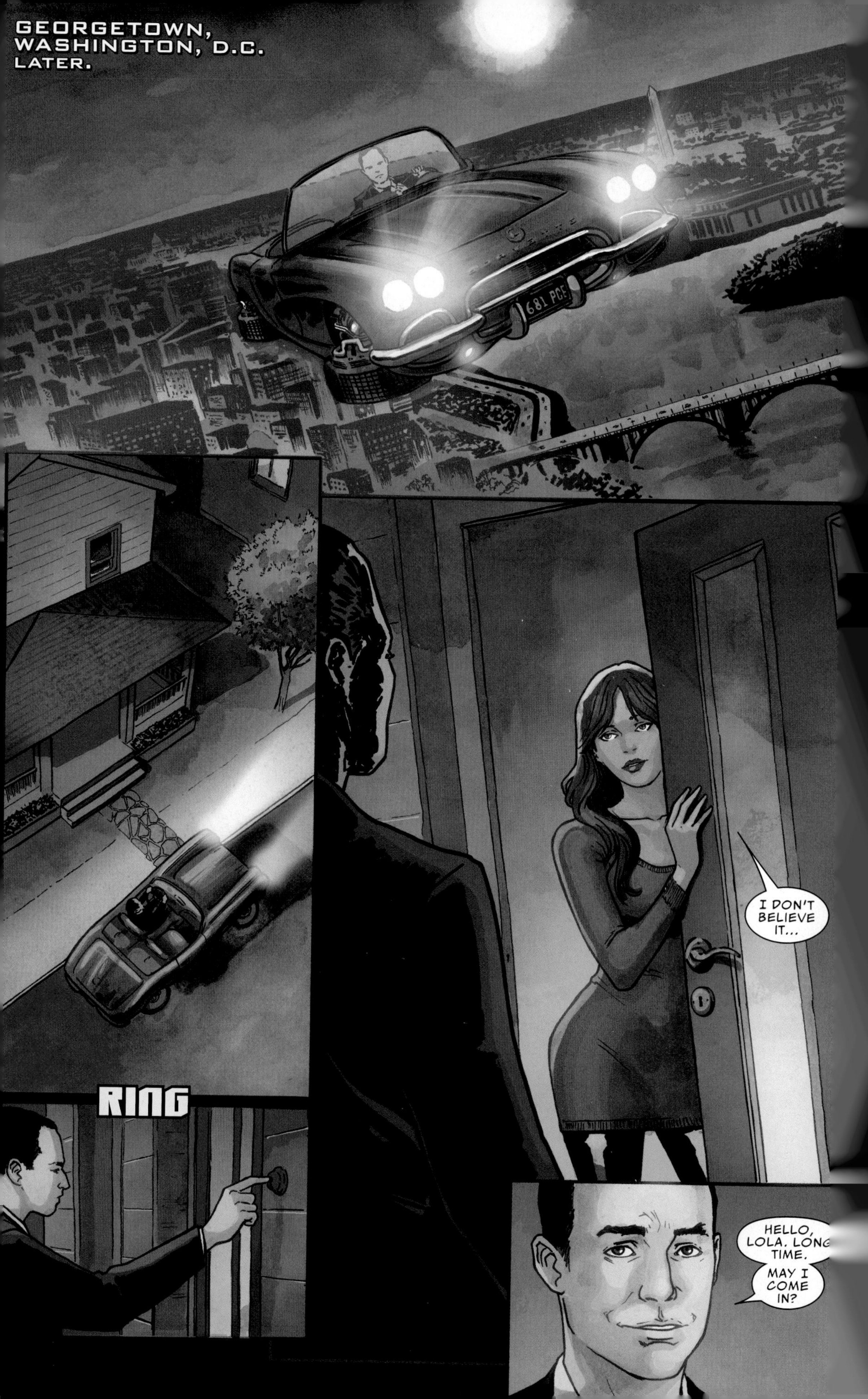
GEORGETOWN, WASHINGTON, D.C. LATER.
681 PCE
RING
I DON'T BELIEVE IT...
HELLO, LOLA. LONG TIME.
MAY I COME IN?

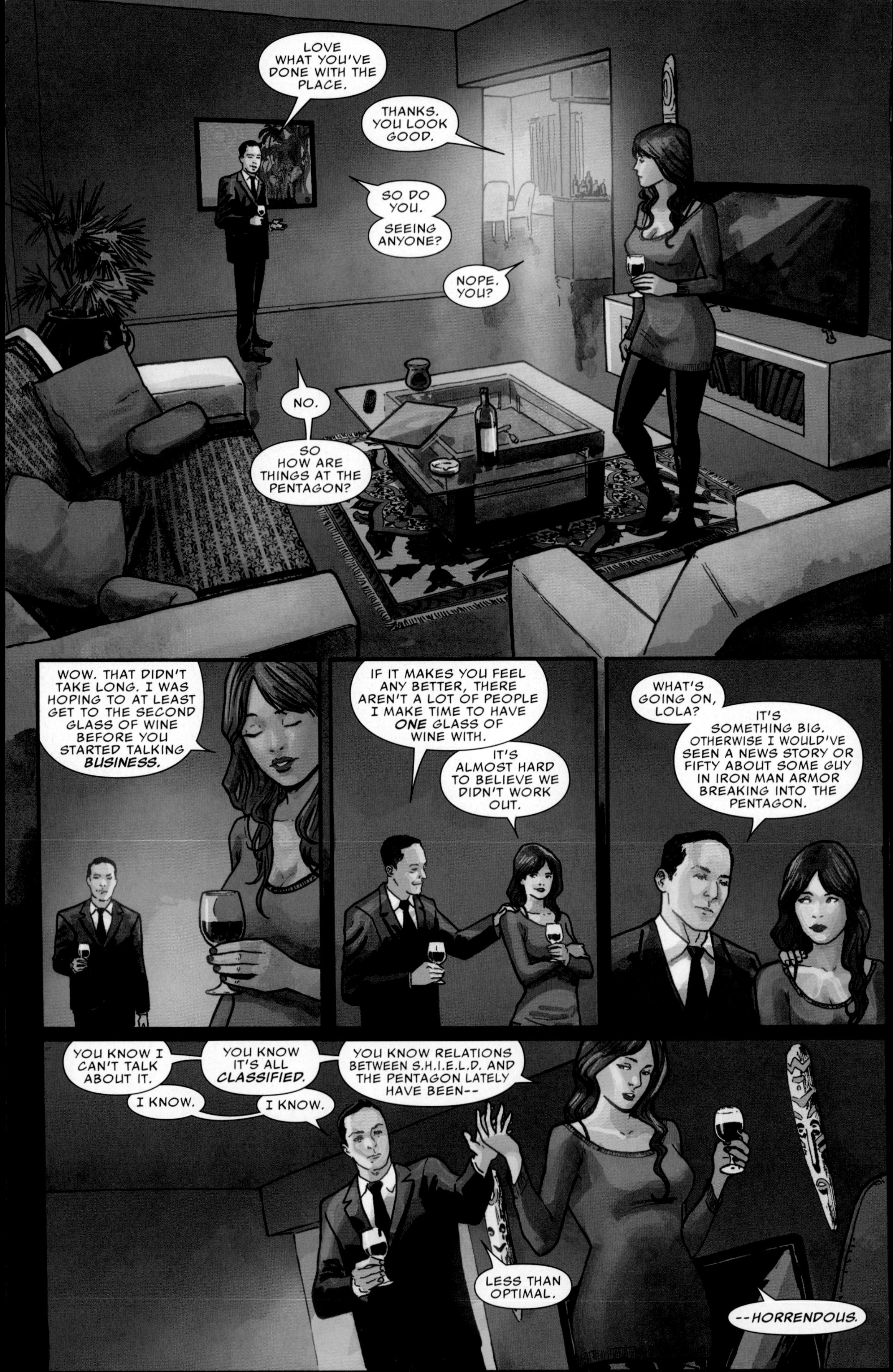
LOVE WHAT YOU'VE DONE WITH THE PLACE.
THANKS. YOU LOOK GOOD.
SO DO YOU.
SEEING ANYONE?
NOPE. YOU?
NO.
SO HOW ARE THINGS AT THE PENTAGON?
WOW. THAT DIDN'T TAKE LONG. I WAS HOPING TO AT LEAST GET TO THE SECOND GLASS OF WINE BEFORE YOU STARTED TALKING *BUSINESS.*
IF IT MAKES YOU FEEL ANY BETTER, THERE AREN'T A LOT OF PEOPLE I MAKE TIME TO HAVE *ONE* GLASS OF WINE WITH.
IT'S ALMOST HARD TO BELIEVE WE DIDN'T WORK OUT.
WHAT'S GOING ON, LOLA?
IT'S SOMETHING BIG. OTHERWISE I WOULD'VE SEEN A NEWS STORY OR FIFTY ABOUT SOME GUY IN IRON MAN ARMOR BREAKING INTO THE PENTAGON.
YOU KNOW I CAN'T TALK ABOUT IT.
I KNOW.
YOU KNOW IT'S ALL *CLASSIFIED.*
I KNOW.
YOU KNOW RELATIONS BETWEEN S.H.I.E.L.D. AND THE PENTAGON LATELY HAVE BEEN--
LESS THAN OPTIMAL.
--*HORRENDOUS.*

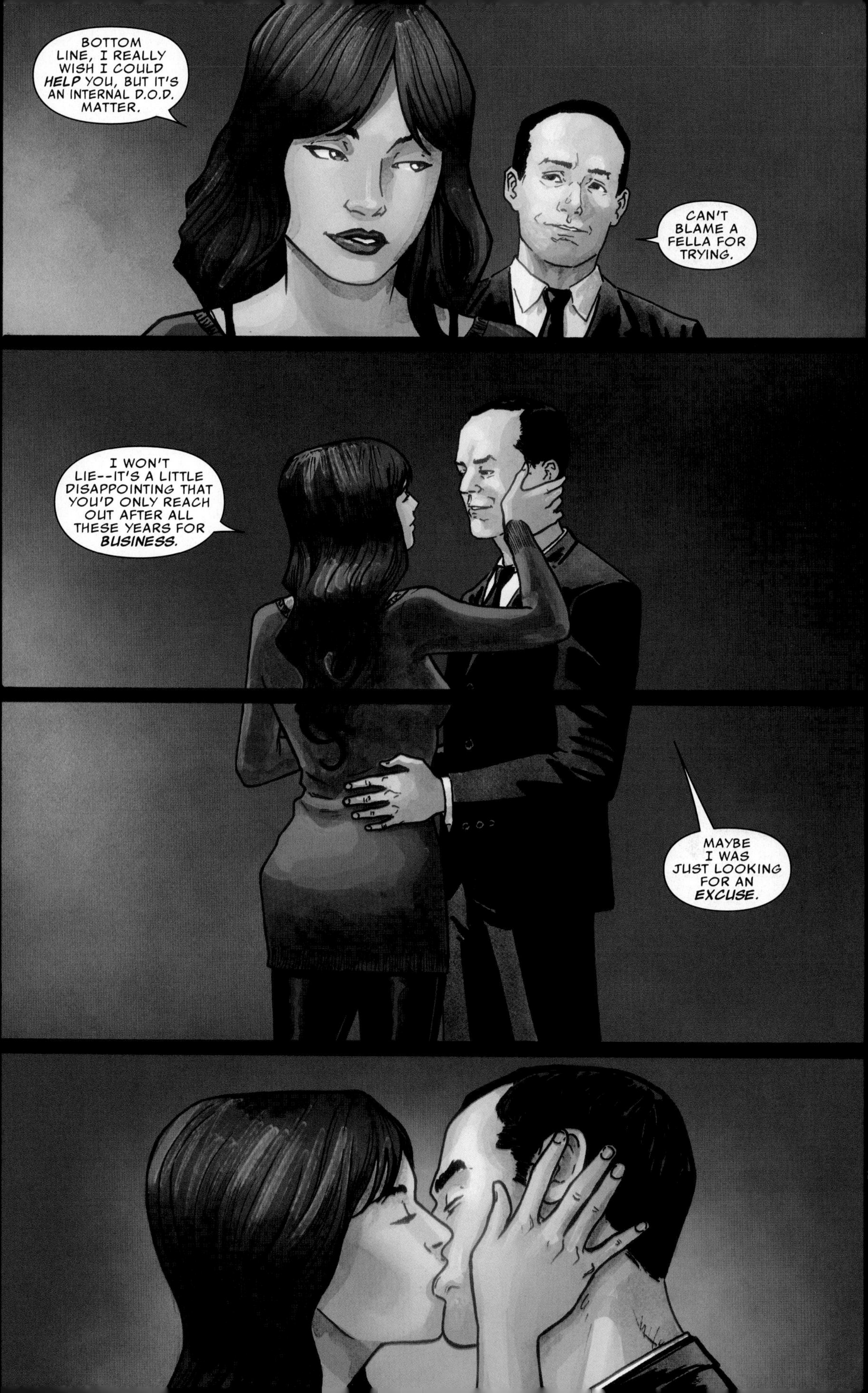
BOTTOM LINE, I REALLY WISH I COULD *HELP* YOU, BUT IT'S AN INTERNAL D.O.D. MATTER.
CAN'T BLAME A FELLA FOR TRYING.
I WON'T LIE--IT'S A LITTLE DISAPPOINTING THAT YOU'D ONLY REACH OUT AFTER ALL THESE YEARS FOR *BUSINESS*.
MAYBE I WAS JUST LOOKING FOR AN *EXCUSE*.

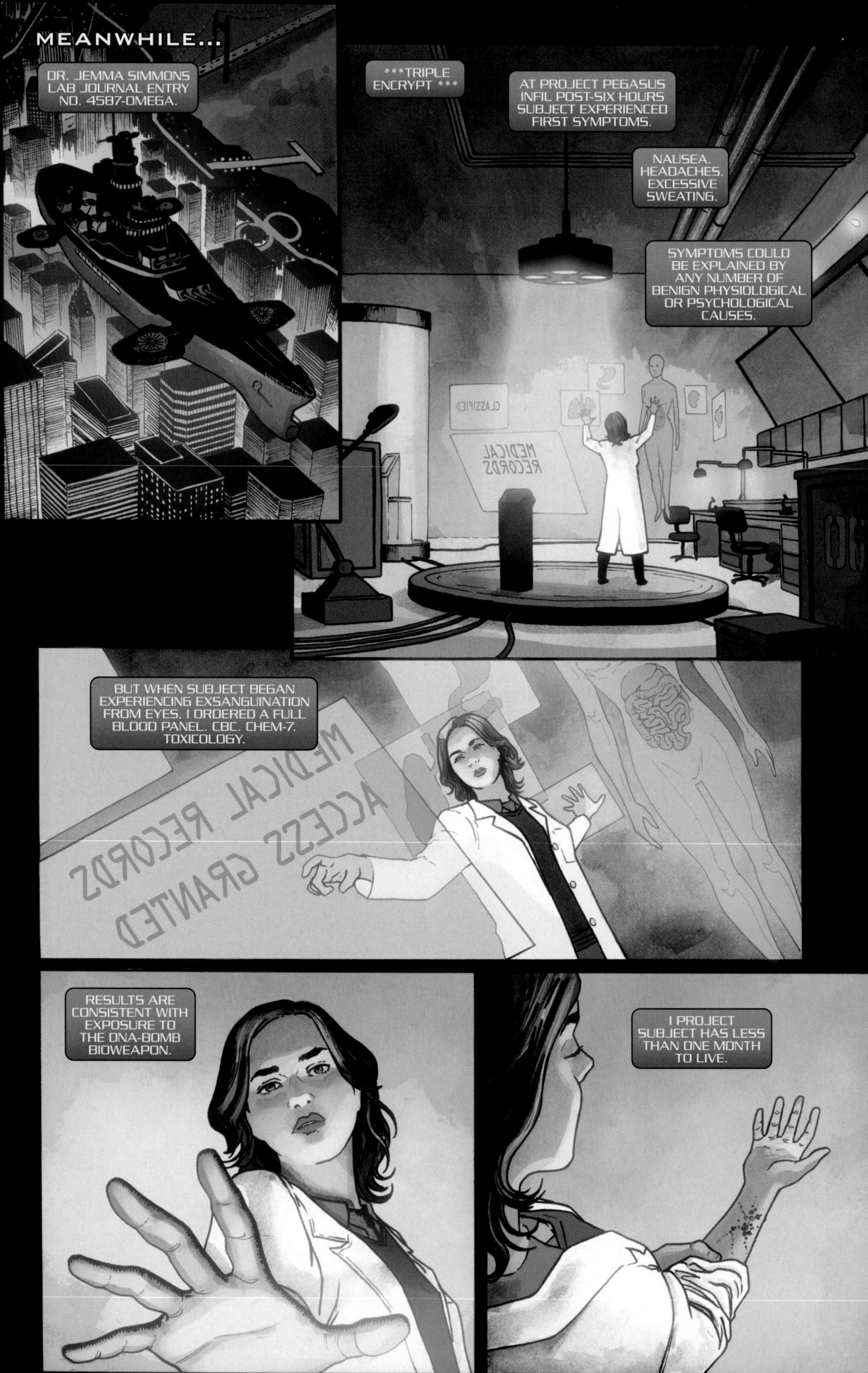
MEANWHILE...
DR. JEMMA SIMMONS LAB JOURNAL ENTRY NO. 4587-OMEGA.
***TRIPLE ENCRYPT ***
AT PROJECT PEGASUS INFIL POST-SIX HOURS SUBJECT EXPERIENCED FIRST SYMPTOMS.
NAUSEA. HEADACHES. EXCESSIVE SWEATING.
SYMPTOMS COULD BE EXPLAINED BY ANY NUMBER OF BENIGN PHYSIOLOGICAL OR PSYCHOLOGICAL CAUSES.
CLASSIFIED
MEDICAL RECORDS
BUT WHEN SUBJECT BEGAN EXPERIENCING EXSANGUINATION FROM EYES, I ORDERED A FULL BLOOD PANEL. CBC. CHEM-7. TOXICOLOGY.
MEDICAL RECORDS ACCESS GRANTED
RESULTS ARE CONSISTENT WITH EXPOSURE TO THE DNA-BOMB BIOWEAPON.
I PROJECT SUBJECT HAS LESS THAN ONE MONTH TO LIVE.

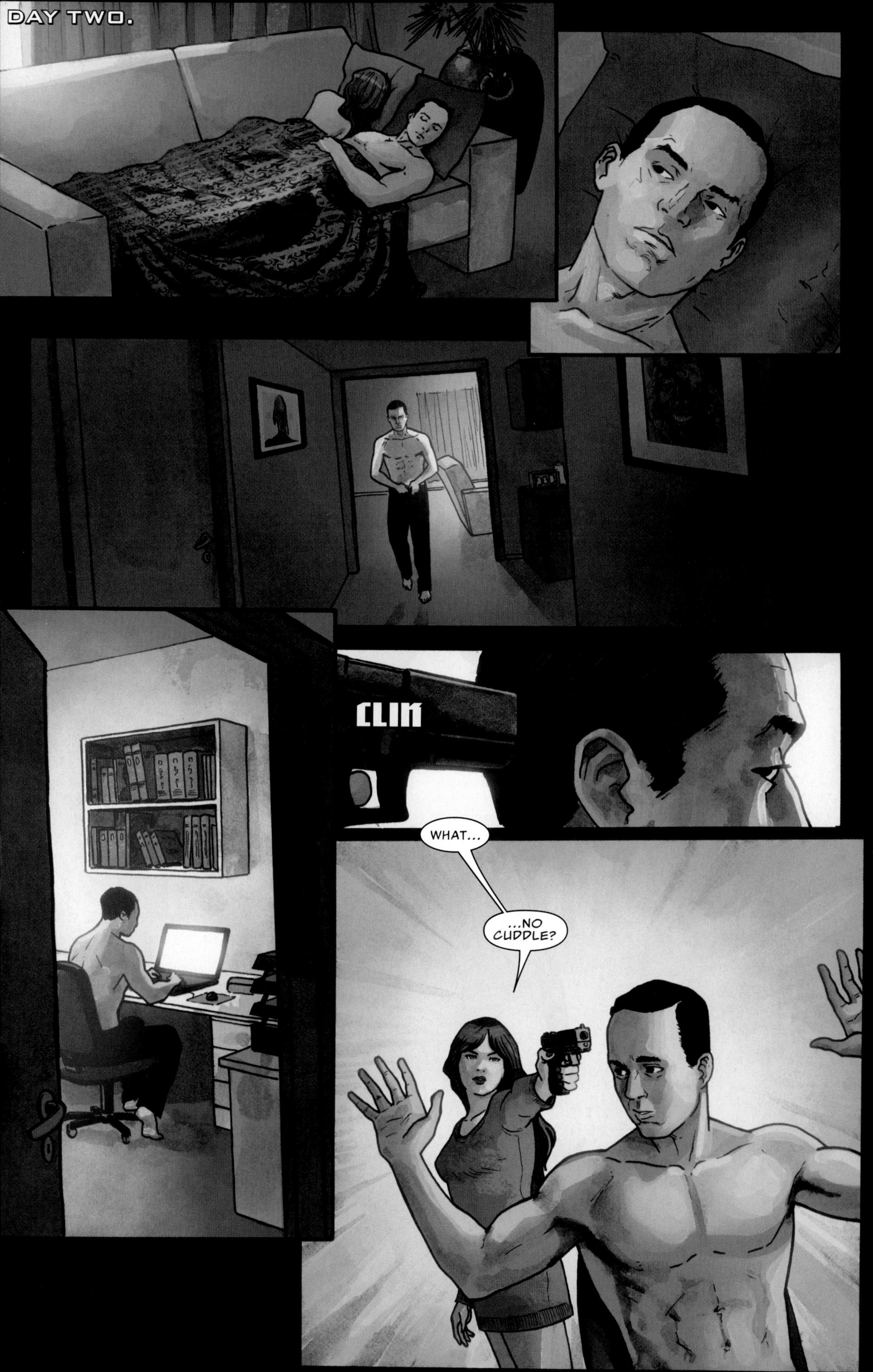
DAY TWO.
CLIK
WHAT...
...NO CUDDLE?

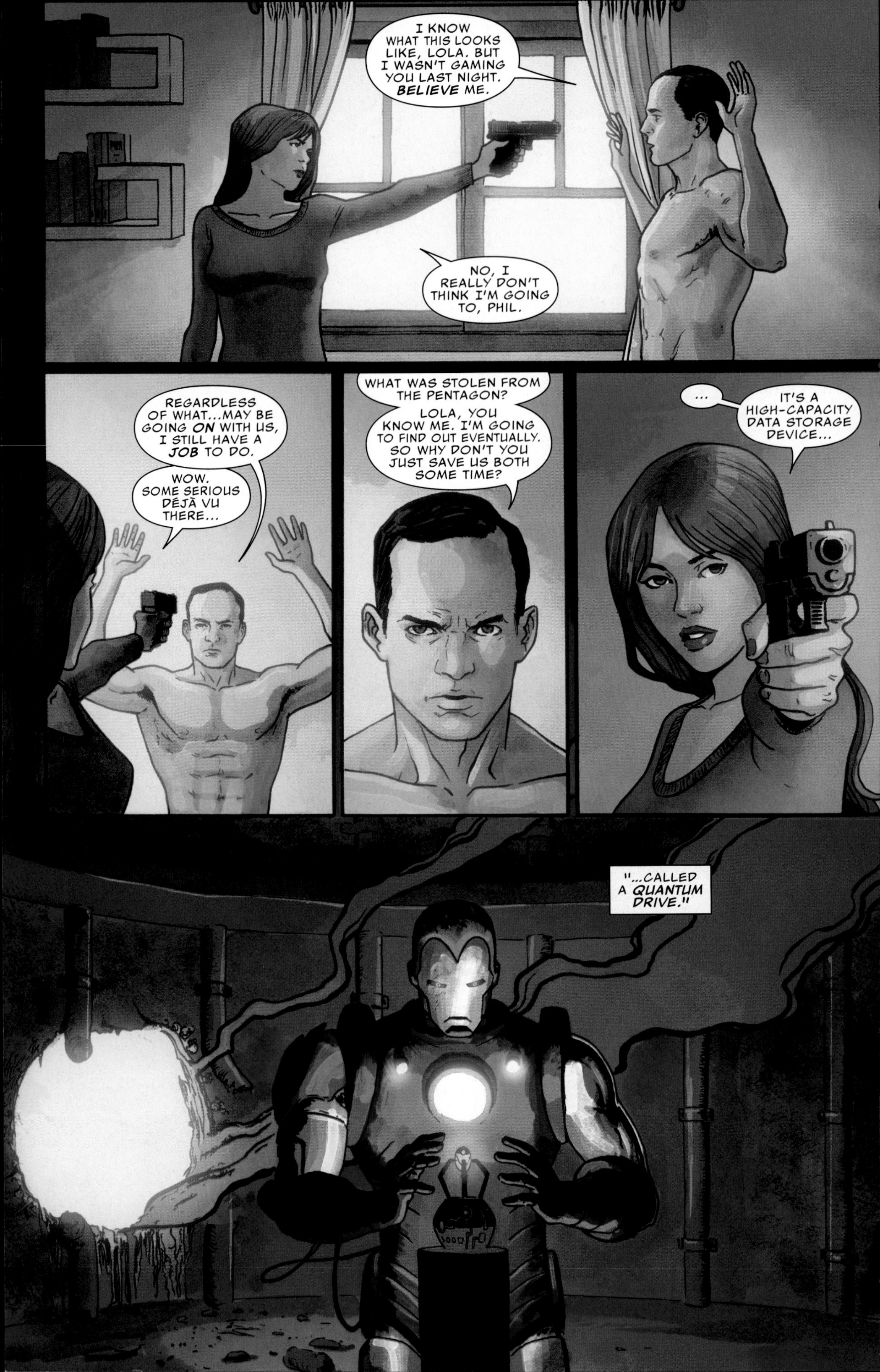
I KNOW WHAT THIS LOOKS LIKE, LOLA. BUT I WASN'T GAMING YOU LAST NIGHT. BELIEVE ME.
NO, I REALLY DON'T THINK I'M GOING TO, PHIL.
REGARDLESS OF WHAT...MAY BE GOING ON WITH US, I STILL HAVE A JOB TO DO.
WOW. SOME SERIOUS DÉJÀ VU THERE...
WHAT WAS STOLEN FROM THE PENTAGON?
LOLA, YOU KNOW ME. I'M GOING TO FIND OUT EVENTUALLY. SO WHY DON'T YOU JUST SAVE US BOTH SOME TIME?
...
IT'S A HIGH-CAPACITY DATA STORAGE DEVICE...
"...CALLED A QUANTUM DRIVE."

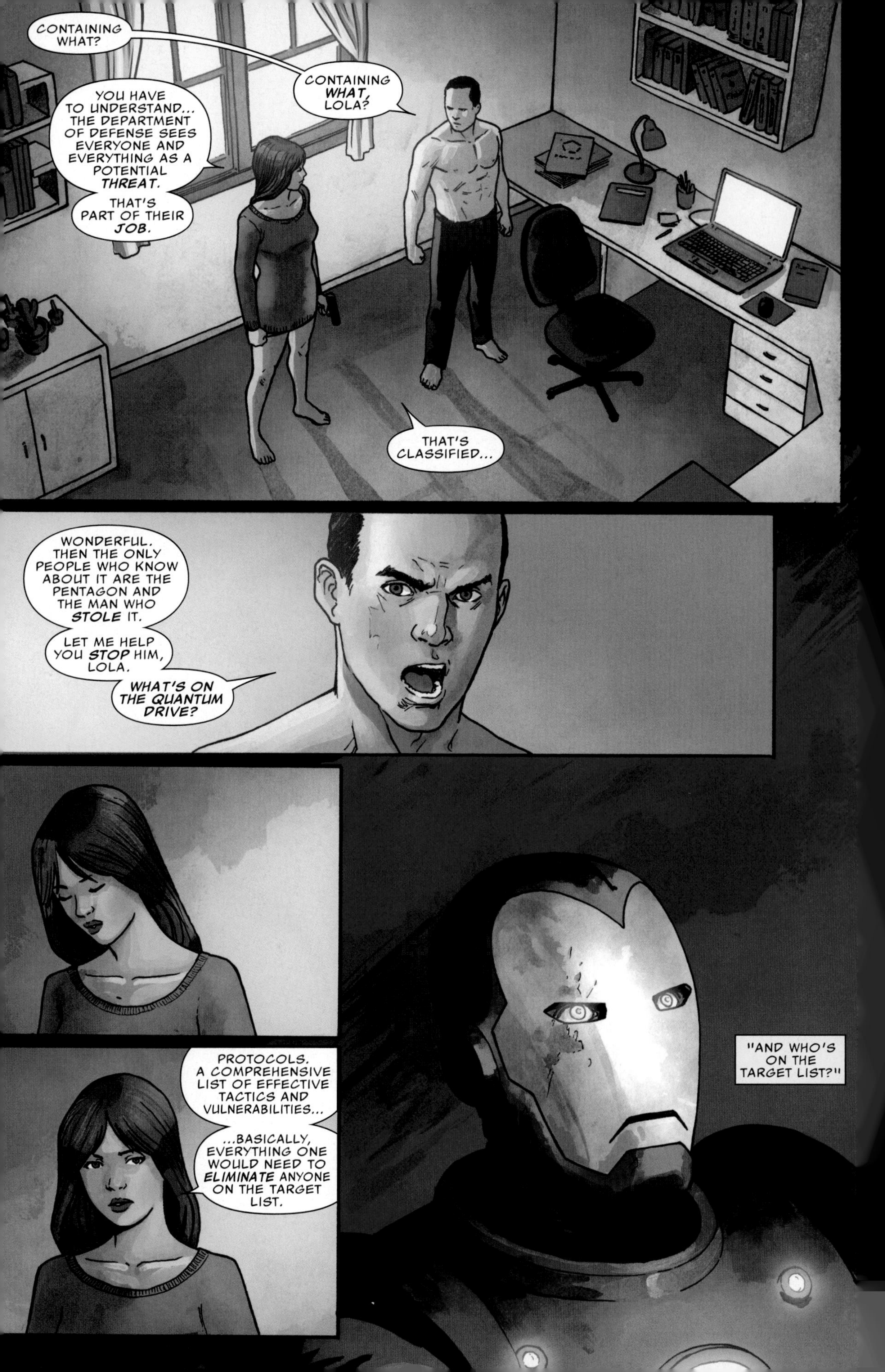
CONTAINING WHAT?
CONTAINING WHAT, LOLA?
YOU HAVE TO UNDERSTAND... THE DEPARTMENT OF DEFENSE SEES EVERYONE AND EVERYTHING AS A POTENTIAL THREAT.
THAT'S PART OF THEIR JOB.
THAT'S CLASSIFIED...
WONDERFUL. THEN THE ONLY PEOPLE WHO KNOW ABOUT IT ARE THE PENTAGON AND THE MAN WHO STOLE IT.
LET ME HELP YOU STOP HIM, LOLA.
WHAT'S ON THE QUANTUM DRIVE?
PROTOCOLS. A COMPREHENSIVE LIST OF EFFECTIVE TACTICS AND VULNERABILITIES...
...BASICALLY, EVERYTHING ONE WOULD NEED TO ELIMINATE ANYONE ON THE TARGET LIST.
"AND WHO'S ON THE TARGET LIST?"

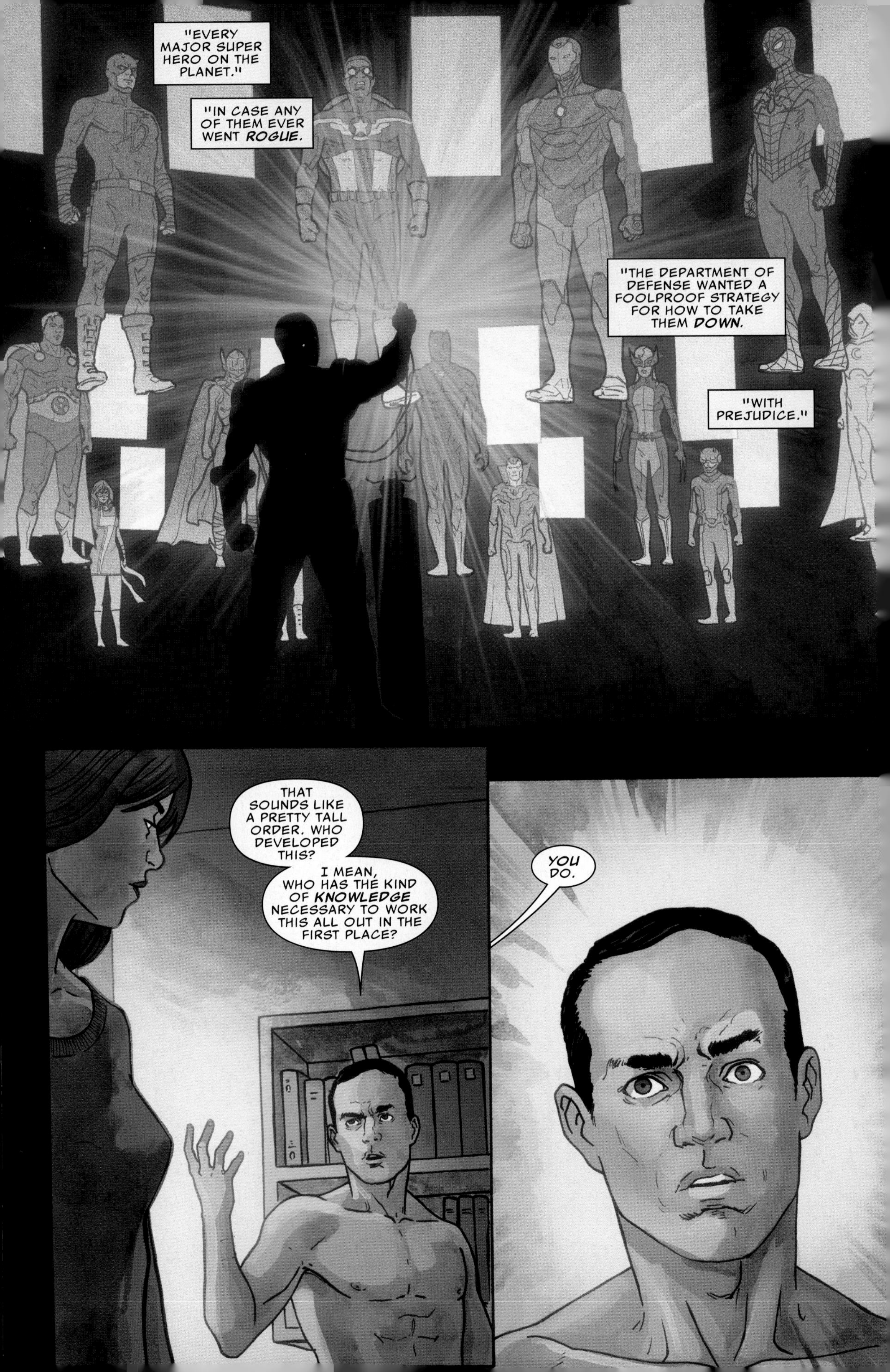
"EVERY MAJOR SUPER HERO ON THE PLANET."
"IN CASE ANY OF THEM EVER WENT ROGUE.
"THE DEPARTMENT OF DEFENSE WANTED A FOOLPROOF STRATEGY FOR HOW TO TAKE THEM DOWN.
"WITH PREJUDICE."
THAT SOUNDS LIKE A PRETTY TALL ORDER. WHO DEVELOPED THIS?
I MEAN, WHO HAS THE KIND OF KNOWLEDGE NECESSARY TO WORK THIS ALL OUT IN THE FIRST PLACE?
YOU DO.

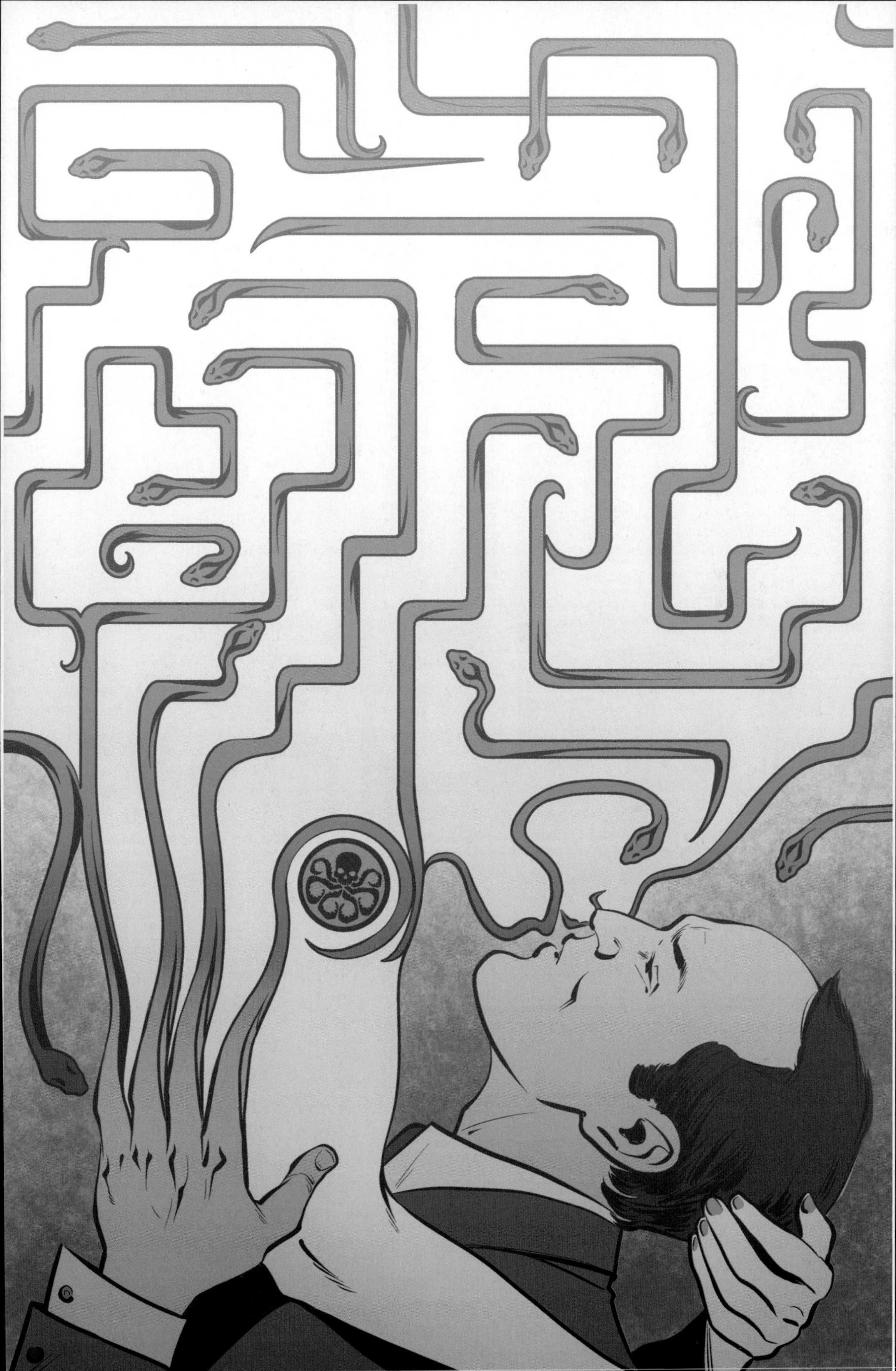

ACTIVE MISSION:
DANGEROUS LIAISONS | 2.

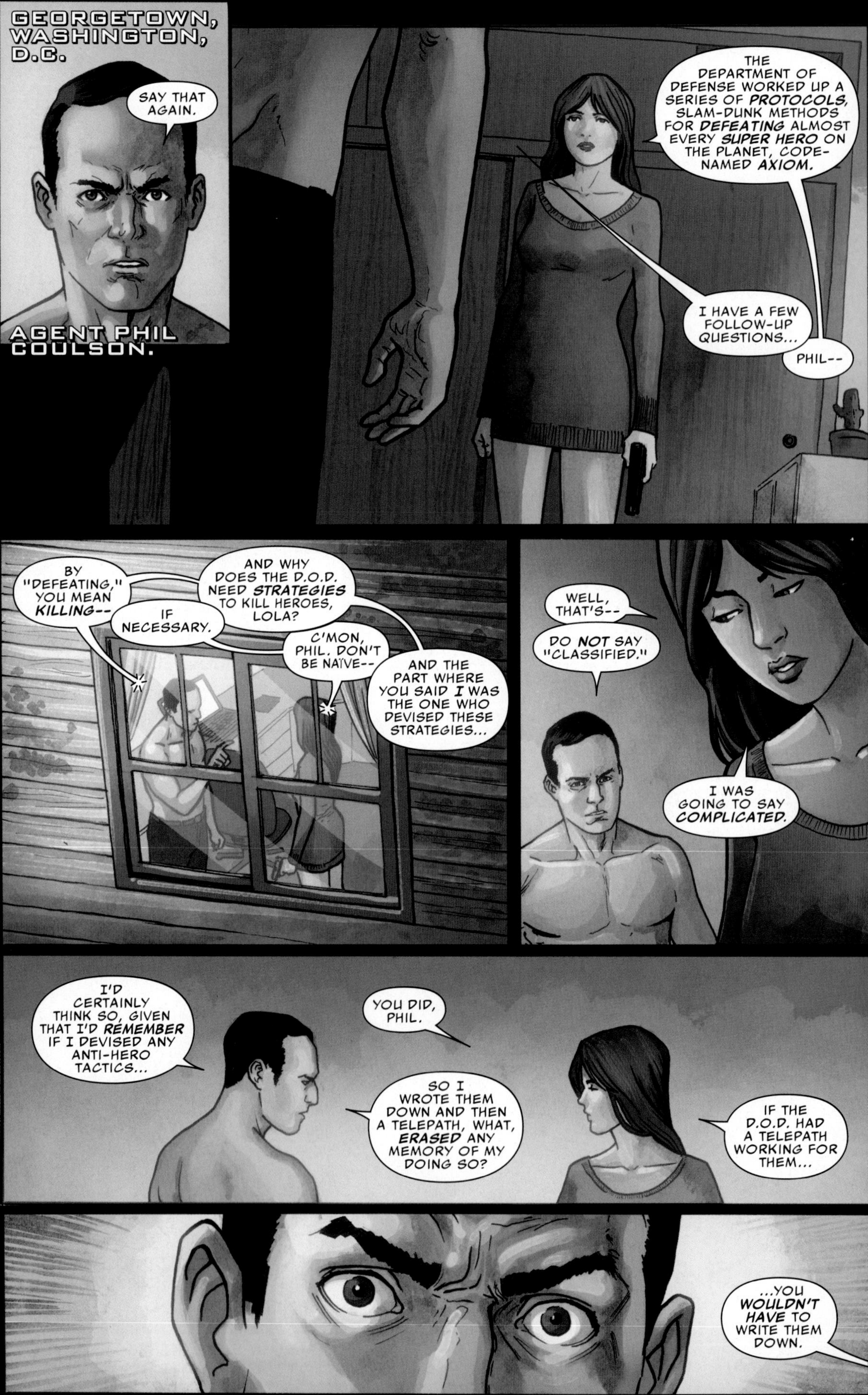
GEORGETOWN, WASHINGTON, D.C.
SAY THAT AGAIN.
AGENT PHIL COULSON.
THE DEPARTMENT OF DEFENSE WORKED UP A SERIES OF PROTOCOLS, SLAM-DUNK METHODS FOR DEFEATING ALMOST EVERY SUPER HERO ON THE PLANET, CODE-NAMED AXIOM.
I HAVE A FEW FOLLOW-UP QUESTIONS...
PHIL--
BY "DEFEATING," YOU MEAN KILLING--
IF NECESSARY.
AND WHY DOES THE D.O.D. NEED STRATEGIES TO KILL HEROES, LOLA?
C'MON, PHIL. DON'T BE NAÏVE--
AND THE PART WHERE YOU SAID I WAS THE ONE WHO DEVISED THESE STRATEGIES...
WELL, THAT'S--
DO NOT SAY "CLASSIFIED."
I WAS GOING TO SAY COMPLICATED.
I'D CERTAINLY THINK SO, GIVEN THAT I'D REMEMBER IF I DEVISED ANY ANTI-HERO TACTICS...
YOU DID, PHIL.
SO I WROTE THEM DOWN AND THEN A TELEPATH, WHAT, ERASED ANY MEMORY OF MY DOING SO?
IF THE D.O.D. HAD A TELEPATH WORKING FOR THEM...
...YOU WOULDN'T HAVE TO WRITE THEM DOWN.

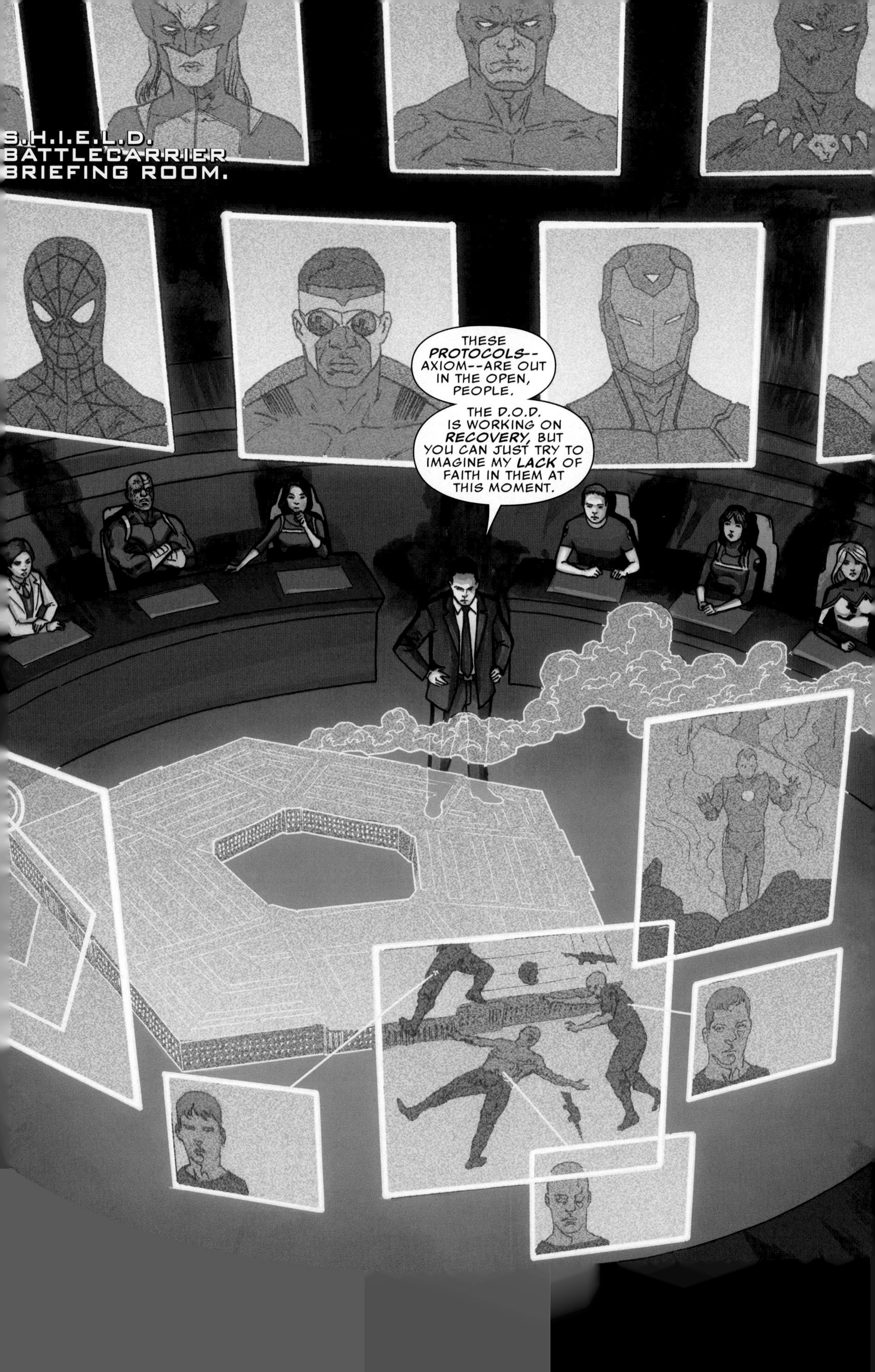
S.H.I.E.L.D. BATTLECARRIER BRIEFING ROOM.
THESE PROTOCOLS--AXIOM--ARE OUT IN THE OPEN, PEOPLE.
THE D.O.D. IS WORKING ON RECOVERY, BUT YOU CAN JUST TRY TO IMAGINE MY LACK OF FAITH IN THEM AT THIS MOMENT.

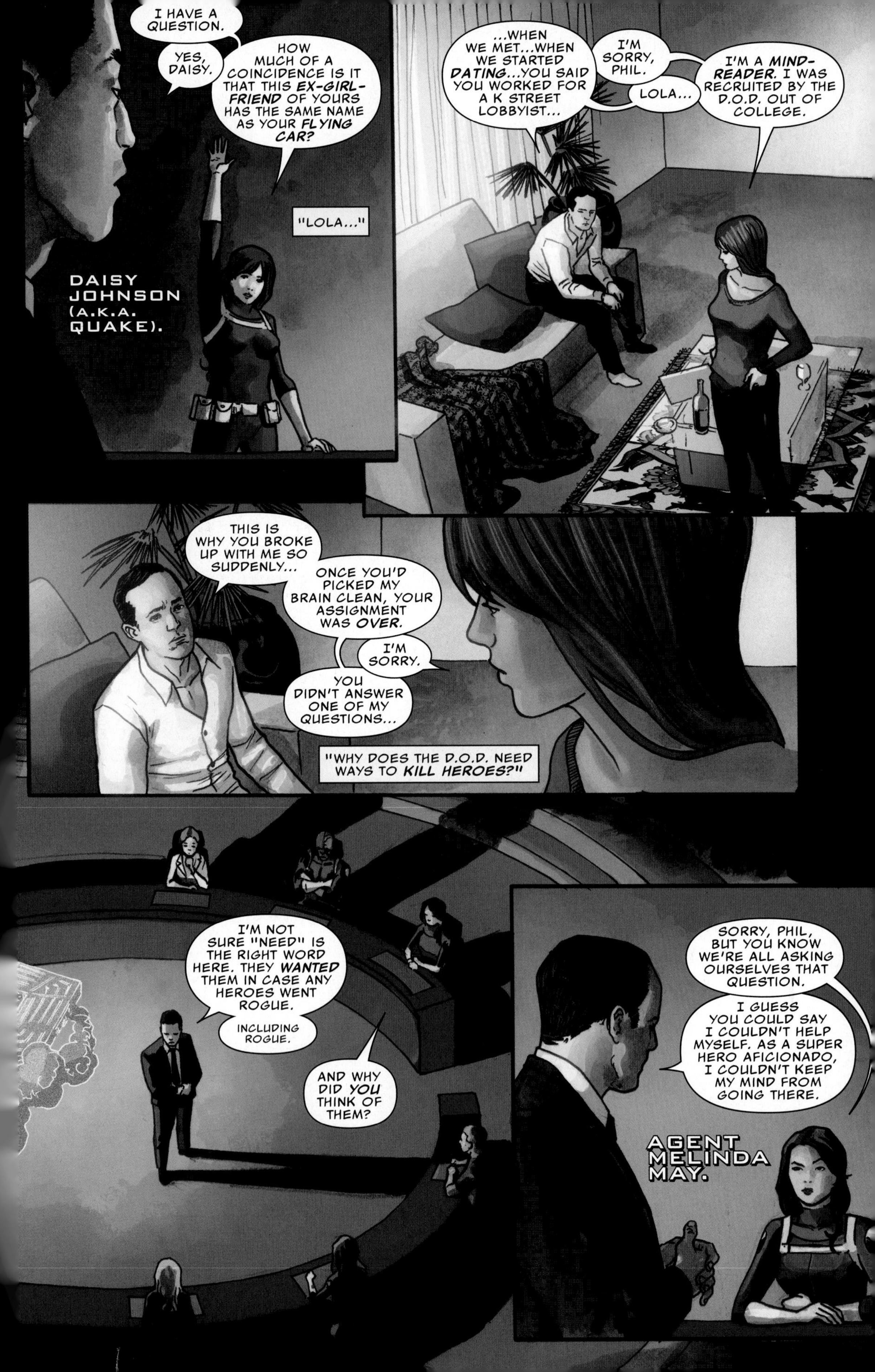

I HAVE A QUESTION.
YES, DAISY.
HOW MUCH OF A COINCIDENCE IS IT THAT THIS EX-GIRL-FRIEND OF YOURS HAS THE SAME NAME AS YOUR FLYING CAR?
"LOLA..."
DAISY JOHNSON (A.K.A. QUAKE).
...WHEN WE MET...WHEN WE STARTED DATING...YOU SAID YOU WORKED FOR A K STREET LOBBYIST...
I'M SORRY, PHIL.
LOLA...
I'M A MIND-READER. I WAS RECRUITED BY THE D.O.D. OUT OF COLLEGE.
THIS IS WHY YOU BROKE UP WITH ME SO SUDDENLY...
ONCE YOU'D PICKED MY BRAIN CLEAN, YOUR ASSIGNMENT WAS OVER.
I'M SORRY.
YOU DIDN'T ANSWER ONE OF MY QUESTIONS...
"WHY DOES THE D.O.D. NEED WAYS TO KILL HEROES?"
I'M NOT SURE "NEED" IS THE RIGHT WORD HERE. THEY WANTED THEM IN CASE ANY HEROES WENT ROGUE.
INCLUDING ROGUE.
AND WHY DID YOU THINK OF THEM?
SORRY, PHIL, BUT YOU KNOW WE'RE ALL ASKING OURSELVES THAT QUESTION.
I GUESS YOU COULD SAY I COULDN'T HELP MYSELF. AS A SUPER HERO AFICIONADO, I COULDN'T KEEP MY MIND FROM GOING THERE.
AGENT MELINDA MAY.

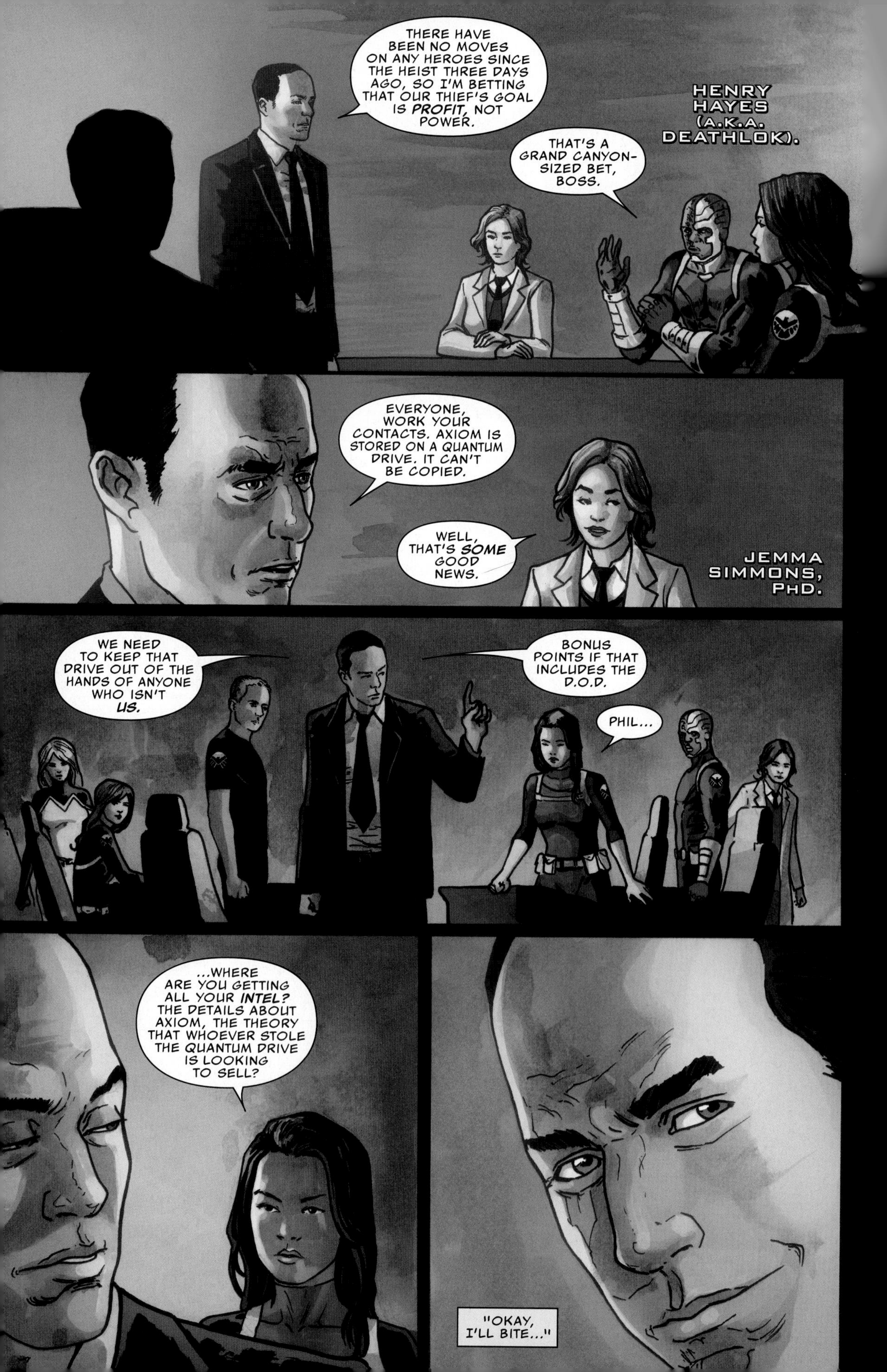
THERE HAVE BEEN NO MOVES ON ANY HEROES SINCE THE HEIST THREE DAYS AGO, SO I'M BETTING THAT OUR THIEF'S GOAL IS PROFIT, NOT POWER.
HENRY HAYES (A.K.A. DEATHLOK).
THAT'S A GRAND CANYON-SIZED BET, BOSS.
EVERYONE, WORK YOUR CONTACTS. AXIOM IS STORED ON A QUANTUM DRIVE. IT CAN'T BE COPIED.
WELL, THAT'S SOME GOOD NEWS.
JEMMA SIMMONS, PHD.
WE NEED TO KEEP THAT DRIVE OUT OF THE HANDS OF ANYONE WHO ISN'T US.
BONUS POINTS IF THAT INCLUDES THE D.O.D.
PHIL...
...WHERE ARE YOU GETTING ALL YOUR INTEL? THE DETAILS ABOUT AXIOM, THE THEORY THAT WHOEVER STOLE THE QUANTUM DRIVE IS LOOKING TO SELL?
"OKAY, I'LL BITE..."

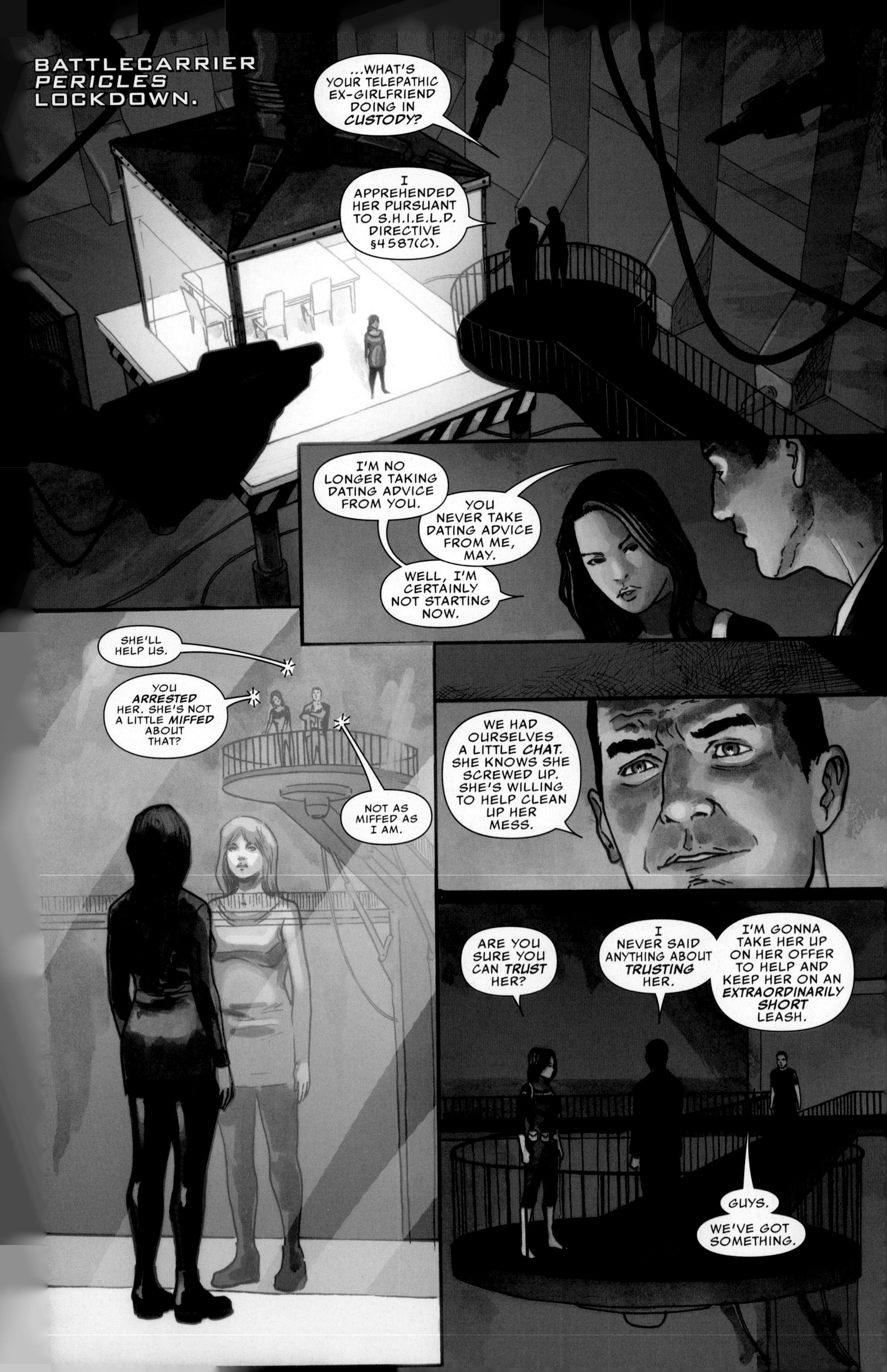
BATTLECARRIER PERICLES LOCKDOWN.
...WHAT'S YOUR TELEPATHIC EX-GIRLFRIEND DOING IN CUSTODY?
I APPREHENDED HER PURSUANT TO S.H.I.E.L.D. DIRECTIVE §4587(C).
I'M NO LONGER TAKING DATING ADVICE FROM YOU.
YOU NEVER TAKE DATING ADVICE FROM ME, MAY.
WELL, I'M CERTAINLY NOT STARTING NOW.
SHE'LL HELP US.
YOU ARRESTED HER. SHE'S NOT A LITTLE MIFFED ABOUT THAT?
NOT AS MIFFED AS I AM.
WE HAD OURSELVES A LITTLE CHAT. SHE KNOWS SHE SCREWED UP. SHE'S WILLING TO HELP CLEAN UP HER MESS.
ARE YOU SURE YOU CAN TRUST HER?
I NEVER SAID ANYTHING ABOUT TRUSTING HER.
I'M GONNA TAKE HER UP ON HER OFFER TO HELP AND KEEP HER ON AN EXTRAORDINARILY SHORT LEASH.
GUYS.
WE'VE GOT SOMETHING.

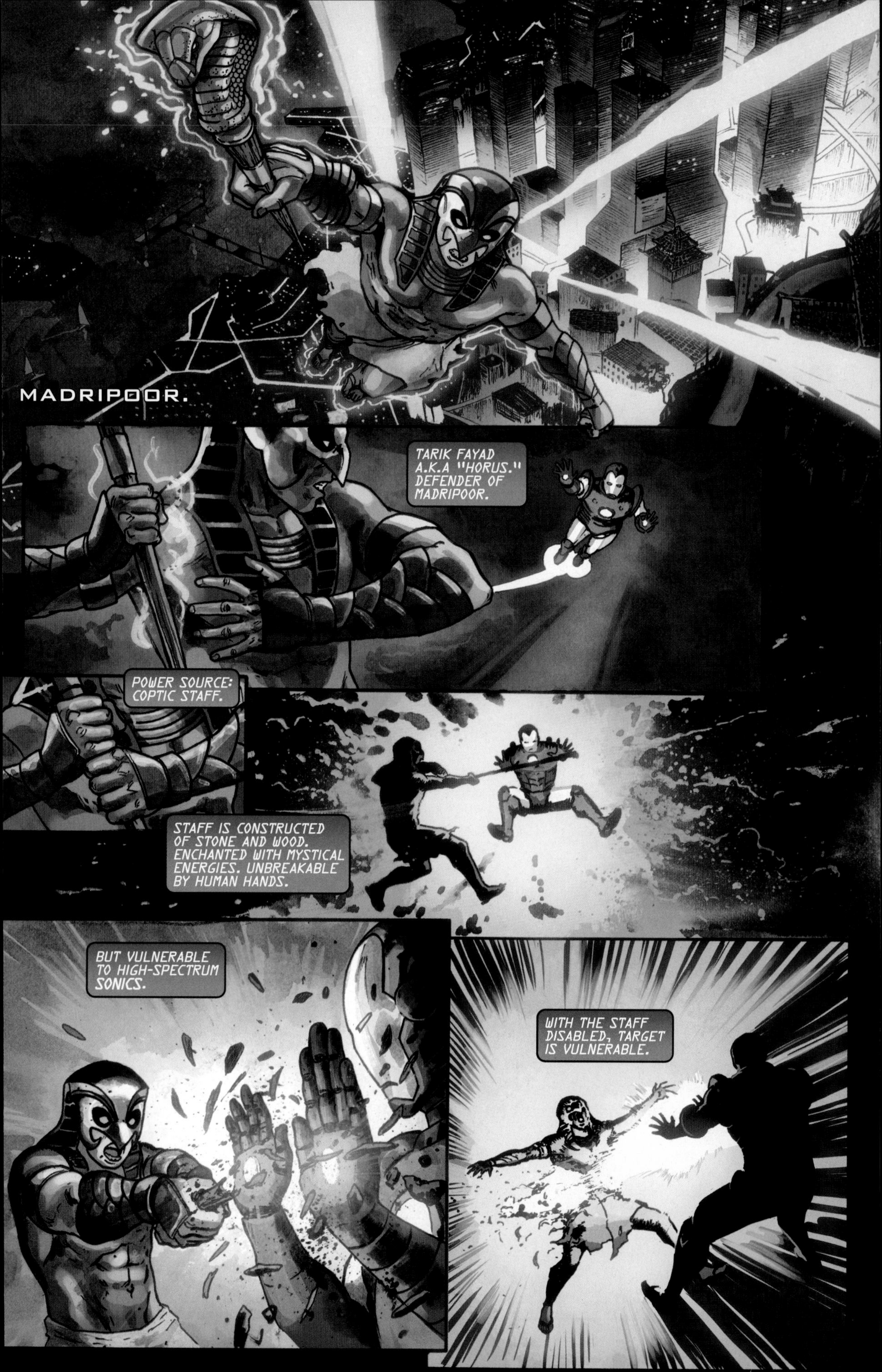
MADRIPOOR.
TARIK FAYAD A.K.A "HORUS." DEFENDER OF MADRIPOOR.
POWER SOURCE: COPTIC STAFF.
STAFF IS CONSTRUCTED OF STONE AND WOOD. ENCHANTED WITH MYSTICAL ENERGIES. UNBREAKABLE BY HUMAN HANDS.
BUT VULNERABLE TO HIGH-SPECTRUM SONICS.
WITH THE STAFF DISABLED, TARGET IS VULNERABLE.

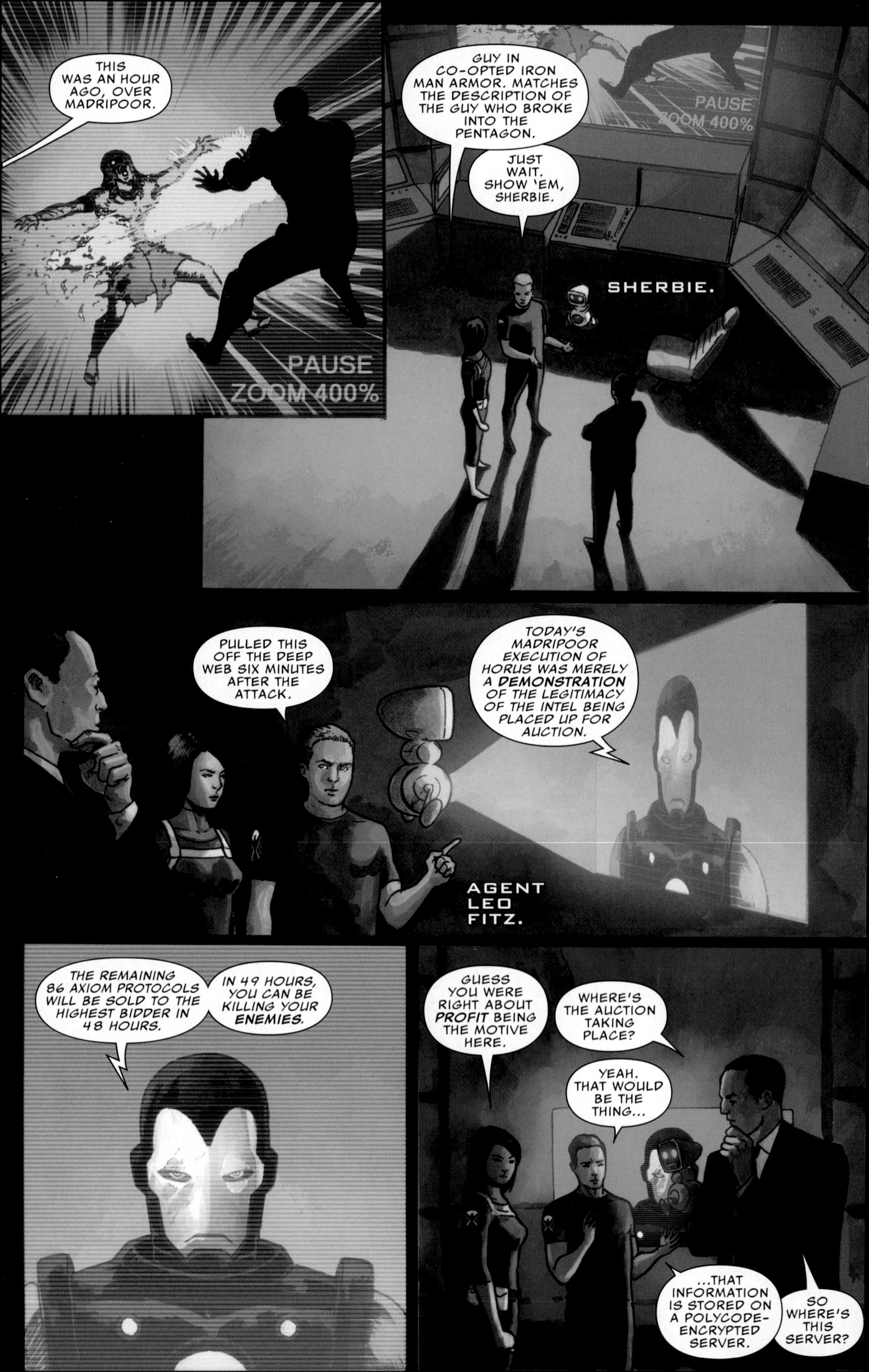
THIS WAS AN HOUR AGO, OVER MADRIPOOR.
PAUSE
ZOOM 400%
GUY IN CO-OPTED IRON MAN ARMOR. MATCHES THE DESCRIPTION OF THE GUY WHO BROKE INTO THE PENTAGON.
JUST WAIT. SHOW 'EM, SHERBIE.
PAUSE
ZOOM 400%
SHERBIE.
PULLED THIS OFF THE DEEP WEB SIX MINUTES AFTER THE ATTACK.
TODAY'S MADRIPOOR EXECUTION OF HORUS WAS MERELY A DEMONSTRATION OF THE LEGITIMACY OF THE INTEL BEING PLACED UP FOR AUCTION.
AGENT LEO FITZ.
THE REMAINING 86 AXIOM PROTOCOLS WILL BE SOLD TO THE HIGHEST BIDDER IN 48 HOURS.
IN 49 HOURS, YOU CAN BE KILLING YOUR ENEMIES.
GUESS YOU WERE RIGHT ABOUT PROFIT BEING THE MOTIVE HERE.
WHERE'S THE AUCTION TAKING PLACE?
YEAH. THAT WOULD BE THE THING...
...THAT INFORMATION IS STORED ON A POLYCODE-ENCRYPTED SERVER.
SO WHERE'S THIS SERVER?

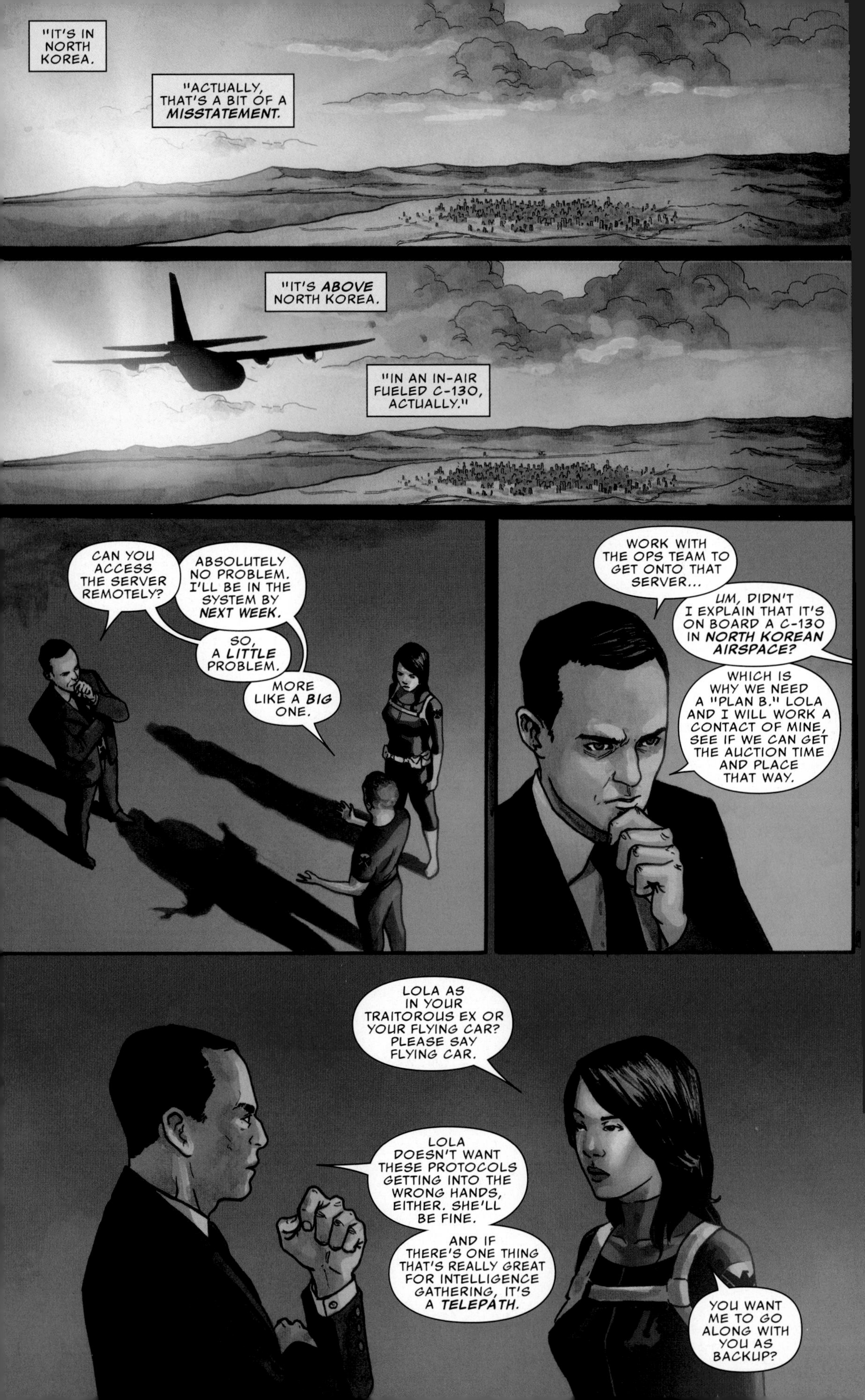
"IT'S IN NORTH KOREA.
"ACTUALLY, THAT'S A BIT OF A MISSTATEMENT.
"IT'S ABOVE NORTH KOREA.
"IN AN IN-AIR FUELED C-130, ACTUALLY."
CAN YOU ACCESS THE SERVER REMOTELY?
ABSOLUTELY NO PROBLEM. I'LL BE IN THE SYSTEM BY NEXT WEEK.
SO, A LITTLE PROBLEM.
MORE LIKE A BIG ONE.
WORK WITH THE OPS TEAM TO GET ONTO THAT SERVER...
UM, DIDN'T I EXPLAIN THAT IT'S ON BOARD A C-130 IN NORTH KOREAN AIRSPACE?
WHICH IS WHY WE NEED A "PLAN B." LOLA AND I WILL WORK A CONTACT OF MINE, SEE IF WE CAN GET THE AUCTION TIME AND PLACE THAT WAY.
LOLA AS IN YOUR TRAITOROUS EX OR YOUR FLYING CAR? PLEASE SAY FLYING CAR.
LOLA DOESN'T WANT THESE PROTOCOLS GETTING INTO THE WRONG HANDS, EITHER. SHE'LL BE FINE.
AND IF THERE'S ONE THING THAT'S REALLY GREAT FOR INTELLIGENCE GATHERING, IT'S A TELEPATH.
YOU WANT ME TO GO ALONG WITH YOU AS BACKUP?

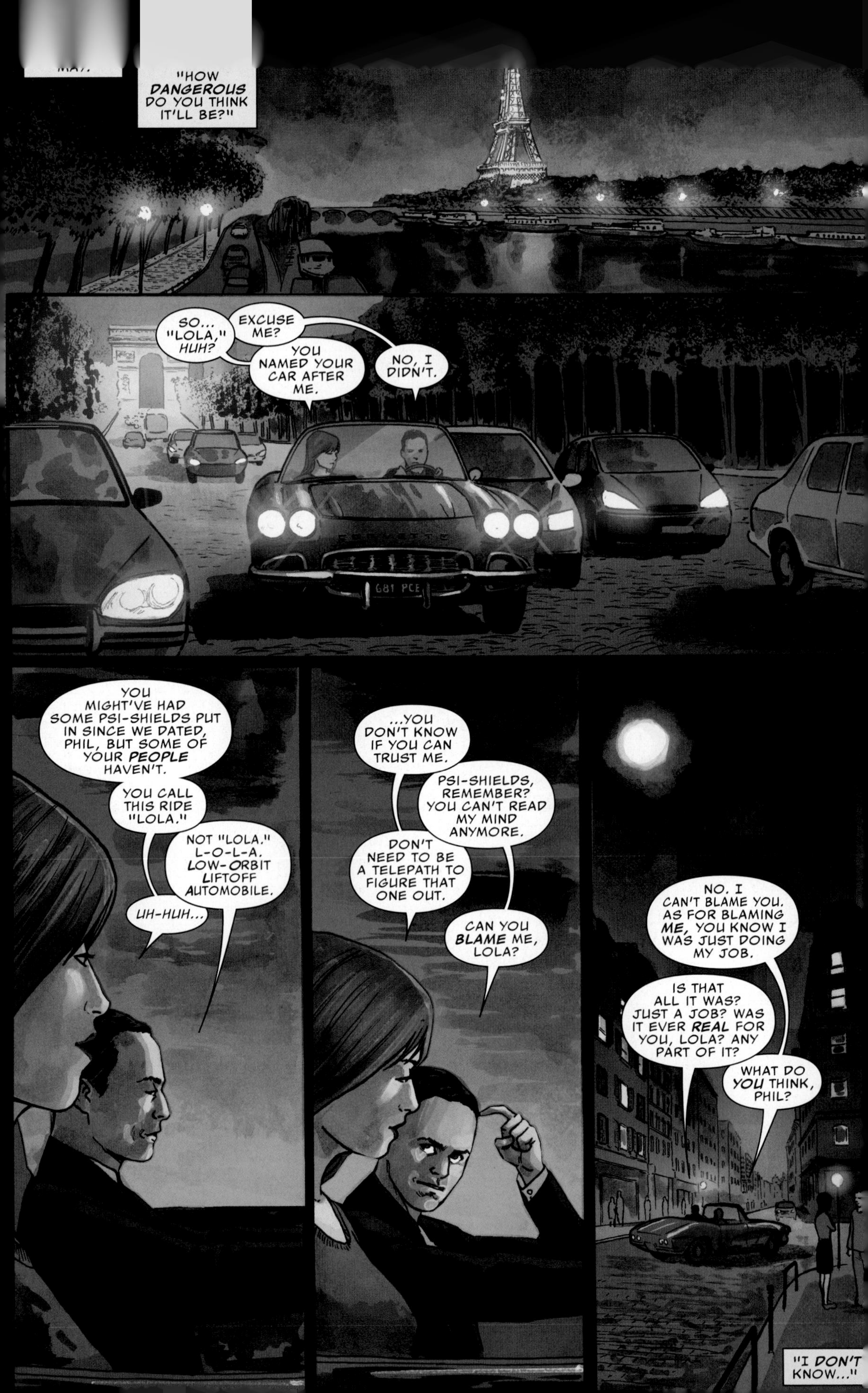
"HOW DANGEROUS DO YOU THINK IT'LL BE?"
SO... "LOLA," HUH?
EXCUSE ME?
YOU NAMED YOUR CAR AFTER ME.
NO, I DIDN'T.
YOU MIGHT'VE HAD SOME PSI-SHIELDS PUT IN SINCE WE DATED, PHIL, BUT SOME OF YOUR PEOPLE HAVEN'T.
YOU CALL THIS RIDE "LOLA."
NOT "LOLA." L-O-L-A. LOW-ORBIT LIFTOFF AUTOMOBILE.
UH-HUH...
...YOU DON'T KNOW IF YOU CAN TRUST ME.
PSI-SHIELDS, REMEMBER? YOU CAN'T READ MY MIND ANYMORE.
DON'T NEED TO BE A TELEPATH TO FIGURE THAT ONE OUT.
CAN YOU BLAME ME, LOLA?
NO. I CAN'T BLAME YOU. AS FOR BLAMING ME, YOU KNOW I WAS JUST DOING MY JOB.
IS THAT ALL IT WAS? JUST A JOB? WAS IT EVER REAL FOR YOU, LOLA? ANY PART OF IT?
WHAT DO YOU THINK, PHIL?
"I DON'T KNOW..."

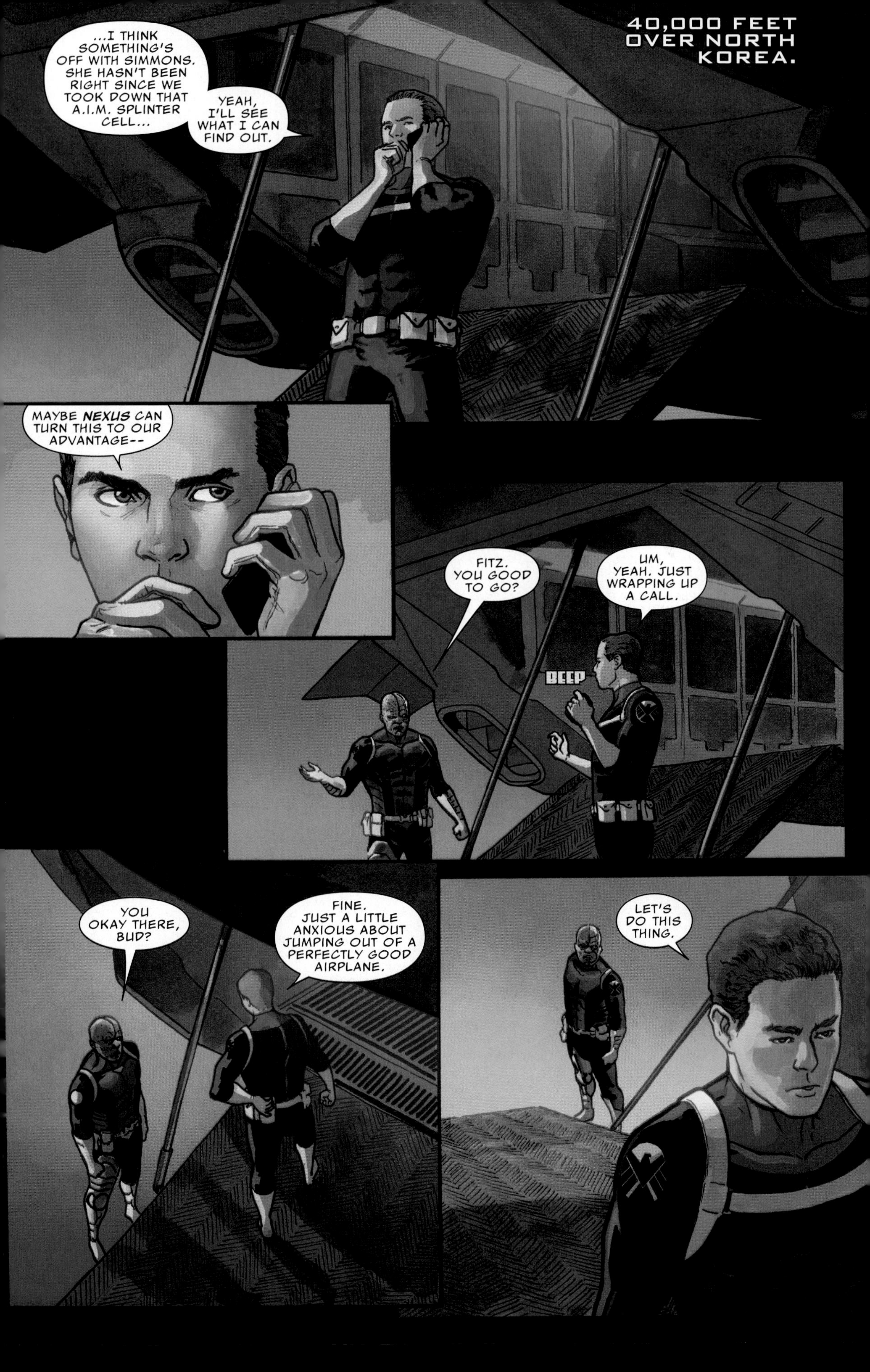
40,000 FEET OVER NORTH KOREA.
...I THINK SOMETHING'S OFF WITH SIMMONS. SHE HASN'T BEEN RIGHT SINCE WE TOOK DOWN THAT A.I.M. SPLINTER CELL...
YEAH, I'LL SEE WHAT I CAN FIND OUT.
MAYBE NEXUS CAN TURN THIS TO OUR ADVANTAGE--
FITZ. YOU GOOD TO GO?
UM, YEAH. JUST WRAPPING UP A CALL.
BEEP
YOU OKAY THERE, BUD?
FINE. JUST A LITTLE ANXIOUS ABOUT JUMPING OUT OF A PERFECTLY GOOD AIRPLANE.
LET'S DO THIS THING.

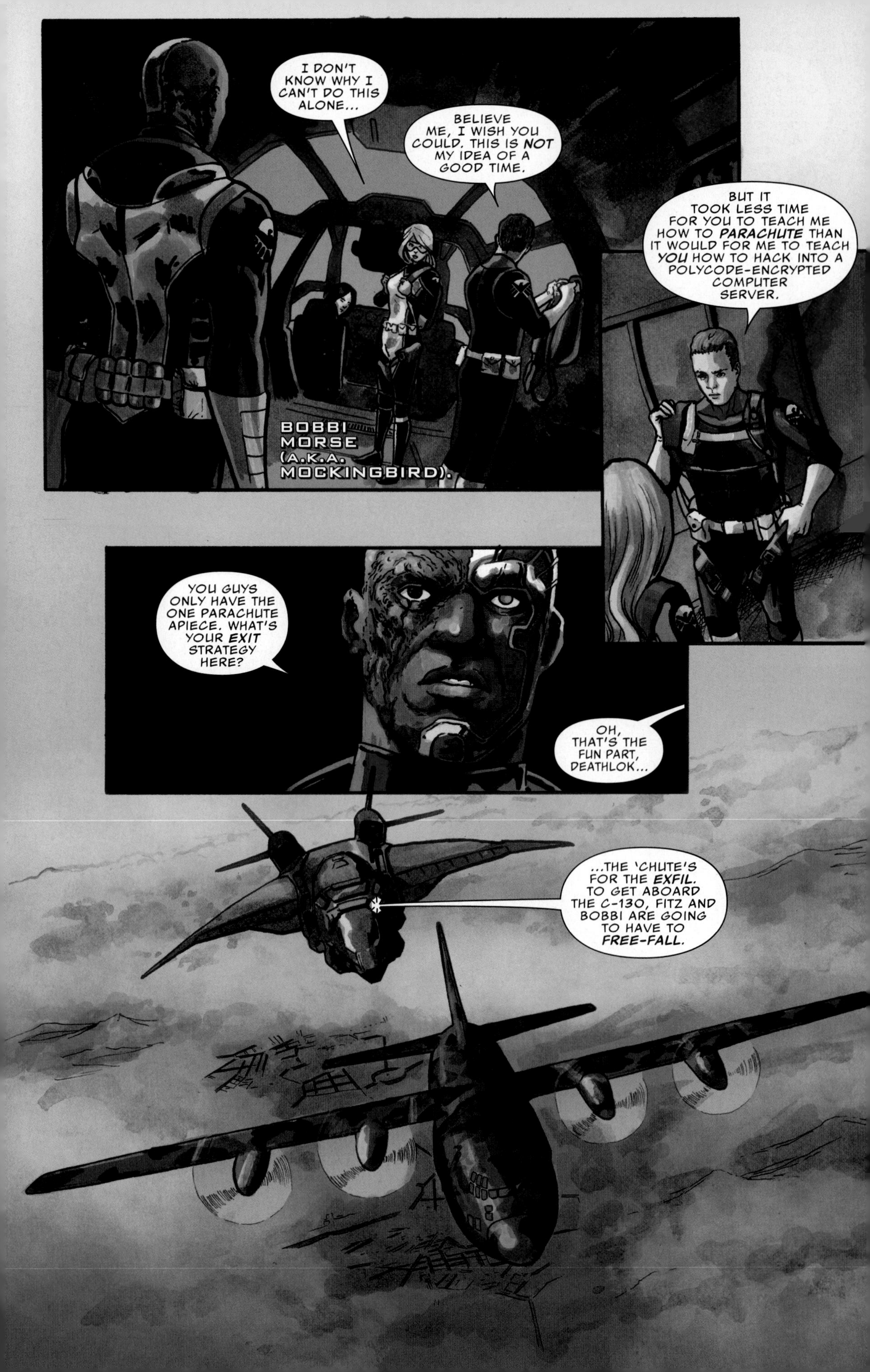
I DON'T KNOW WHY I CAN'T DO THIS ALONE...
BELIEVE ME, I WISH YOU COULD. THIS IS NOT MY IDEA OF A GOOD TIME.
BOBBI MORSE (A.K.A. MOCKINGBIRD).
BUT IT TOOK LESS TIME FOR YOU TO TEACH ME HOW TO PARACHUTE THAN IT WOULD FOR ME TO TEACH YOU HOW TO HACK INTO A POLYCODE-ENCRYPTED COMPUTER SERVER.
YOU GUYS ONLY HAVE THE ONE PARACHUTE APIECE. WHAT'S YOUR EXIT STRATEGY HERE?
OH, THAT'S THE FUN PART, DEATHLOK...
...THE 'CHUTE'S FOR THE EXFIL. TO GET ABOARD THE C-130, FITZ AND BOBBI ARE GOING TO HAVE TO FREE-FALL.

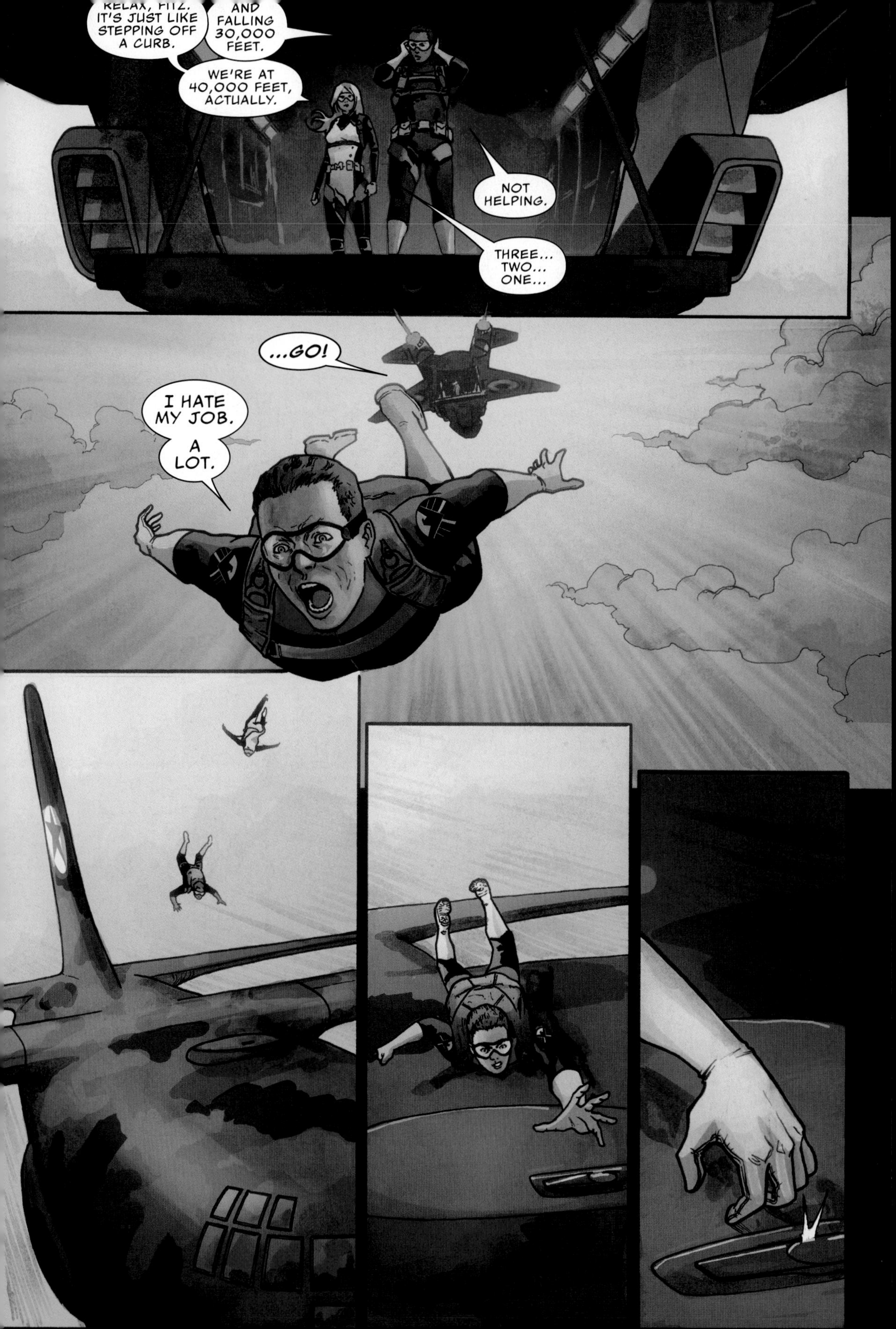
RELAX, FITZ. IT'S JUST LIKE STEPPING OFF A CURB.
AND FALLING 30,000 FEET.
WE'RE AT 40,000 FEET, ACTUALLY.
NOT HELPING.
THREE... TWO... ONE...
...GO!
I HATE MY JOB.
A LOT.

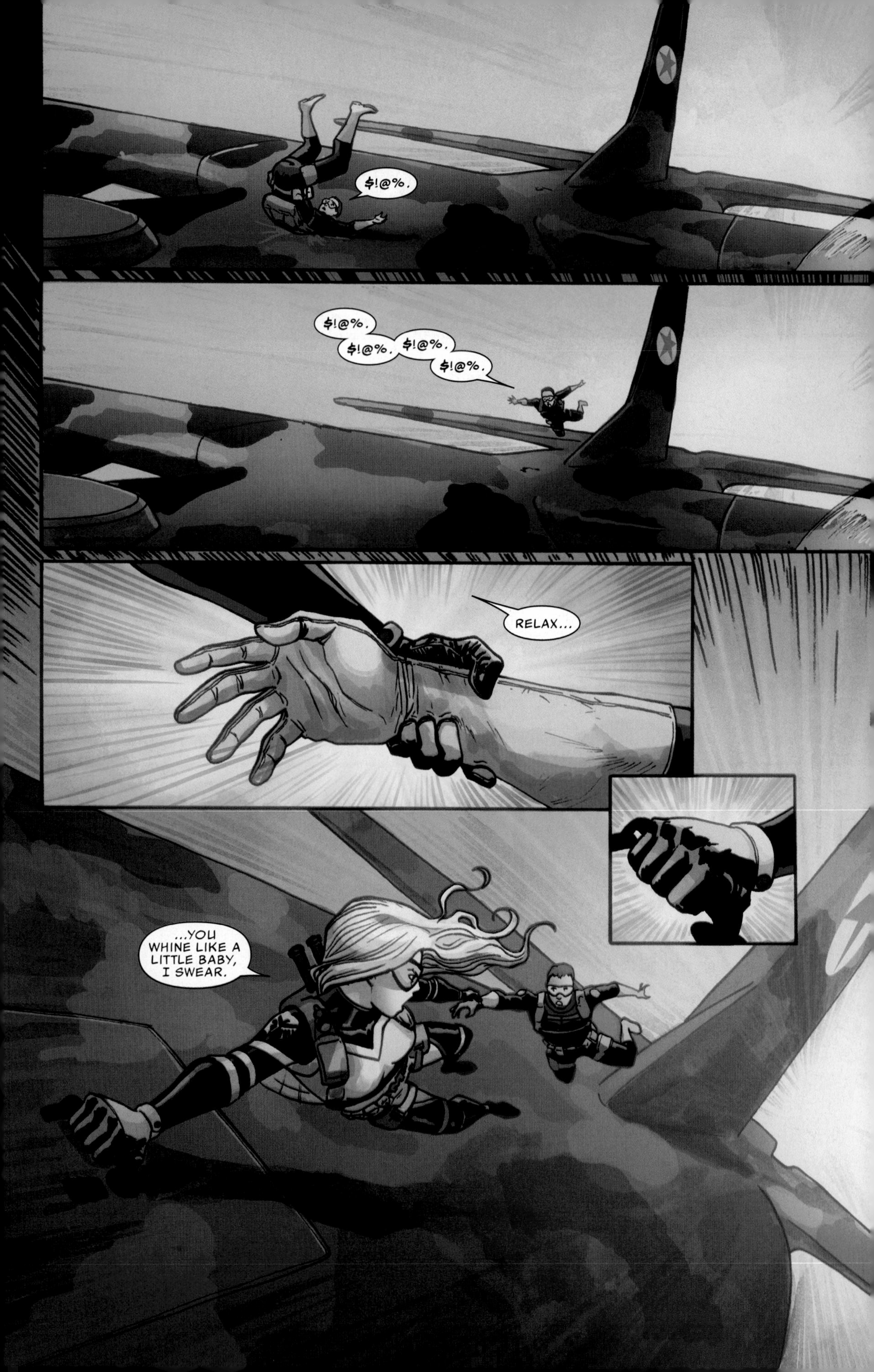
$!@%.
$!@%.
$!@%.
$!@%.
$!@%.
RELAX...
...YOU WHINE LIKE A LITTLE BABY, I SWEAR.

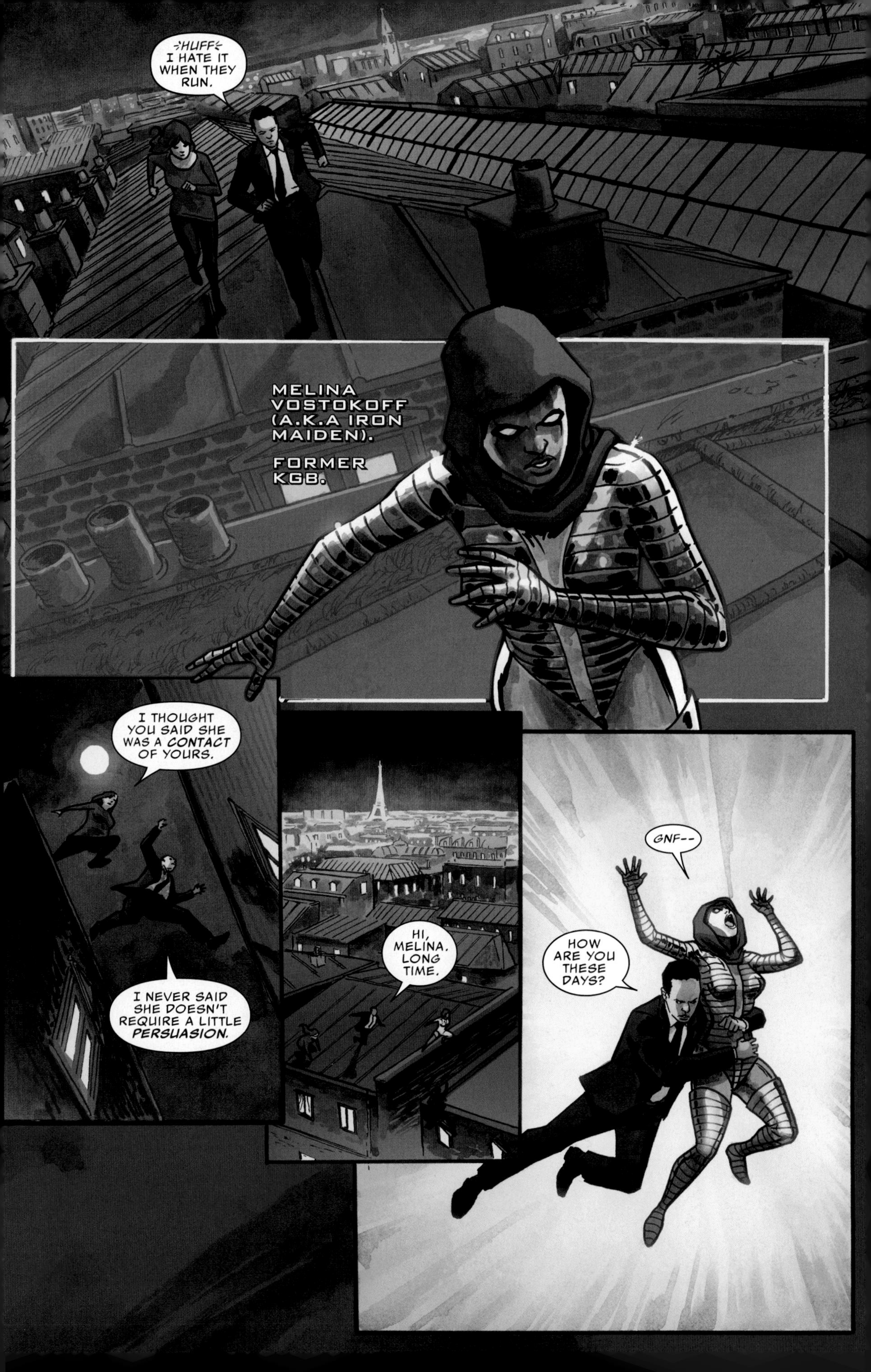

HUFF
I HATE IT WHEN THEY RUN.
MELINA VOSTOKOFF (A.K.A IRON MAIDEN).
FORMER KGB.
I THOUGHT YOU SAID SHE WAS A CONTACT OF YOURS.
I NEVER SAID SHE DOESN'T REQUIRE A LITTLE PERSUASION.
HI, MELINA. LONG TIME.
GNF--
HOW ARE YOU THESE DAYS?

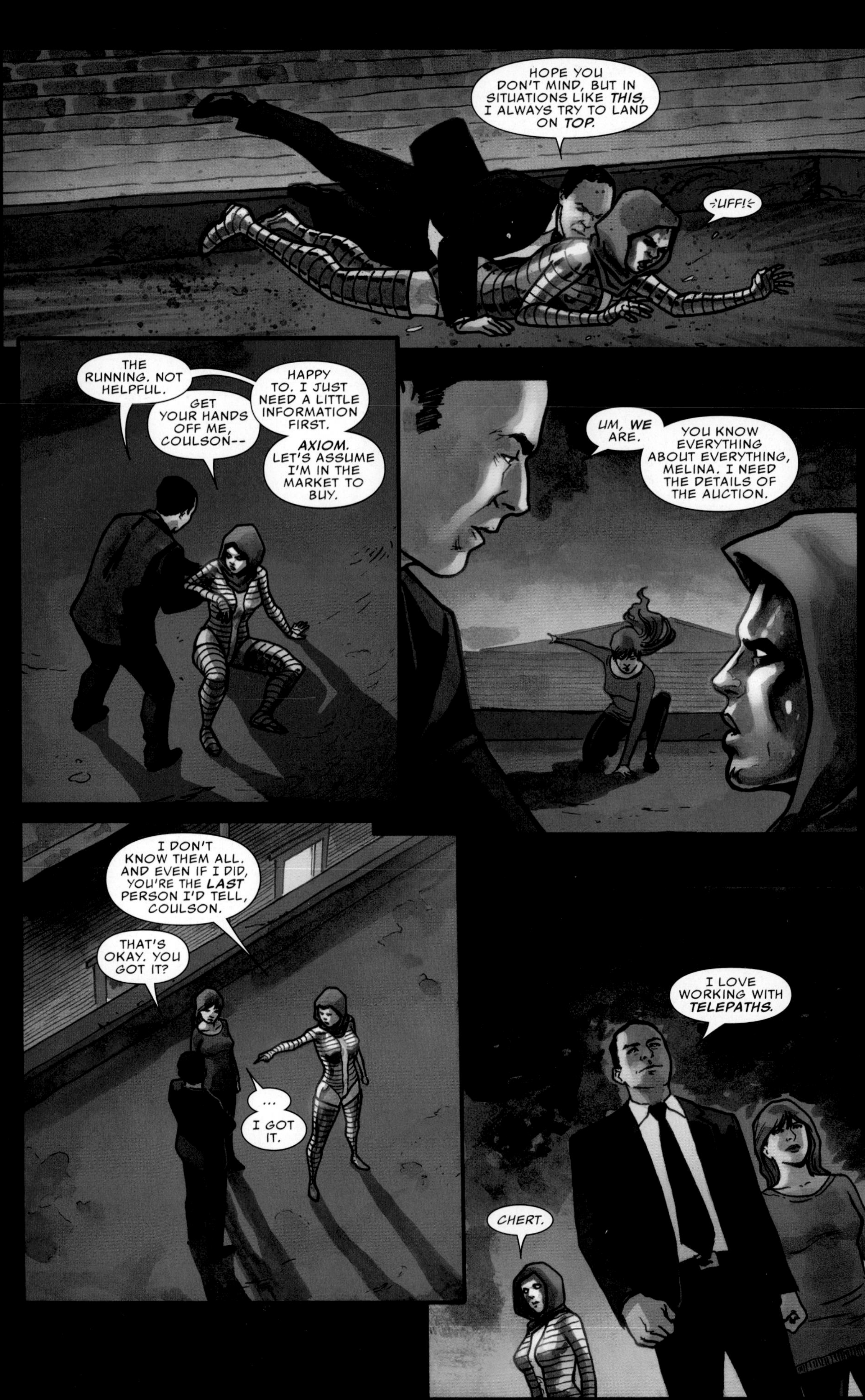
HOPE YOU DON'T MIND, BUT IN SITUATIONS LIKE *THIS*, I ALWAYS TRY TO LAND ON *TOP*.
UFF!
THE RUNNING. NOT HELPFUL.
GET YOUR HANDS OFF ME, COULSON--
HAPPY TO. I JUST NEED A LITTLE INFORMATION FIRST.
AXIOM. LET'S ASSUME I'M IN THE MARKET TO BUY.
UM, *WE* ARE.
YOU KNOW EVERYTHING ABOUT EVERYTHING, MELINA. I NEED THE DETAILS OF THE AUCTION.
I DON'T KNOW THEM ALL. AND EVEN IF I DID, YOU'RE THE *LAST* PERSON I'D TELL, COULSON.
THAT'S OKAY. YOU GOT IT?
... I GOT IT.
I LOVE WORKING WITH *TELEPATHS*.
CHERT.

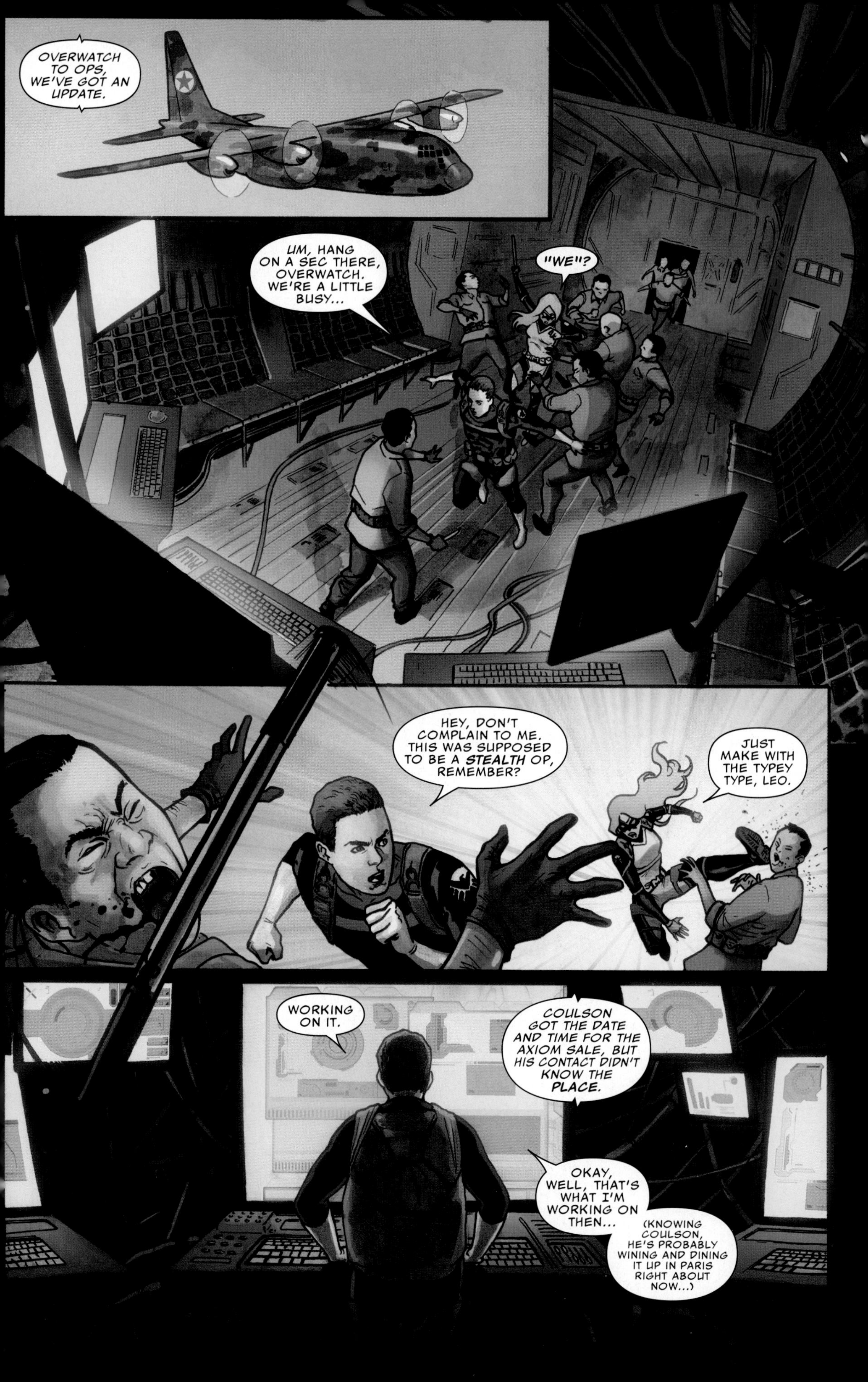
OVERWATCH TO OPS, WE'VE GOT AN UPDATE.
UM, HANG ON A SEC THERE, OVERWATCH. WE'RE A LITTLE BUSY...
"WE"?
HEY, DON'T COMPLAIN TO ME. THIS WAS SUPPOSED TO BE A STEALTH OP, REMEMBER?
JUST MAKE WITH THE TYPEY TYPE, LEO.
WORKING ON IT.
COULSON GOT THE DATE AND TIME FOR THE AXIOM SALE, BUT HIS CONTACT DIDN'T KNOW THE PLACE.
OKAY, WELL, THAT'S WHAT I'M WORKING ON THEN...
(KNOWING COULSON, HE'S PROBABLY WINING AND DINING IT UP IN PARIS RIGHT ABOUT NOW...)

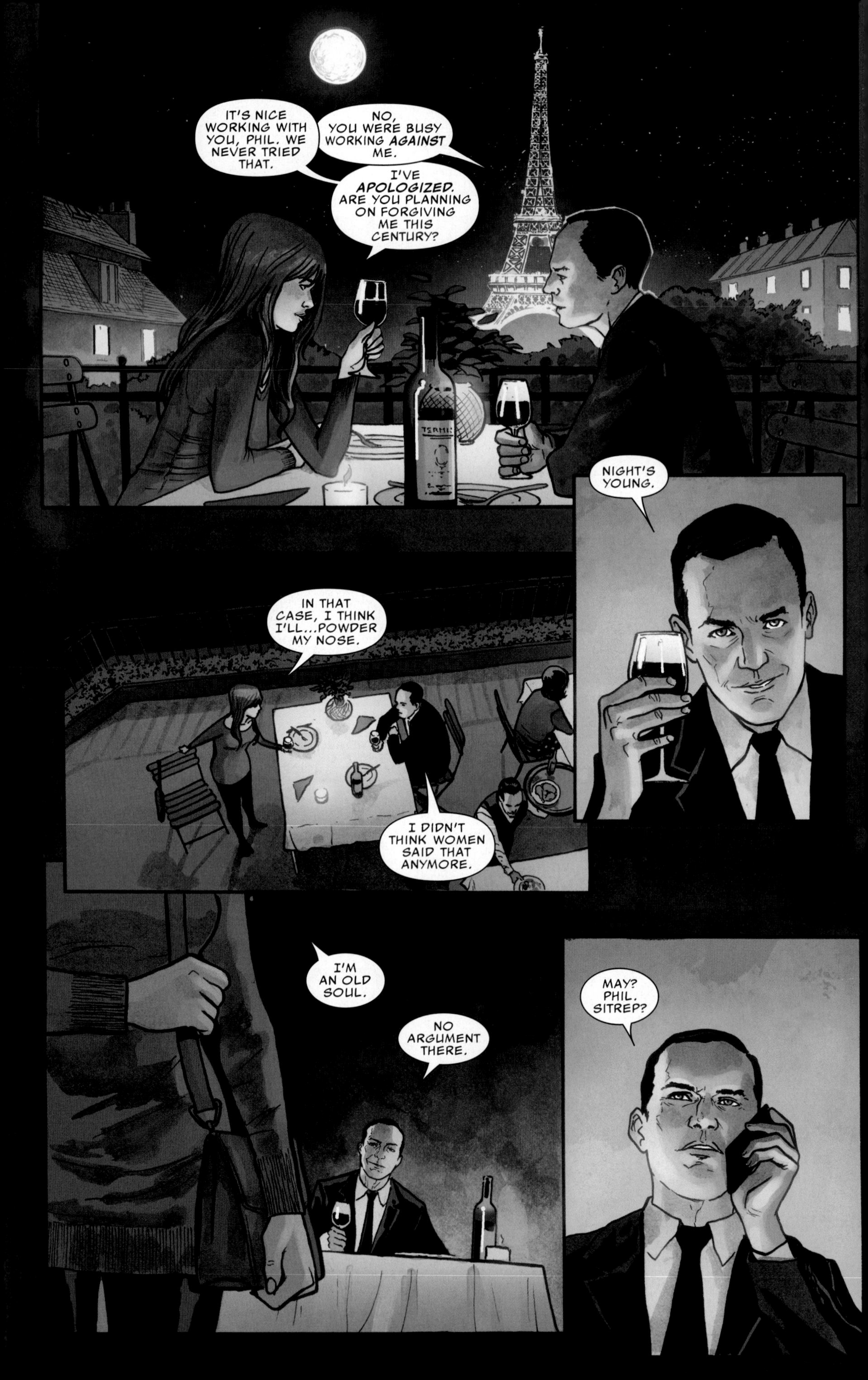
IT'S NICE WORKING WITH YOU, PHIL. WE NEVER TRIED THAT.
NO, YOU WERE BUSY WORKING AGAINST ME.
I'VE APOLOGIZED. ARE YOU PLANNING ON FORGIVING ME THIS CENTURY?
NIGHT'S YOUNG.
IN THAT CASE, I THINK I'LL...POWDER MY NOSE.
I DIDN'T THINK WOMEN SAID THAT ANYMORE.
I'M AN OLD SOUL.
NO ARGUMENT THERE.
MAY? PHIL. SITREP?

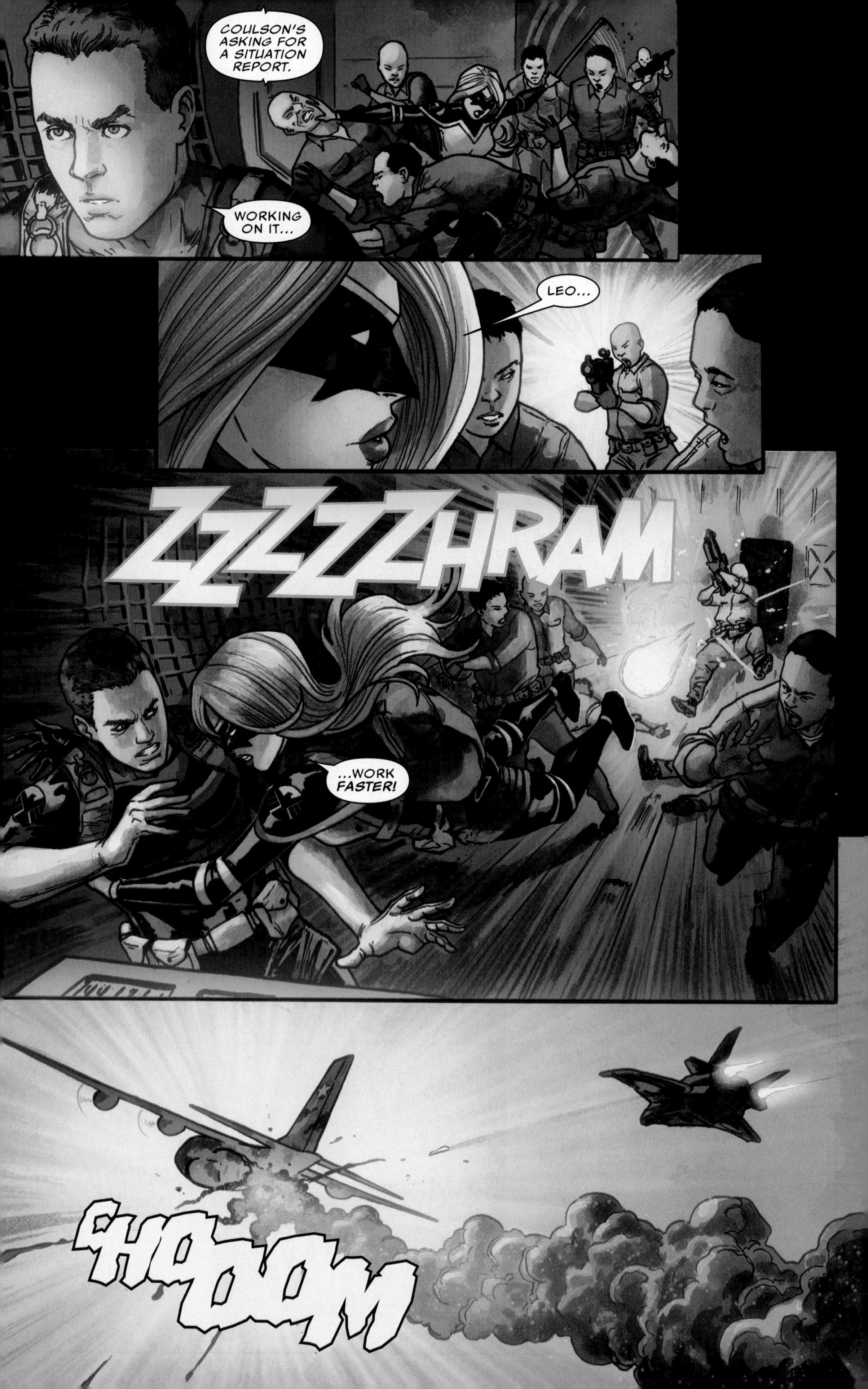
COULSON'S ASKING FOR A SITUATION REPORT.
WORKING ON IT...
LEO...
ZZZZZHRAM
...WORK FASTER!
CHOOOM

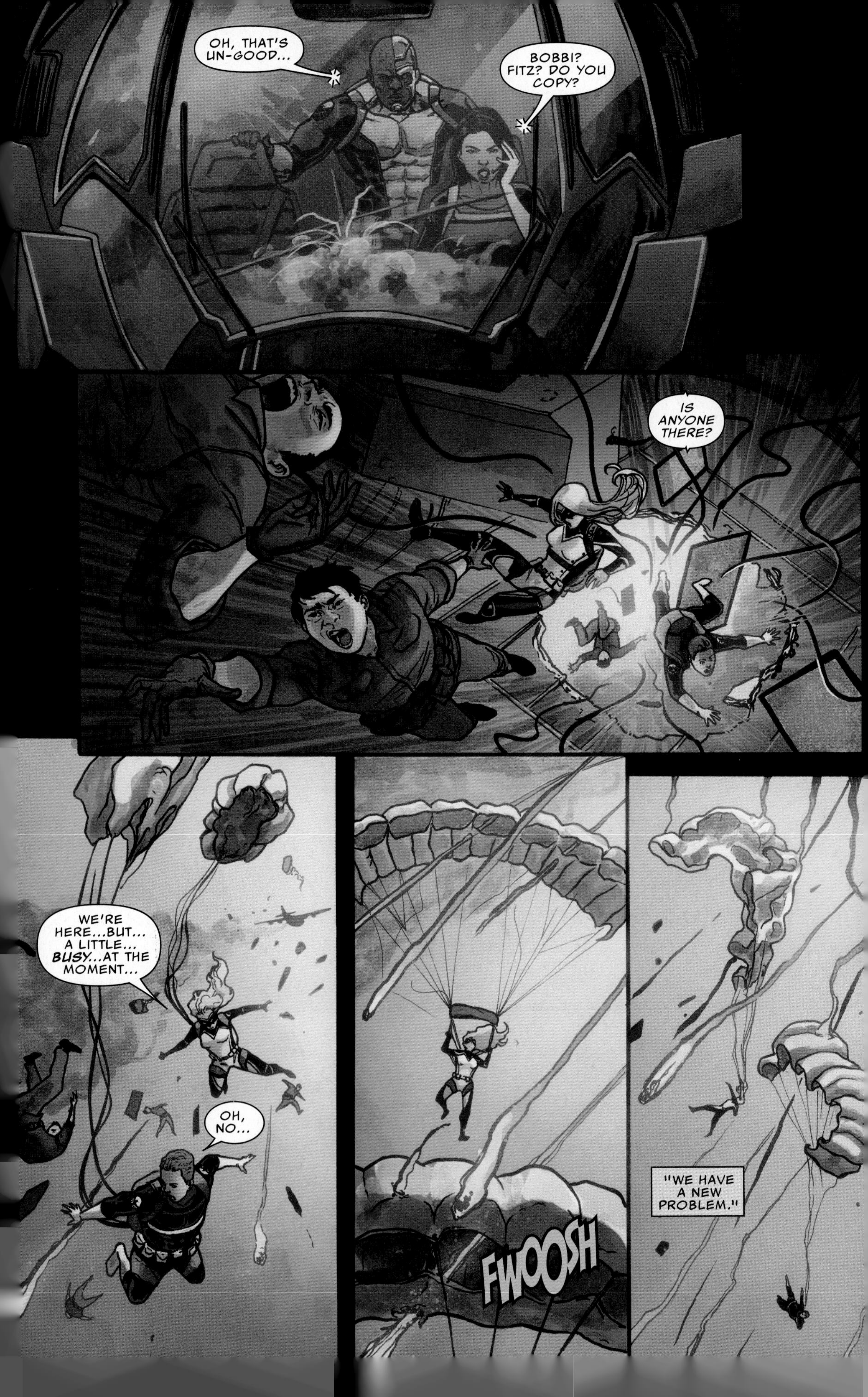
OH, THAT'S UN-GOOD...
BOBBI? FITZ? DO YOU COPY?
IS ANYONE THERE?
WE'RE HERE...BUT... A LITTLE... BUSY...AT THE MOMENT...
OH, NO...
FWOOSH
"WE HAVE A NEW PROBLEM."

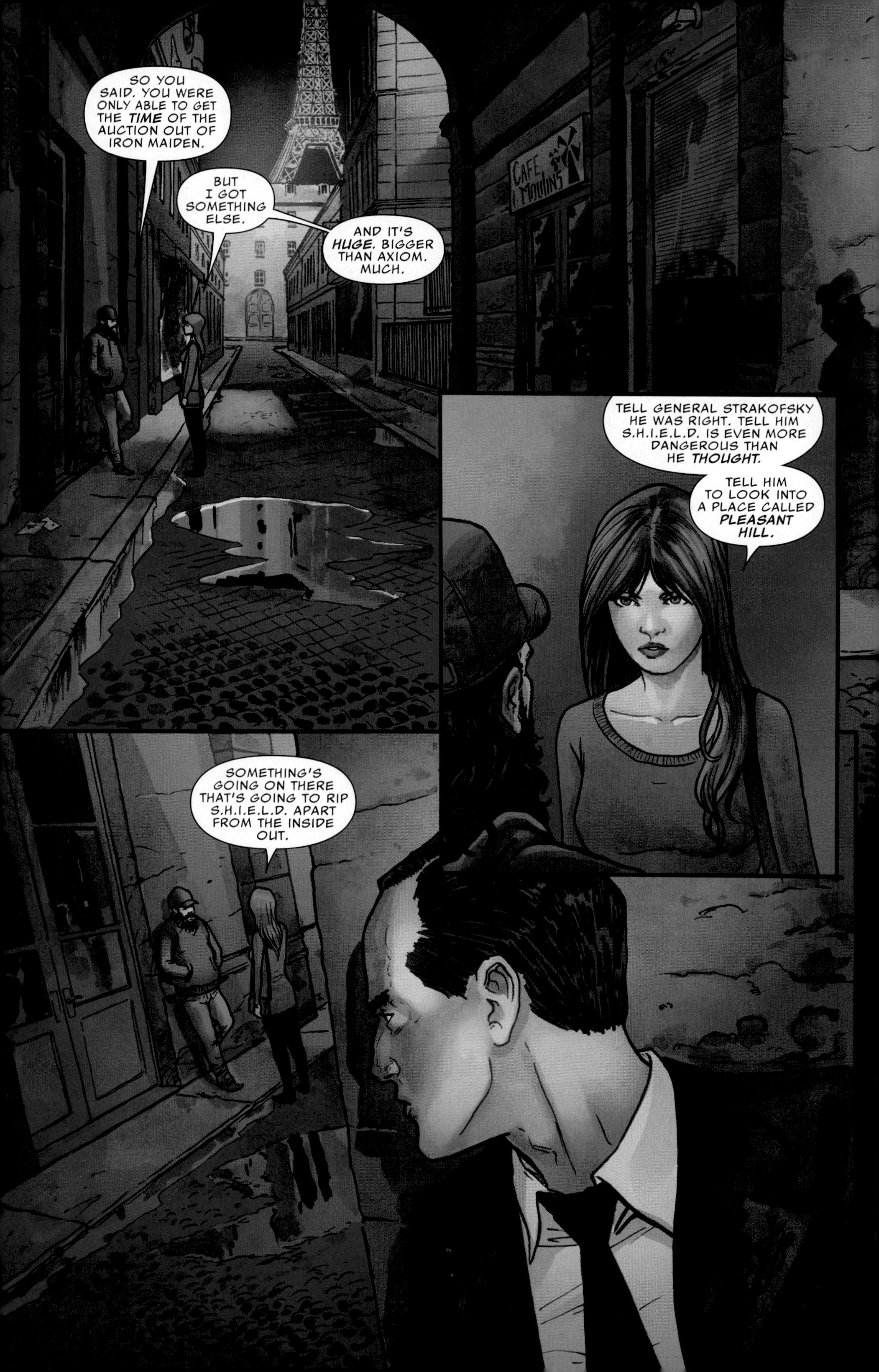
SO YOU SAID. YOU WERE ONLY ABLE TO GET THE TIME OUT OF THE AUCTION OUT OF IRON MAIDEN.
BUT I GOT SOMETHING ELSE.
AND IT'S HUGE. BIGGER THAN AXIOM. MUCH.
CAFE MOULINS
TELL GENERAL STRAKOFSKY HE WAS RIGHT. TELL HIM S.H.I.E.L.D. IS EVEN MORE DANGEROUS THAN HE THOUGHT.
TELL HIM TO LOOK INTO A PLACE CALLED PLEASANT HILL.
SOMETHING'S GOING ON THERE THAT'S GOING TO RIP S.H.I.E.L.D. APART FROM THE INSIDE OUT.

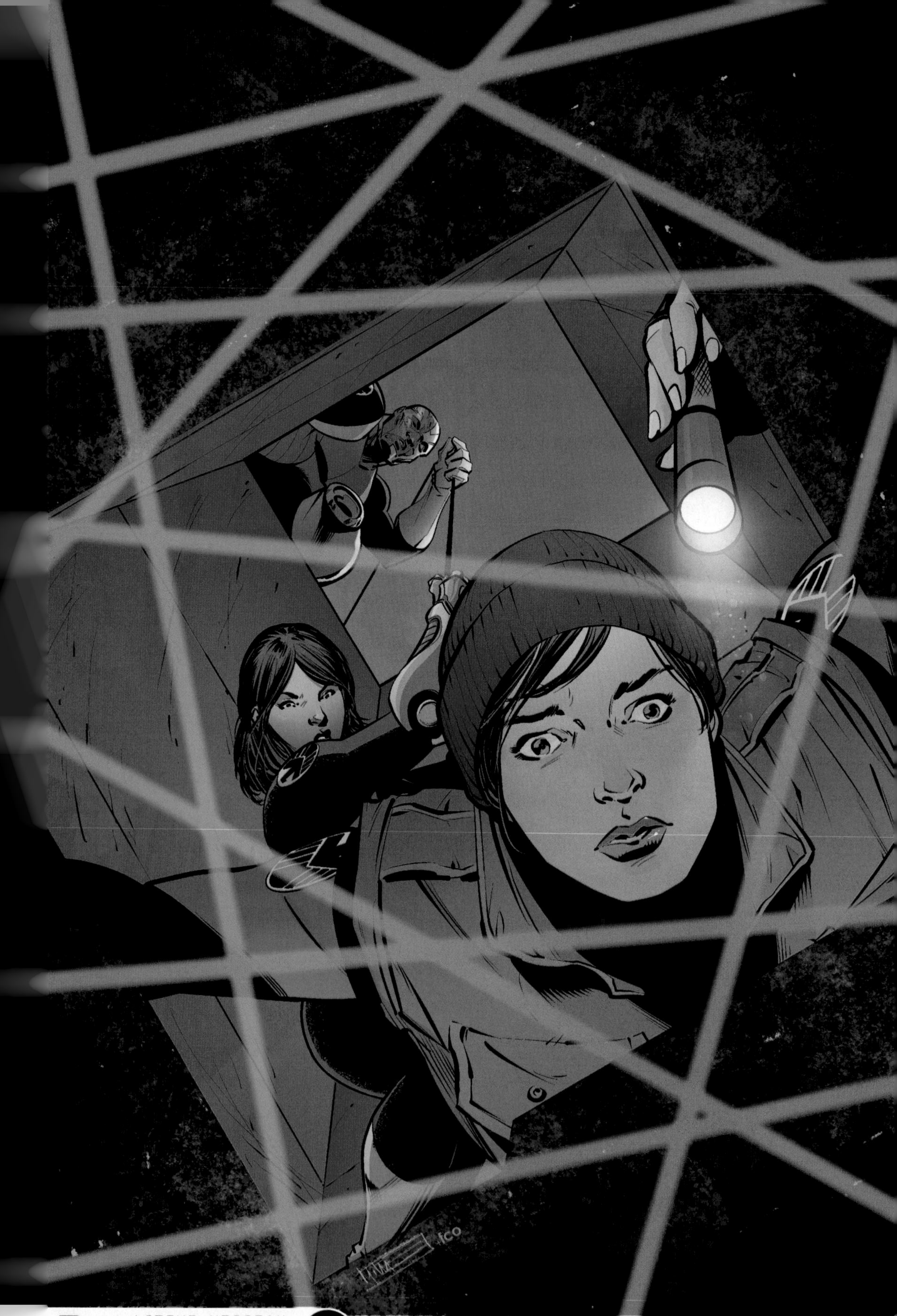

3. ACTIVE MISSION: FREE FALL

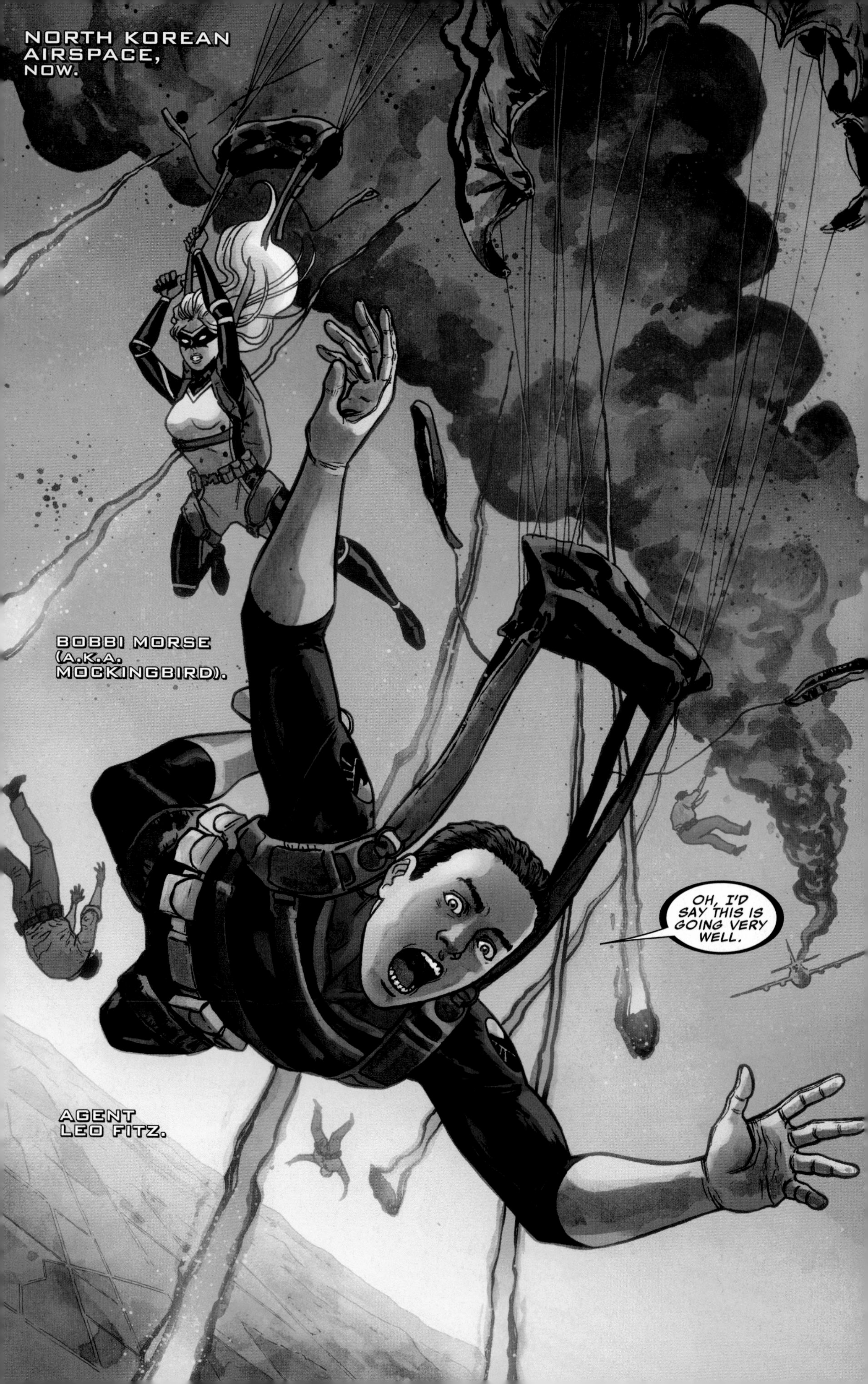
NORTH KOREAN AIRSPACE, NOW.
BOBBI MORSE (A.K.A. MOCKINGBIRD).
OH, I'D SAY THIS IS GOING VERY WELL.
AGENT LEO FITZ.

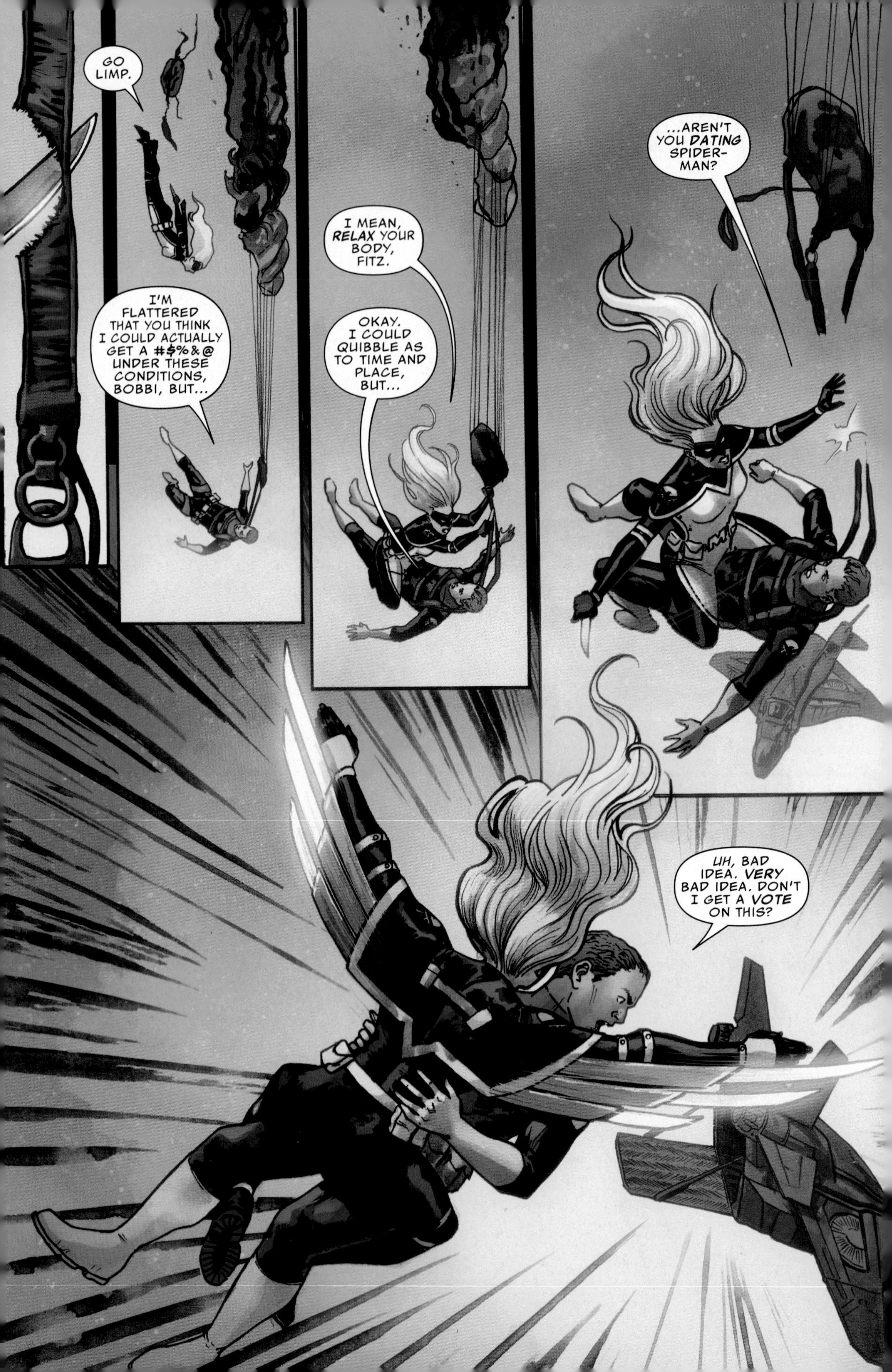
GO LIMP.
I'M FLATTERED THAT YOU THINK I COULD ACTUALLY GET A #$%&@ UNDER THESE CONDITIONS, BOBBI, BUT...
I MEAN, RELAX YOUR BODY, FITZ.
OKAY. I COULD QUIBBLE AS TO TIME AND PLACE, BUT...
...AREN'T YOU DATING SPIDER-MAN?
UH, BAD IDEA. VERY BAD IDEA. DON'T I GET A VOTE ON THIS?

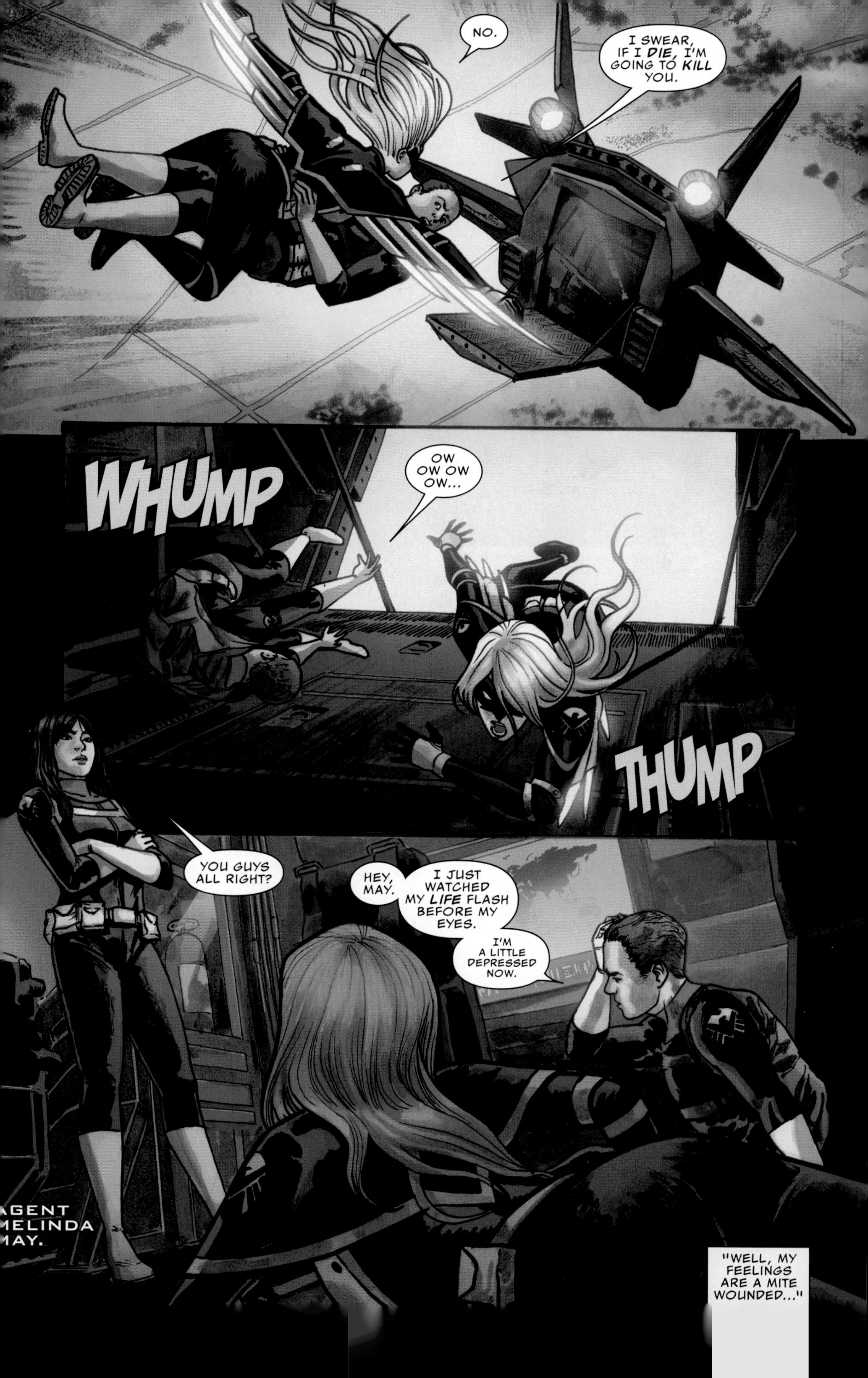
NO.
I SWEAR, IF I DIE, I'M GOING TO KILL YOU.
WHUMP
OW OW OW OW...
THUMP
YOU GUYS ALL RIGHT?
HEY, MAY.
I JUST WATCHED MY LIFE FLASH BEFORE MY EYES.
I'M A LITTLE DEPRESSED NOW.
AGENT MELINDA MAY.
"WELL, MY FEELINGS ARE A MITE WOUNDED..."

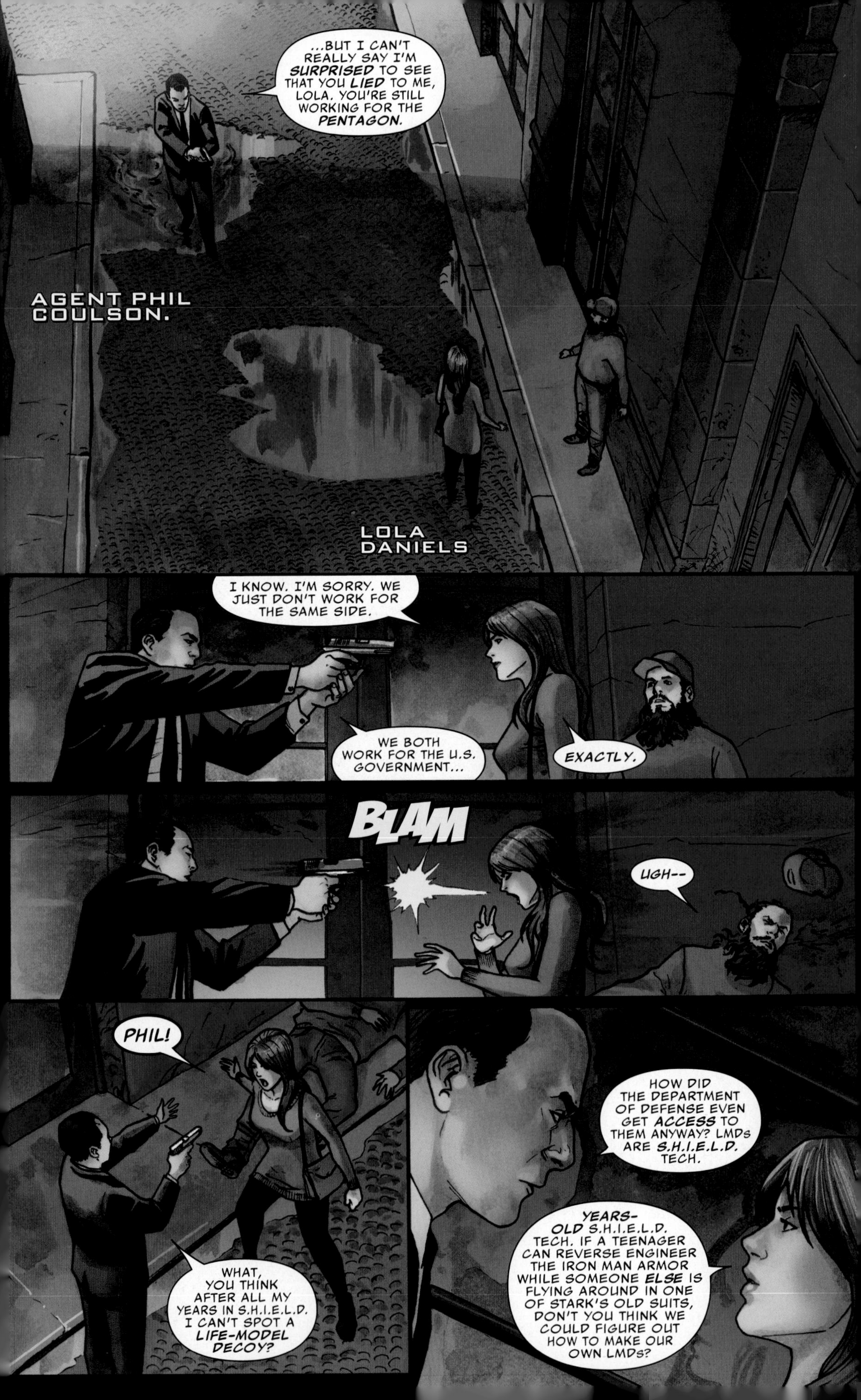
...BUT I CAN'T REALLY SAY I'M SURPRISED TO SEE THAT YOU LIED TO ME, LOLA. YOU'RE STILL WORKING FOR THE PENTAGON.
AGENT PHIL COULSON.
LOLA DANIELS
I KNOW. I'M SORRY. WE JUST DON'T WORK FOR THE SAME SIDE.
WE BOTH WORK FOR THE U.S. GOVERNMENT...
EXACTLY.
BLAM
UGH--
PHIL!
WHAT, YOU THINK AFTER ALL MY YEARS IN S.H.I.E.L.D. I CAN'T SPOT A LIFE-MODEL DECOY?
HOW DID THE DEPARTMENT OF DEFENSE EVEN GET ACCESS TO THEM ANYWAY? LMDs ARE S.H.I.E.L.D. TECH.
YEARS-OLD S.H.I.E.L.D. TECH. IF A TEENAGER CAN REVERSE ENGINEER THE IRON MAN ARMOR WHILE SOMEONE ELSE IS FLYING AROUND IN ONE OF STARK'S OLD SUITS, DON'T YOU THINK WE COULD FIGURE OUT HOW TO MAKE OUR OWN LMDs?

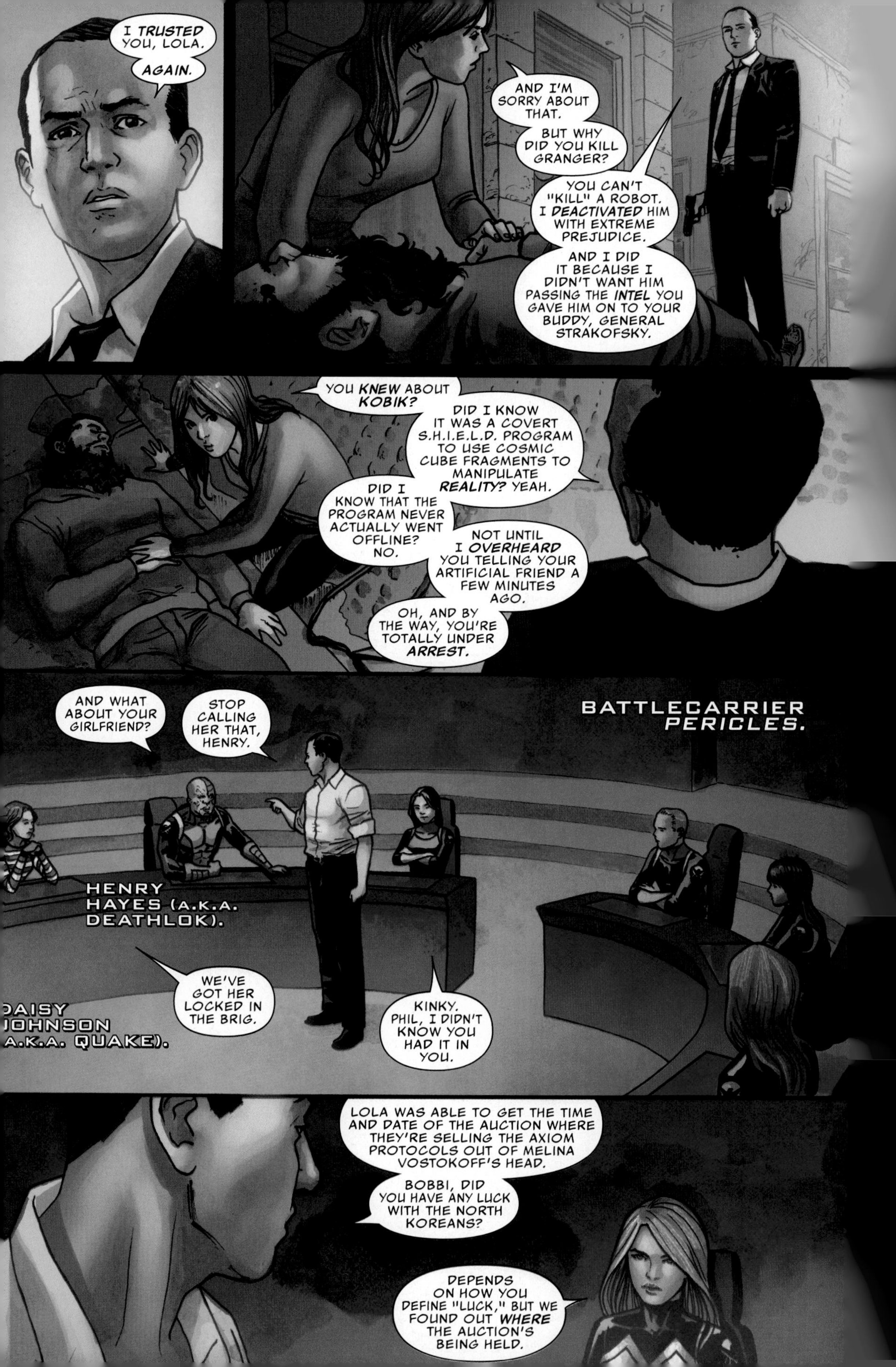
I TRUSTED YOU, LOLA.
AGAIN.
AND I'M SORRY ABOUT THAT.
BUT WHY DID YOU KILL GRANGER?
YOU CAN'T "KILL" A ROBOT. I DEACTIVATED HIM WITH EXTREME PREJUDICE.
AND I DID IT BECAUSE I DIDN'T WANT HIM PASSING THE INTEL YOU GAVE HIM ON TO YOUR BUDDY, GENERAL STRAKOFSKY.
YOU KNEW ABOUT KOBIK?
DID I KNOW IT WAS A COVERT S.H.I.E.L.D. PROGRAM TO USE COSMIC CUBE FRAGMENTS TO MANIPULATE REALITY? YEAH.
DID I KNOW THAT THE PROGRAM NEVER ACTUALLY WENT OFFLINE? NO.
NOT UNTIL I OVERHEARD YOU TELLING YOUR ARTIFICIAL FRIEND A FEW MINUTES AGO.
OH, AND BY THE WAY, YOU'RE TOTALLY UNDER ARREST.
BATTLECARRIER PERICLES.
AND WHAT ABOUT YOUR GIRLFRIEND?
STOP CALLING HER THAT, HENRY.
HENRY HAYES (A.K.A. DEATHLOK).
WE'VE GOT HER LOCKED IN THE BRIG.
DAISY JOHNSON (A.K.A. QUAKE).
KINKY. PHIL, I DIDN'T KNOW YOU HAD IT IN YOU.
LOLA WAS ABLE TO GET THE TIME AND DATE OF THE AUCTION WHERE THEY'RE SELLING THE AXIOM PROTOCOLS OUT OF MELINA VOSTOKOFF'S HEAD.
BOBBI, DID YOU HAVE ANY LUCK WITH THE NORTH KOREANS?
DEPENDS ON HOW YOU DEFINE "LUCK," BUT WE FOUND OUT WHERE THE AUCTION'S BEING HELD.

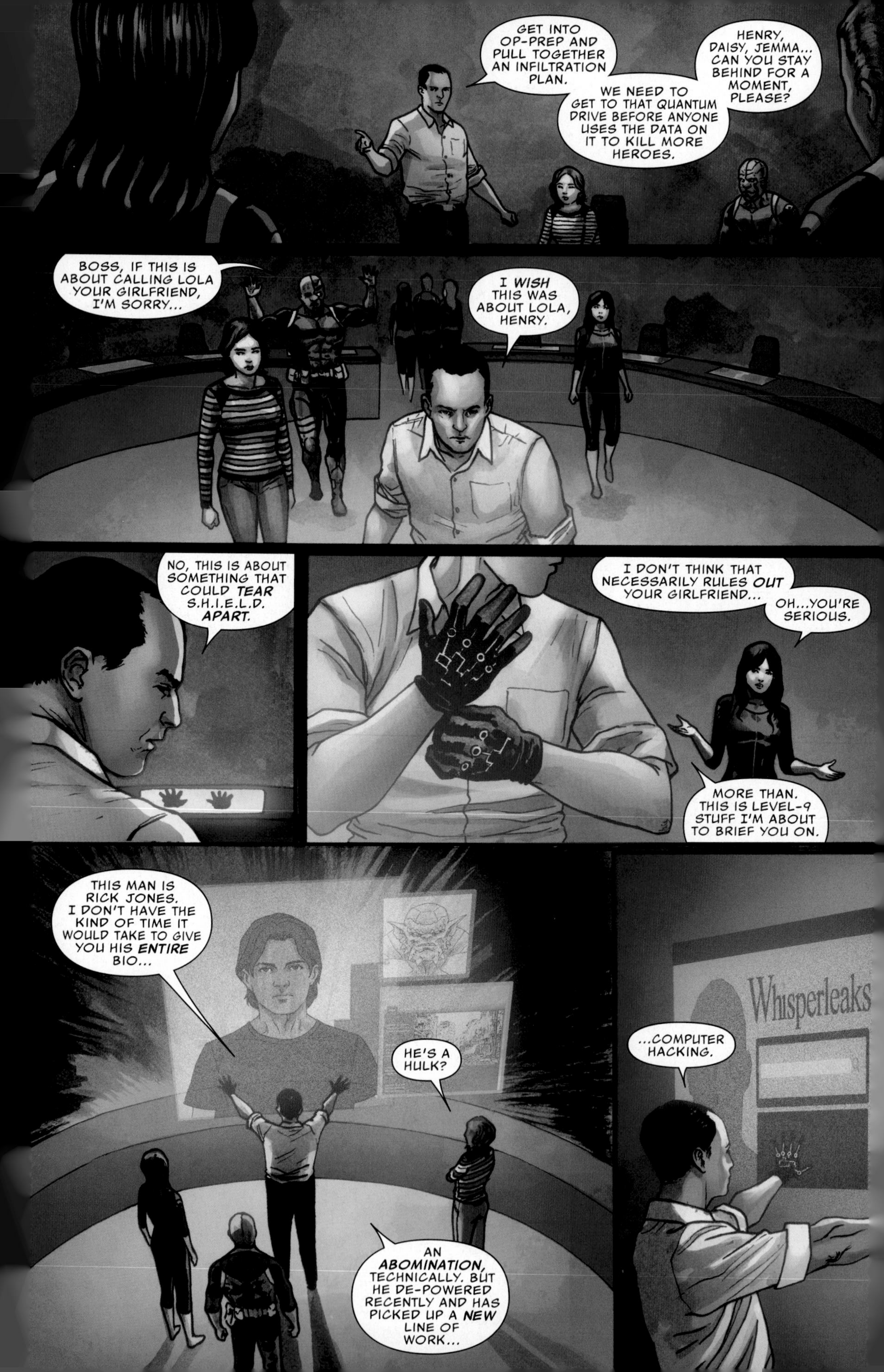
GET INTO OP-PREP AND PULL TOGETHER AN INFILTRATION PLAN.
WE NEED TO GET TO THAT QUANTUM DRIVE BEFORE ANYONE USES THE DATA ON IT TO KILL MORE HEROES.
HENRY, DAISY, JEMMA... CAN YOU STAY BEHIND FOR A MOMENT, PLEASE?
BOSS, IF THIS IS ABOUT CALLING LOLA YOUR GIRLFRIEND, I'M SORRY...
I WISH THIS WAS ABOUT LOLA, HENRY.
NO, THIS IS ABOUT SOMETHING THAT COULD TEAR S.H.I.E.L.D. APART.
I DON'T THINK THAT NECESSARILY RULES OUT YOUR GIRLFRIEND...
OH...YOU'RE SERIOUS.
MORE THAN. THIS IS LEVEL-9 STUFF I'M ABOUT TO BRIEF YOU ON.
THIS MAN IS RICK JONES. I DON'T HAVE THE KIND OF TIME IT WOULD TAKE TO GIVE YOU HIS ENTIRE BIO...
HE'S A HULK?
AN ABOMINATION, TECHNICALLY. BUT HE DE-POWERED RECENTLY AND HAS PICKED UP A NEW LINE OF WORK...
Whisperleaks
...COMPUTER HACKING.

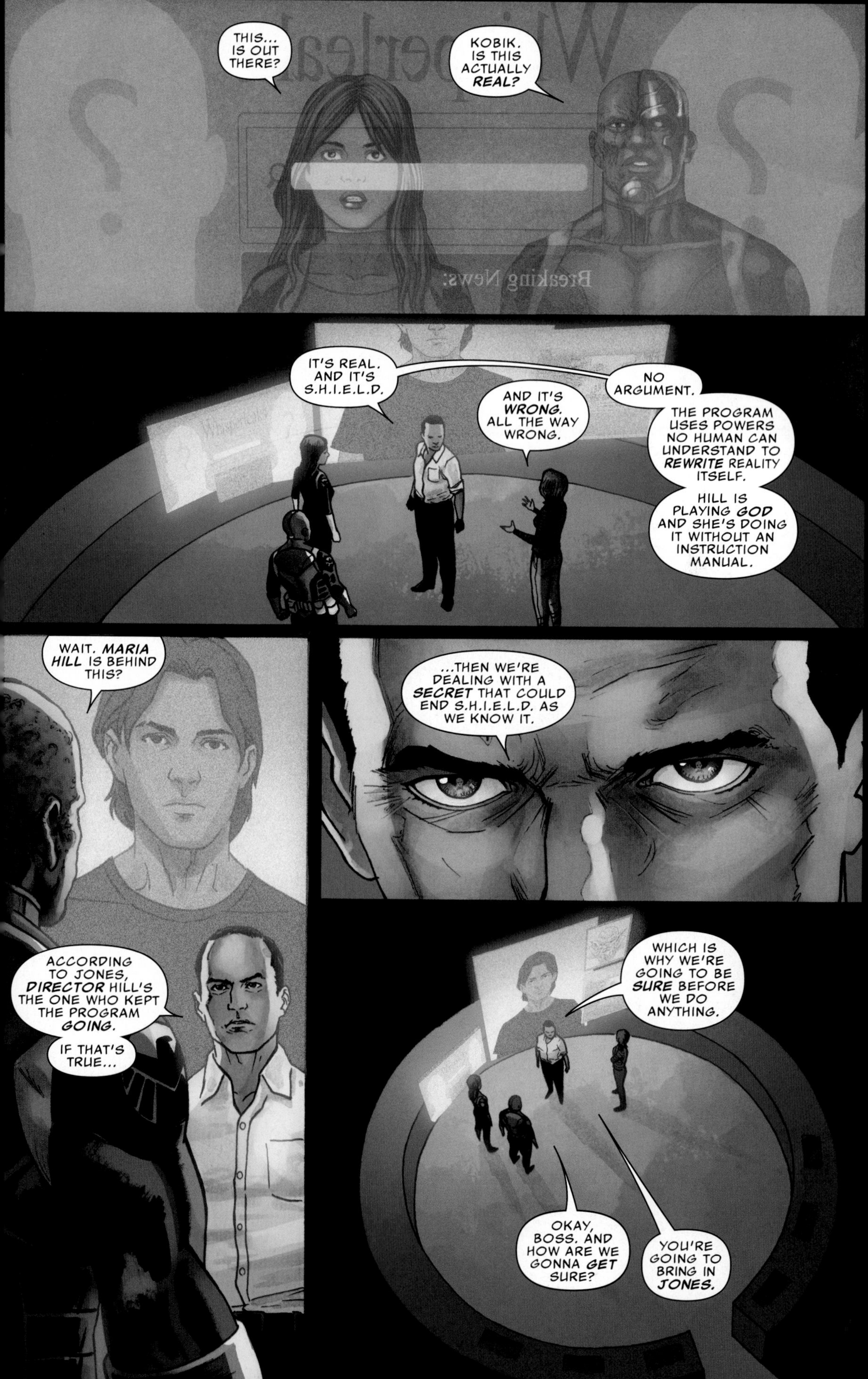
THIS... IS OUT THERE?
KOBIK. IS THIS ACTUALLY REAL?
Breaking News:
IT'S REAL. AND IT'S S.H.I.E.L.D.
NO ARGUMENT.
AND IT'S WRONG. ALL THE WAY WRONG.
THE PROGRAM USES POWERS NO HUMAN CAN UNDERSTAND TO REWRITE REALITY ITSELF.
HILL IS PLAYING GOD AND SHE'S DOING IT WITHOUT AN INSTRUCTION MANUAL.
WAIT. MARIA HILL IS BEHIND THIS?
ACCORDING TO JONES, DIRECTOR HILL'S THE ONE WHO KEPT THE PROGRAM GOING.
IF THAT'S TRUE...
...THEN WE'RE DEALING WITH A SECRET THAT COULD END S.H.I.E.L.D. AS WE KNOW IT.
WHICH IS WHY WE'RE GOING TO BE SURE BEFORE WE DO ANYTHING.
OKAY, BOSS. AND HOW ARE WE GONNA GET SURE?
YOU'RE GOING TO BRING IN JONES.

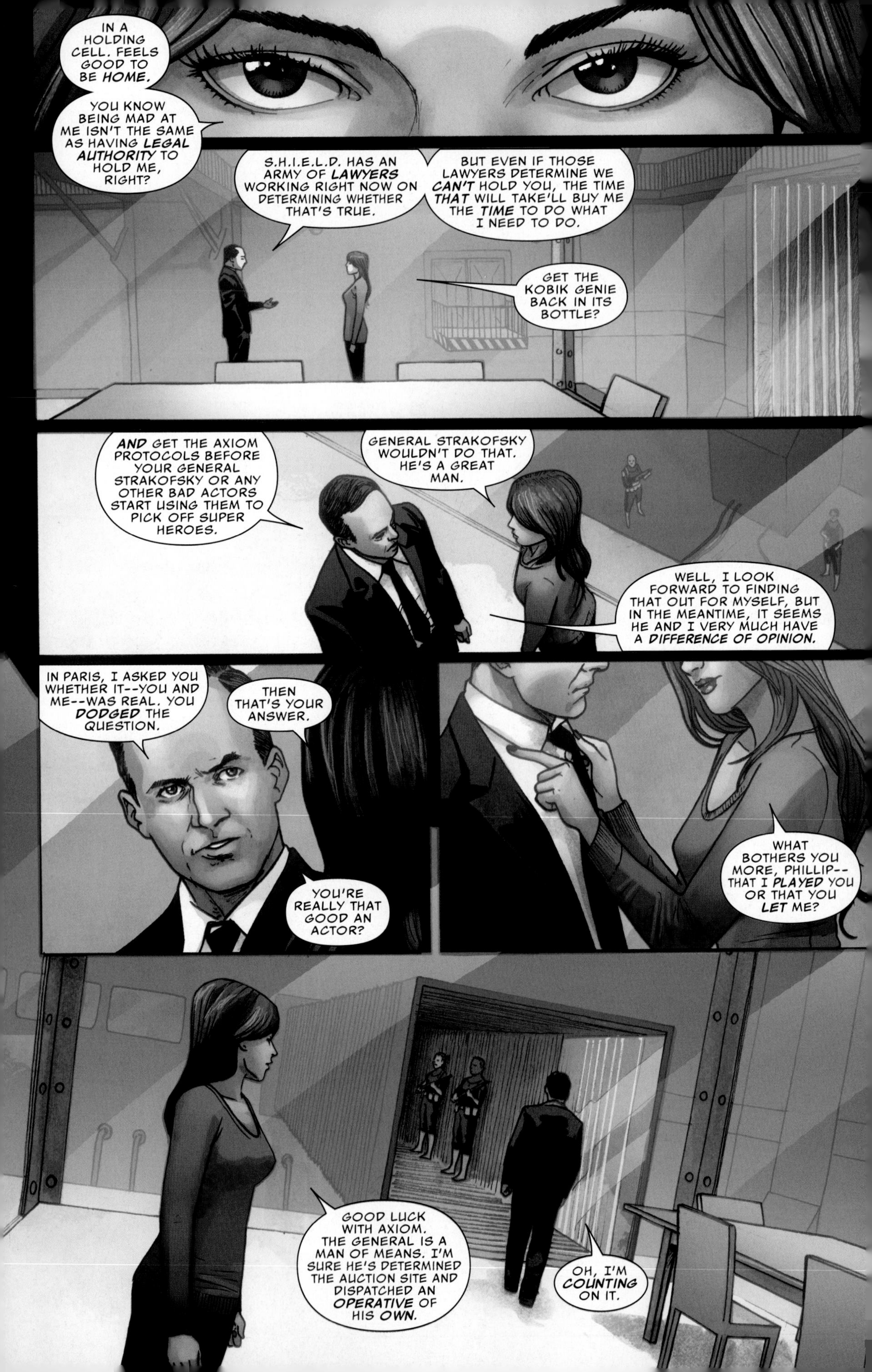
IN A HOLDING CELL. FEELS GOOD TO BE HOME.
YOU KNOW BEING MAD AT ME ISN'T THE SAME AS HAVING LEGAL AUTHORITY TO HOLD ME, RIGHT?
S.H.I.E.L.D. HAS AN ARMY OF LAWYERS WORKING RIGHT NOW ON DETERMINING WHETHER THAT'S TRUE.
BUT EVEN IF THOSE LAWYERS DETERMINE WE CAN'T HOLD YOU, THE TIME THAT WILL TAKE'LL BUY ME THE TIME TO DO WHAT I NEED TO DO.
GET THE KOBIK GENIE BACK IN ITS BOTTLE?
AND GET THE AXIOM PROTOCOLS BEFORE YOUR GENERAL STRAKOFSKY OR ANY OTHER BAD ACTORS START USING THEM TO PICK OFF SUPER HEROES.
GENERAL STRAKOFSKY WOULDN'T DO THAT. HE'S A GREAT MAN.
WELL, I LOOK FORWARD TO FINDING THAT OUT FOR MYSELF, BUT IN THE MEANTIME, IT SEEMS HE AND I VERY MUCH HAVE A DIFFERENCE OF OPINION.
IN PARIS, I ASKED YOU WHETHER IT--YOU AND ME--WAS REAL. YOU DODGED THE QUESTION.
THEN THAT'S YOUR ANSWER.
YOU'RE REALLY THAT GOOD AN ACTOR?
WHAT BOTHERS YOU MORE, PHILLIP--THAT I PLAYED YOU OR THAT YOU LET ME?
GOOD LUCK WITH AXIOM. THE GENERAL IS A MAN OF MEANS. I'M SURE HE'S DETERMINED THE AUCTION SITE AND DISPATCHED AN OPERATIVE OF HIS OWN.
OH, I'M COUNTING ON IT.

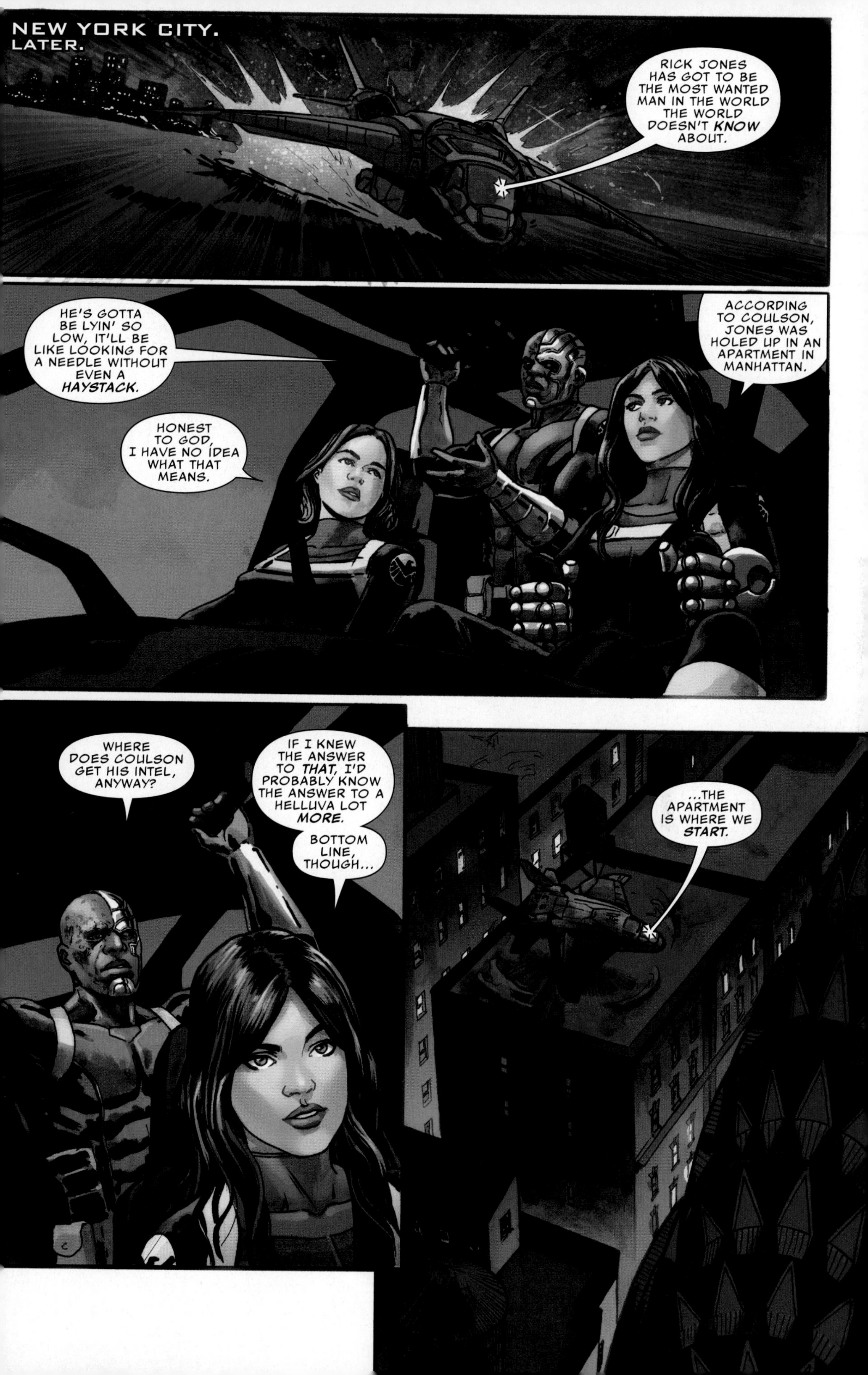
NEW YORK CITY. LATER.
RICK JONES HAS GOT TO BE THE MOST WANTED MAN IN THE WORLD THE WORLD DOESN'T KNOW ABOUT.
HE'S GOTTA BE LYIN' SO LOW, IT'LL BE LIKE LOOKING FOR A NEEDLE WITHOUT EVEN A HAYSTACK.
ACCORDING TO COULSON, JONES WAS HOLED UP IN AN APARTMENT IN MANHATTAN.
HONEST TO GOD, I HAVE NO IDEA WHAT THAT MEANS.
WHERE DOES COULSON GET HIS INTEL, ANYWAY?
IF I KNEW THE ANSWER TO THAT, I'D PROBABLY KNOW THE ANSWER TO A HELLUVA LOT MORE.
BOTTOM LINE, THOUGH...
...THE APARTMENT IS WHERE WE START.

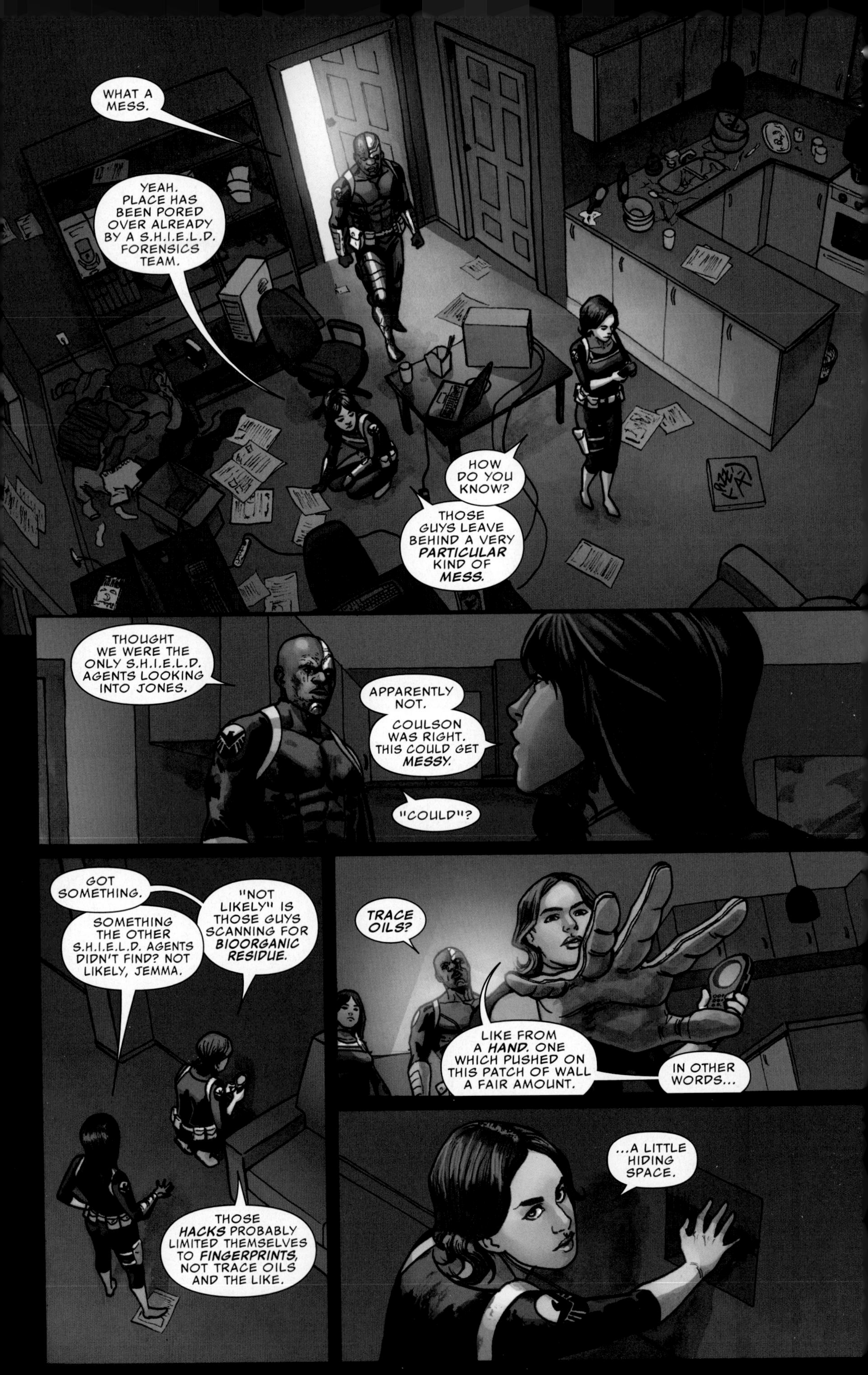
WHAT A MESS.
YEAH. PLACE HAS BEEN PORED OVER ALREADY BY A S.H.I.E.L.D. FORENSICS TEAM.
HOW DO YOU KNOW?
THOSE GUYS LEAVE BEHIND A VERY PARTICULAR KIND OF MESS.
THOUGHT WE WERE THE ONLY S.H.I.E.L.D. AGENTS LOOKING INTO JONES.
APPARENTLY NOT.
COULSON WAS RIGHT. THIS COULD GET MESSY.
"COULD"?
GOT SOMETHING.
SOMETHING THE OTHER S.H.I.E.L.D. AGENTS DIDN'T FIND? NOT LIKELY, JEMMA.
"NOT LIKELY" IS THOSE GUYS SCANNING FOR BIOORGANIC RESIDUE.
THOSE HACKS PROBABLY LIMITED THEMSELVES TO FINGERPRINTS, NOT TRACE OILS AND THE LIKE.
TRACE OILS?
LIKE FROM A HAND. ONE WHICH PUSHED ON THIS PATCH OF WALL A FAIR AMOUNT.
IN OTHER WORDS...
...A LITTLE HIDING SPACE.

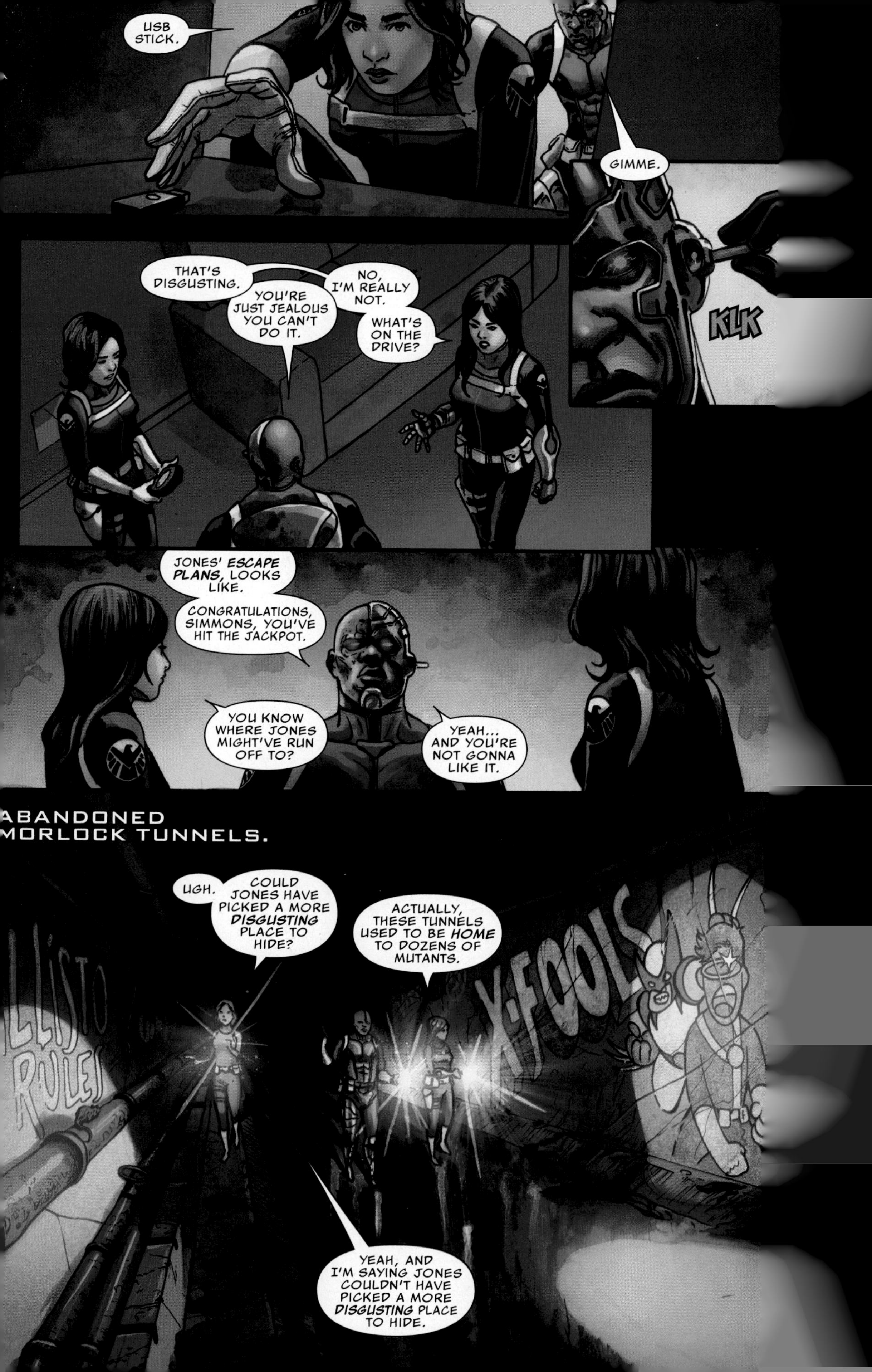
USB STICK.
GIMME.
KLK
THAT'S DISGUSTING.
YOU'RE JUST JEALOUS YOU CAN'T DO IT.
NO, I'M REALLY NOT.
WHAT'S ON THE DRIVE?
JONES' ESCAPE PLANS, LOOKS LIKE.
CONGRATULATIONS, SIMMONS, YOU'VE HIT THE JACKPOT.
YOU KNOW WHERE JONES MIGHT'VE RUN OFF TO?
YEAH... AND YOU'RE NOT GONNA LIKE IT.
ABANDONED MORLOCK TUNNELS.
UGH.
COULD JONES HAVE PICKED A MORE DISGUSTING PLACE TO HIDE?
ACTUALLY, THESE TUNNELS USED TO BE HOME TO DOZENS OF MUTANTS.
X-FOOLS
RULE!
YEAH, AND I'M SAYING JONES COULDN'T HAVE PICKED A MORE DISGUSTING PLACE TO HIDE.

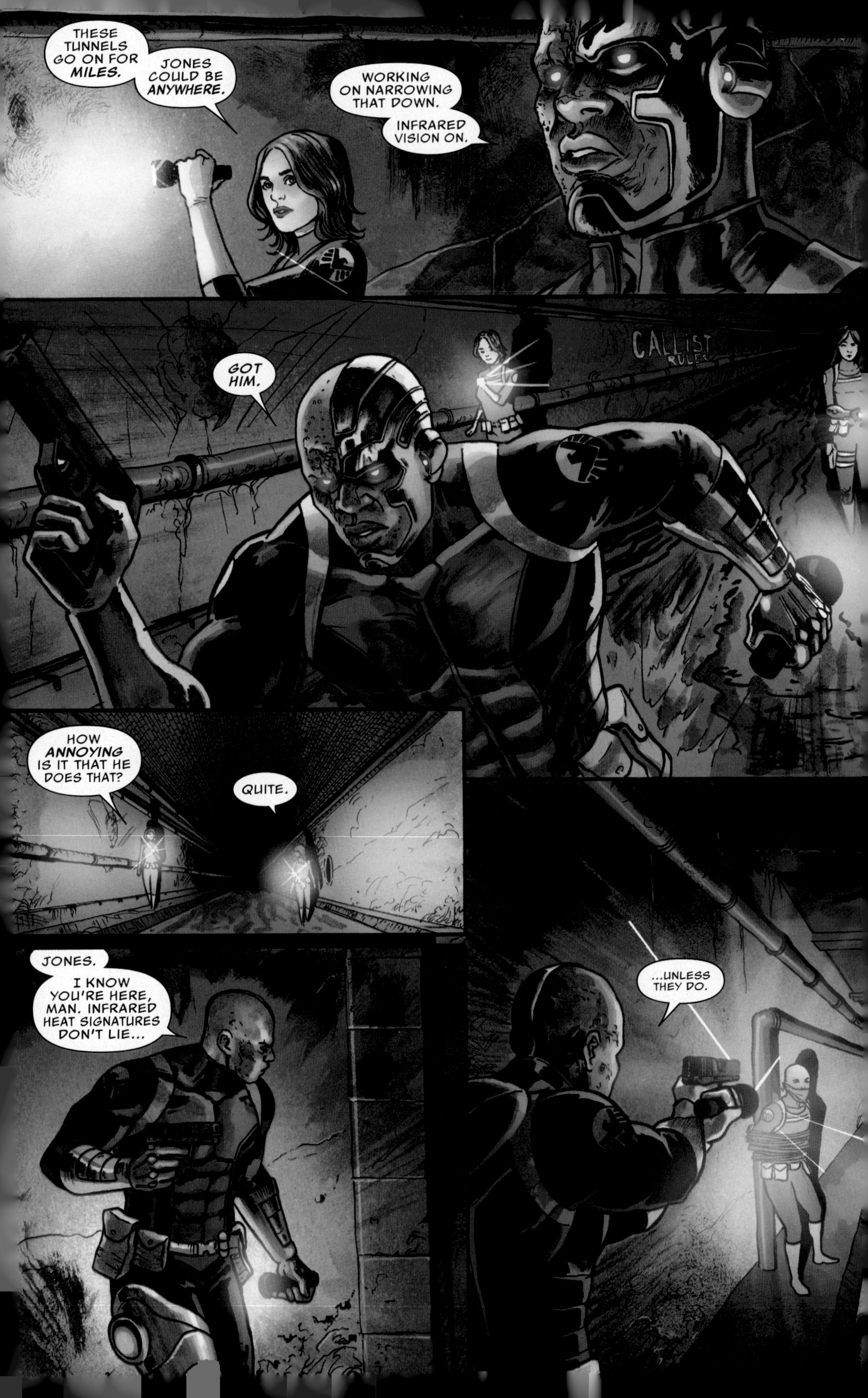

THESE TUNNELS GO ON FOR MILES.
JONES COULD BE ANYWHERE.
WORKING ON NARROWING THAT DOWN.
INFRARED VISION ON.
GOT HIM.
CALLIST RULES
HOW ANNOYING IS IT THAT HE DOES THAT?
QUITE.
JONES.
I KNOW YOU'RE HERE, MAN. INFRARED HEAT SIGNATURES DON'T LIE...
...UNLESS THEY DO.

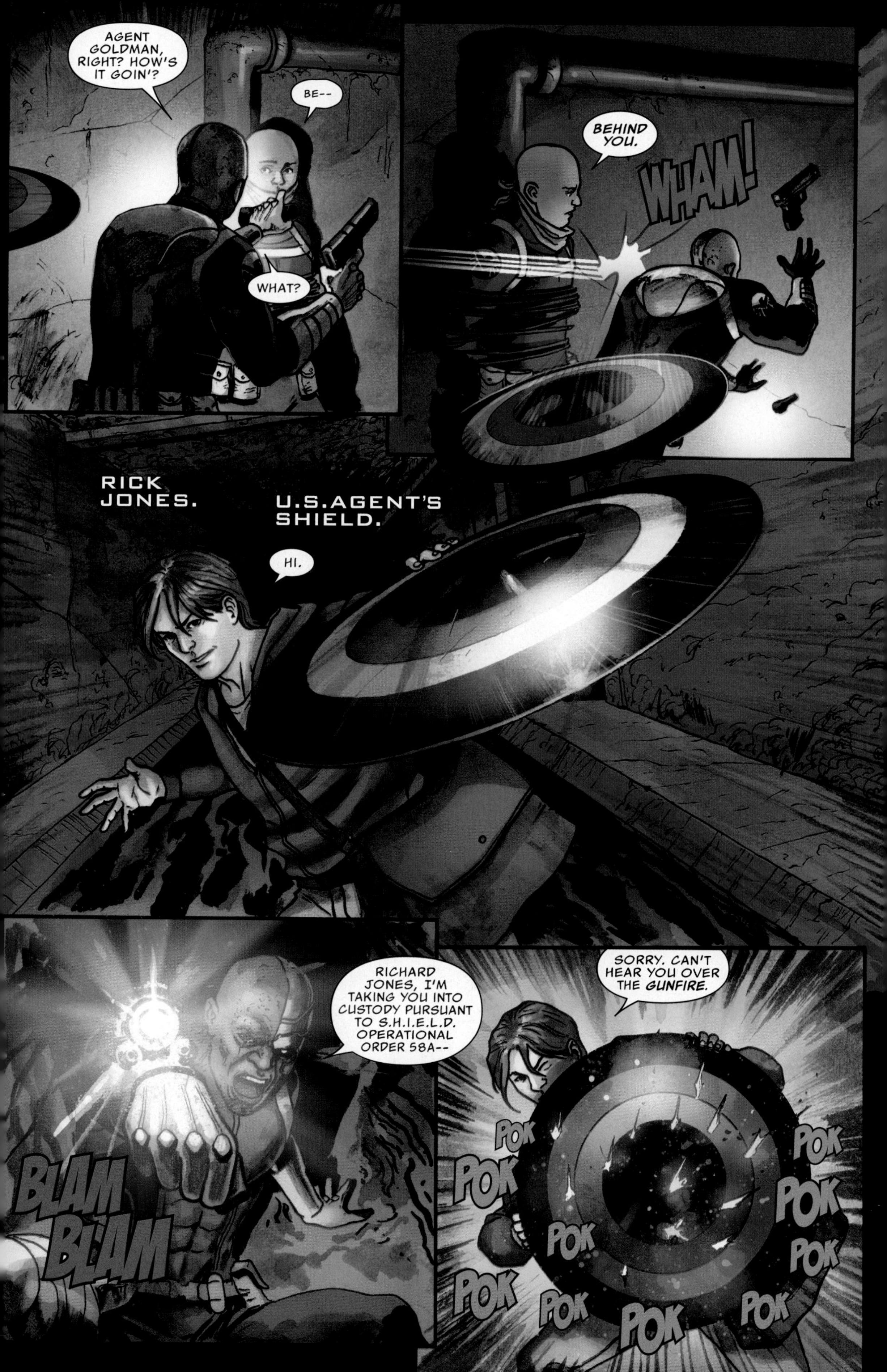
AGENT GOLDMAN, RIGHT? HOW'S IT GOIN'?
BE--
WHAT?
BEHIND YOU.
WHAM!
RICK JONES.
U.S.AGENT'S SHIELD.
HI.
RICHARD JONES, I'M TAKING YOU INTO CUSTODY PURSUANT TO S.H.I.E.L.D. OPERATIONAL ORDER 58A--
BLAM BLAM
SORRY. CAN'T HEAR YOU OVER THE GUNFIRE.
POK POK POK POK POK POK POK POK POK POK POK POK

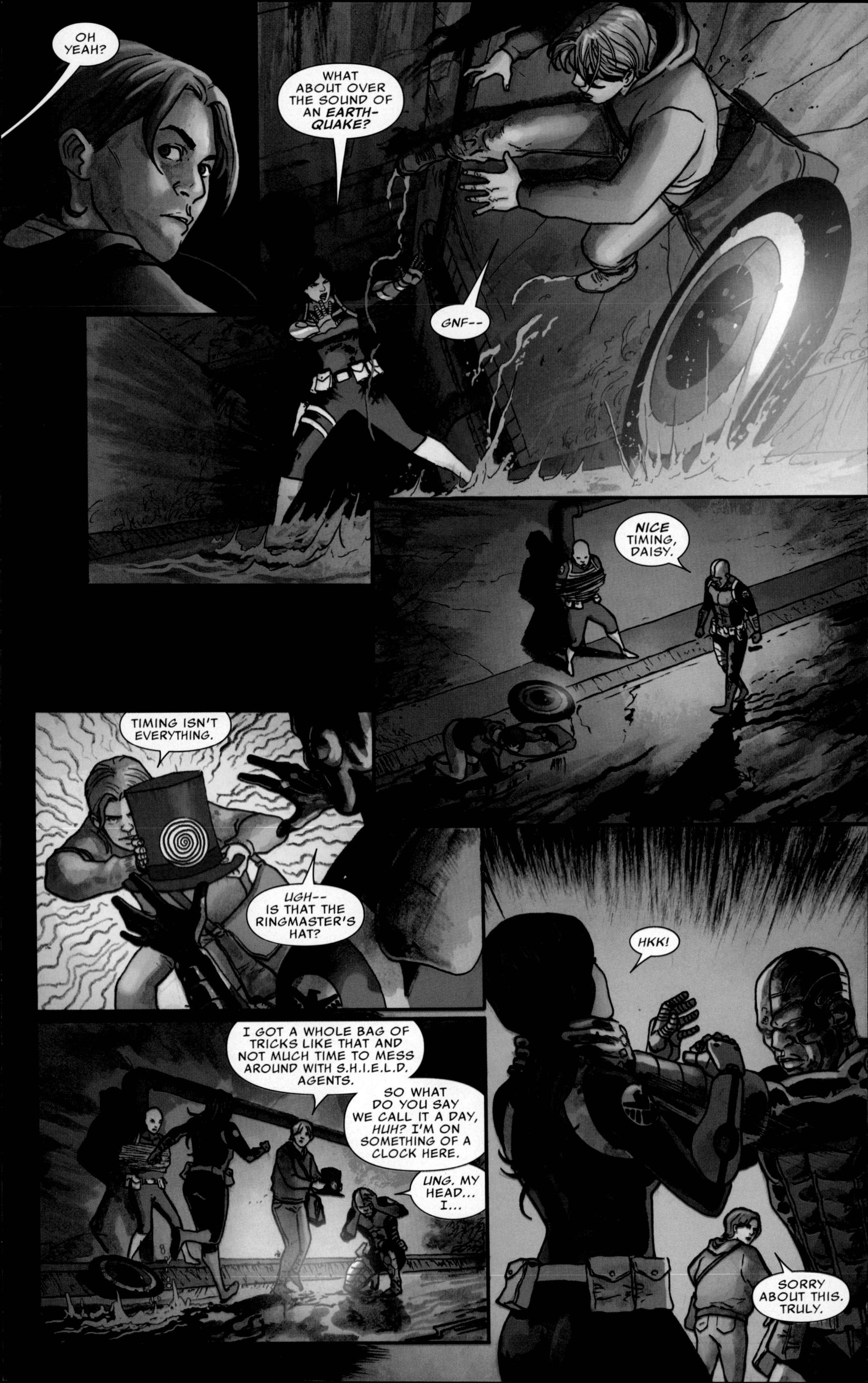
OH YEAH?
WHAT ABOUT OVER THE SOUND OF AN *EARTH-QUAKE?*
GNF--
NICE TIMING, DAISY.
TIMING ISN'T EVERYTHING.
UGH-- IS THAT THE RINGMASTER'S HAT?
HKK!
I GOT A WHOLE BAG OF TRICKS LIKE THAT AND NOT MUCH TIME TO MESS AROUND WITH S.H.I.E.L.D. AGENTS.
SO WHAT DO YOU SAY WE CALL IT A DAY, *HUH?* I'M ON SOMETHING OF A CLOCK HERE.
UNG. MY HEAD... I...
SORRY ABOUT THIS. TRULY.

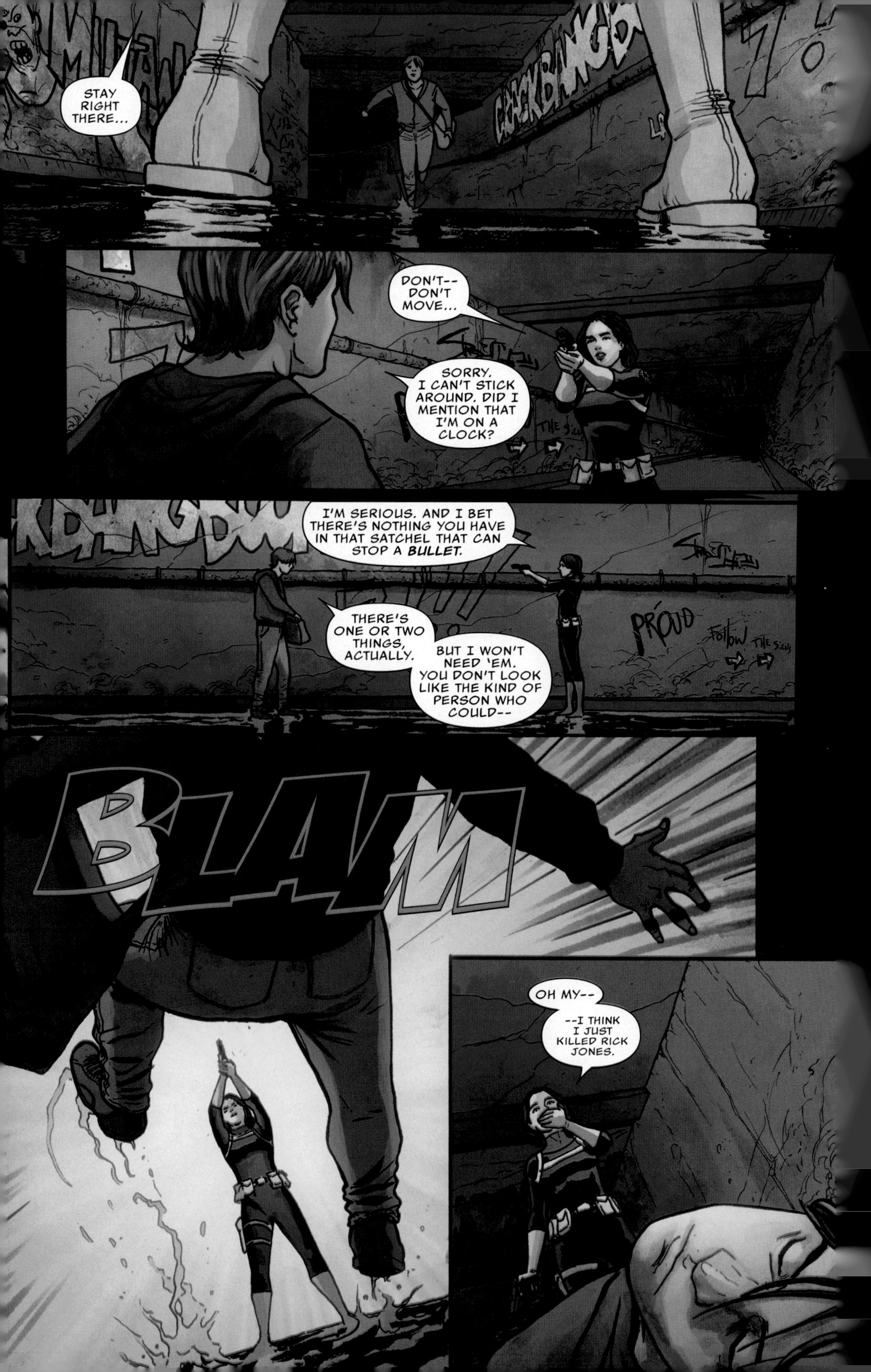
STAY RIGHT THERE...
DON'T-- DON'T MOVE...
SORRY. I CAN'T STICK AROUND. DID I MENTION THAT I'M ON A CLOCK?
I'M SERIOUS. AND I BET THERE'S NOTHING YOU HAVE IN THAT SATCHEL THAT CAN STOP A ***BULLET***.
THERE'S ONE OR TWO THINGS, ACTUALLY.
BUT I WON'T NEED 'EM. YOU DON'T LOOK LIKE THE KIND OF PERSON WHO COULD--
BLAM
OH MY--
--I THINK I JUST KILLED RICK JONES.

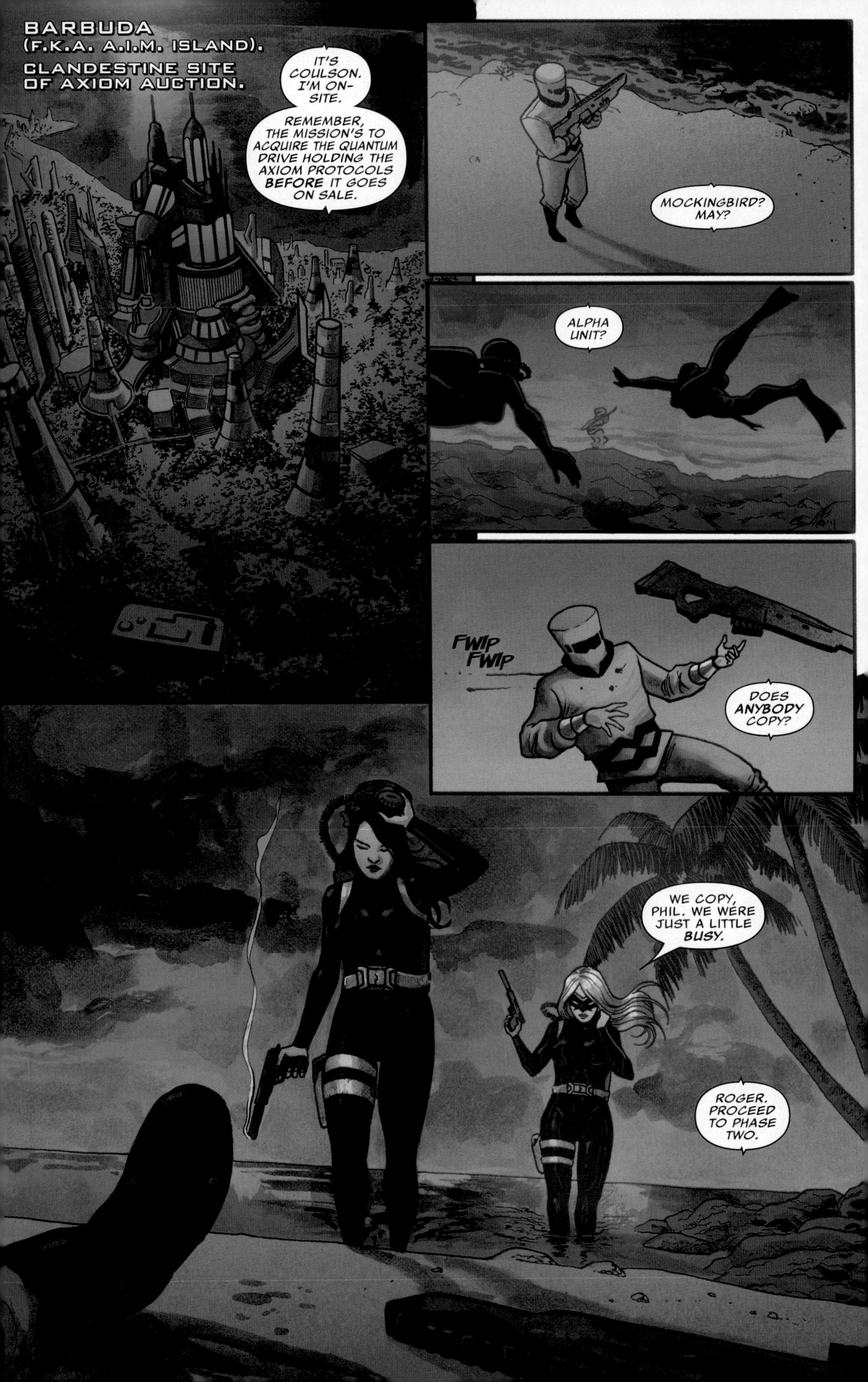
BARBUDA
(F.K.A. A.I.M. ISLAND).
CLANDESTINE SITE OF AXIOM AUCTION.
IT'S COULSON. I'M ON-SITE.
REMEMBER, THE MISSION'S TO ACQUIRE THE QUANTUM DRIVE HOLDING THE AXIOM PROTOCOLS BEFORE IT GOES ON SALE.
MOCKINGBIRD? MAY?
ALPHA UNIT?
FWIP FWIP
DOES ANYBODY COPY?
WE COPY, PHIL. WE WERE JUST A LITTLE BUSY.
ROGER. PROCEED TO PHASE TWO.

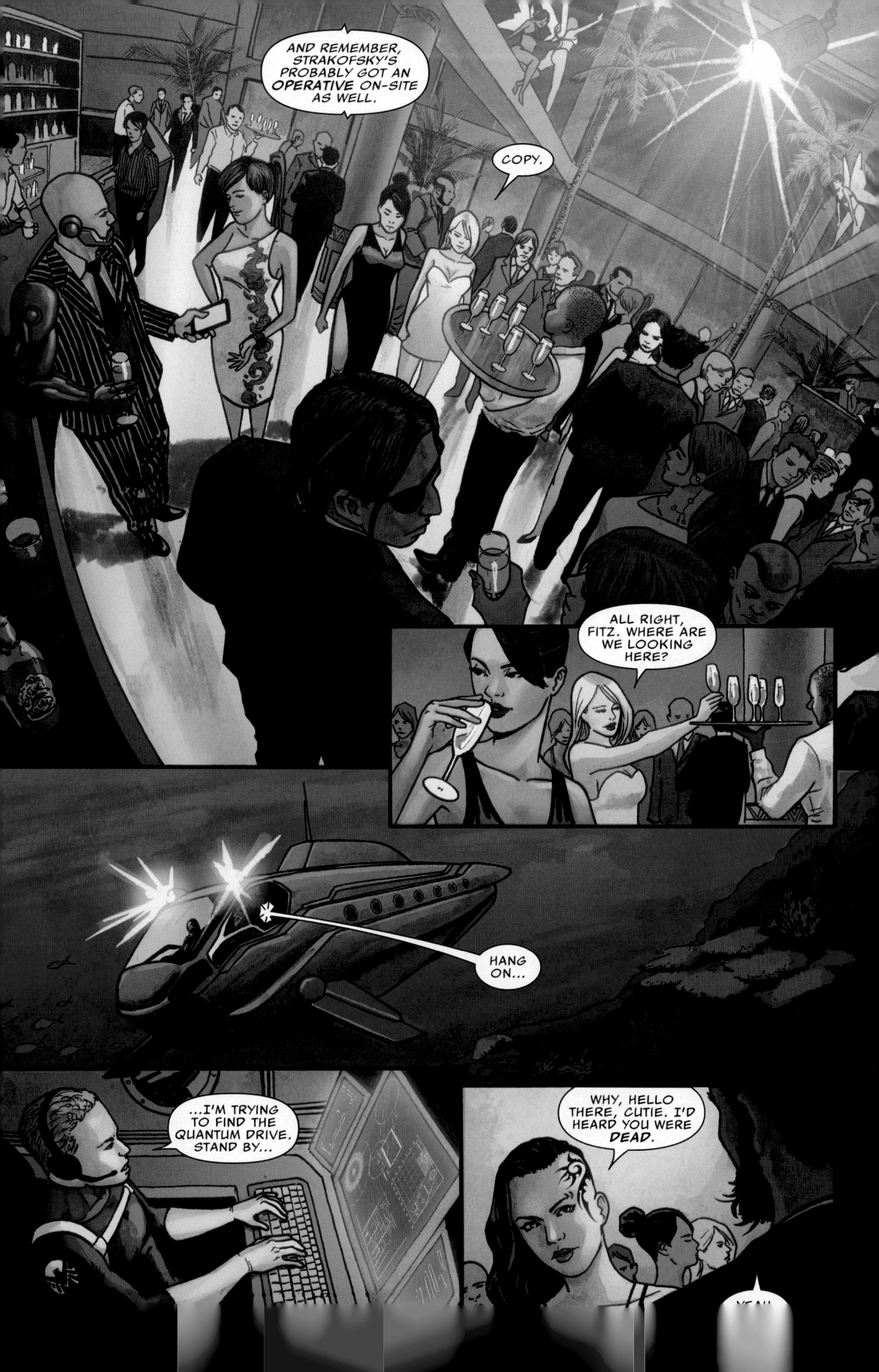
AND REMEMBER, STRAKOFSKY'S PROBABLY GOT AN OPERATIVE ON-SITE AS WELL.
COPY.
ALL RIGHT, FITZ. WHERE ARE WE LOOKING HERE?
HANG ON...
...I'M TRYING TO FIND THE QUANTUM DRIVE. STAND BY...
WHY, HELLO THERE, CUTIE. I'D HEARD YOU WERE DEAD.

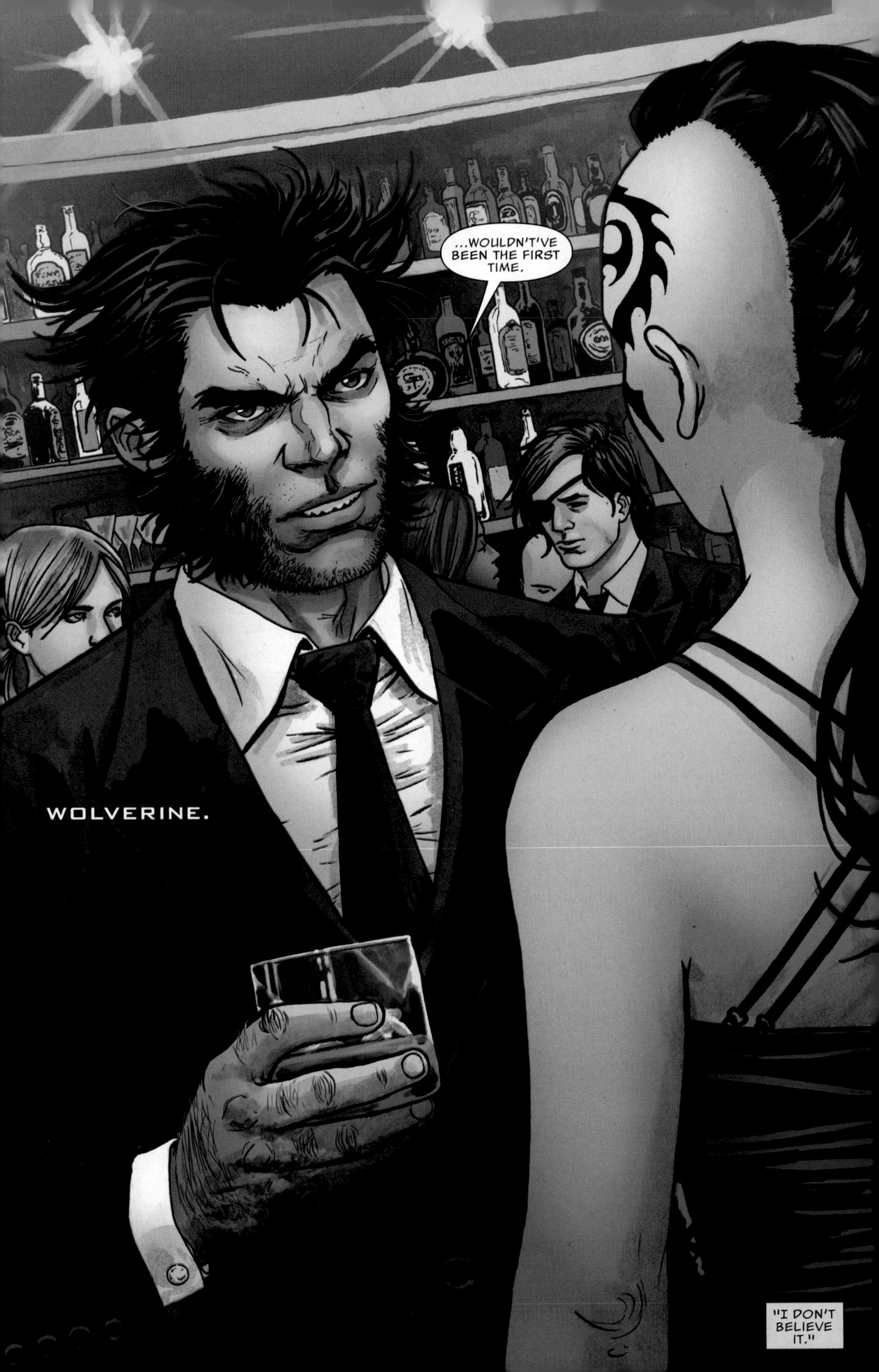

...WOULDN'T'VE BEEN THE FIRST TIME.
WOLVERINE.
"I DON'T BELIEVE IT."

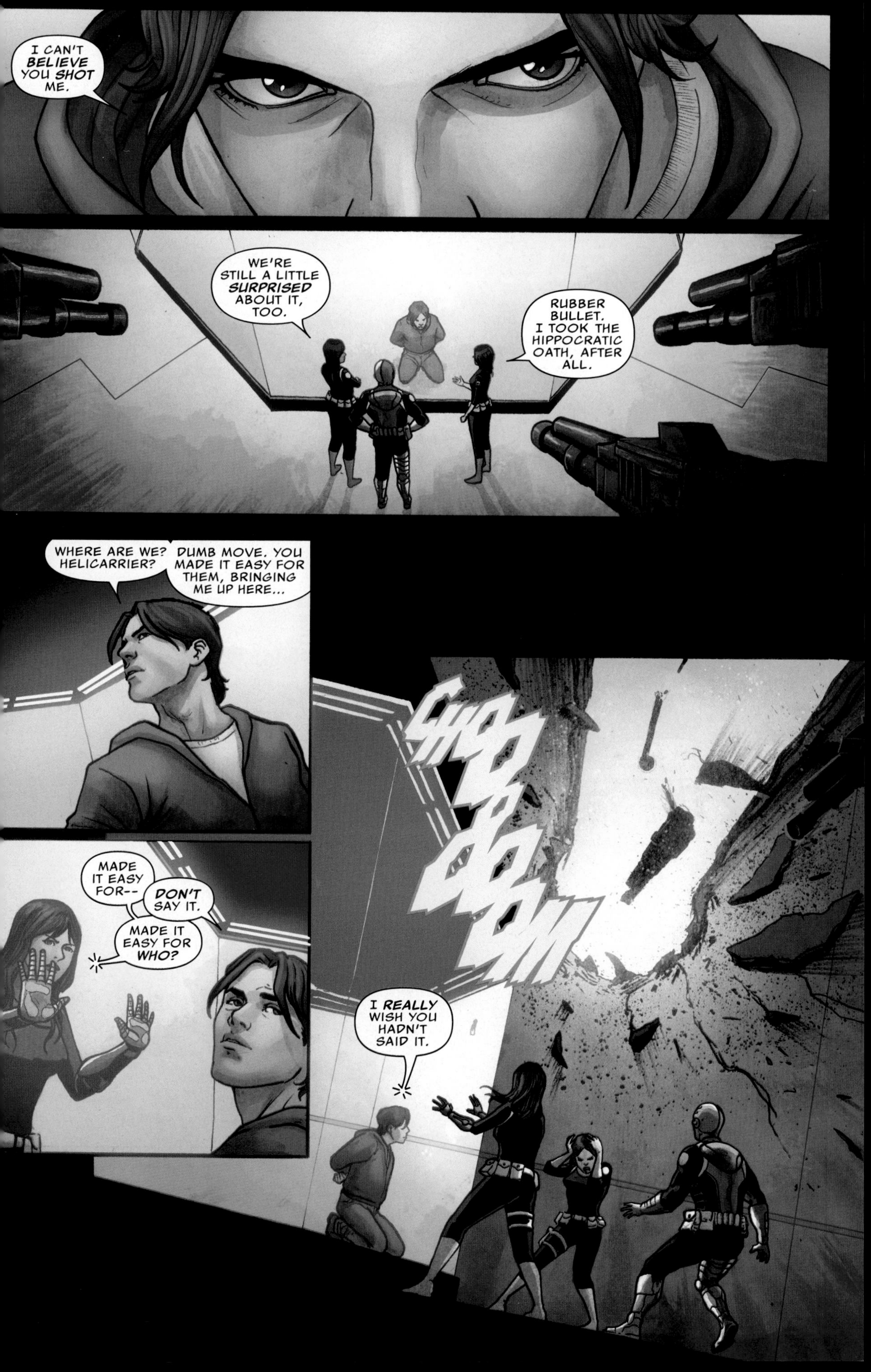
I CAN'T BELIEVE YOU SHOT ME.
WE'RE STILL A LITTLE SURPRISED ABOUT IT, TOO.
RUBBER BULLET. I TOOK THE HIPPOCRATIC OATH, AFTER ALL.
WHERE ARE WE? HELICARRIER?
DUMB MOVE. YOU MADE IT EASY FOR THEM, BRINGING ME UP HERE...
MADE IT EASY FOR--
DON'T SAY IT.
MADE IT EASY FOR WHO?
CHOOOOOOM
I REALLY WISH YOU HADN'T SAID IT.

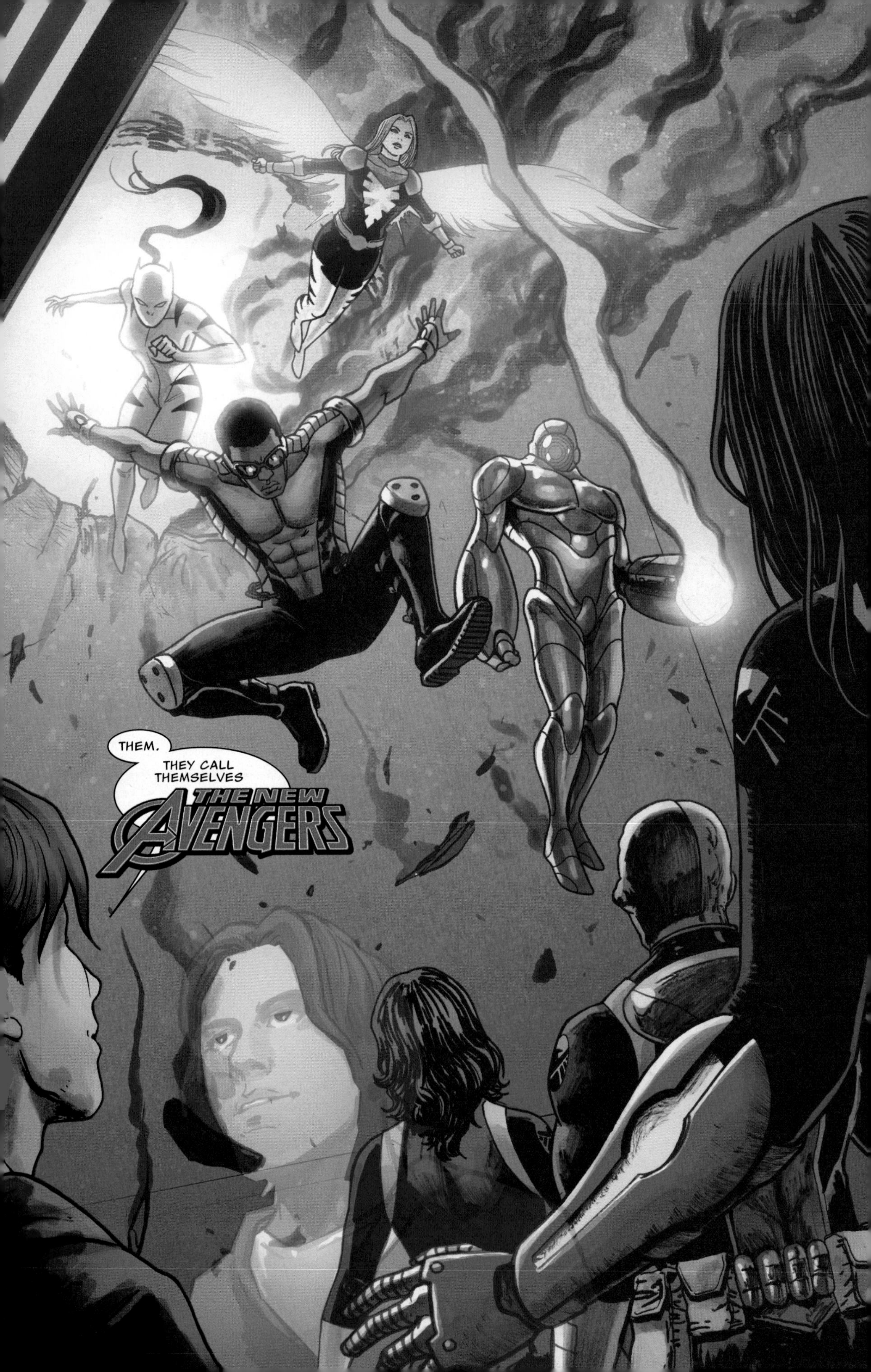
THEM.
THEY CALL THEMSELVES
THE NEW AVENGERS

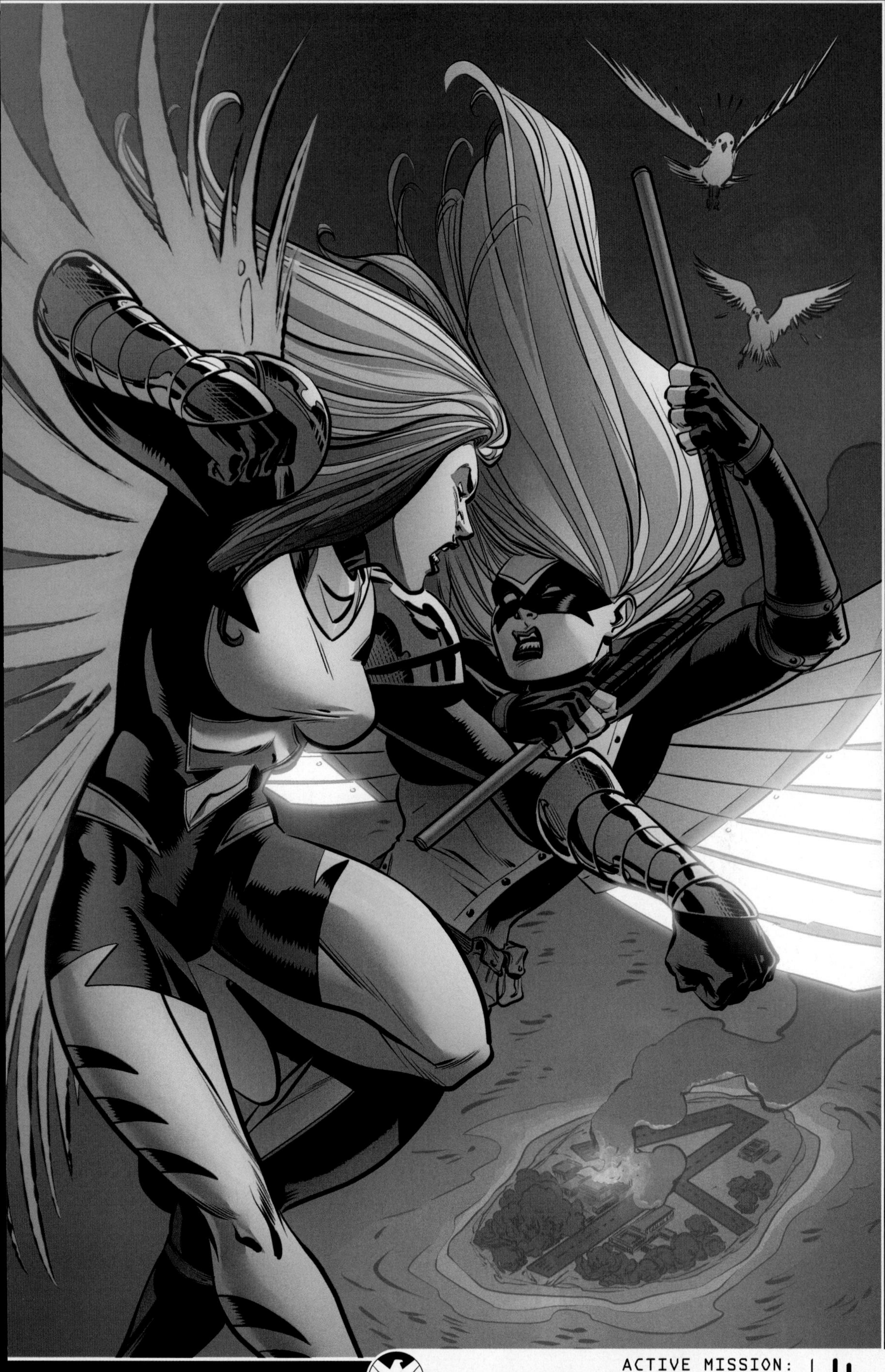

ACTIVE MISSION:
REVERSALS OF FORTUNE | 4.

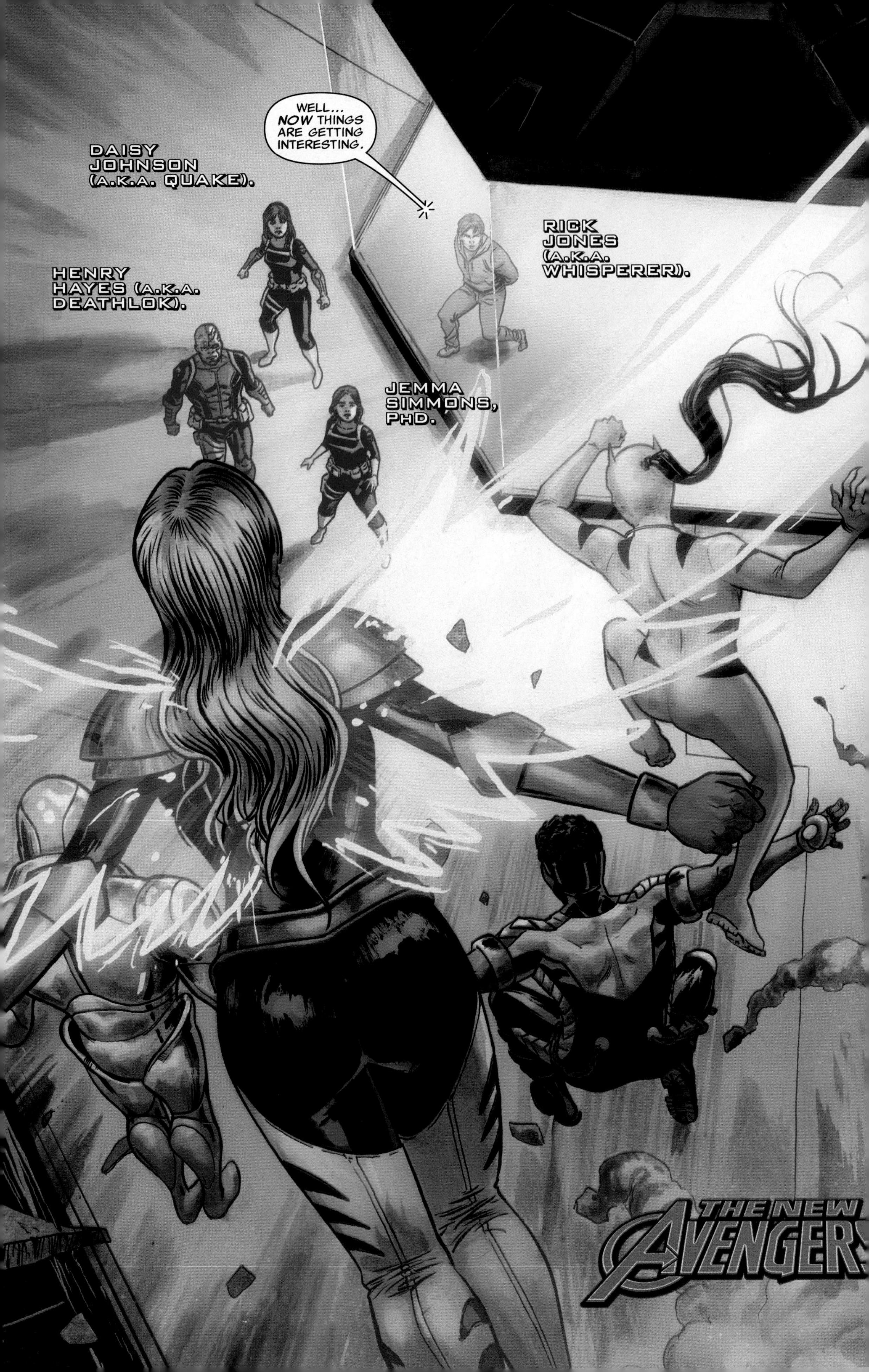
DAISY JOHNSON (A.K.A. QUAKE).
WELL... NOW THINGS ARE GETTING INTERESTING.
RICK JONES (A.K.A. WHISPERER).
HENRY HAYES (A.K.A. DEATHLOK).
JEMMA SIMMONS, PHD.
THE NEW AVENGERS

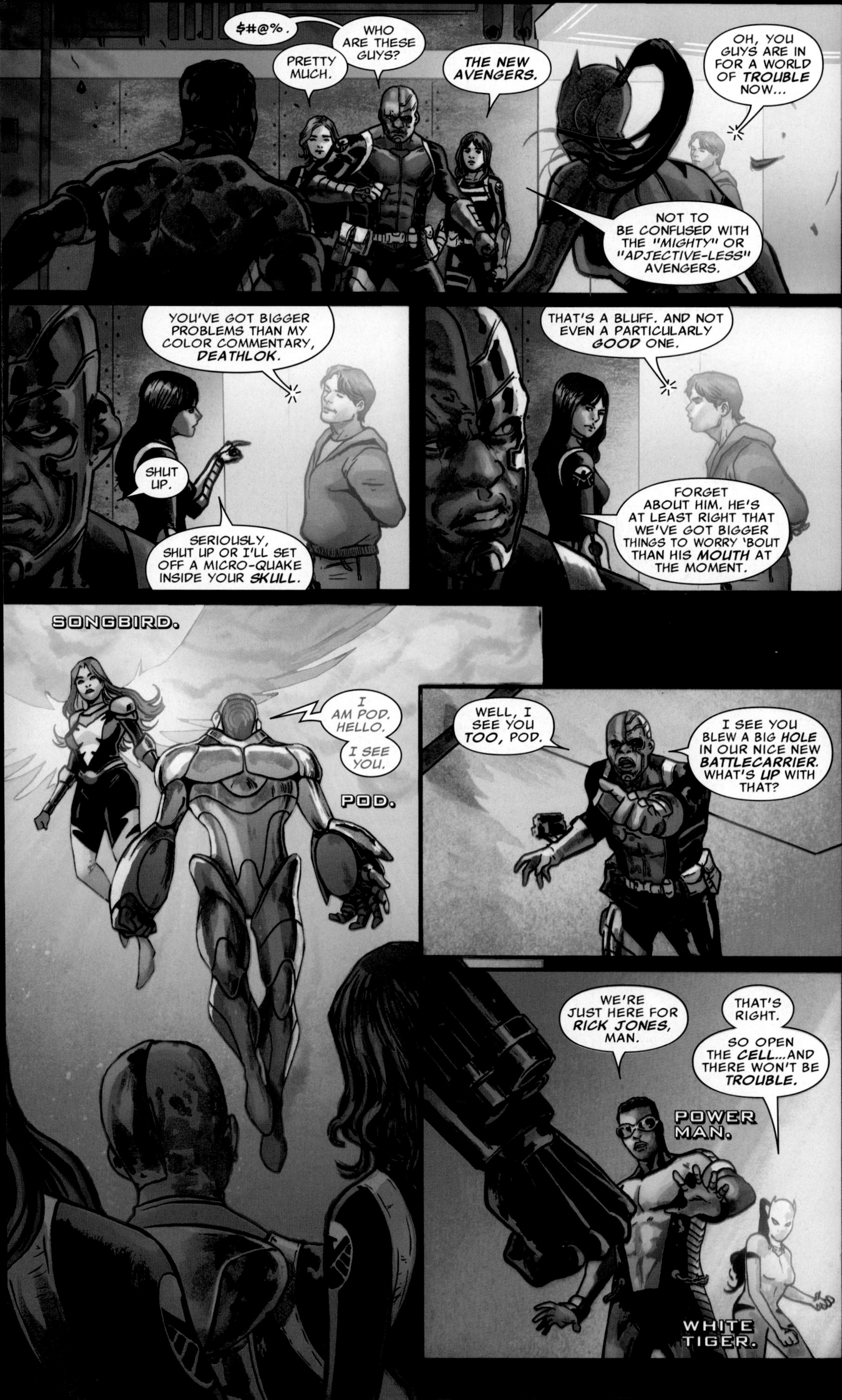
$#@%.
WHO ARE THESE GUYS?
PRETTY MUCH.
THE NEW AVENGERS.
OH, YOU GUYS ARE IN FOR A WORLD OF TROUBLE NOW...
NOT TO BE CONFUSED WITH THE "MIGHTY" OR "ADJECTIVE-LESS" AVENGERS.
YOU'VE GOT BIGGER PROBLEMS THAN MY COLOR COMMENTARY, DEATHLOK.
SHUT UP.
SERIOUSLY, SHUT UP OR I'LL SET OFF A MICRO-QUAKE INSIDE YOUR SKULL.
THAT'S A BLUFF. AND NOT EVEN A PARTICULARLY GOOD ONE.
FORGET ABOUT HIM. HE'S AT LEAST RIGHT THAT WE'VE GOT BIGGER THINGS TO WORRY 'BOUT THAN HIS MOUTH AT THE MOMENT.
SONGBIRD.
I AM POD. HELLO.
I SEE YOU.
POD.
WELL, I SEE YOU TOO, POD.
I SEE YOU BLEW A BIG HOLE IN OUR NICE NEW BATTLECARRIER. WHAT'S UP WITH THAT?
WE'RE JUST HERE FOR RICK JONES, MAN.
THAT'S RIGHT.
SO OPEN THE CELL...AND THERE WON'T BE TROUBLE.
POWER MAN.
WHITE TIGER.

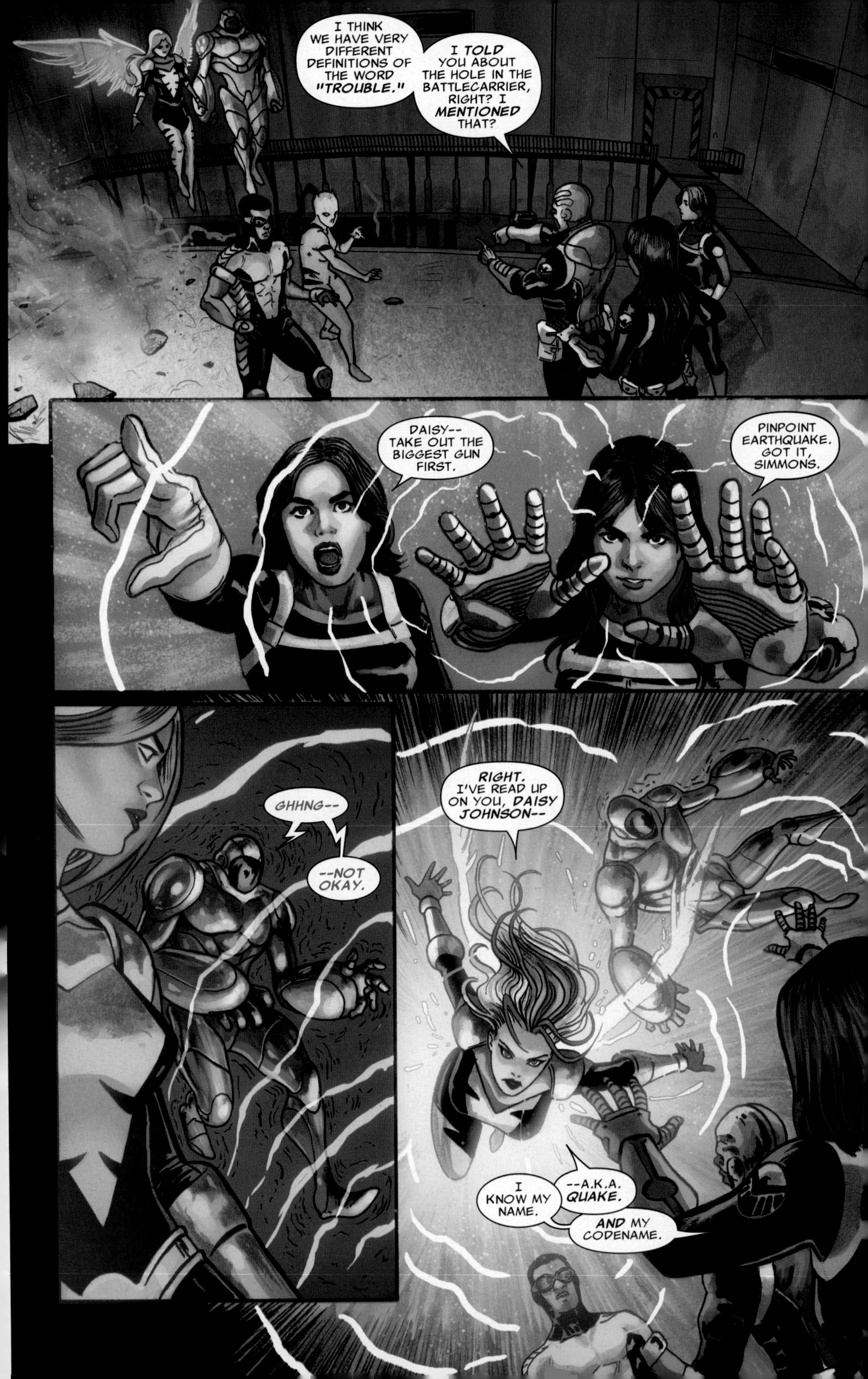
I THINK WE HAVE VERY DIFFERENT DEFINITIONS OF THE WORD "TROUBLE."
I TOLD YOU ABOUT THE HOLE IN THE BATTLECARRIER, RIGHT? I MENTIONED THAT?
DAISY-- TAKE OUT THE BIGGEST GUN FIRST.
PINPOINT EARTHQUAKE. GOT IT, SIMMONS.
GHHNG--
--NOT OKAY.
RIGHT. I'VE READ UP ON YOU, DAISY JOHNSON--
--A.K.A. QUAKE.
I KNOW MY NAME.
AND MY CODENAME.

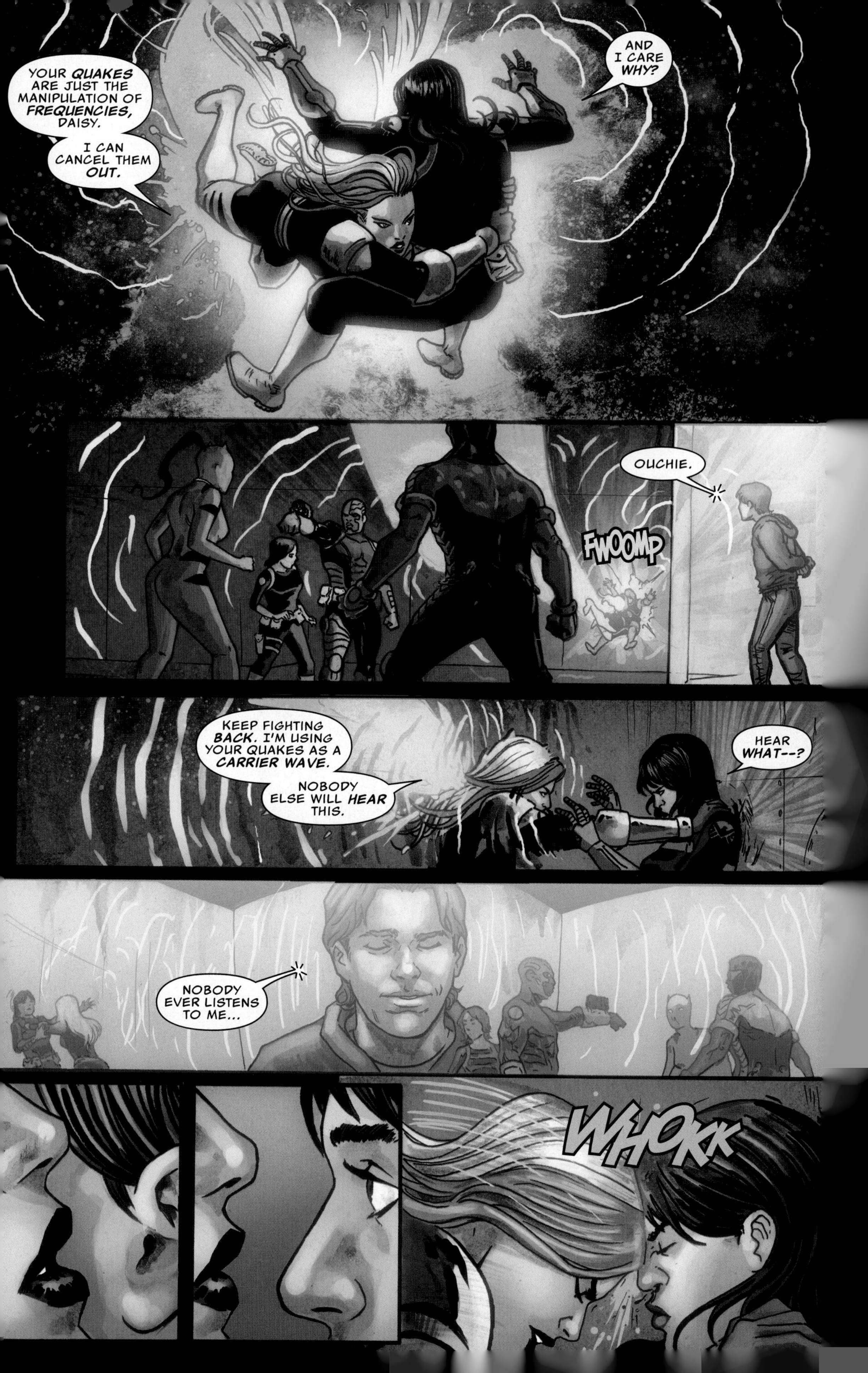
YOUR QUAKES ARE JUST THE MANIPULATION OF FREQUENCIES, DAISY.
I CAN CANCEL THEM OUT.
AND I CARE WHY?
OUCHIE.
FWOOMP
KEEP FIGHTING BACK. I'M USING YOUR QUAKES AS A CARRIER WAVE.
NOBODY ELSE WILL HEAR THIS.
HEAR WHAT--?
NOBODY EVER LISTENS TO ME...
WHOKK

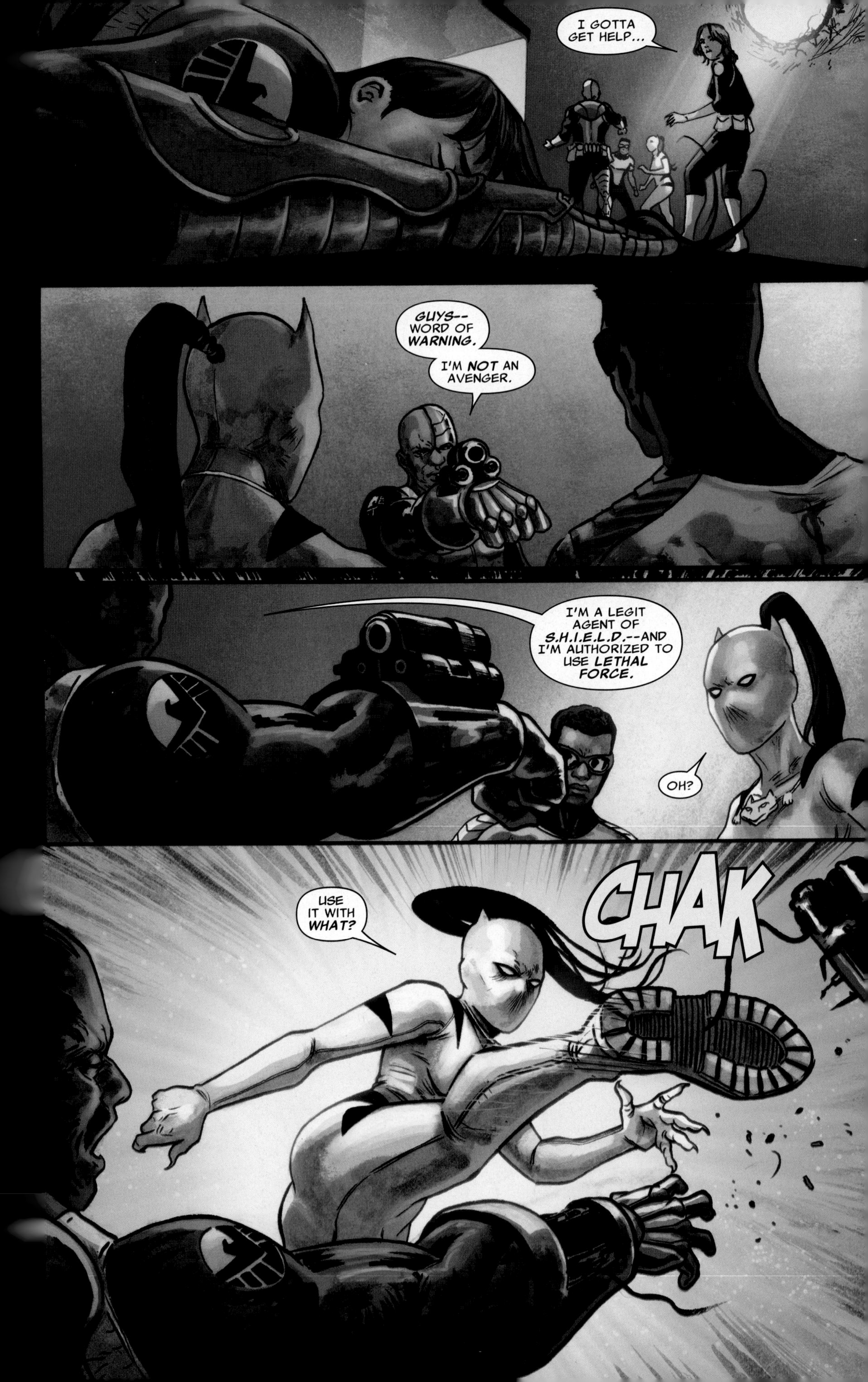
I GOTTA GET HELP...
GUYS-- WORD OF WARNING.
I'M NOT AN AVENGER.
I'M A LEGIT AGENT OF S.H.I.E.L.D.--AND I'M AUTHORIZED TO USE LETHAL FORCE.
OH?
USE IT WITH WHAT?
CHAK

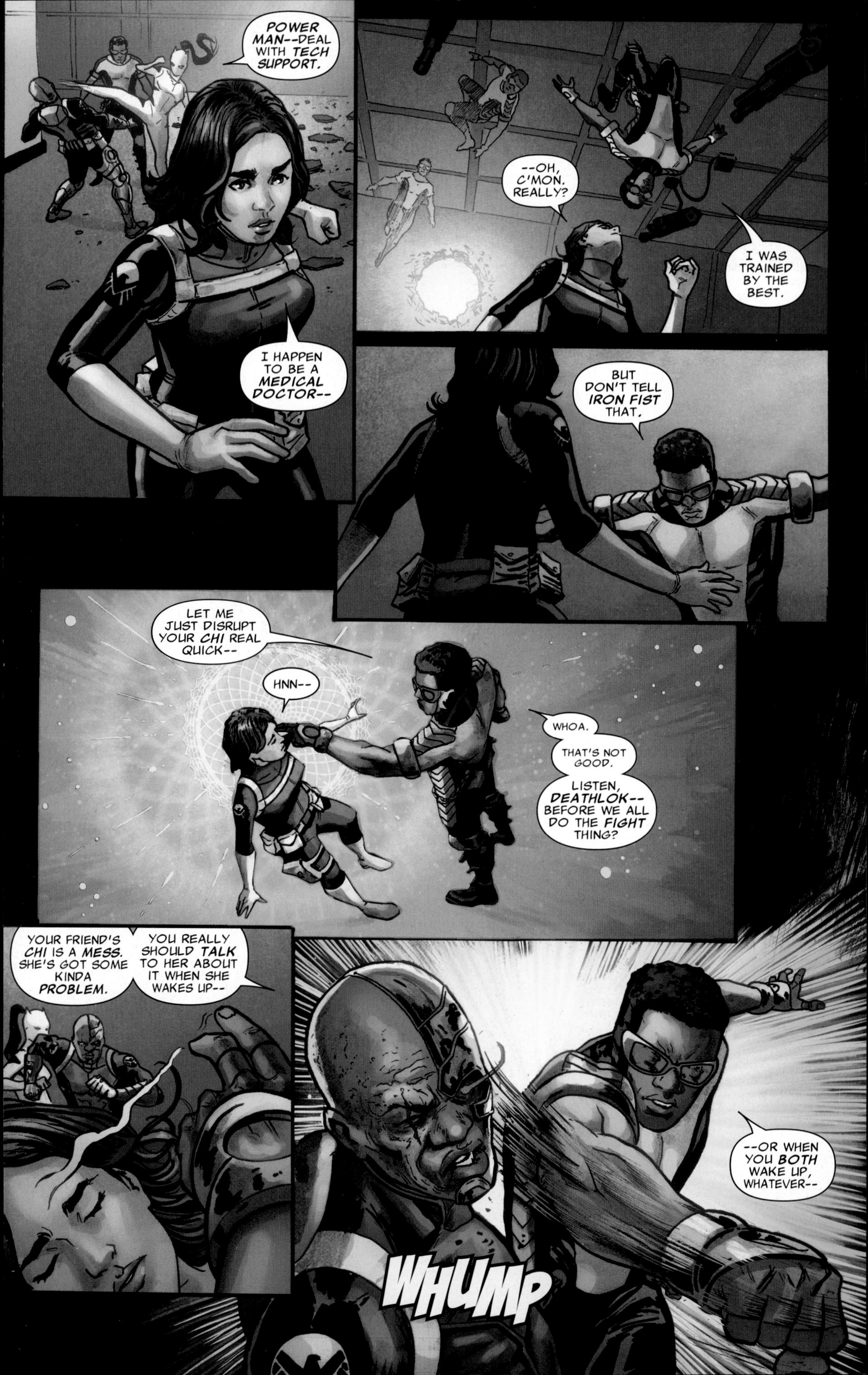
POWER MAN--DEAL WITH TECH SUPPORT.
I HAPPEN TO BE A MEDICAL DOCTOR--
--OH, C'MON. REALLY?
I WAS TRAINED BY THE BEST.
BUT DON'T TELL IRON FIST THAT.
LET ME JUST DISRUPT YOUR CHI REAL QUICK--
HNN--
WHOA.
THAT'S NOT GOOD.
LISTEN, DEATHLOK--BEFORE WE ALL DO THE FIGHT THING?
YOUR FRIEND'S CHI IS A MESS. SHE'S GOT SOME KINDA PROBLEM.
YOU REALLY SHOULD TALK TO HER ABOUT IT WHEN SHE WAKES UP--
--OR WHEN YOU BOTH WAKE UP, WHATEVER--
WHUMP

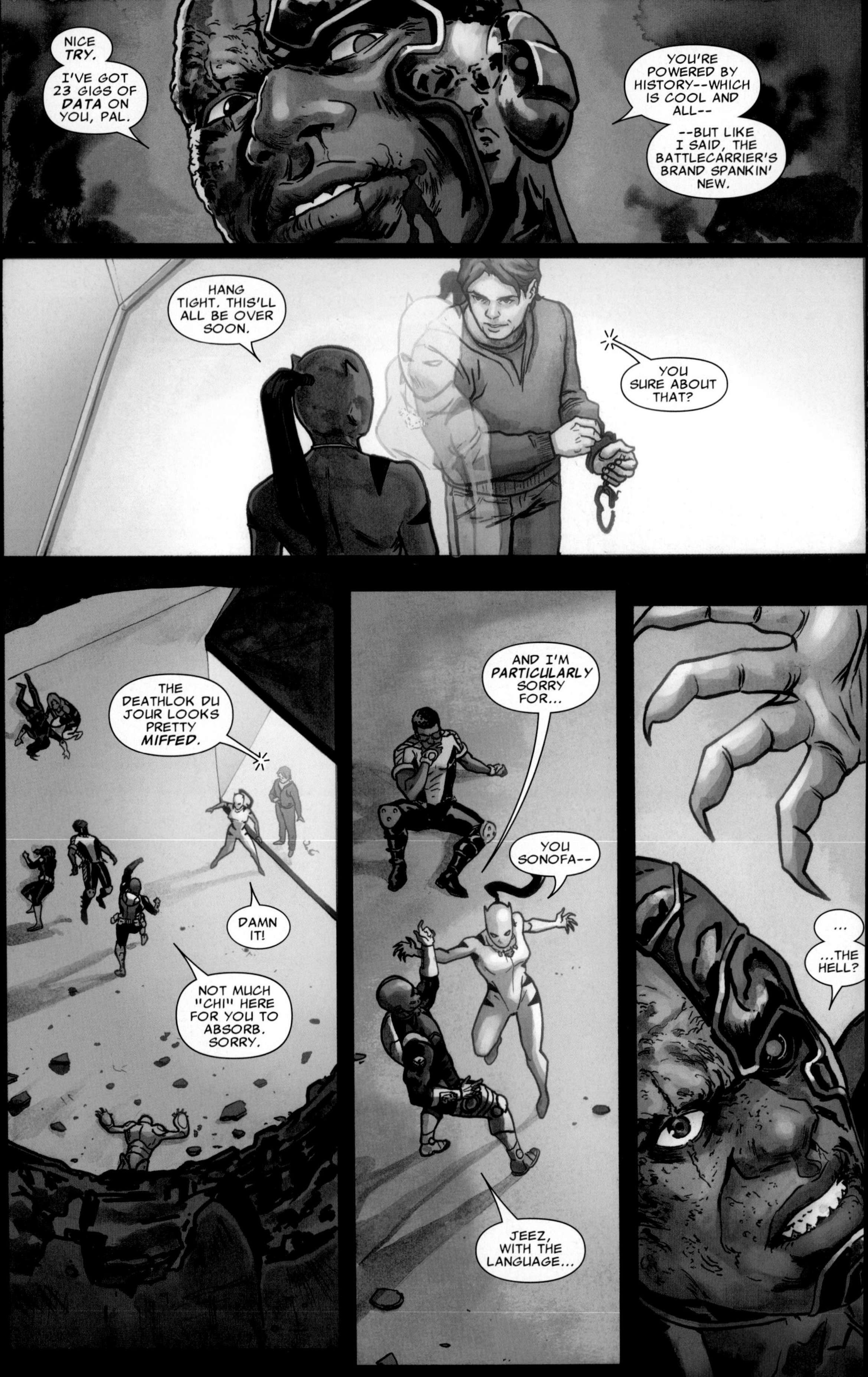
NICE TRY.
I'VE GOT 23 GIGS OF DATA ON YOU, PAL.
YOU'RE POWERED BY HISTORY--WHICH IS COOL AND ALL--
--BUT LIKE I SAID, THE BATTLECARRIER'S BRAND SPANKIN' NEW.
HANG TIGHT. THIS'LL ALL BE OVER SOON.
YOU SURE ABOUT THAT?
THE DEATHLOK DU JOUR LOOKS PRETTY MIFFED.
DAMN IT!
NOT MUCH "CHI" HERE FOR YOU TO ABSORB. SORRY.
AND I'M PARTICULARLY SORRY FOR...
YOU SONOFA--
JEEZ, WITH THE LANGUAGE...
...
...THE HELL?

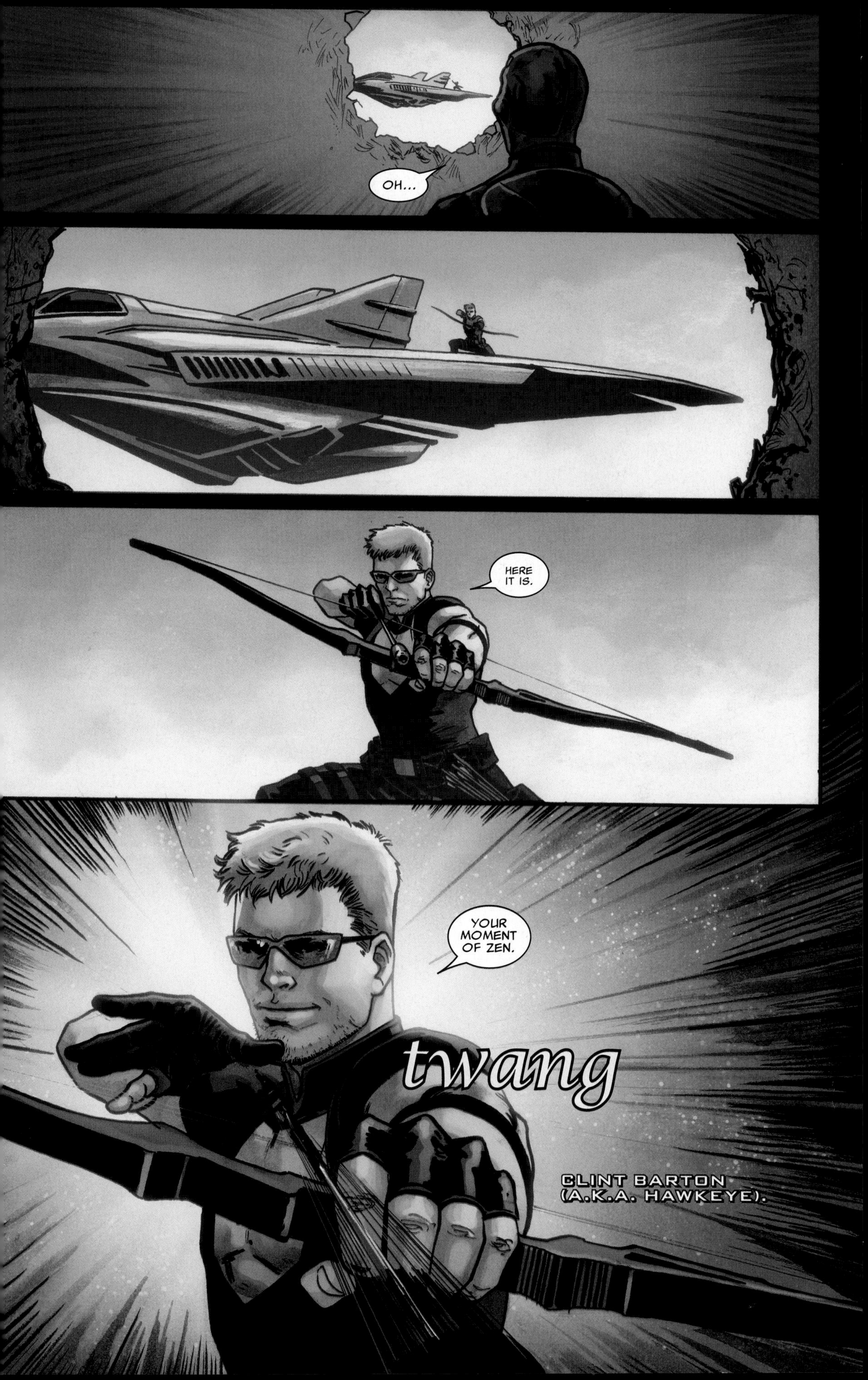
OH...
HERE IT IS.
YOUR MOMENT OF ZEN.
twang
CLINT BARTON (A.K.A. HAWKEYE).

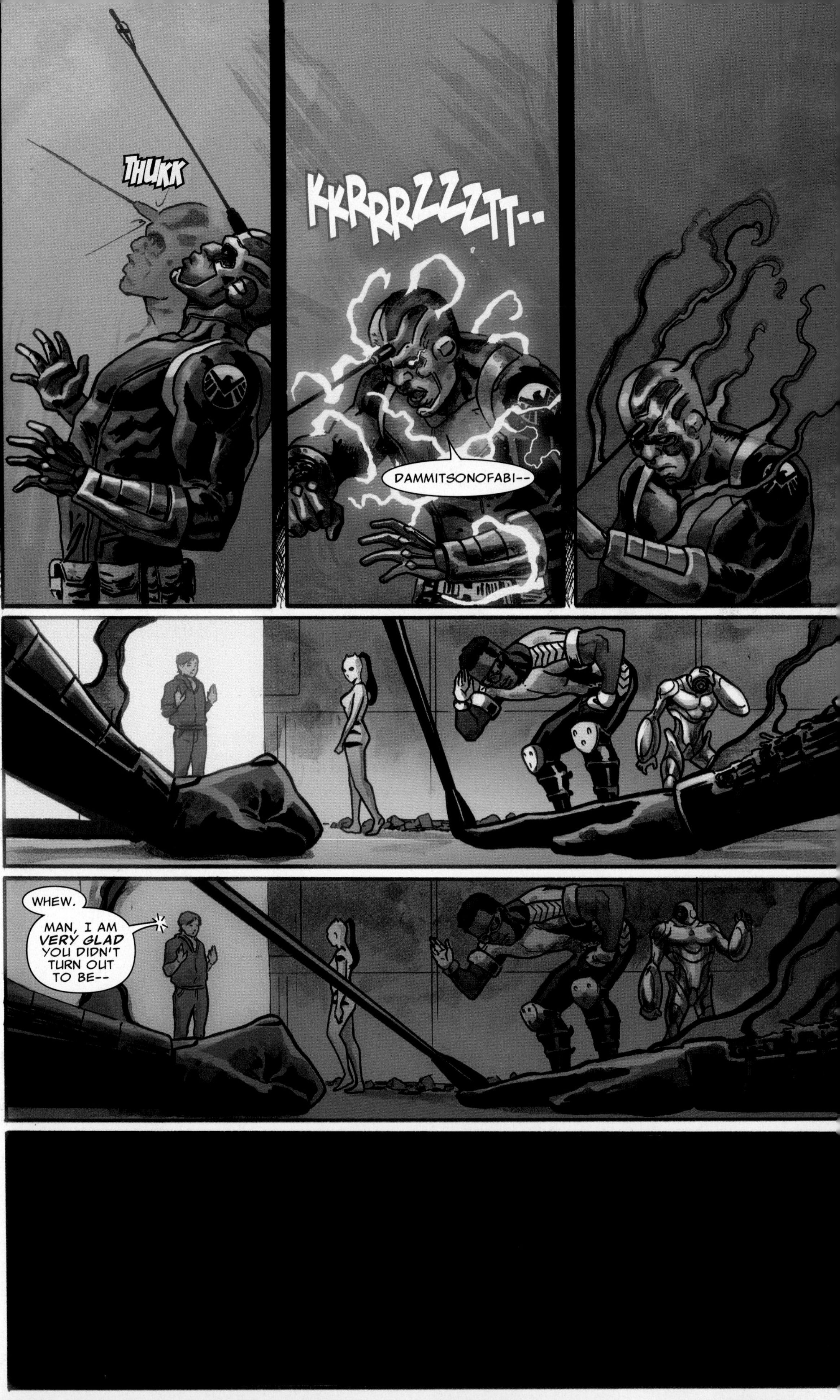
THUKK
KKRRRZZZZTT--
DAMMITSONOFABI--
WHEW.
MAN, I AM VERY GLAD YOU DIDN'T TURN OUT TO BE--

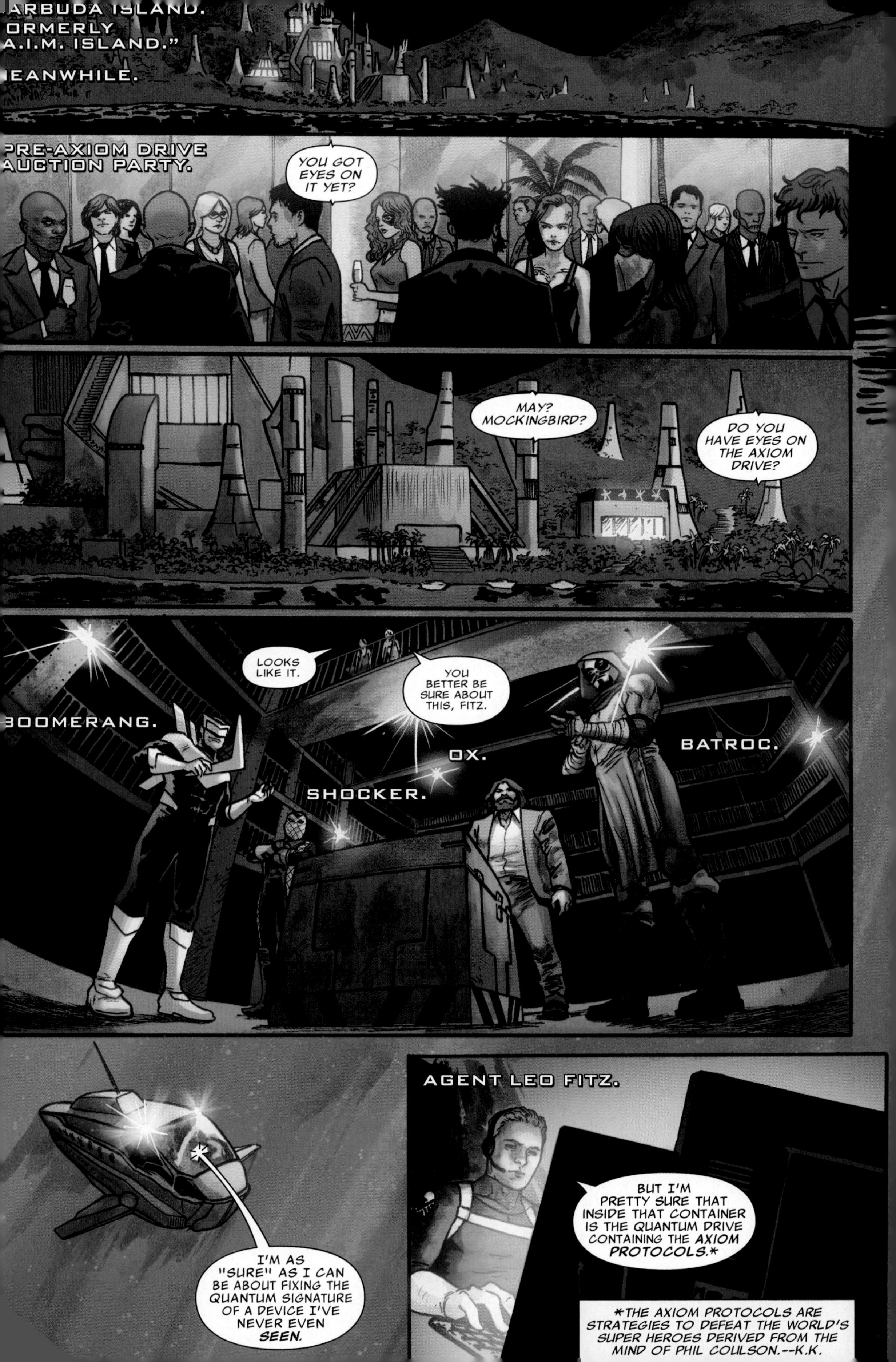
ARBUDA ISLAND. ORMERLY A.I.M. ISLAND."
EANWHILE.
PRE-AXIOM DRIVE AUCTION PARTY.
YOU GOT EYES ON IT YET?
MAY? MOCKINGBIRD?
DO YOU HAVE EYES ON THE AXIOM DRIVE?
LOOKS LIKE IT.
YOU BETTER BE SURE ABOUT THIS, FITZ.
BOOMERANG.
SHOCKER.
OX.
BATROC.
AGENT LEO FITZ.
I'M AS "SURE" AS I CAN BE ABOUT FIXING THE QUANTUM SIGNATURE OF A DEVICE I'VE NEVER EVEN SEEN.
BUT I'M PRETTY SURE THAT INSIDE THAT CONTAINER IS THE QUANTUM DRIVE CONTAINING THE AXIOM PROTOCOLS.*
*THE AXIOM PROTOCOLS ARE STRATEGIES TO DEFEAT THE WORLD'S SUPER HEROES DERIVED FROM THE MIND OF PHIL COULSON.--K.K.

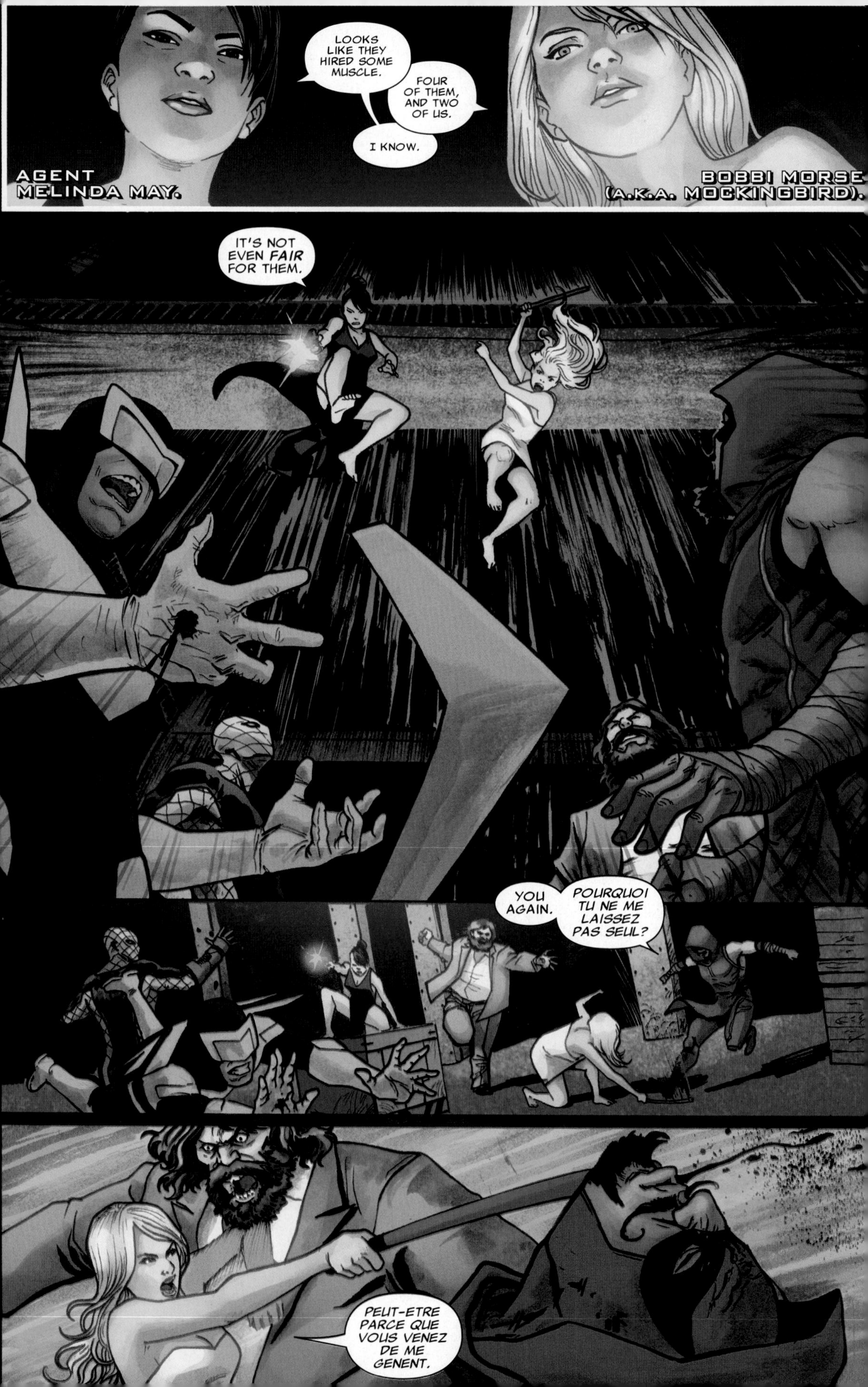
LOOKS LIKE THEY HIRED SOME MUSCLE.
FOUR OF THEM, AND TWO OF US.
I KNOW.
AGENT MELINDA MAY.
BOBBI MORSE (A.K.A. MOCKINGBIRD).
IT'S NOT EVEN FAIR FOR THEM.
YOU AGAIN.
POURQUOI TU NE ME LAISSEZ PAS SEUL?
PEUT-ETRE PARCE QUE VOUS VENEZ DE ME GENENT.

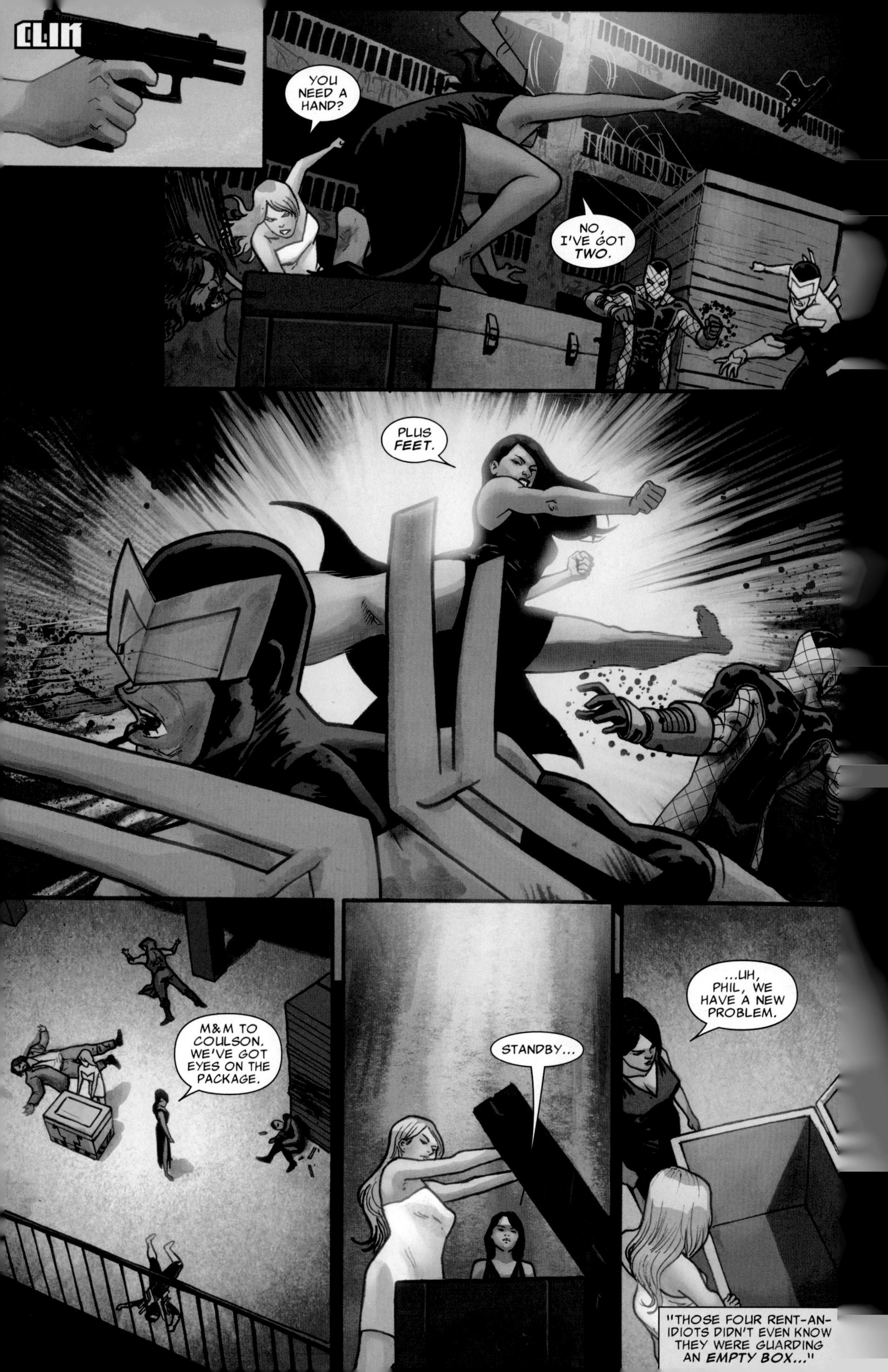
CLIK
YOU NEED A HAND?
NO, I'VE GOT TWO.
PLUS FEET.
M&M TO COULSON. WE'VE GOT EYES ON THE PACKAGE.
STANDBY...
...UH, PHIL, WE HAVE A NEW PROBLEM.
"THOSE FOUR RENT-AN-IDIOTS DIDN'T EVEN KNOW THEY WERE GUARDING AN EMPTY BOX..."

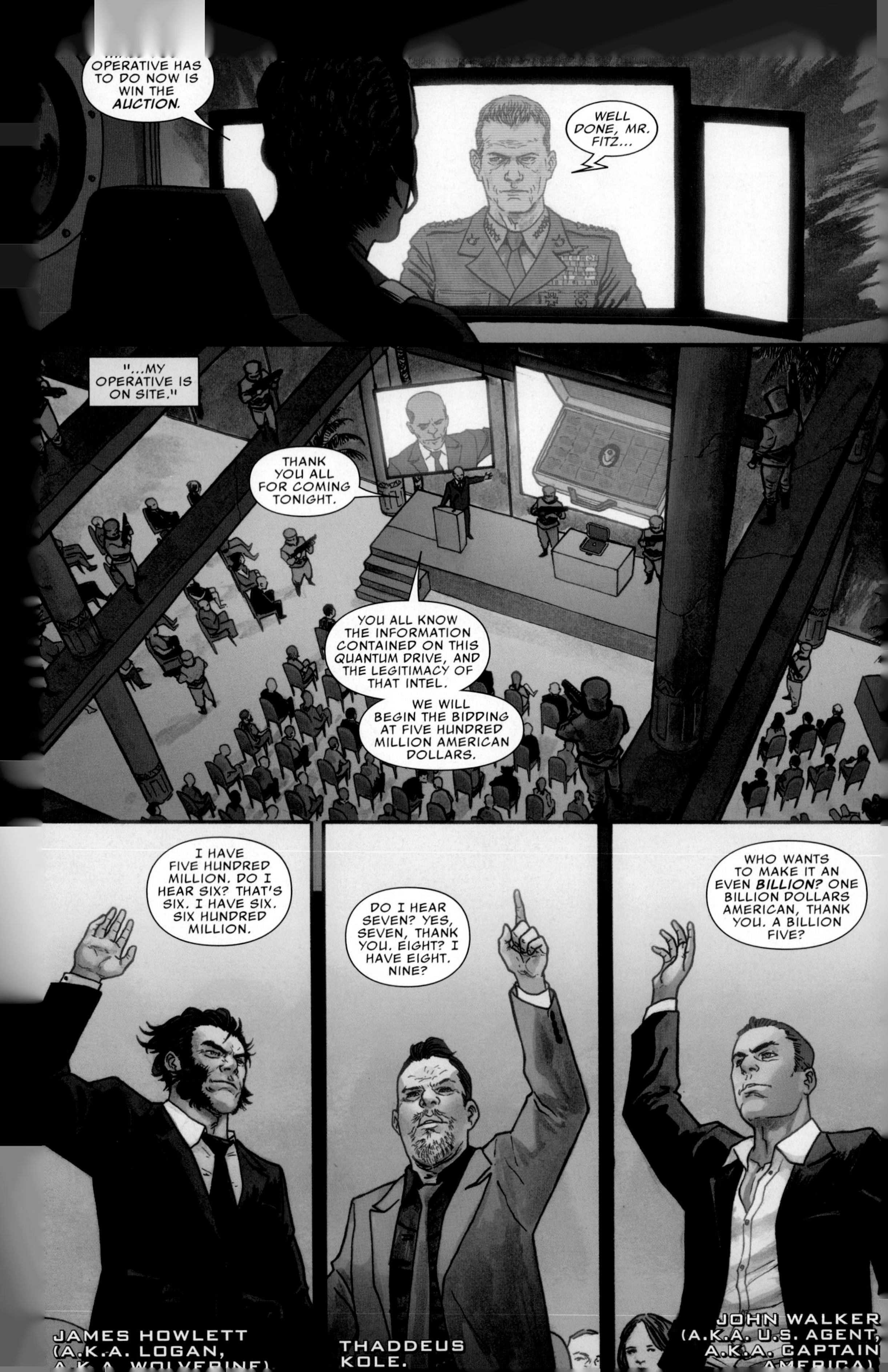
OPERATIVE HAS TO DO NOW IS WIN THE AUCTION.
WELL DONE, MR. FITZ...
"...MY OPERATIVE IS ON SITE."
THANK YOU ALL FOR COMING TONIGHT.
YOU ALL KNOW THE INFORMATION CONTAINED ON THIS QUANTUM DRIVE, AND THE LEGITIMACY OF THAT INTEL.
WE WILL BEGIN THE BIDDING AT FIVE HUNDRED MILLION AMERICAN DOLLARS.
I HAVE FIVE HUNDRED MILLION. DO I HEAR SIX? THAT'S SIX. I HAVE SIX. SIX HUNDRED MILLION.
DO I HEAR SEVEN? YES, SEVEN, THANK YOU. EIGHT? I HAVE EIGHT. NINE?
WHO WANTS TO MAKE IT AN EVEN BILLION? ONE BILLION DOLLARS AMERICAN, THANK YOU. A BILLION FIVE?
JAMES HOWLETT (A.K.A. LOGAN,
THADDEUS KOLE.
JOHN WALKER (A.K.A. U.S. AGENT, A.K.A. CAPTAIN

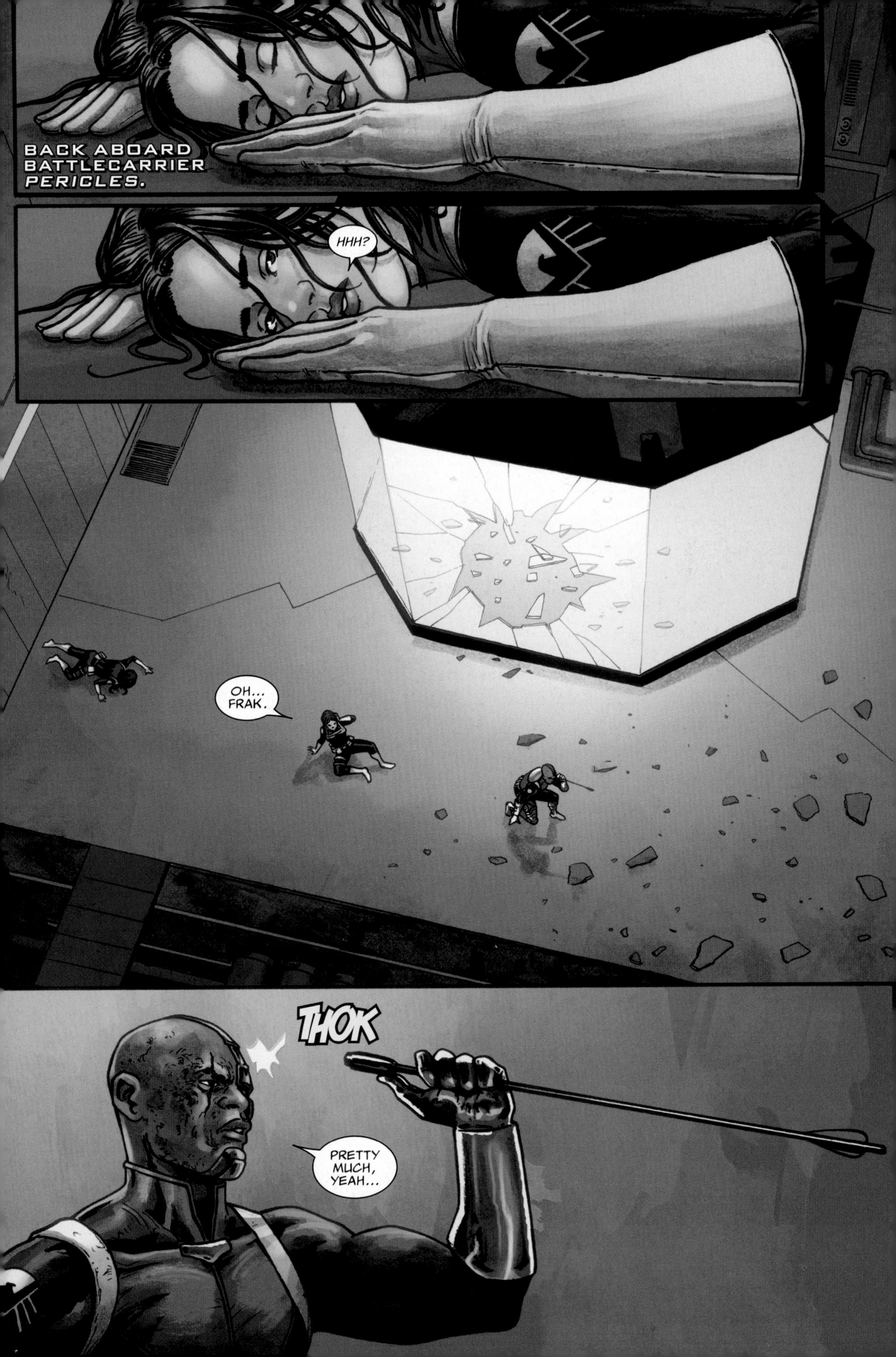
BACK ABOARD BATTLECARRIER *PERICLES.*
HHH?
OH... FRAK.
THOK
PRETTY MUCH, YEAH...

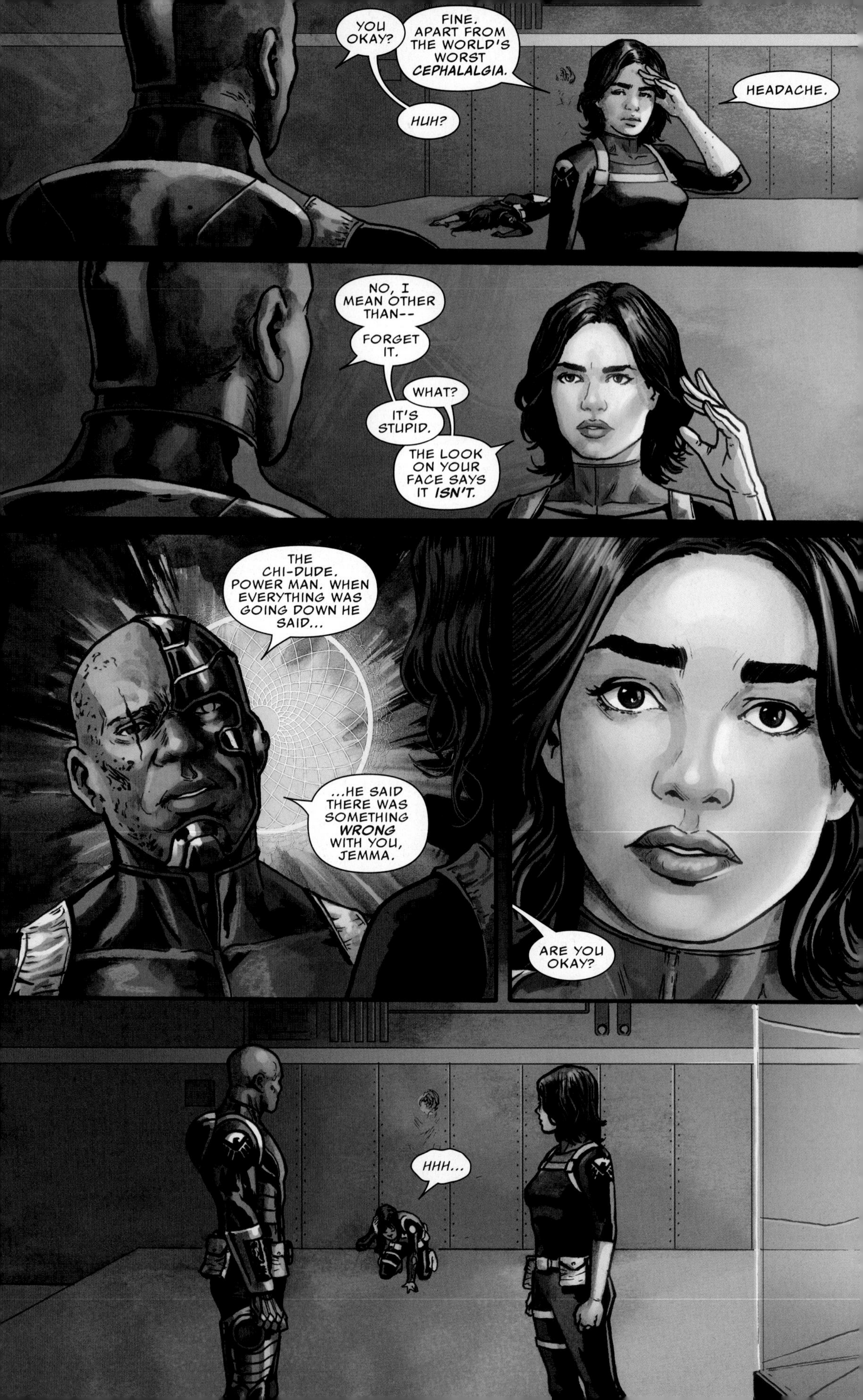
YOU OKAY?
FINE. APART FROM THE WORLD'S WORST CEPHALALGIA.
HUH?
HEADACHE.
NO, I MEAN OTHER THAN--
FORGET IT.
WHAT?
IT'S STUPID.
THE LOOK ON YOUR FACE SAYS IT ISN'T.
THE CHI-DUDE. POWER MAN. WHEN EVERYTHING WAS GOING DOWN HE SAID...
...HE SAID THERE WAS SOMETHING WRONG WITH YOU, JEMMA.
ARE YOU OKAY?
HHH...

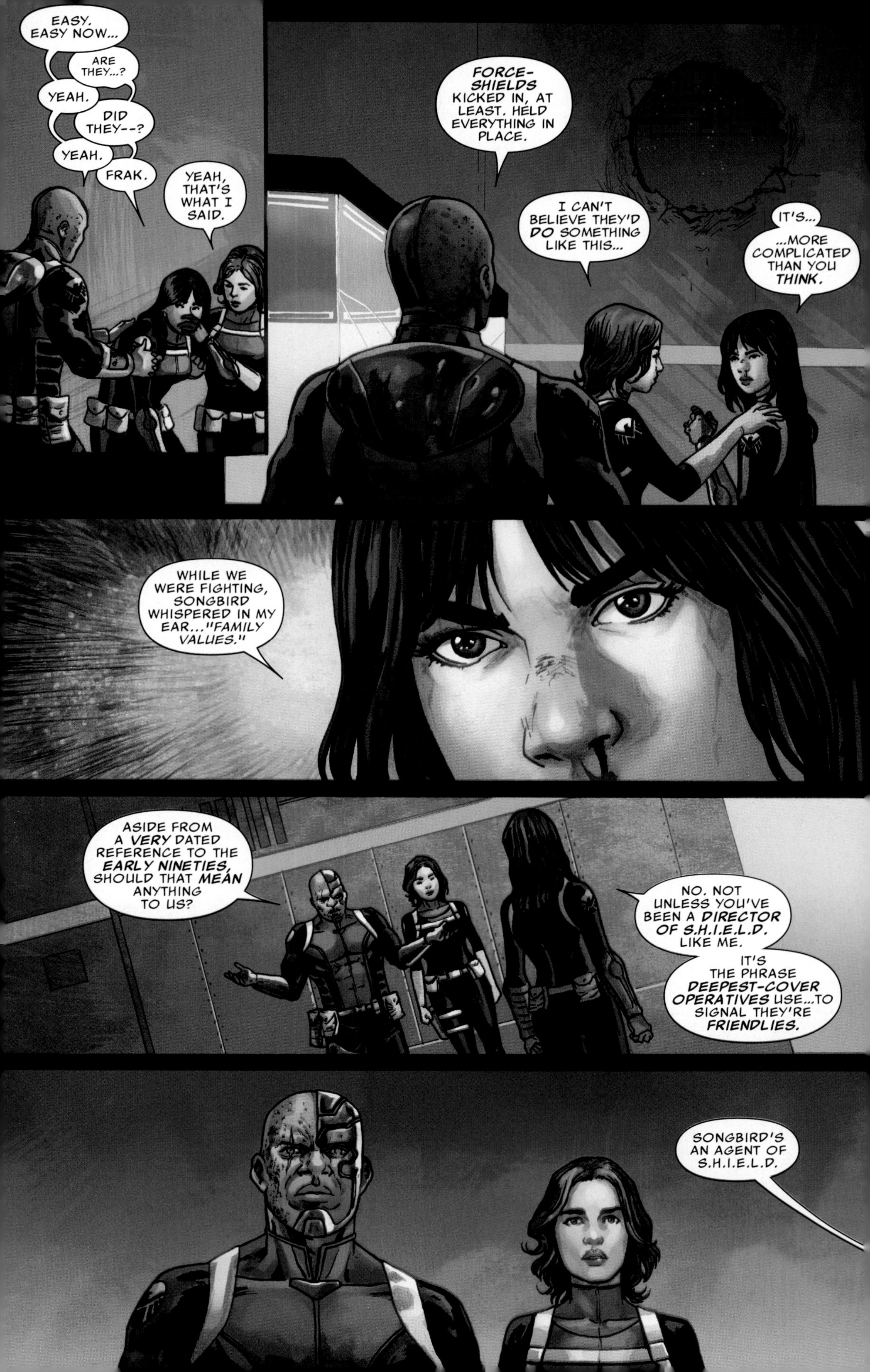
EASY. EASY NOW...
ARE THEY...?
YEAH.
DID THEY--?
YEAH.
FRAK.
YEAH, THAT'S WHAT I SAID.
FORCE-SHIELDS KICKED IN, AT LEAST. HELD EVERYTHING IN PLACE.
I CAN'T BELIEVE THEY'D DO SOMETHING LIKE THIS...
IT'S...
...MORE COMPLICATED THAN YOU THINK.
WHILE WE WERE FIGHTING, SONGBIRD WHISPERED IN MY EAR..."FAMILY VALUES."
ASIDE FROM A VERY DATED REFERENCE TO THE EARLY NINETIES, SHOULD THAT MEAN ANYTHING TO US?
NO. NOT UNLESS YOU'VE BEEN A DIRECTOR OF S.H.I.E.L.D. LIKE ME.
IT'S THE PHRASE DEEPEST-COVER OPERATIVES USE...TO SIGNAL THEY'RE FRIENDLIES.
SONGBIRD'S AN AGENT OF S.H.I.E.L.D.

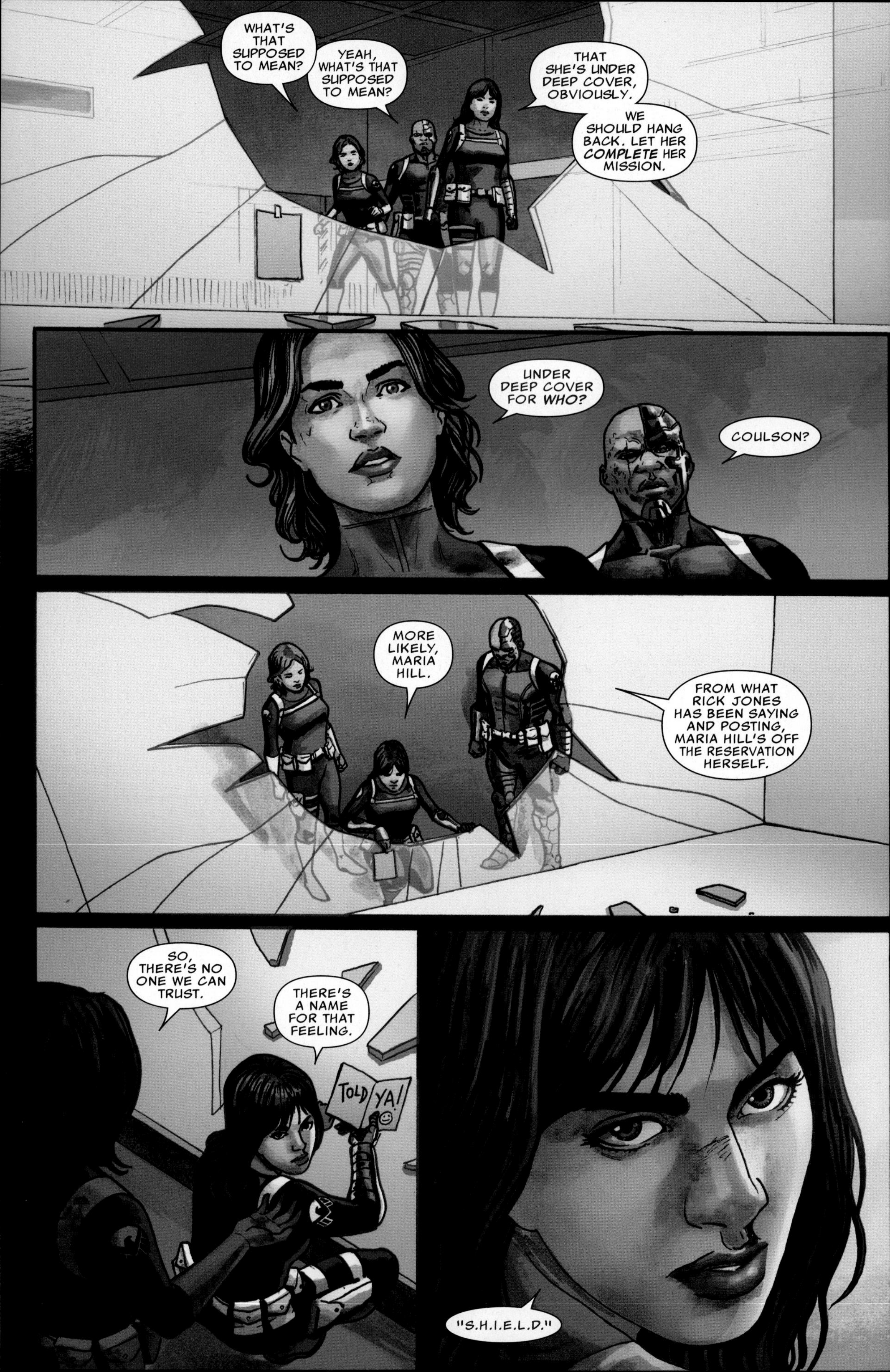
WHAT'S THAT SUPPOSED TO MEAN?
YEAH, WHAT'S THAT SUPPOSED TO MEAN?
THAT SHE'S UNDER DEEP COVER, OBVIOUSLY.
WE SHOULD HANG BACK. LET HER COMPLETE HER MISSION.
UNDER DEEP COVER FOR WHO?
COULSON?
MORE LIKELY, MARIA HILL.
FROM WHAT RICK JONES HAS BEEN SAYING AND POSTING, MARIA HILL'S OFF THE RESERVATION HERSELF.
SO, THERE'S NO ONE WE CAN TRUST.
THERE'S A NAME FOR THAT FEELING.
TOLD YA!
"S.H.I.E.L.D."

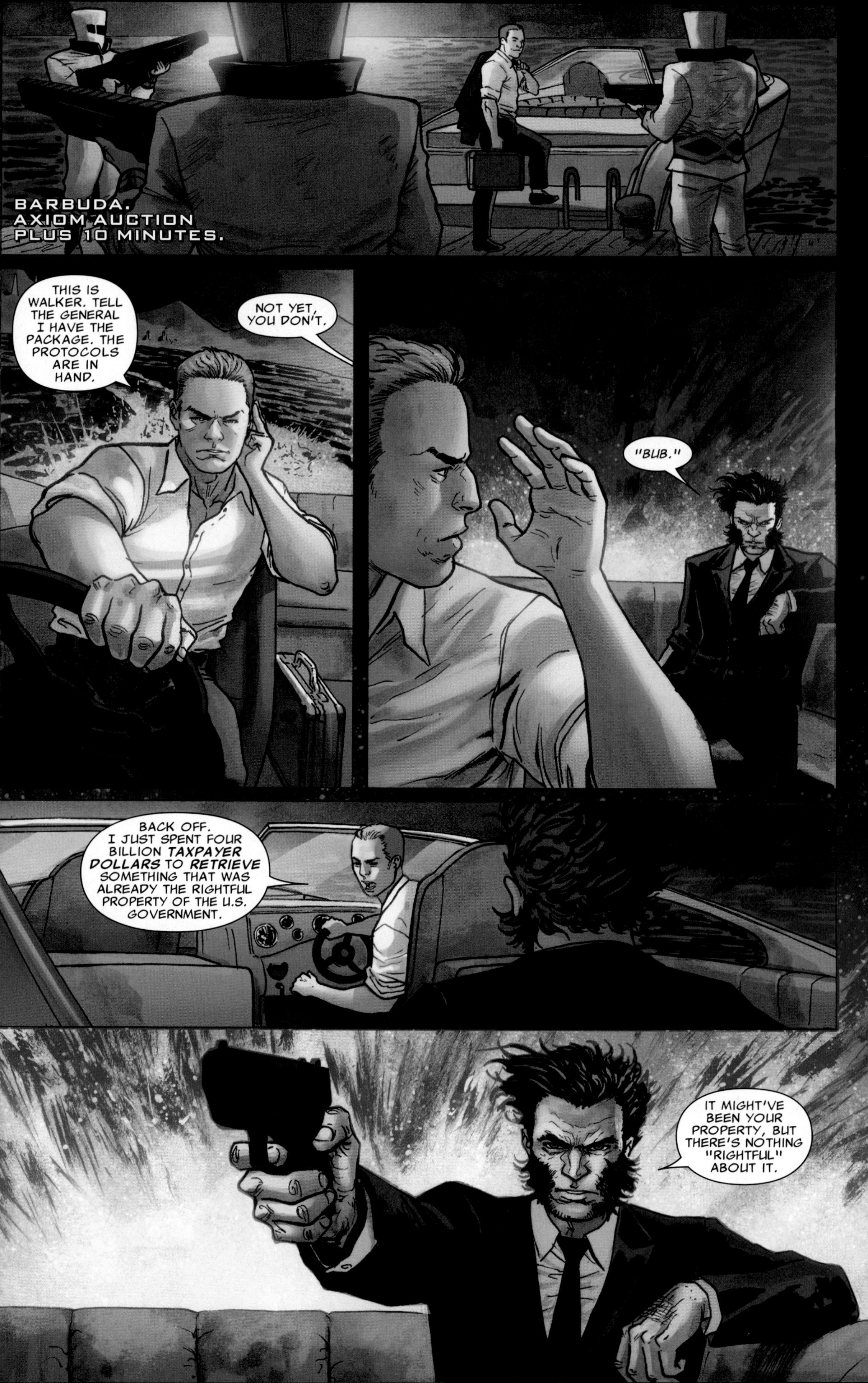
BARBUDA. AXIOM AUCTION PLUS 10 MINUTES.
THIS IS WALKER. TELL THE GENERAL I HAVE THE PACKAGE. THE PROTOCOLS ARE IN HAND.
NOT YET, YOU DON'T.
"BUB."
BACK OFF. I JUST SPENT FOUR BILLION TAXPAYER DOLLARS TO RETRIEVE SOMETHING THAT WAS ALREADY THE RIGHTFUL PROPERTY OF THE U.S. GOVERNMENT.
IT MIGHT'VE BEEN YOUR PROPERTY, BUT THERE'S NOTHING "RIGHTFUL" ABOUT IT.

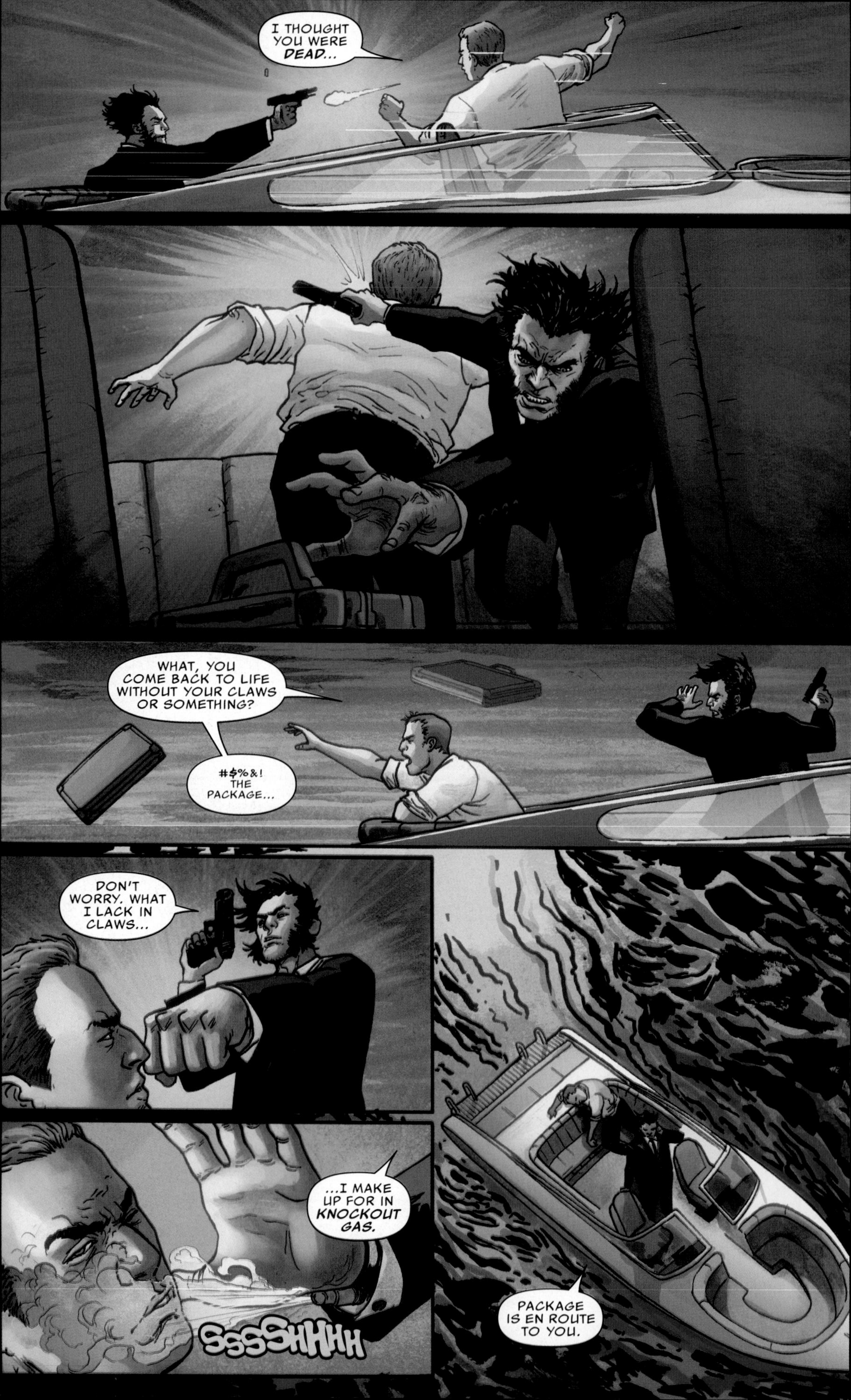
I THOUGHT YOU WERE DEAD...
WHAT, YOU COME BACK TO LIFE WITHOUT YOUR CLAWS OR SOMETHING?
#$%&! THE PACKAGE...
DON'T WORRY. WHAT I LACK IN CLAWS...
...I MAKE UP FOR IN KNOCKOUT GAS.
SSSSHHHH
PACKAGE IS EN ROUTE TO YOU.

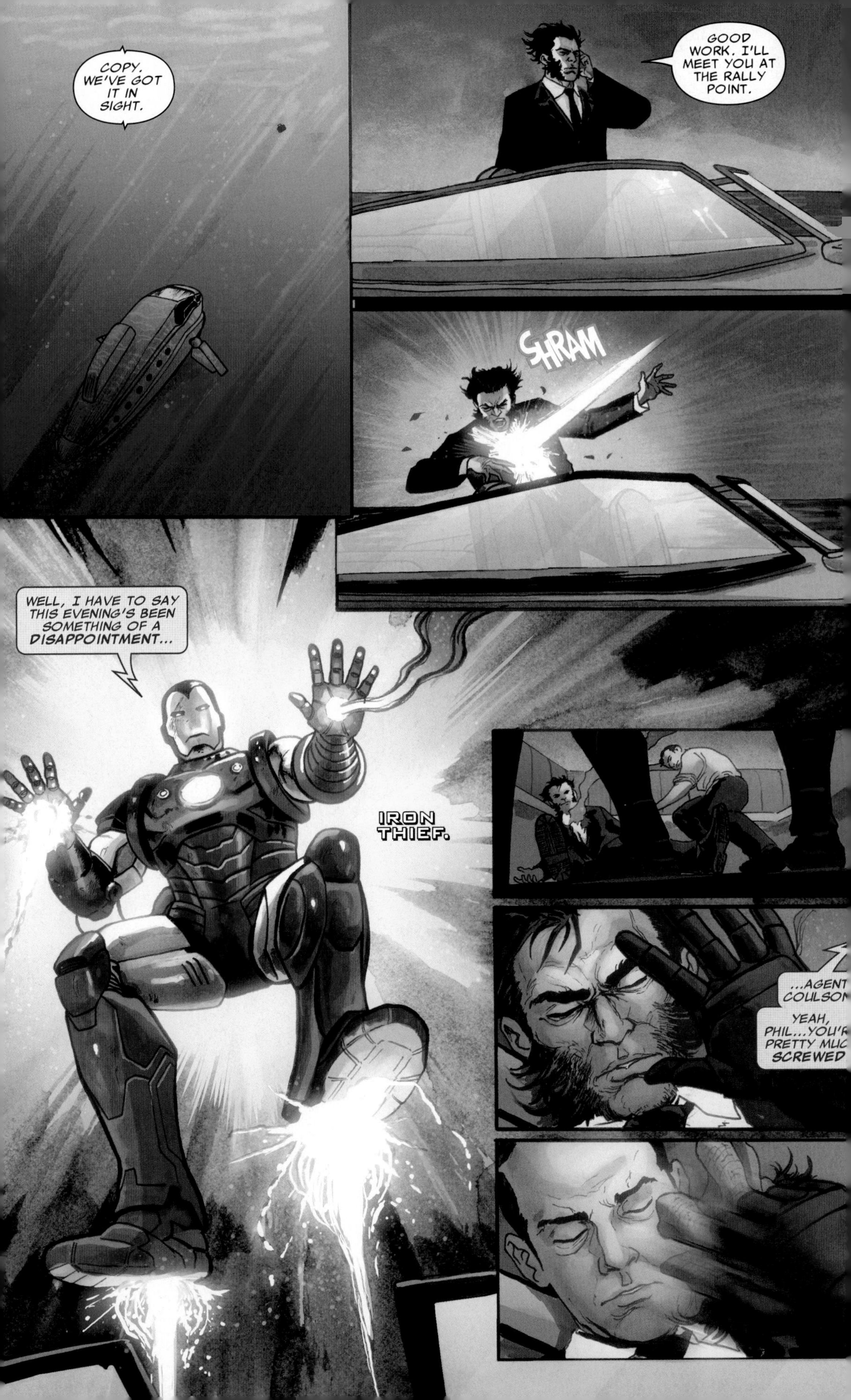
COPY. WE'VE GOT IT IN SIGHT.
GOOD WORK. I'LL MEET YOU AT THE RALLY POINT.
SHRAM
WELL, I HAVE TO SAY THIS EVENING'S BEEN SOMETHING OF A DISAPPOINTMENT...
IRON THIEF.
...AGENT COULSON
YEAH, PHIL...YOU'R PRETTY MUC SCREWED

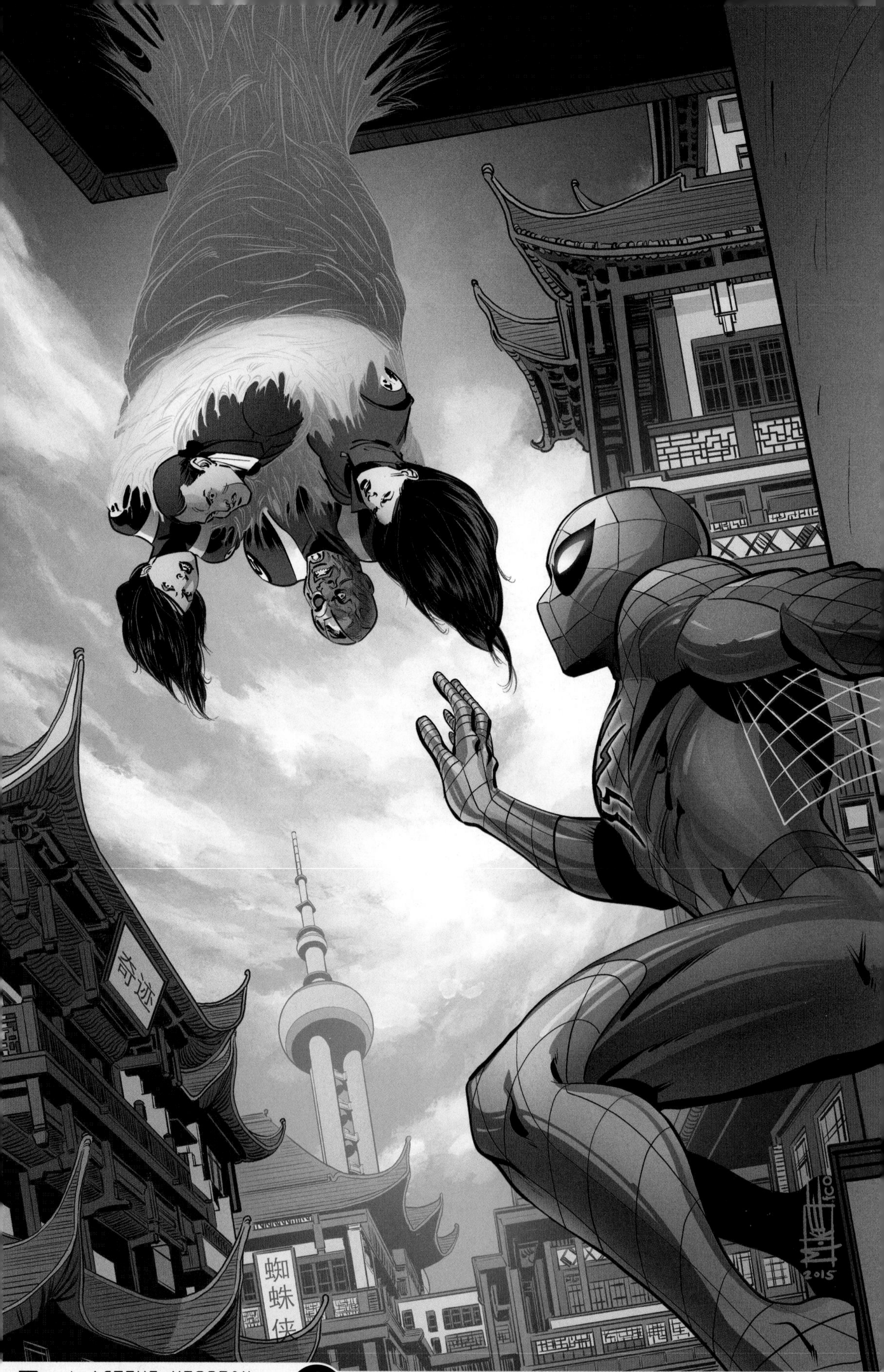
奇迹
蜘蛛侠
2015

ACTIVE MISSION:

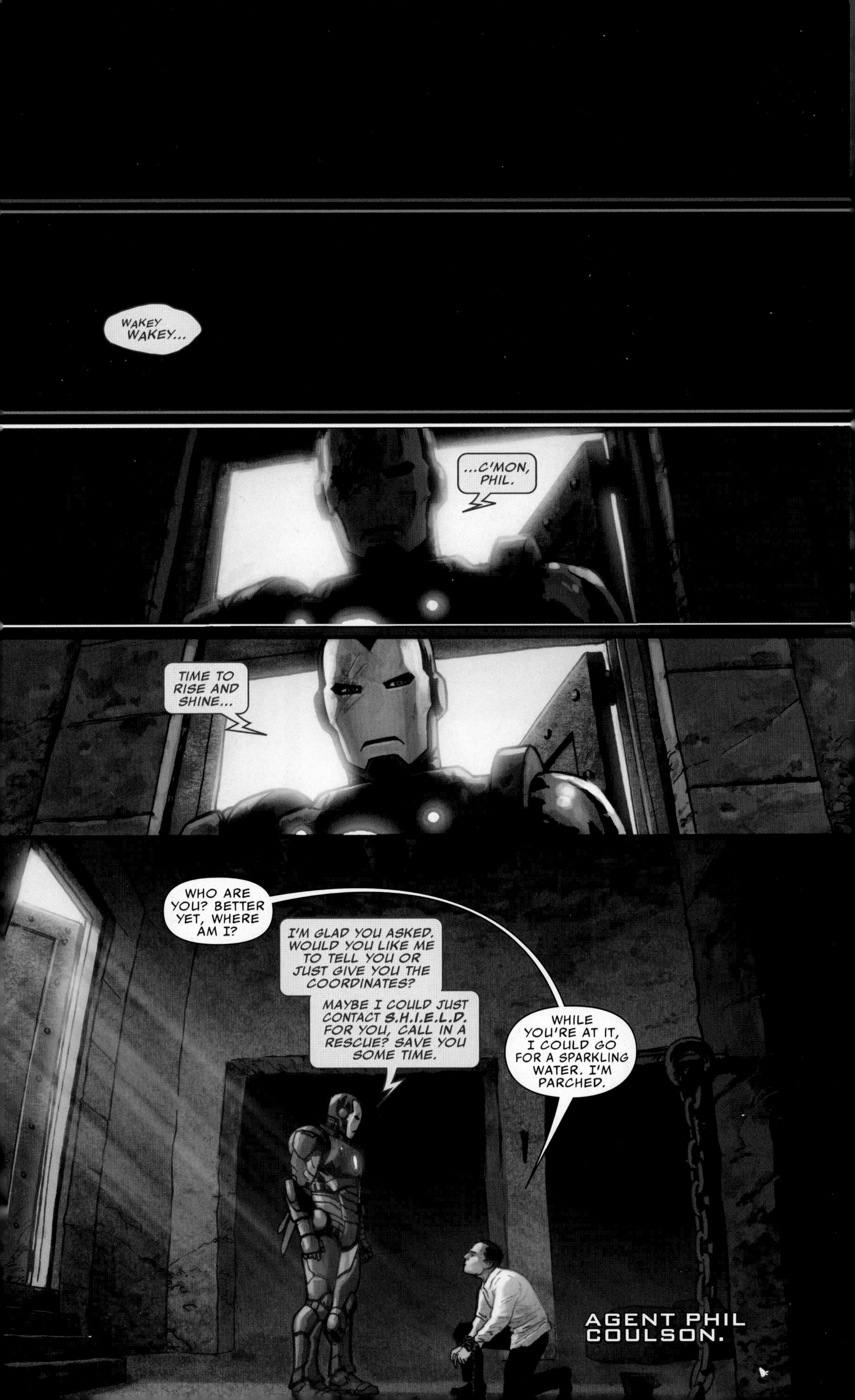
WAKEY WAKEY...
...C'MON, PHIL.
TIME TO RISE AND SHINE...
WHO ARE YOU? BETTER YET, WHERE AM I?
I'M GLAD YOU ASKED. WOULD YOU LIKE ME TO TELL YOU OR JUST GIVE YOU THE COORDINATES?
MAYBE I COULD JUST CONTACT S.H.I.E.L.D. FOR YOU, CALL IN A RESCUE? SAVE YOU SOME TIME.
WHILE YOU'RE AT IT, I COULD GO FOR A SPARKLING WATER. I'M PARCHED.
AGENT PHIL COULSON.

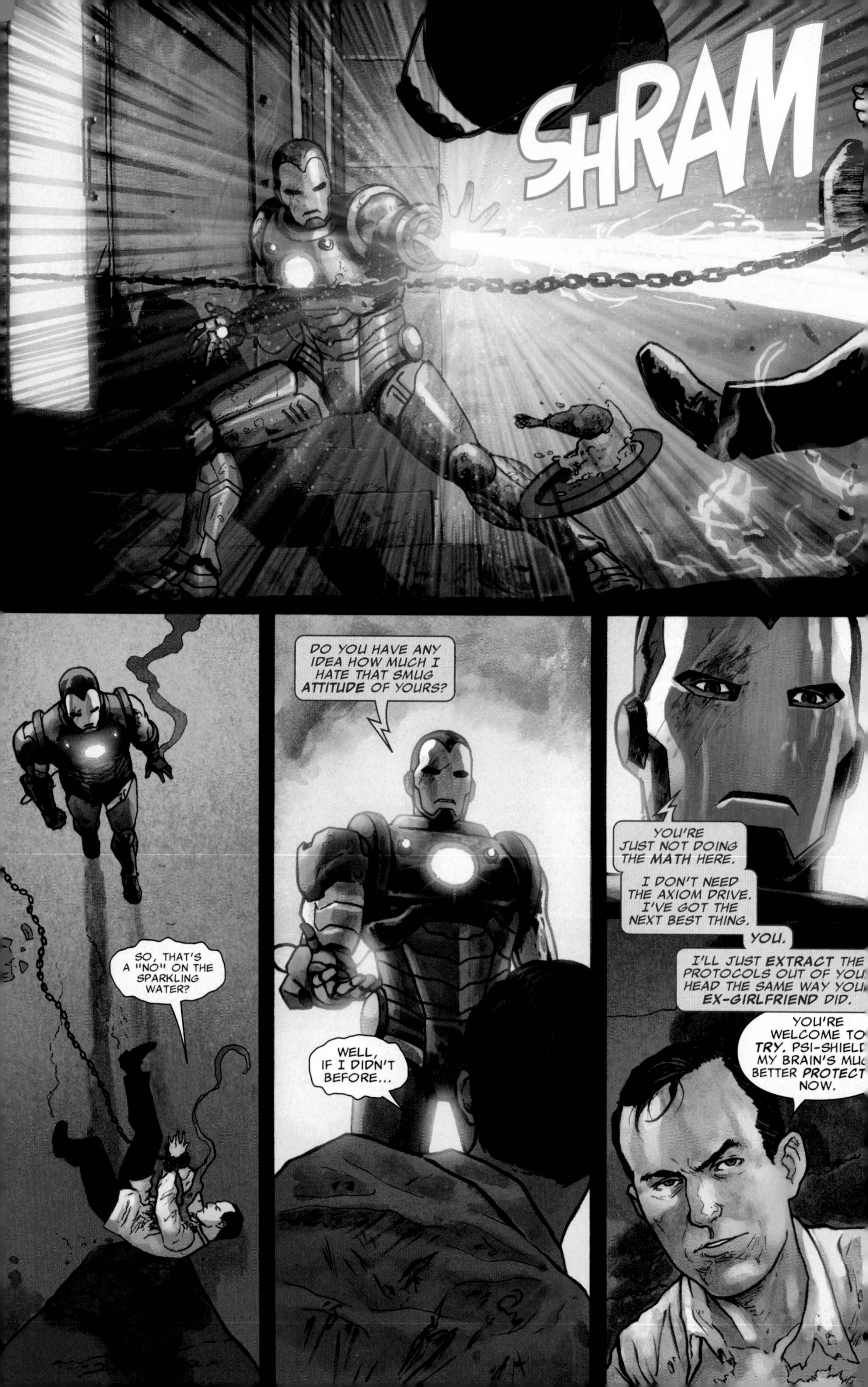
SHRAM
SO, THAT'S A "NO" ON THE SPARKLING WATER?
DO YOU HAVE ANY IDEA HOW MUCH I HATE THAT SMUG ATTITUDE OF YOURS?
WELL, IF I DIDN'T BEFORE...
YOU'RE JUST NOT DOING THE MATH HERE.
I DON'T NEED THE AXIOM DRIVE. I'VE GOT THE NEXT BEST THING.
YOU.
I'LL JUST EXTRACT THE PROTOCOLS OUT OF YOU HEAD THE SAME WAY YOU EX-GIRLFRIEND DID.
YOU'RE WELCOME TO TRY. PSI-SHIELD MY BRAIN'S MU BETTER PROTECT NOW.

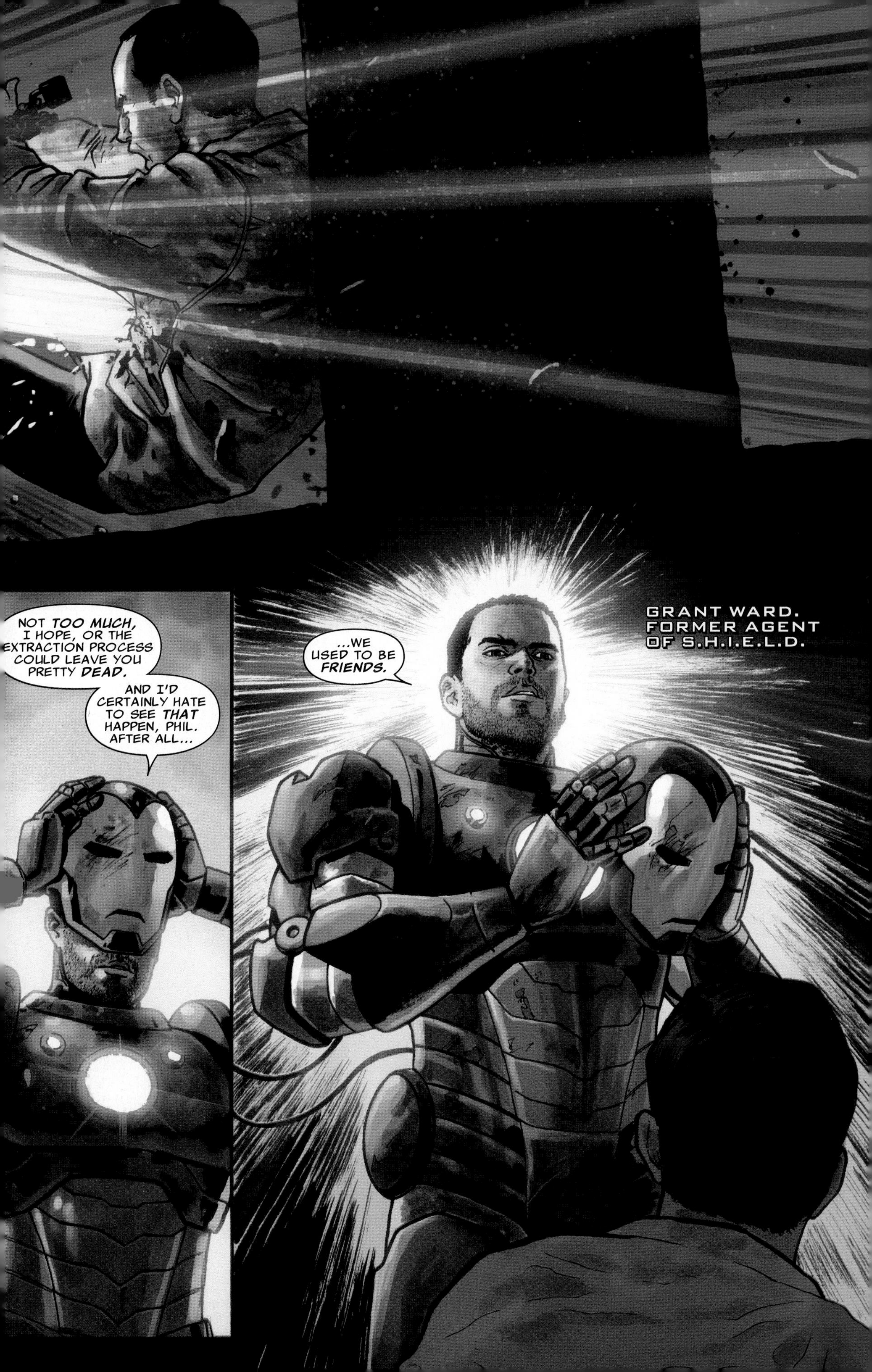

NOT TOO MUCH, I HOPE, OR THE EXTRACTION PROCESS COULD LEAVE YOU PRETTY DEAD.
AND I'D CERTAINLY HATE TO SEE THAT HAPPEN, PHIL. AFTER ALL...
...WE USED TO BE FRIENDS.
GRANT WARD. FORMER AGENT OF S.H.I.E.L.D.

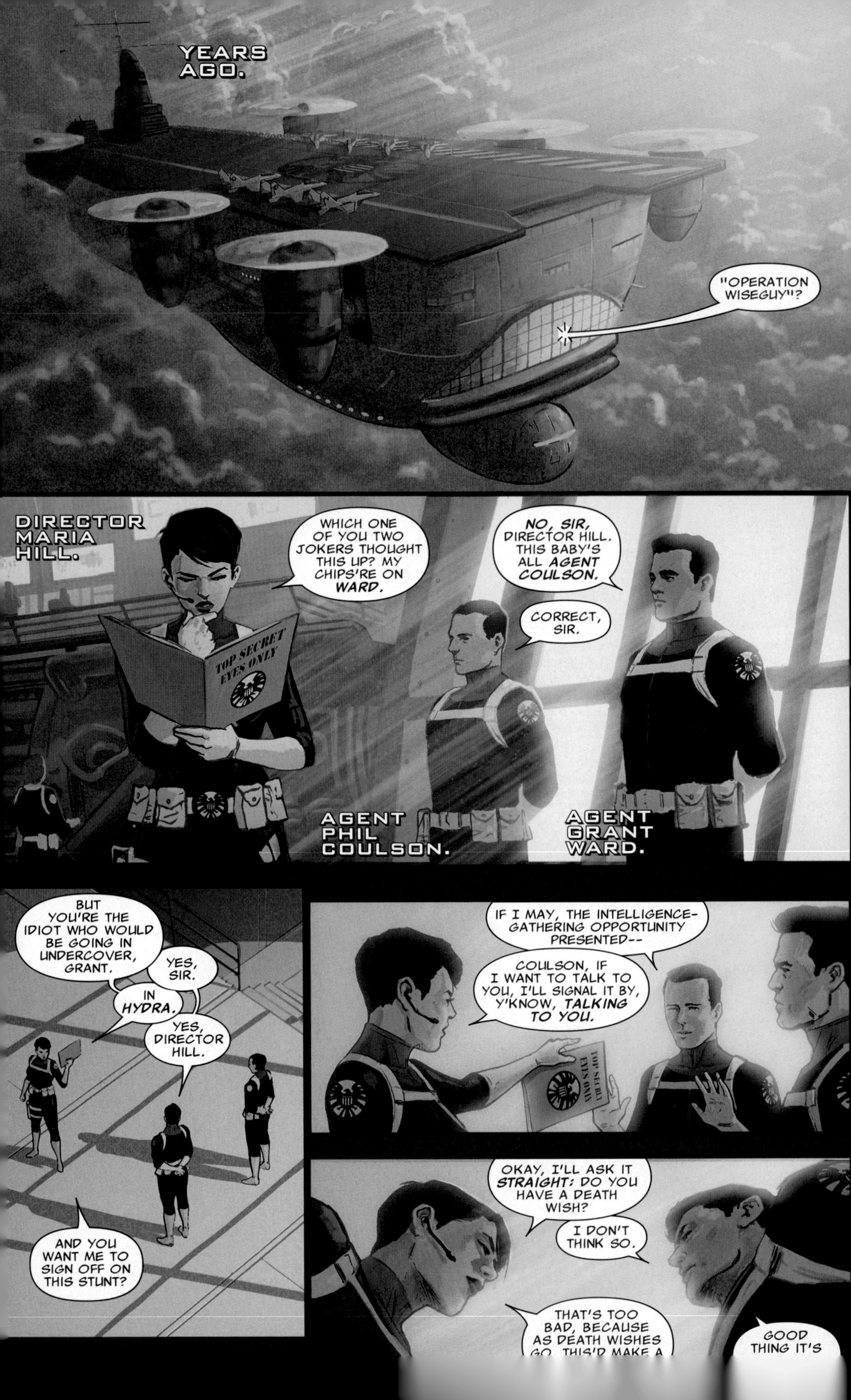
YEARS AGO.
"OPERATION WISEGUY"?
DIRECTOR MARIA HILL.
WHICH ONE OF YOU TWO JOKERS THOUGHT THIS UP? MY CHIPS'RE ON WARD.
NO, SIR, DIRECTOR HILL. THIS BABY'S ALL AGENT COULSON.
CORRECT, SIR.
TOP SECRET EYES ONLY
AGENT PHIL COULSON.
AGENT GRANT WARD.
BUT YOU'RE THE IDIOT WHO WOULD BE GOING IN UNDERCOVER, GRANT.
YES, SIR.
IN HYDRA.
YES, DIRECTOR HILL.
AND YOU WANT ME TO SIGN OFF ON THIS STUNT?
IF I MAY, THE INTELLIGENCE-GATHERING OPPORTUNITY PRESENTED--
COULSON, IF I WANT TO TALK TO YOU, I'LL SIGNAL IT BY, Y'KNOW, TALKING TO YOU.
OKAY, I'LL ASK IT STRAIGHT: DO YOU HAVE A DEATH WISH?
I DON'T THINK SO.
THAT'S TOO BAD, BECAUSE AS DEATH WISHES
GOOD THING IT'S

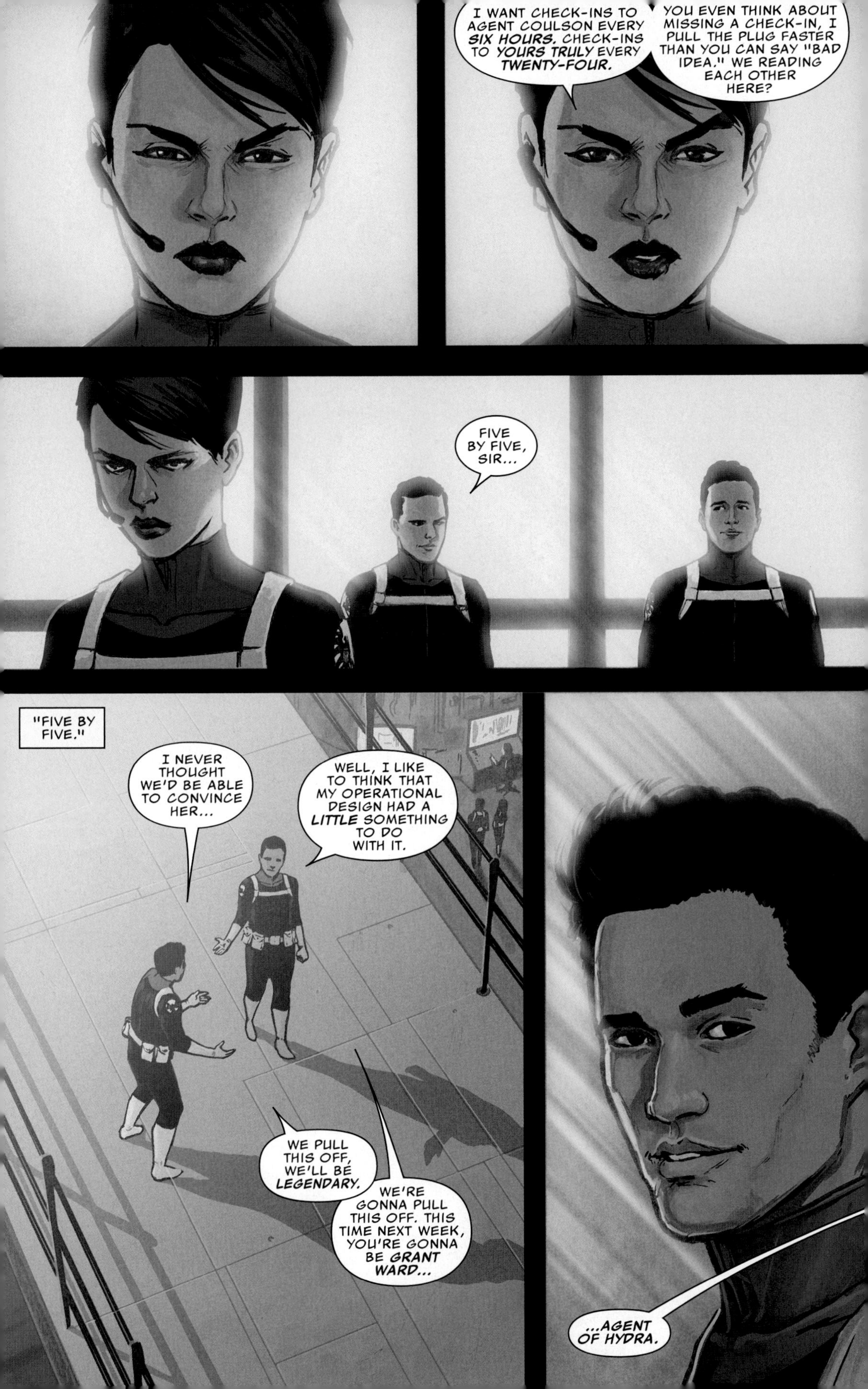
I WANT CHECK-INS TO AGENT COULSON EVERY SIX HOURS. CHECK-INS TO YOURS TRULY EVERY TWENTY-FOUR.
YOU EVEN THINK ABOUT MISSING A CHECK-IN, I PULL THE PLUG FASTER THAN YOU CAN SAY "BAD IDEA." WE READING EACH OTHER HERE?
FIVE BY FIVE, SIR...
"FIVE BY FIVE."
I NEVER THOUGHT WE'D BE ABLE TO CONVINCE HER...
WELL, I LIKE TO THINK THAT MY OPERATIONAL DESIGN HAD A LITTLE SOMETHING TO DO WITH IT.
WE PULL THIS OFF, WE'LL BE LEGENDARY.
WE'RE GONNA PULL THIS OFF. THIS TIME NEXT WEEK, YOU'RE GONNA BE GRANT WARD...
...AGENT OF HYDRA.

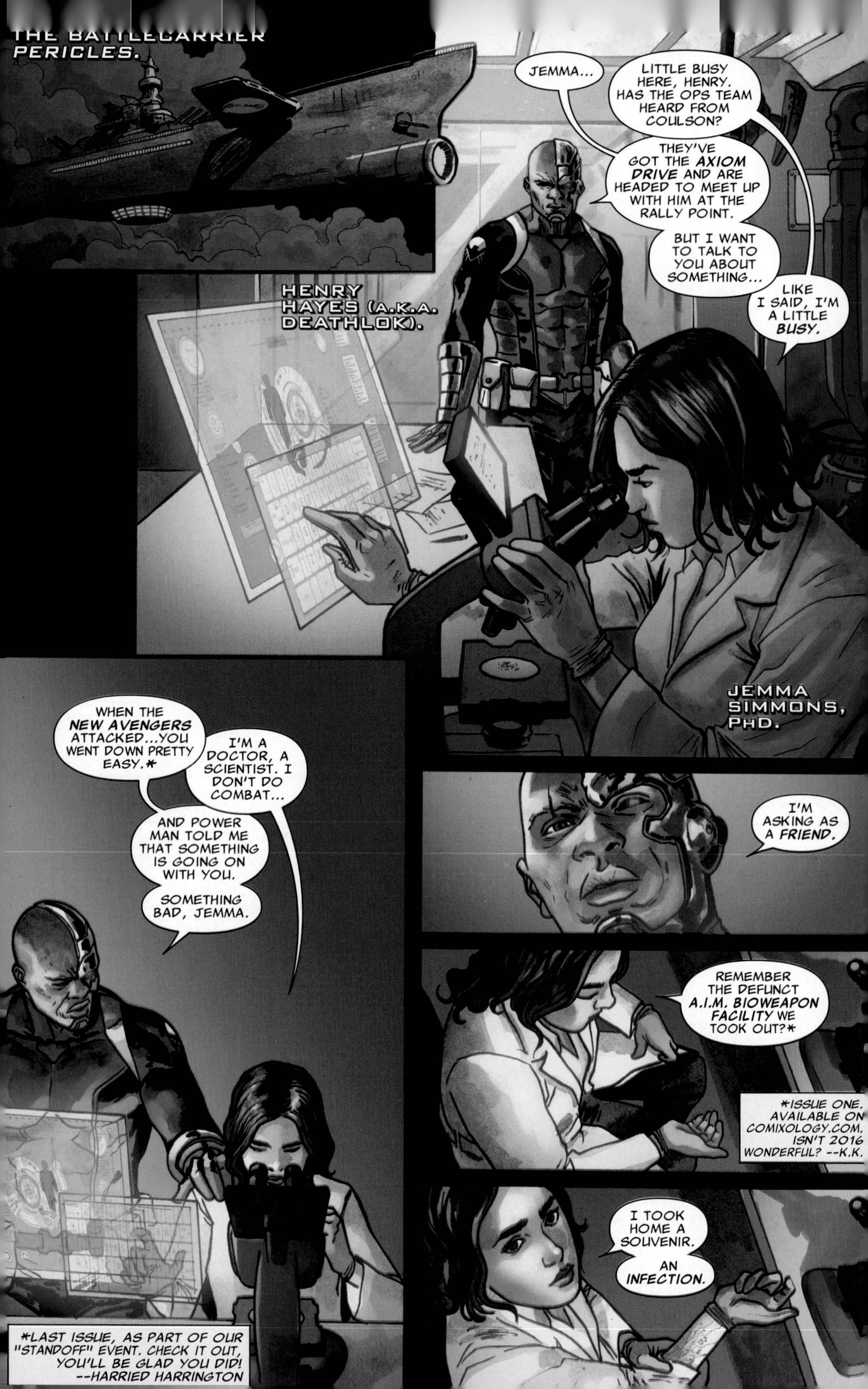
THE BATTLECARRIER PERICLES.
JEMMA...
LITTLE BUSY HERE, HENRY. HAS THE OPS TEAM HEARD FROM COULSON?
THEY'VE GOT THE AXIOM DRIVE AND ARE HEADED TO MEET UP WITH HIM AT THE RALLY POINT.
BUT I WANT TO TALK TO YOU ABOUT SOMETHING...
LIKE I SAID, I'M A LITTLE BUSY.
HENRY HAYES (A.K.A. DEATHLOK).
JEMMA SIMMONS, PHD.
WHEN THE NEW AVENGERS ATTACKED...YOU WENT DOWN PRETTY EASY.*
I'M A DOCTOR, A SCIENTIST. I DON'T DO COMBAT...
AND POWER MAN TOLD ME THAT SOMETHING IS GOING ON WITH YOU.
SOMETHING BAD, JEMMA.
*LAST ISSUE, AS PART OF OUR "STANDOFF" EVENT. CHECK IT OUT, YOU'LL BE GLAD YOU DID! --HARRIED HARRINGTON
I'M ASKING AS A FRIEND.
REMEMBER THE DEFUNCT A.I.M. BIOWEAPON FACILITY WE TOOK OUT?*
*ISSUE ONE. AVAILABLE ON COMIXOLOGY.COM. ISN'T 2016 WONDERFUL? --K.K.
I TOOK HOME A SOUVENIR.
AN INFECTION.

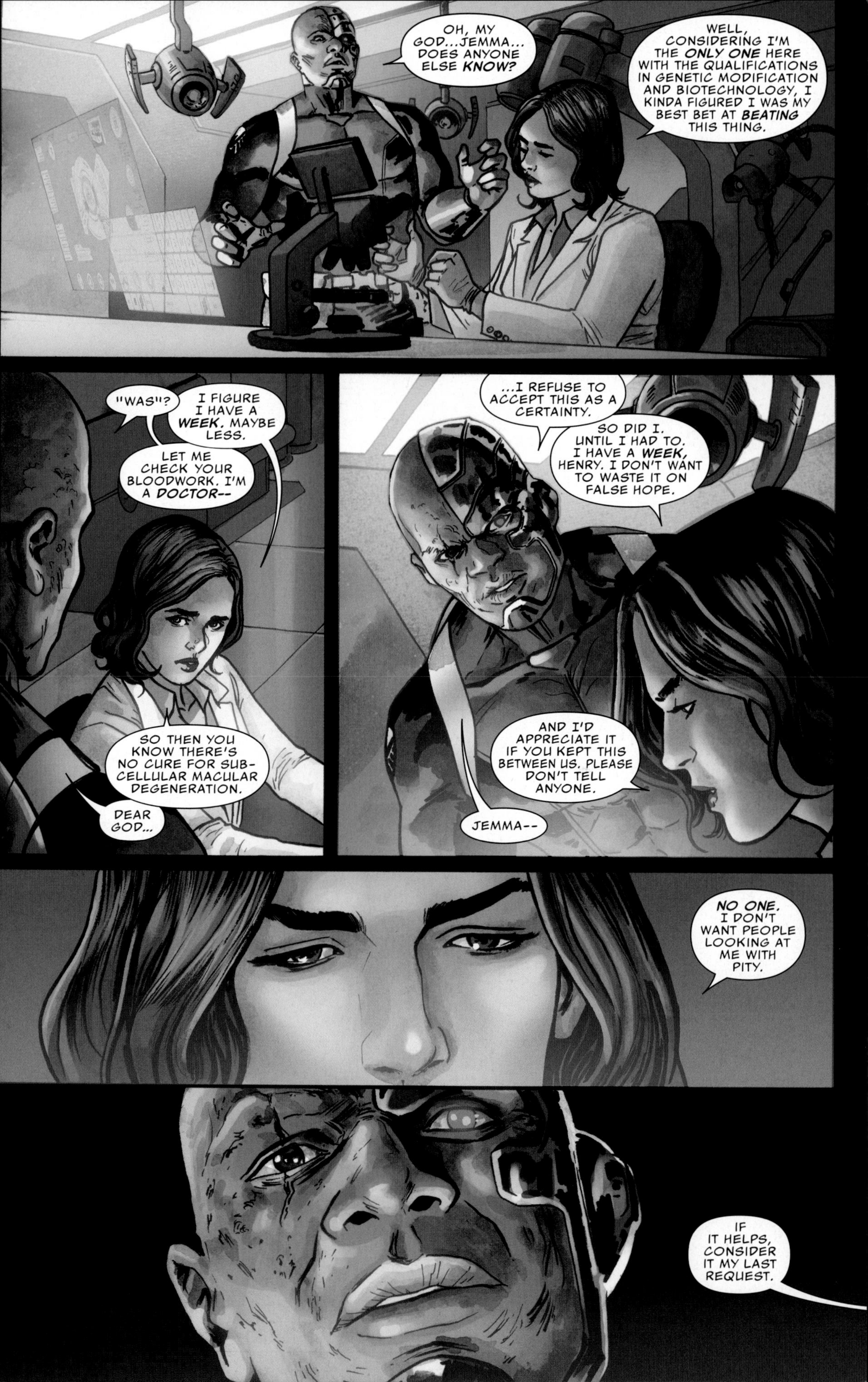

OH, MY GOD...JEMMA... DOES ANYONE ELSE KNOW?
WELL, CONSIDERING I'M THE ONLY ONE HERE WITH THE QUALIFICATIONS IN GENETIC MODIFICATION AND BIOTECHNOLOGY, I KINDA FIGURED I WAS MY BEST BET AT BEATING THIS THING.
"WAS"?
I FIGURE I HAVE A WEEK. MAYBE LESS.
LET ME CHECK YOUR BLOODWORK. I'M A DOCTOR--
SO THEN YOU KNOW THERE'S NO CURE FOR SUB-CELLULAR MACULAR DEGENERATION.
DEAR GOD...
...I REFUSE TO ACCEPT THIS AS A CERTAINTY.
SO DID I. UNTIL I HAD TO. I HAVE A WEEK, HENRY. I DON'T WANT TO WASTE IT ON FALSE HOPE.
AND I'D APPRECIATE IT IF YOU KEPT THIS BETWEEN US. PLEASE DON'T TELL ANYONE.
JEMMA--
NO ONE. I DON'T WANT PEOPLE LOOKING AT ME WITH PITY.
IF IT HELPS, CONSIDER IT MY LAST REQUEST.

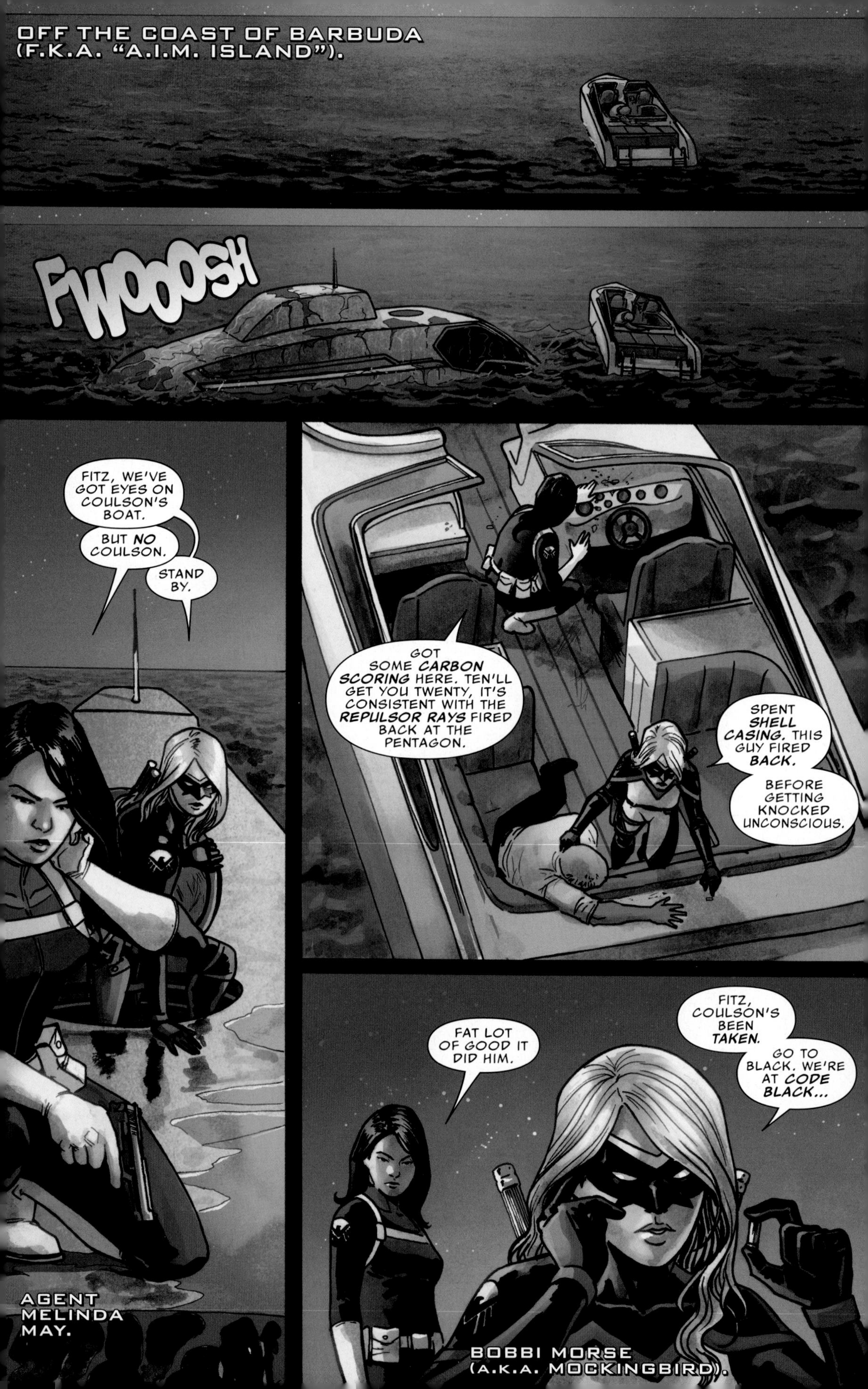
OFF THE COAST OF BARBUDA (F.K.A. "A.I.M. ISLAND").
FWOOOSH
FITZ, WE'VE GOT EYES ON COULSON'S BOAT.
BUT NO COULSON.
STAND BY.
AGENT MELINDA MAY.
GOT SOME CARBON SCORING HERE. TEN'LL GET YOU TWENTY, IT'S CONSISTENT WITH THE REPULSOR RAYS FIRED BACK AT THE PENTAGON.
SPENT SHELL CASING. THIS GUY FIRED BACK.
BEFORE GETTING KNOCKED UNCONSCIOUS.
FAT LOT OF GOOD IT DID HIM.
FITZ, COULSON'S BEEN TAKEN.
GO TO BLACK. WE'RE AT CODE BLACK...
BOBBI MORSE (A.K.A. MOCKINGBIRD).

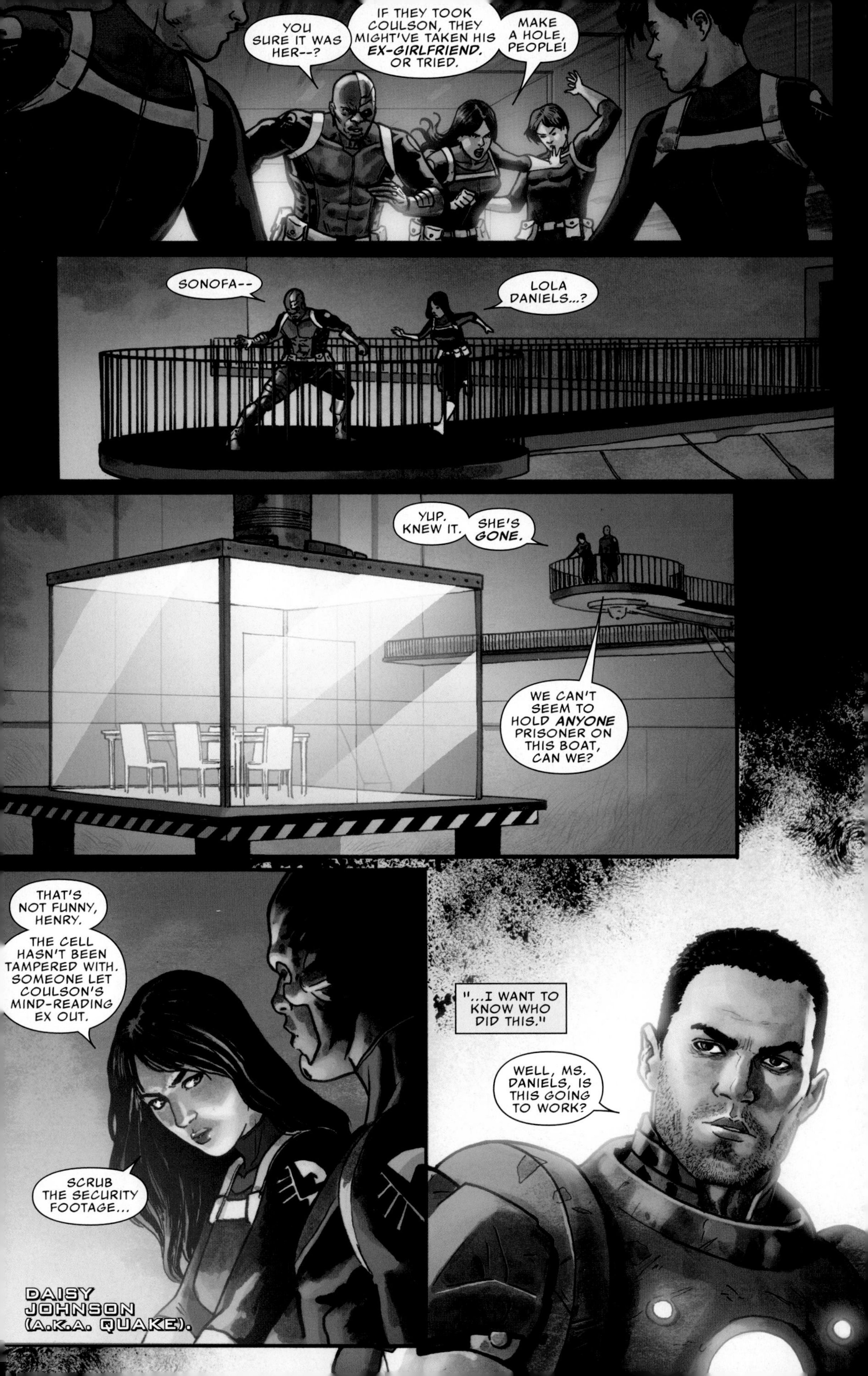
YOU SURE IT WAS HER--?
IF THEY TOOK COULSON, THEY MIGHT'VE TAKEN HIS EX-GIRLFRIEND. OR TRIED.
MAKE A HOLE, PEOPLE!
SONOFA--
LOLA DANIELS...?
YUP. KNEW IT.
SHE'S GONE.
WE CAN'T SEEM TO HOLD ANYONE PRISONER ON THIS BOAT, CAN WE?
THAT'S NOT FUNNY, HENRY.
THE CELL HASN'T BEEN TAMPERED WITH. SOMEONE LET COULSON'S MIND-READING EX OUT.
SCRUB THE SECURITY FOOTAGE...
DAISY JOHNSON (A.K.A. QUAKE).
"...I WANT TO KNOW WHO DID THIS."
WELL, MS. DANIELS, IS THIS GOING TO WORK?

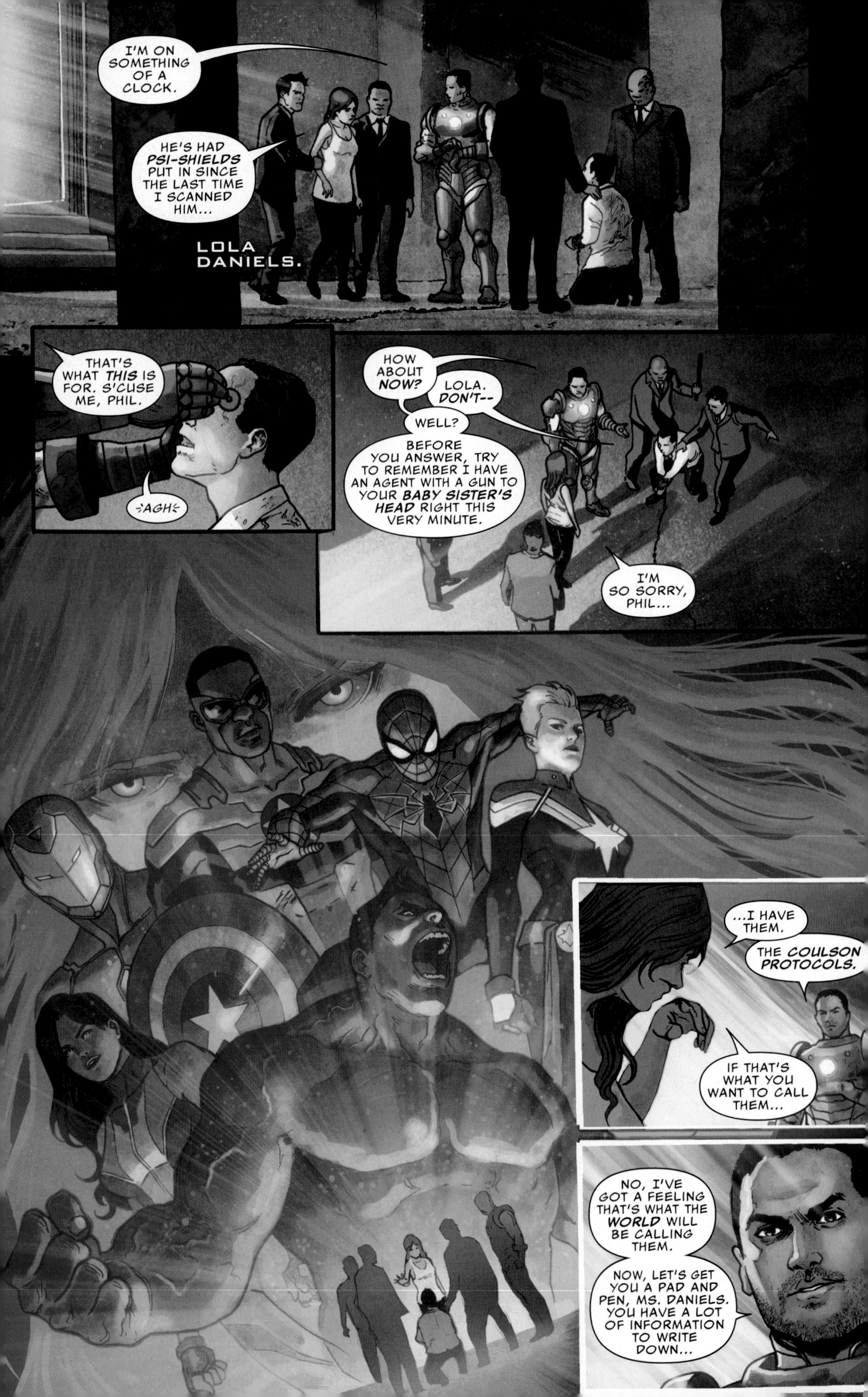
I'M ON SOMETHING OF A CLOCK.
HE'S HAD PSI-SHIELDS PUT IN SINCE THE LAST TIME I SCANNED HIM...
LOLA DANIELS.
THAT'S WHAT THIS IS FOR. S'CUSE ME, PHIL.
AGH
HOW ABOUT NOW?
LOLA. DON'T--
WELL?
BEFORE YOU ANSWER, TRY TO REMEMBER I HAVE AN AGENT WITH A GUN TO YOUR BABY SISTER'S HEAD RIGHT THIS VERY MINUTE.
I'M SO SORRY, PHIL...
...I HAVE THEM.
THE COULSON PROTOCOLS.
IF THAT'S WHAT YOU WANT TO CALL THEM...
NO, I'VE GOT A FEELING THAT'S WHAT THE WORLD WILL BE CALLING THEM.
NOW, LET'S GET YOU A PAD AND PEN, MS. DANIELS. YOU HAVE A LOT OF INFORMATION TO WRITE DOWN...

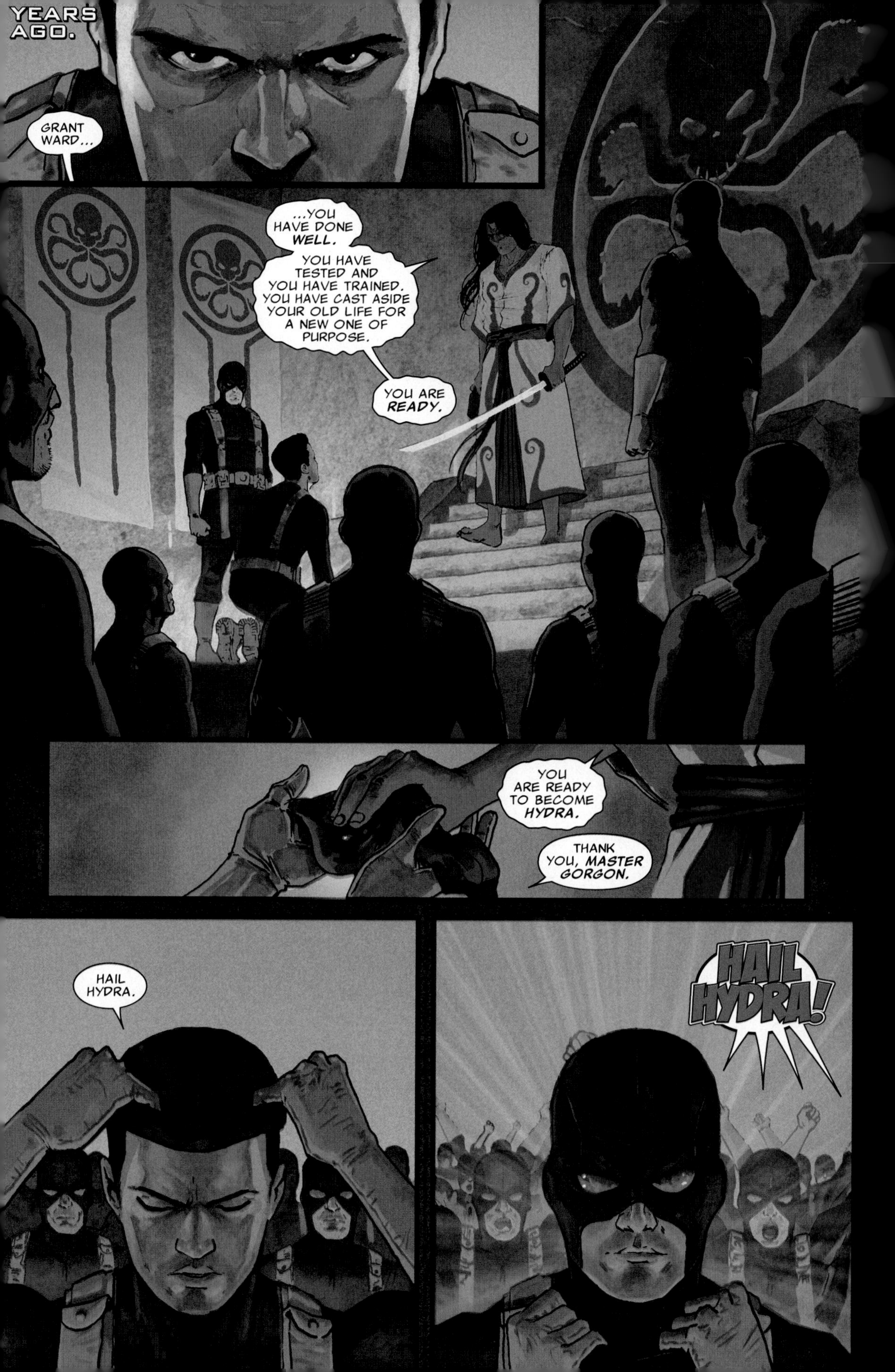
YEARS AGO.
GRANT WARD...
...YOU HAVE DONE WELL.
YOU HAVE TESTED AND YOU HAVE TRAINED. YOU HAVE CAST ASIDE YOUR OLD LIFE FOR A NEW ONE OF PURPOSE.
YOU ARE READY.
YOU ARE READY TO BECOME HYDRA.
THANK YOU, MASTER GORGON.
HAIL HYDRA.
HAIL HYDRA!

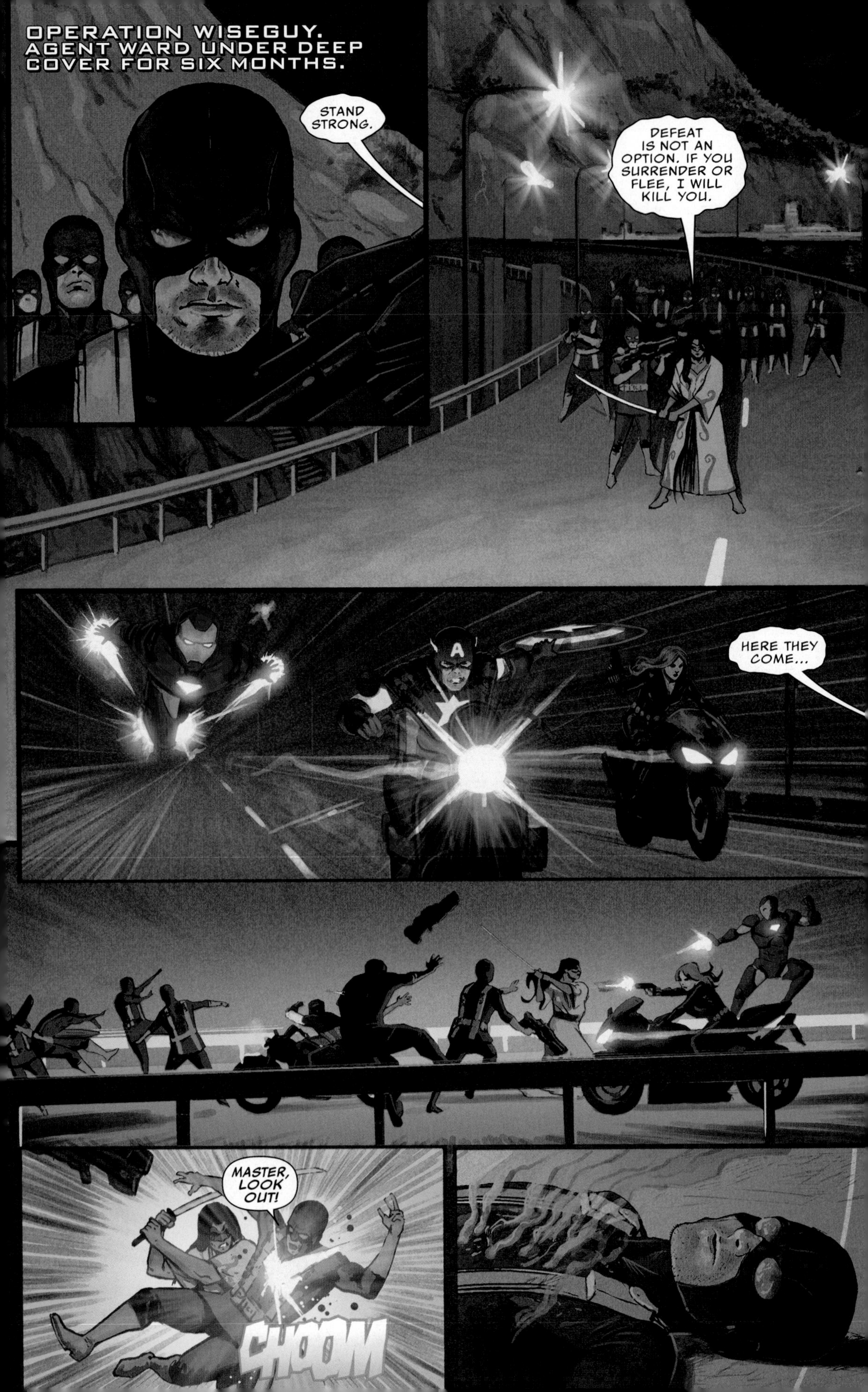
OPERATION WISEGUY. AGENT WARD UNDER DEEP COVER FOR SIX MONTHS.
STAND STRONG.
DEFEAT IS NOT AN OPTION. IF YOU SURRENDER OR FLEE, I WILL KILL YOU.
HERE THEY COME...
MASTER, LOOK OUT!
CHOOM

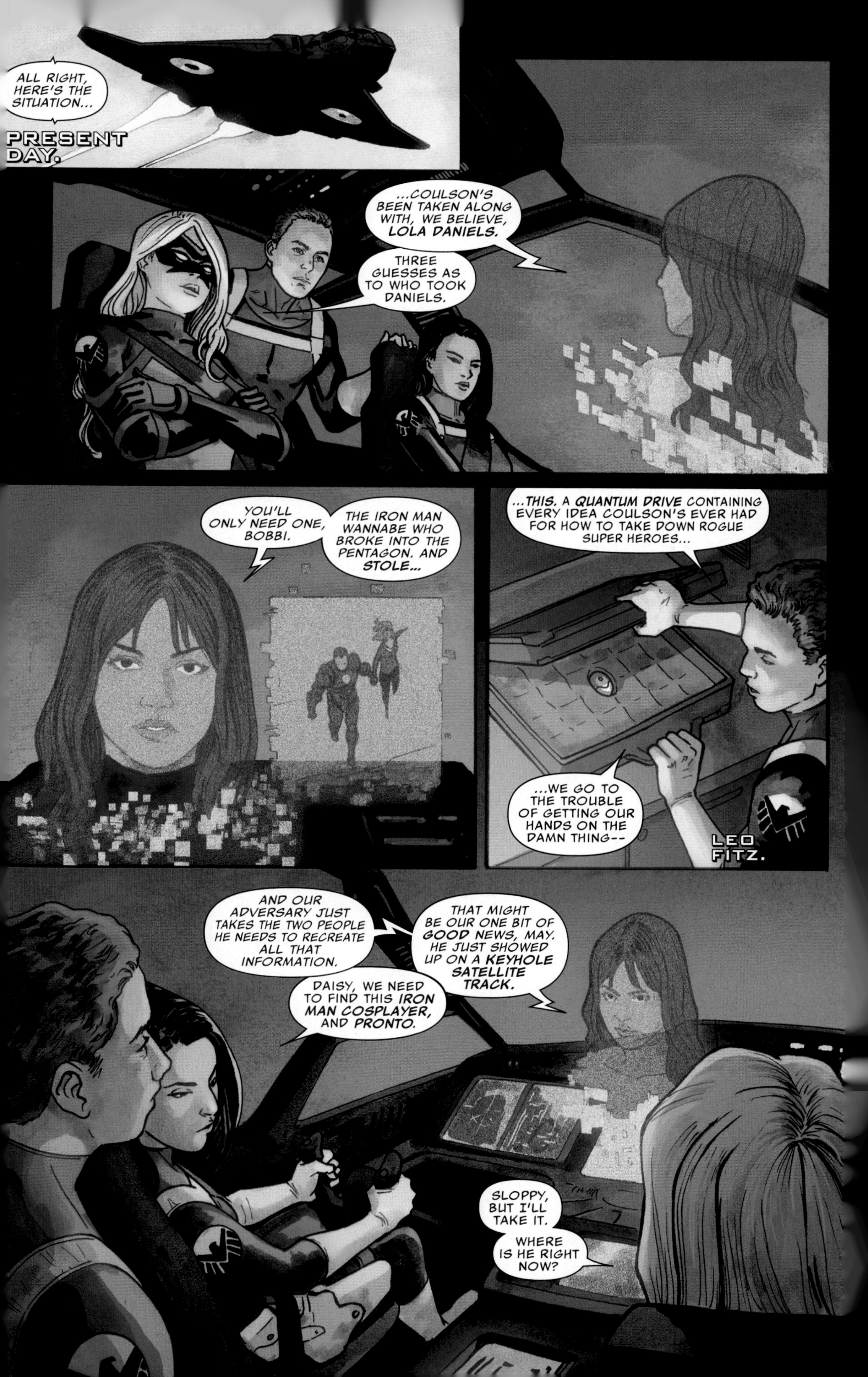
ALL RIGHT, HERE'S THE SITUATION...
PRESENT DAY.
...COULSON'S BEEN TAKEN ALONG WITH, WE BELIEVE, LOLA DANIELS.
THREE GUESSES AS TO WHO TOOK DANIELS.
YOU'LL ONLY NEED ONE, BOBBI.
THE IRON MAN WANNABE WHO BROKE INTO THE PENTAGON. AND STOLE...
...THIS. A QUANTUM DRIVE CONTAINING EVERY IDEA COULSON'S EVER HAD FOR HOW TO TAKE DOWN ROGUE SUPER HEROES...
...WE GO TO THE TROUBLE OF GETTING OUR HANDS ON THE DAMN THING--
LEO FITZ.
AND OUR ADVERSARY JUST TAKES THE TWO PEOPLE HE NEEDS TO RECREATE ALL THAT INFORMATION.
THAT MIGHT BE OUR ONE BIT OF GOOD NEWS, MAY. HE JUST SHOWED UP ON A KEYHOLE SATELLITE TRACK.
DAISY, WE NEED TO FIND THIS IRON MAN COSPLAYER, AND PRONTO.
SLOPPY, BUT I'LL TAKE IT.
WHERE IS HE RIGHT NOW?

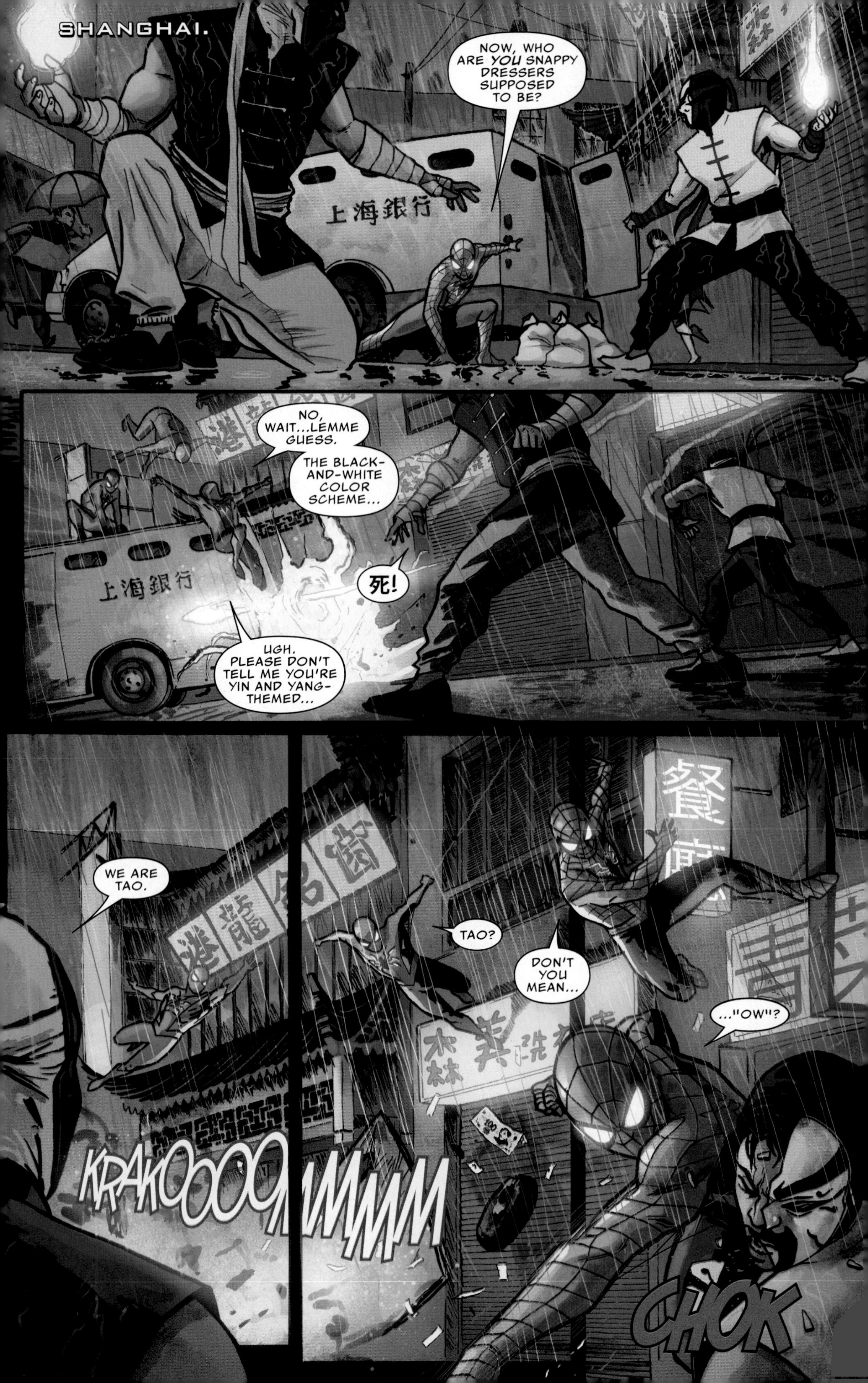
SHANGHAI.
NOW, WHO ARE YOU SNAPPY DRESSERS SUPPOSED TO BE?
上海銀行
NO, WAIT...LEMME GUESS.
THE BLACK-AND-WHITE COLOR SCHEME...
死!
UGH. PLEASE DON'T TELL ME YOU'RE YIN AND YANG-THEMED...
WE ARE TAO.
TAO?
DON'T YOU MEAN...
..."OW"?
KRAKOOOOMMMMM
CHOK

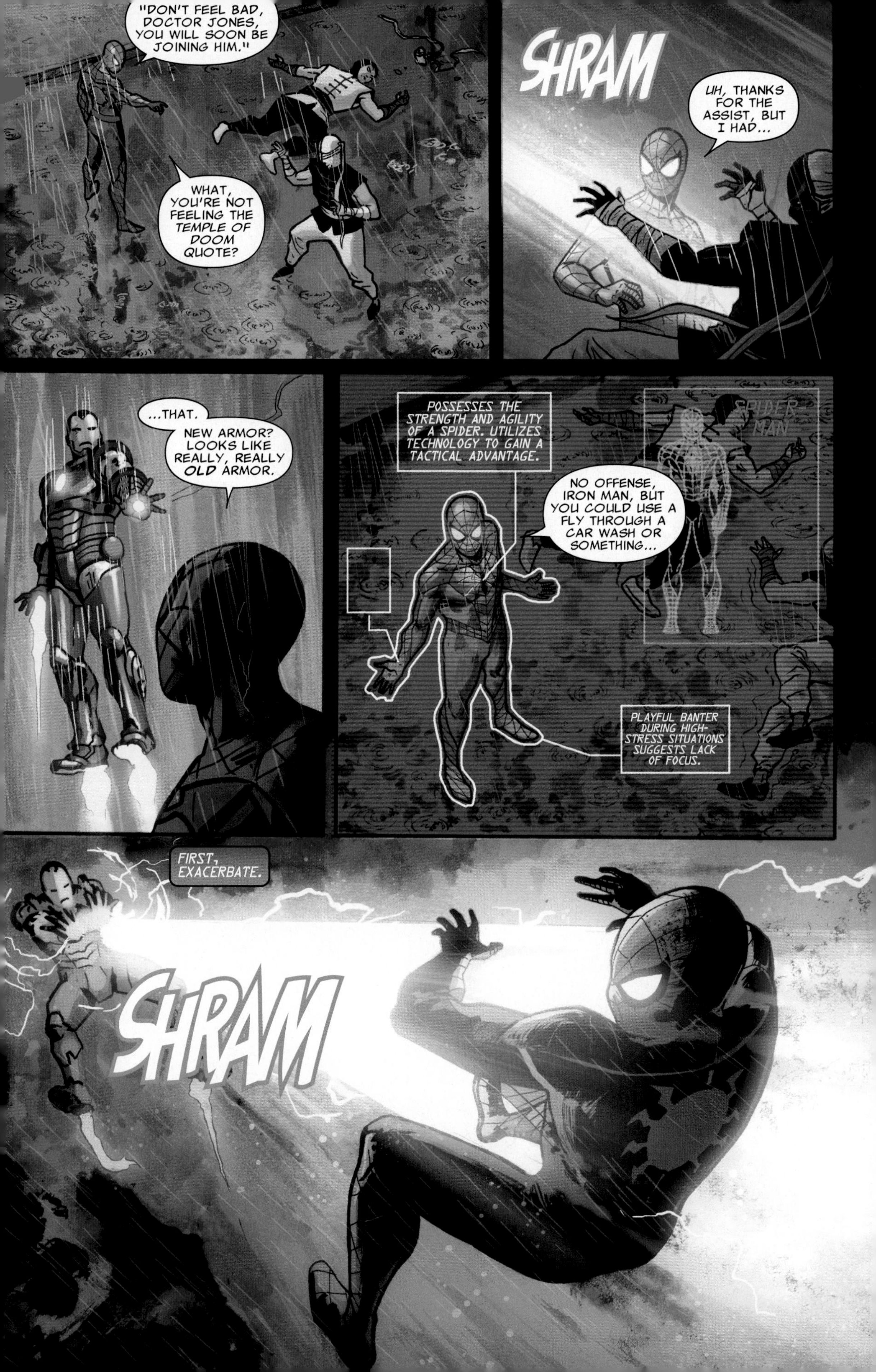
"DON'T FEEL BAD, DOCTOR JONES, YOU WILL SOON BE JOINING HIM."
WHAT, YOU'RE NOT FEELING THE TEMPLE OF DOOM QUOTE?
SHRAM
UH, THANKS FOR THE ASSIST, BUT I HAD...
...THAT.
NEW ARMOR? LOOKS LIKE REALLY, REALLY OLD ARMOR.
POSSESSES THE STRENGTH AND AGILITY OF A SPIDER. UTILIZES TECHNOLOGY TO GAIN A TACTICAL ADVANTAGE.
SPIDER-MAN
NO OFFENSE, IRON MAN, BUT YOU COULD USE A FLY THROUGH A CAR WASH OR SOMETHING...
PLAYFUL BANTER DURING HIGH-STRESS SITUATIONS SUGGESTS LACK OF FOCUS.
FIRST, EXACERBATE.
SHRAM

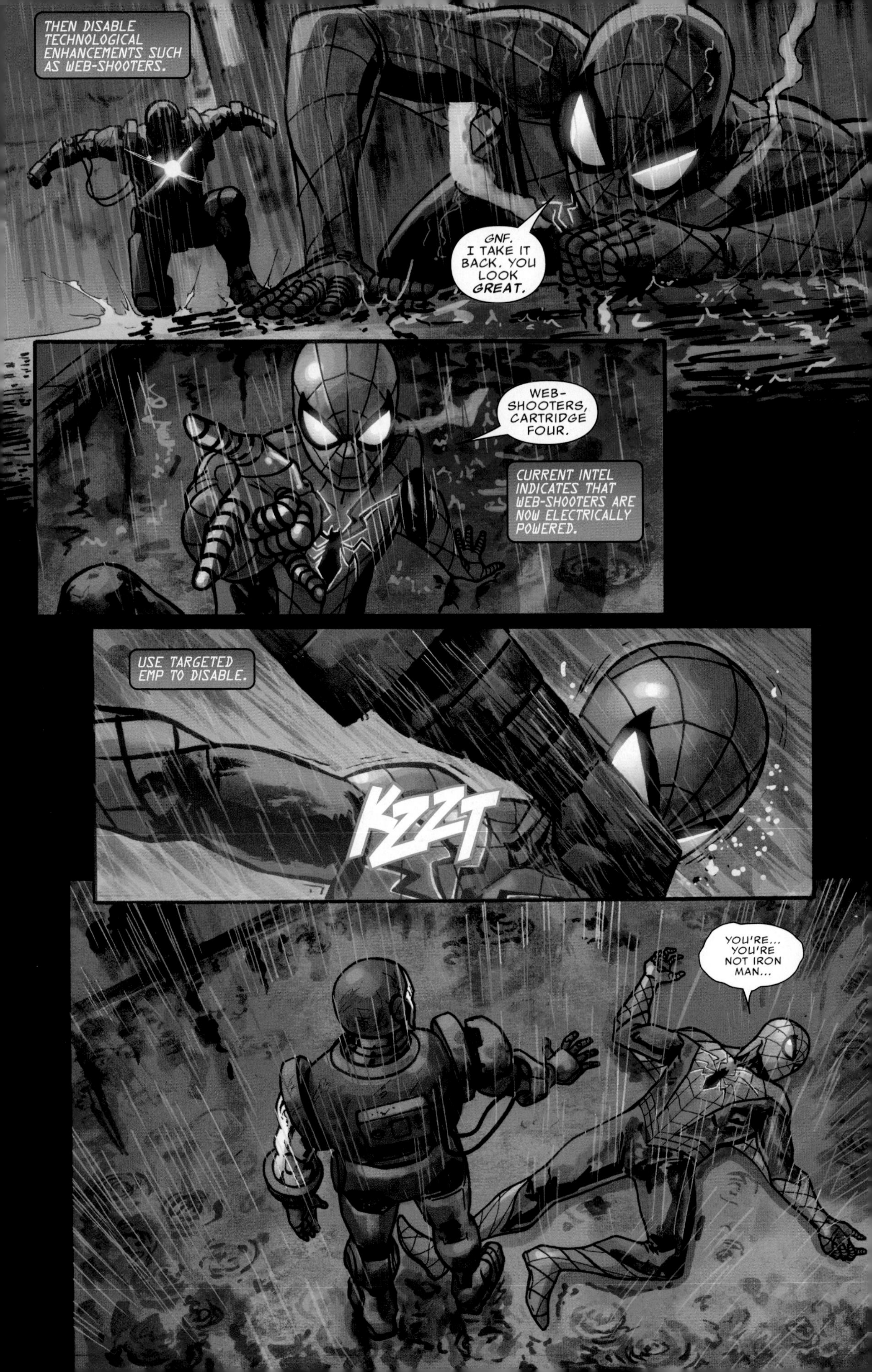
THEN DISABLE TECHNOLOGICAL ENHANCEMENTS SUCH AS WEB-SHOOTERS.
GNF. I TAKE IT BACK. YOU LOOK GREAT.
WEB-SHOOTERS, CARTRIDGE FOUR.
CURRENT INTEL INDICATES THAT WEB-SHOOTERS ARE NOW ELECTRICALLY POWERED.
USE TARGETED EMP TO DISABLE.
KZZT
YOU'RE... YOU'RE NOT IRON MAN...

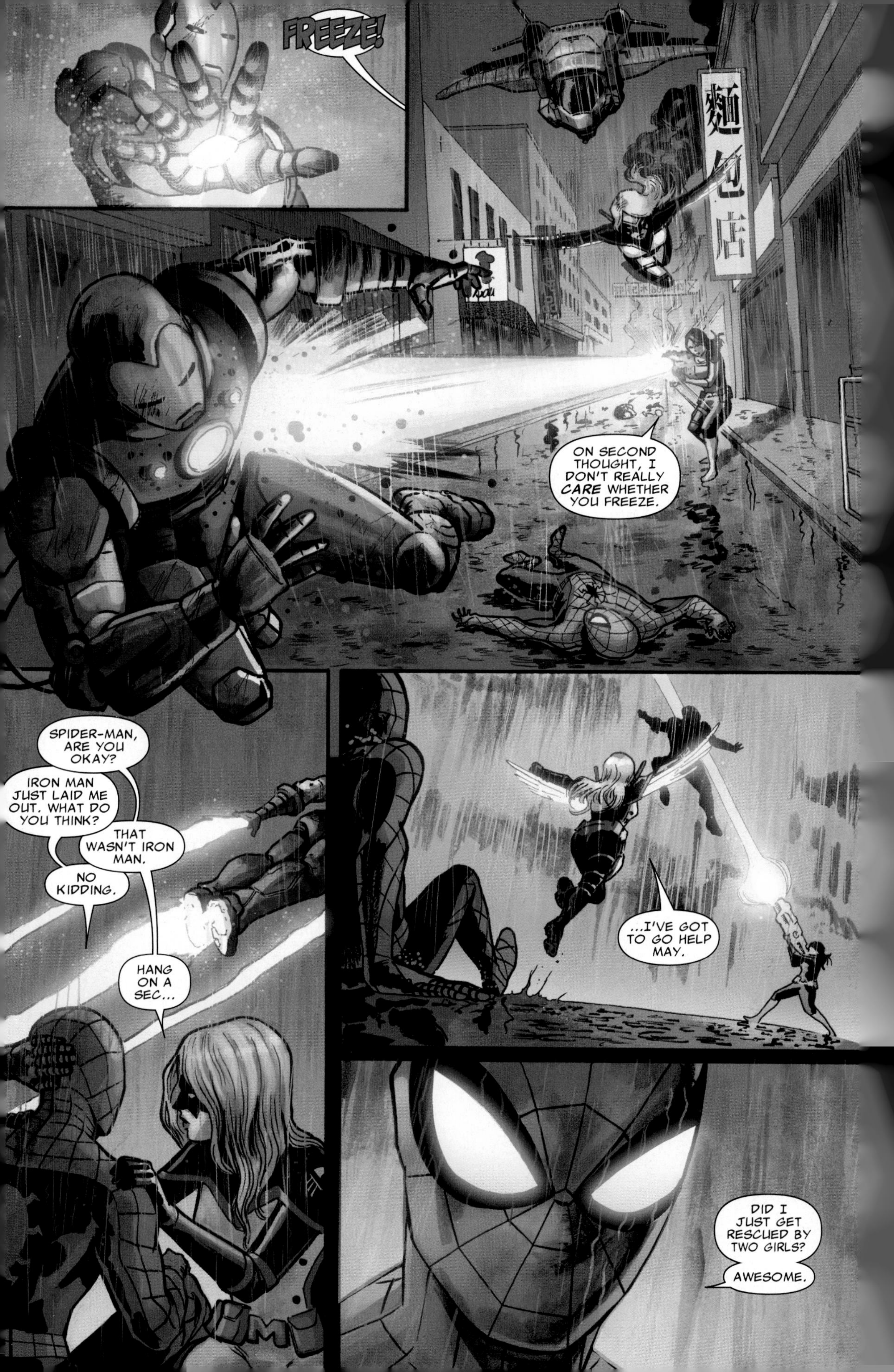
FREEZE!
麵包店
ON SECOND THOUGHT, I DON'T REALLY CARE WHETHER YOU FREEZE.
SPIDER-MAN, ARE YOU OKAY?
IRON MAN JUST LAID ME OUT. WHAT DO YOU THINK?
THAT WASN'T IRON MAN.
NO KIDDING.
HANG ON A SEC...
...I'VE GOT TO GO HELP MAY.
DID I JUST GET RESCUED BY TWO GIRLS?
AWESOME.

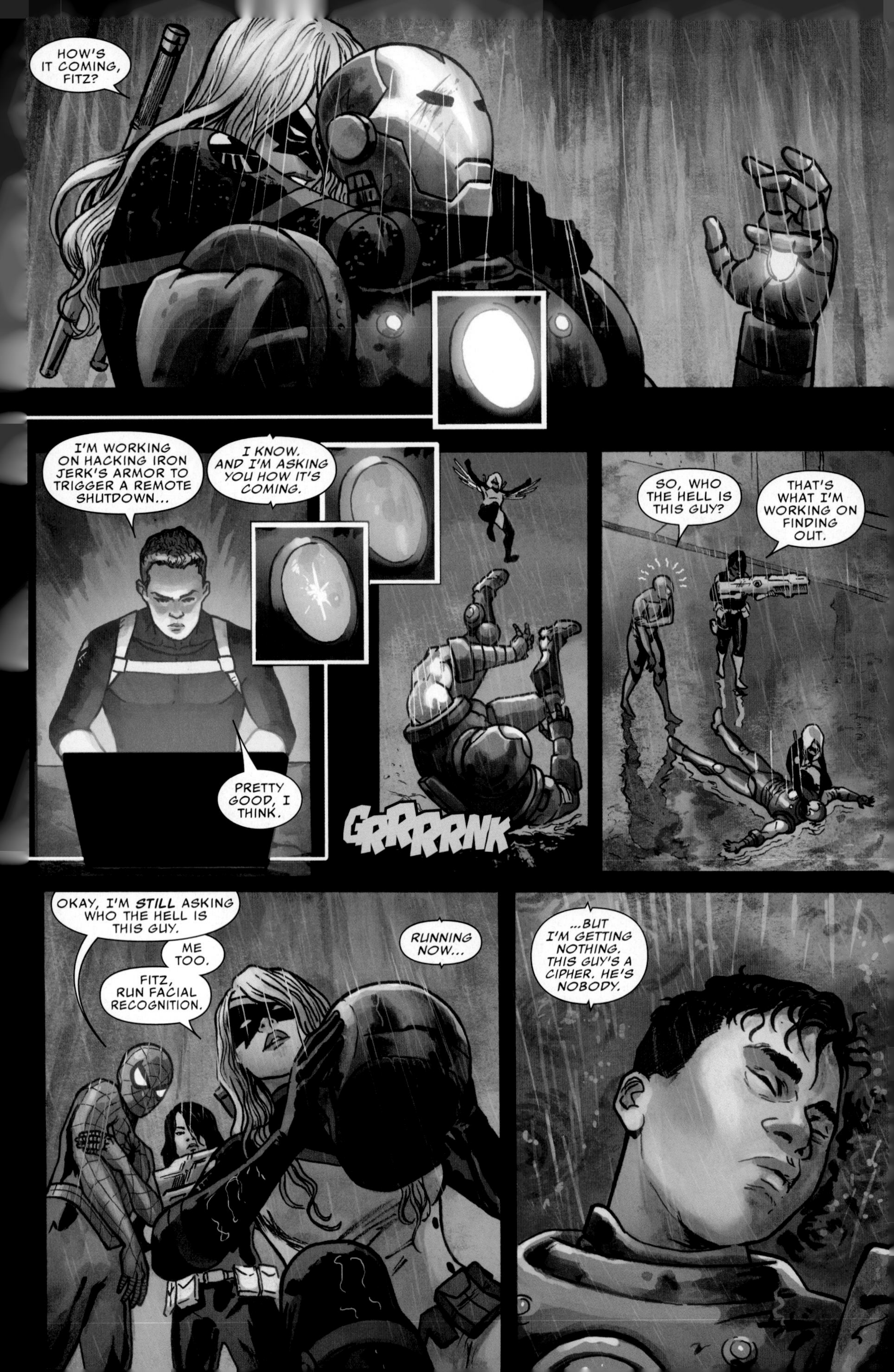
HOW'S IT COMING, FITZ?
I'M WORKING ON HACKING IRON JERK'S ARMOR TO TRIGGER A REMOTE SHUTDOWN...
I KNOW. AND I'M ASKING YOU HOW IT'S COMING.
PRETTY GOOD, I THINK.
GRRRRRNK
SO, WHO THE HELL IS THIS GUY?
THAT'S WHAT I'M WORKING ON FINDING OUT.
OKAY, I'M STILL ASKING WHO THE HELL IS THIS GUY.
ME TOO.
FITZ, RUN FACIAL RECOGNITION.
RUNNING NOW...
...BUT I'M GETTING NOTHING. THIS GUY'S A CIPHER. HE'S NOBODY.

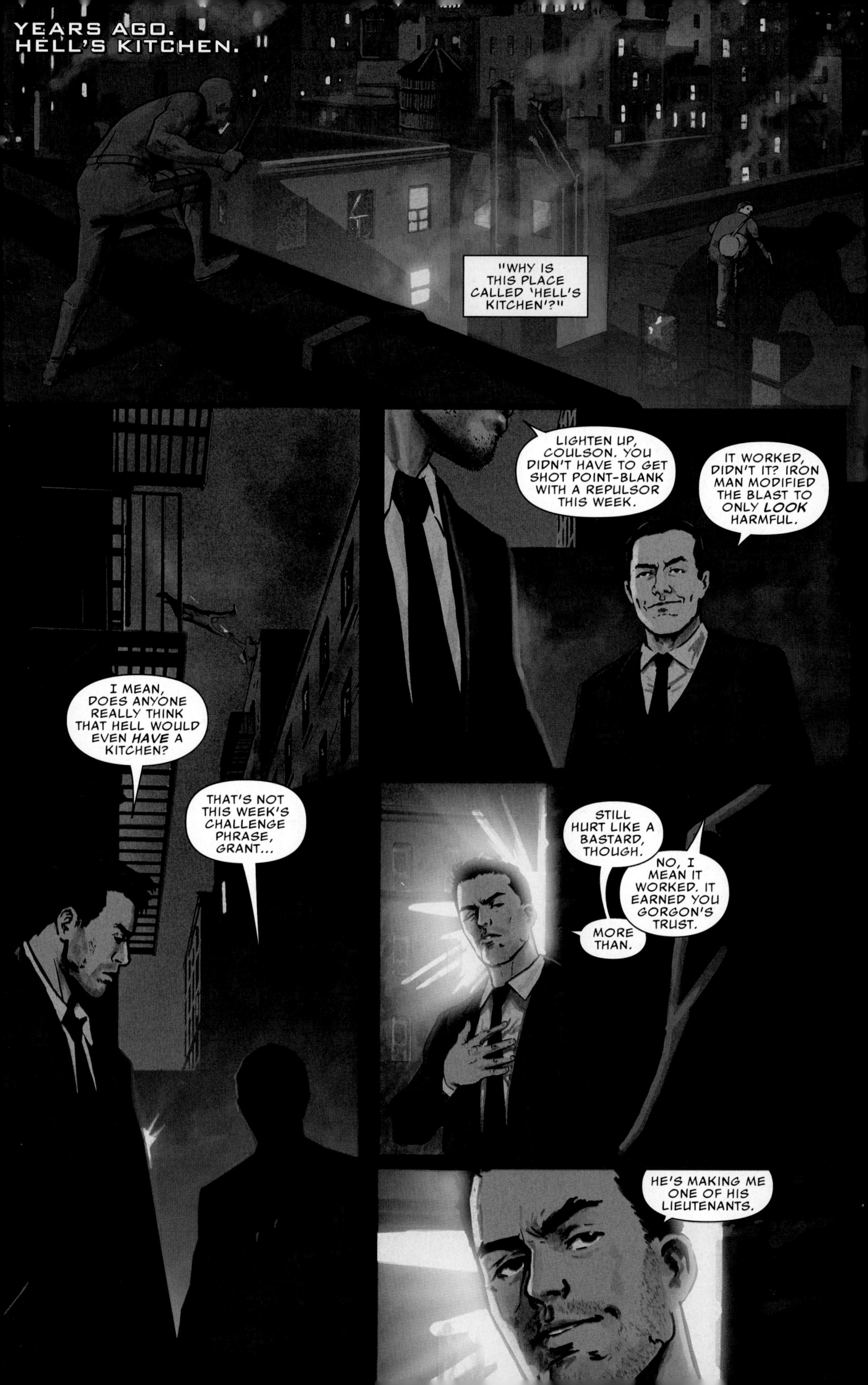
YEARS AGO.
HELL'S KITCHEN.
"WHY IS THIS PLACE CALLED 'HELL'S KITCHEN'?"
LIGHTEN UP, COULSON. YOU DIDN'T HAVE TO GET SHOT POINT-BLANK WITH A REPULSOR THIS WEEK.
IT WORKED, DIDN'T IT? IRON MAN MODIFIED THE BLAST TO ONLY LOOK HARMFUL.
I MEAN, DOES ANYONE REALLY THINK THAT HELL WOULD EVEN HAVE A KITCHEN?
THAT'S NOT THIS WEEK'S CHALLENGE PHRASE, GRANT...
STILL HURT LIKE A BASTARD, THOUGH.
NO, I MEAN IT WORKED. IT EARNED YOU GORGON'S TRUST.
MORE THAN.
HE'S MAKING ME ONE OF HIS LIEUTENANTS.

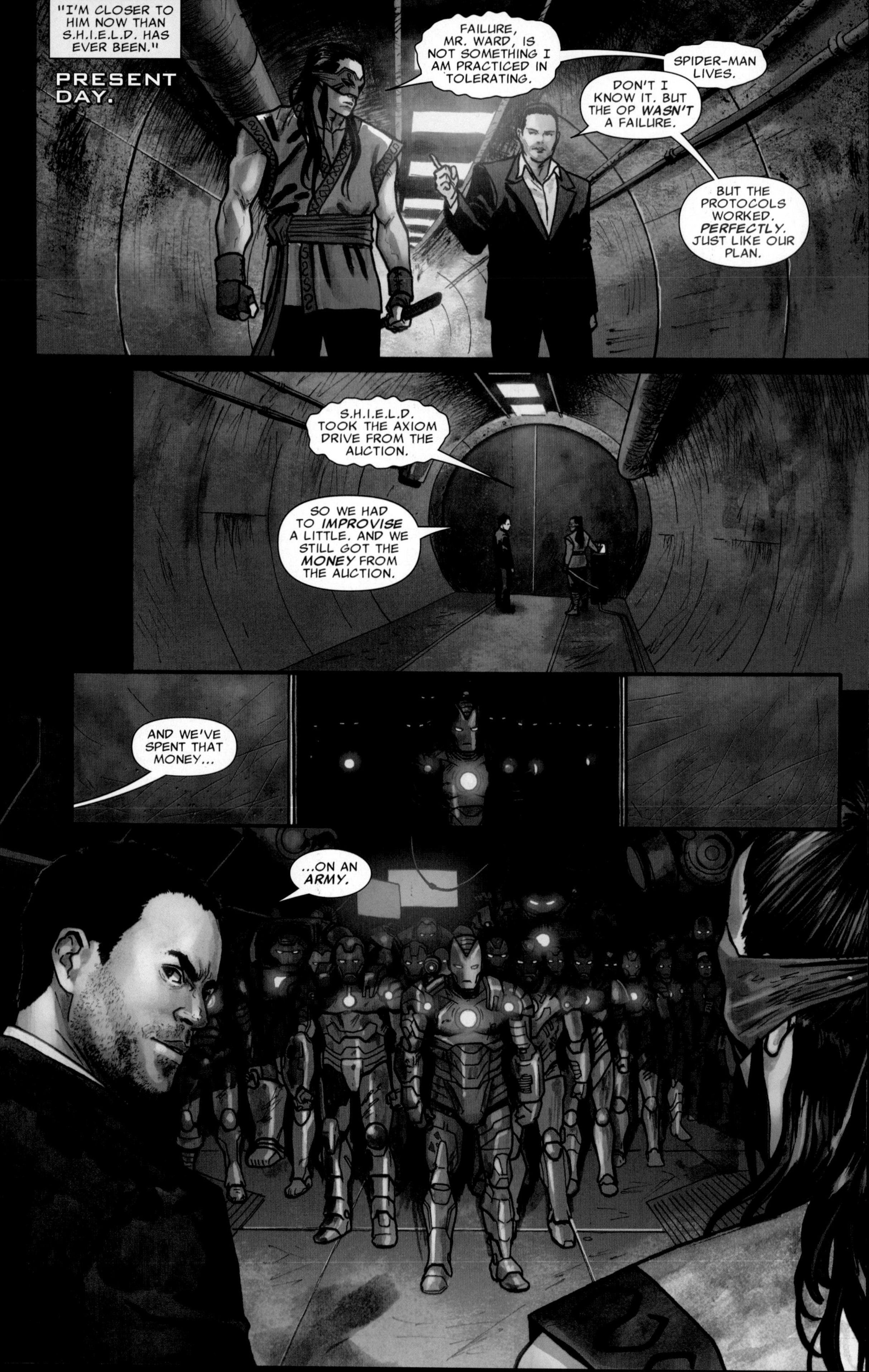
"I'M CLOSER TO HIM NOW THAN S.H.I.E.L.D. HAS EVER BEEN."
PRESENT DAY.
FAILURE, MR. WARD, IS NOT SOMETHING I AM PRACTICED IN TOLERATING.
SPIDER-MAN LIVES.
DON'T I KNOW IT. BUT THE OP WASN'T A FAILURE.
BUT THE PROTOCOLS WORKED. PERFECTLY. JUST LIKE OUR PLAN.
S.H.I.E.L.D. TOOK THE AXIOM DRIVE FROM THE AUCTION.
SO WE HAD TO IMPROVISE A LITTLE. AND WE STILL GOT THE MONEY FROM THE AUCTION.
AND WE'VE SPENT THAT MONEY...
...ON AN ARMY.

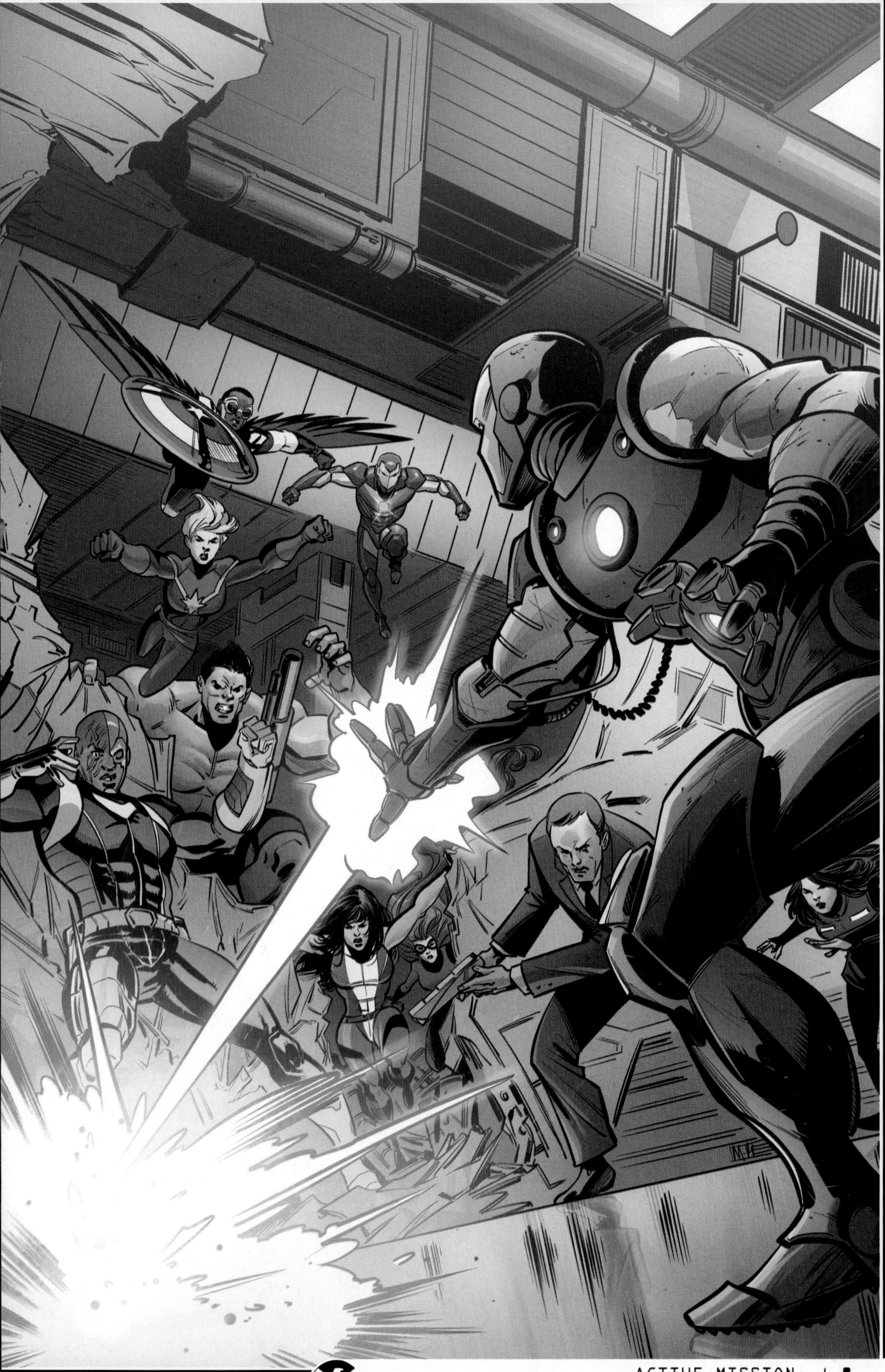

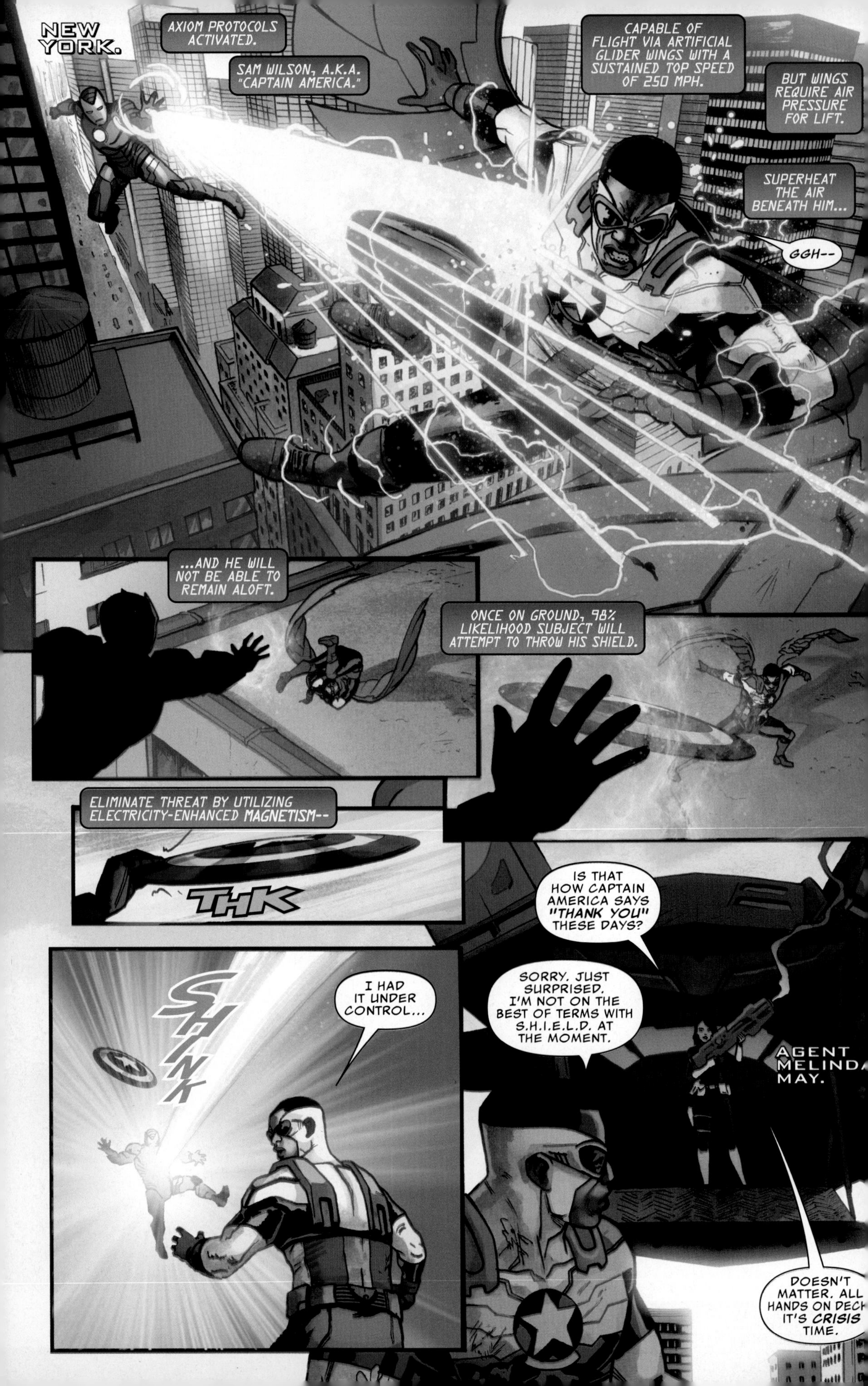
NEW YORK.
AXIOM PROTOCOLS ACTIVATED.
SAM WILSON, A.K.A. "CAPTAIN AMERICA."
CAPABLE OF FLIGHT VIA ARTIFICIAL GLIDER WINGS WITH A SUSTAINED TOP SPEED OF 250 MPH.
BUT WINGS REQUIRE AIR PRESSURE FOR LIFT.
SUPERHEAT THE AIR BENEATH HIM...
GGH--
...AND HE WILL NOT BE ABLE TO REMAIN ALOFT.
ONCE ON GROUND, 98% LIKELIHOOD SUBJECT WILL ATTEMPT TO THROW HIS SHIELD.
ELIMINATE THREAT BY UTILIZING ELECTRICITY-ENHANCED MAGNETISM--
THK
SHINK
I HAD IT UNDER CONTROL...
IS THAT HOW CAPTAIN AMERICA SAYS "THANK YOU" THESE DAYS?
SORRY. JUST SURPRISED. I'M NOT ON THE BEST OF TERMS WITH S.H.I.E.L.D. AT THE MOMENT.
AGENT MELINDA MAY.
DOESN'T MATTER. ALL HANDS ON DECK. IT'S CRISIS TIME.

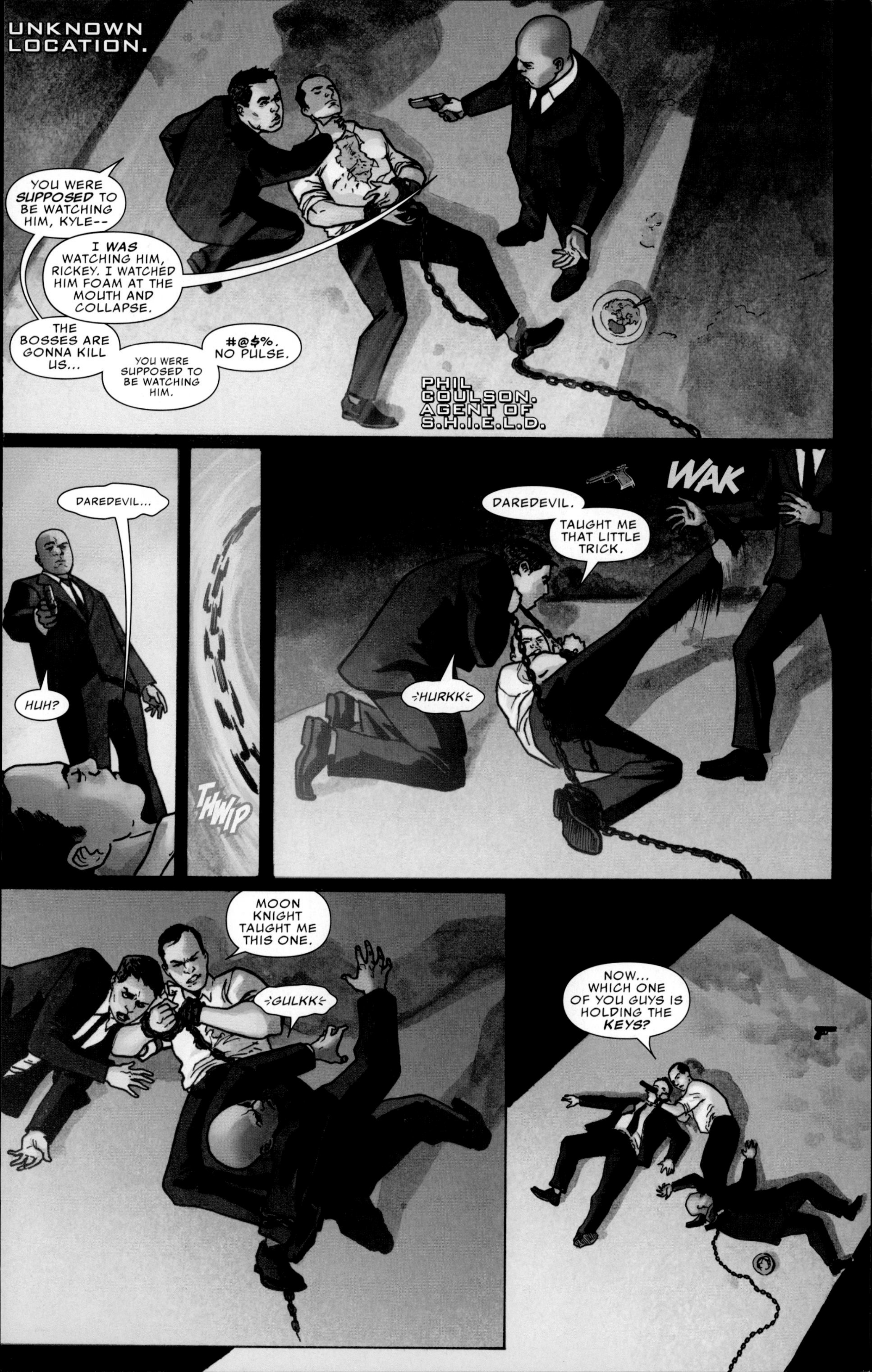
UNKNOWN LOCATION.
YOU WERE SUPPOSED TO BE WATCHING HIM, KYLE--
I WAS WATCHING HIM, RICKEY. I WATCHED HIM FOAM AT THE MOUTH AND COLLAPSE.
THE BOSSES ARE GONNA KILL US...
YOU WERE SUPPOSED TO BE WATCHING HIM.
#@$%. NO PULSE.
PHIL COULSON. AGENT OF S.H.I.E.L.D.
DAREDEVIL...
HUH?
THWIP
WAK
DAREDEVIL.
TAUGHT ME THAT LITTLE TRICK.
HURKK
MOON KNIGHT TAUGHT ME THIS ONE.
GULKK
NOW... WHICH ONE OF YOU GUYS IS HOLDING THE KEYS?

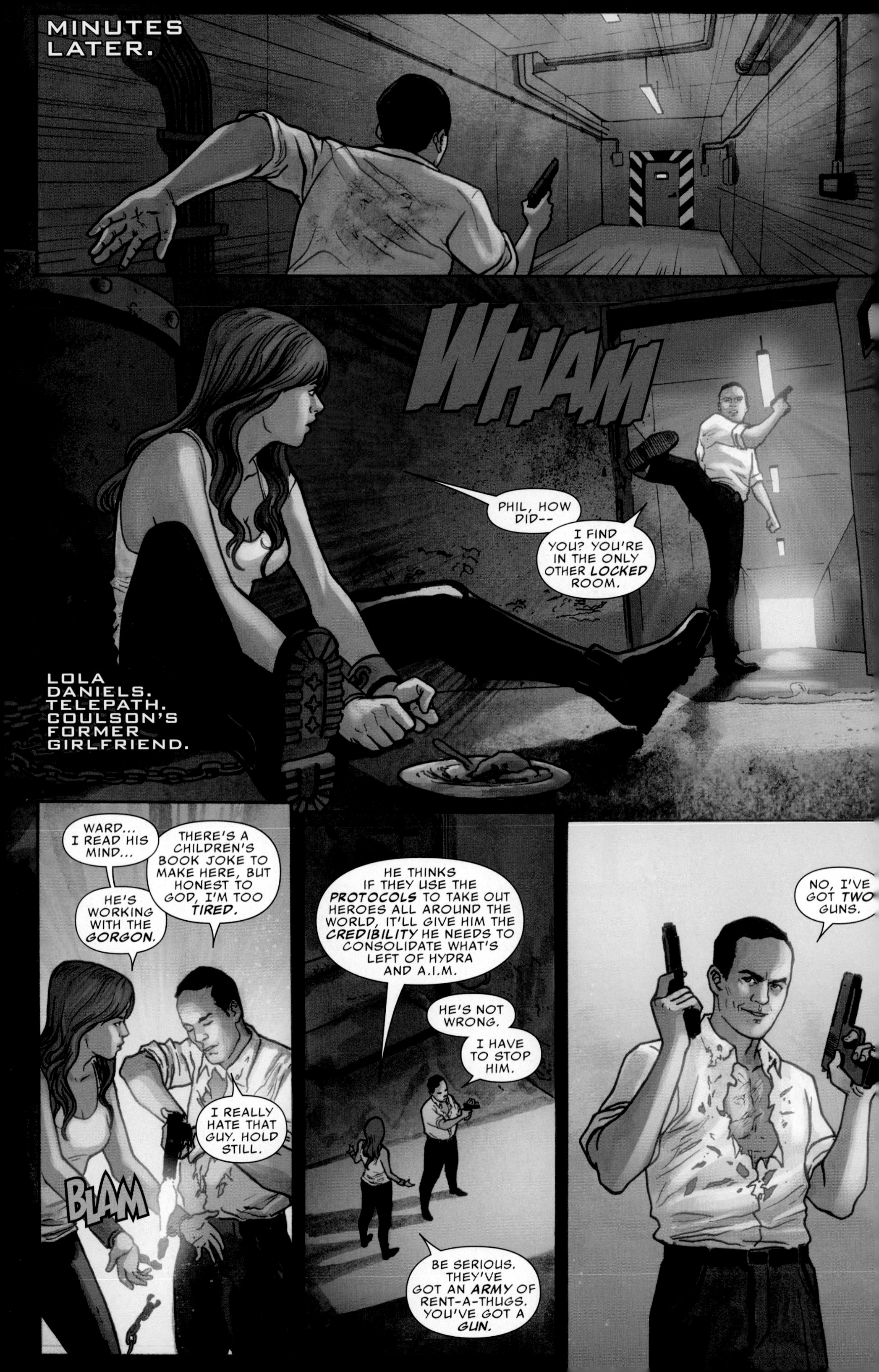
MINUTES LATER.
WHAM
PHIL, HOW DID--
I FIND YOU? YOU'RE IN THE ONLY OTHER LOCKED ROOM.
LOLA DANIELS. TELEPATH. COULSON'S FORMER GIRLFRIEND.
WARD... I READ HIS MIND...
HE'S WORKING WITH THE GORGON.
THERE'S A CHILDREN'S BOOK JOKE TO MAKE HERE, BUT HONEST TO GOD, I'M TOO TIRED.
I REALLY HATE THAT GUY. HOLD STILL.
BLAM
HE THINKS IF THEY USE THE PROTOCOLS TO TAKE OUT HEROES ALL AROUND THE WORLD, IT'LL GIVE HIM THE CREDIBILITY HE NEEDS TO CONSOLIDATE WHAT'S LEFT OF HYDRA AND A.I.M.
HE'S NOT WRONG.
I HAVE TO STOP HIM.
BE SERIOUS. THEY'VE GOT AN ARMY OF RENT-A-THUGS. YOU'VE GOT A GUN.
NO, I'VE GOT TWO GUNS.

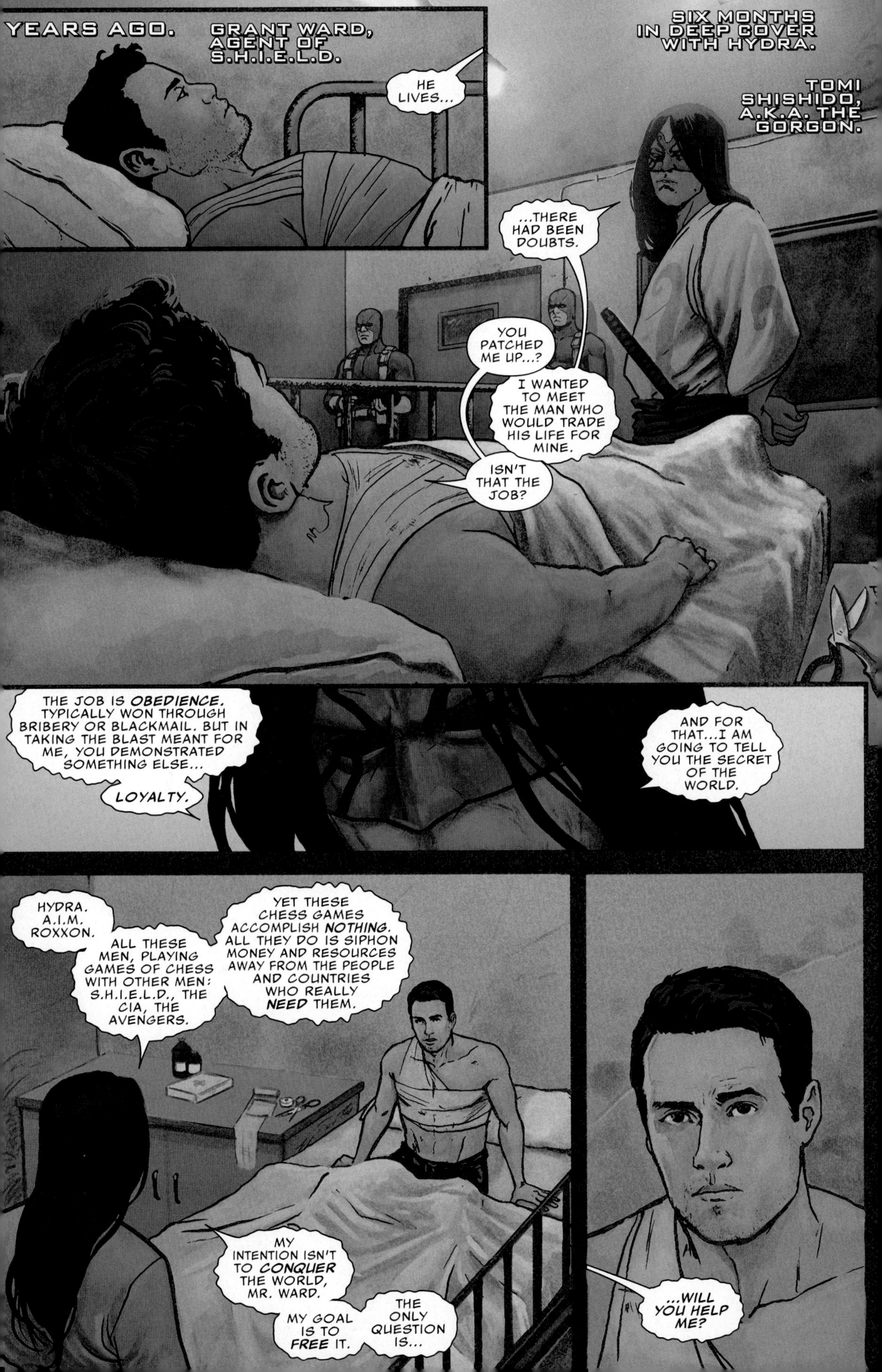
YEARS AGO.
GRANT WARD, AGENT OF S.H.I.E.L.D.
SIX MONTHS IN DEEP COVER WITH HYDRA.
HE LIVES...
TOMI SHISHIDO, A.K.A. THE GORGON.
...THERE HAD BEEN DOUBTS.
YOU PATCHED ME UP...?
I WANTED TO MEET THE MAN WHO WOULD TRADE HIS LIFE FOR MINE.
ISN'T THAT THE JOB?
THE JOB IS OBEDIENCE. TYPICALLY WON THROUGH BRIBERY OR BLACKMAIL. BUT IN TAKING THE BLAST MEANT FOR ME, YOU DEMONSTRATED SOMETHING ELSE...
LOYALTY.
AND FOR THAT...I AM GOING TO TELL YOU THE SECRET OF THE WORLD.
HYDRA. A.I.M. ROXXON.
ALL THESE MEN, PLAYING GAMES OF CHESS WITH OTHER MEN: S.H.I.E.L.D., THE CIA, THE AVENGERS.
YET THESE CHESS GAMES ACCOMPLISH NOTHING. ALL THEY DO IS SIPHON MONEY AND RESOURCES AWAY FROM THE PEOPLE AND COUNTRIES WHO REALLY NEED THEM.
MY INTENTION ISN'T TO CONQUER THE WORLD, MR. WARD.
MY GOAL IS TO FREE IT.
THE ONLY QUESTION IS...
...WILL YOU HELP ME?

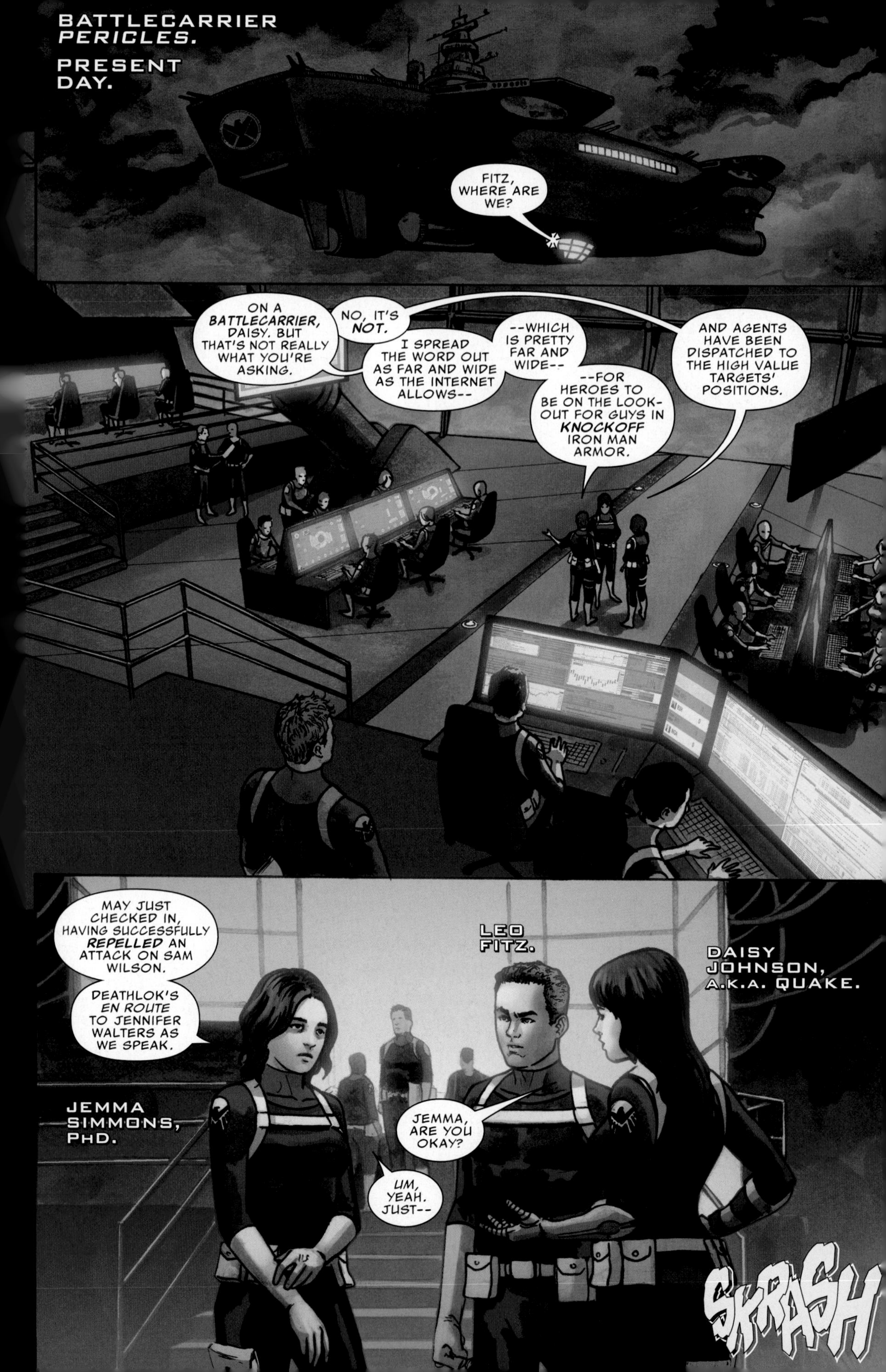
BATTLECARRIER *PERICLES*.
PRESENT DAY.
FITZ, WHERE ARE WE?
ON A *BATTLECARRIER*, DAISY. BUT THAT'S NOT REALLY WHAT YOU'RE ASKING.
NO, IT'S *NOT.*
I SPREAD THE WORD OUT AS FAR AND WIDE AS THE INTERNET ALLOWS--
--WHICH IS PRETTY FAR AND WIDE--
--FOR HEROES TO BE ON THE LOOK-OUT FOR GUYS IN *KNOCKOFF* IRON MAN ARMOR.
AND AGENTS HAVE BEEN DISPATCHED TO THE HIGH VALUE TARGETS' POSITIONS.
MAY JUST CHECKED IN, HAVING SUCCESSFULLY *REPELLED* AN ATTACK ON SAM WILSON.
DEATHLOK'S *EN ROUTE* TO JENNIFER WALTERS AS WE SPEAK.
LEO FITZ.
DAISY JOHNSON, A.K.A. QUAKE.
JEMMA SIMMONS, PHD.
JEMMA, ARE YOU OKAY?
UM, YEAH. JUST--
SKRASH

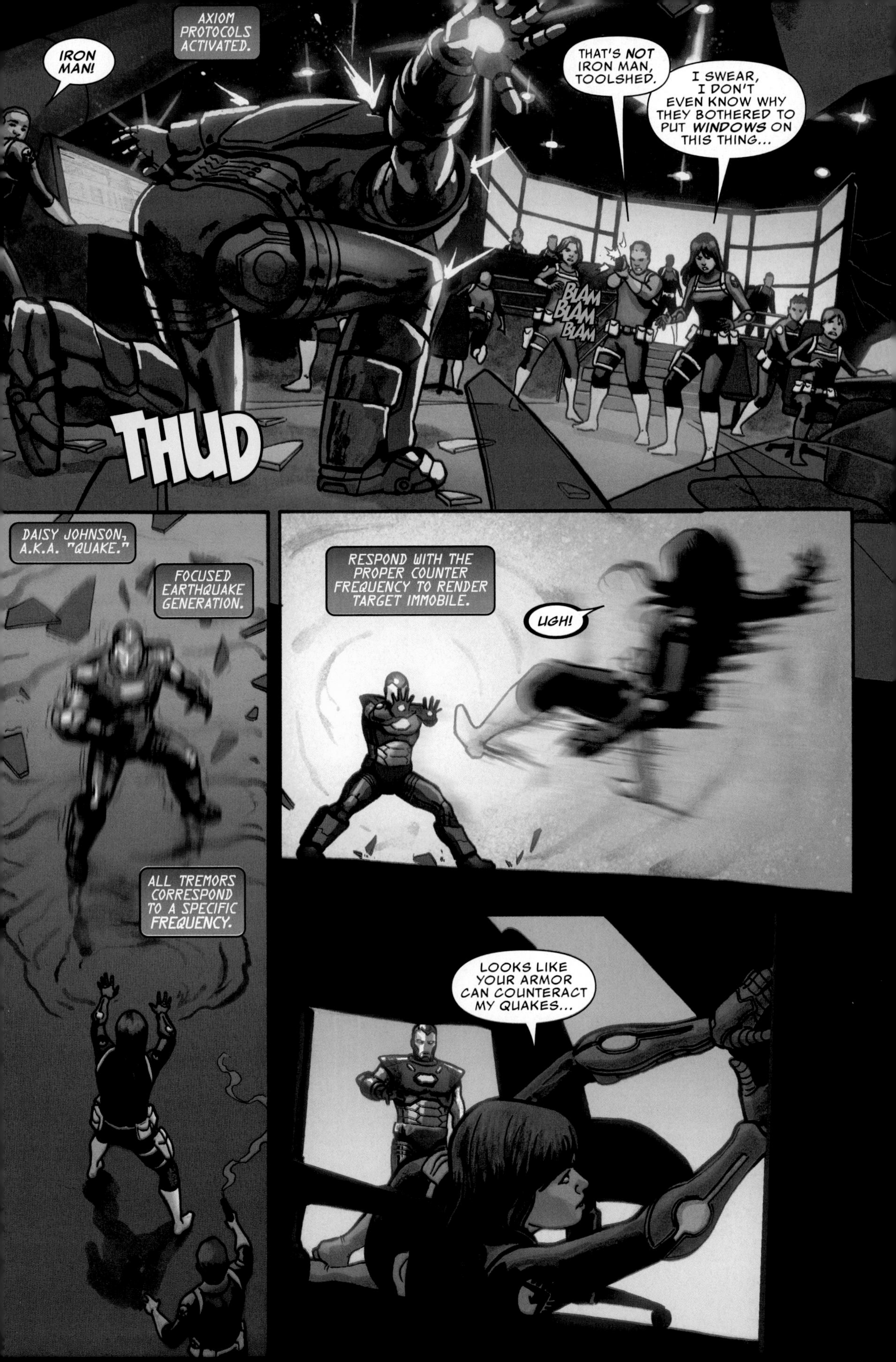
IRON MAN!
AXIOM PROTOCOLS ACTIVATED.
THAT'S NOT IRON MAN, TOOLSHED.
I SWEAR, I DON'T EVEN KNOW WHY THEY BOTHERED TO PUT WINDOWS ON THIS THING...
BLAM BLAM BLAM
THUD
DAISY JOHNSON, A.K.A. "QUAKE."
FOCUSED EARTHQUAKE GENERATION.
ALL TREMORS CORRESPOND TO A SPECIFIC FREQUENCY.
RESPOND WITH THE PROPER COUNTER FREQUENCY TO RENDER TARGET IMMOBILE.
UGH!
LOOKS LIKE YOUR ARMOR CAN COUNTERACT MY QUAKES...

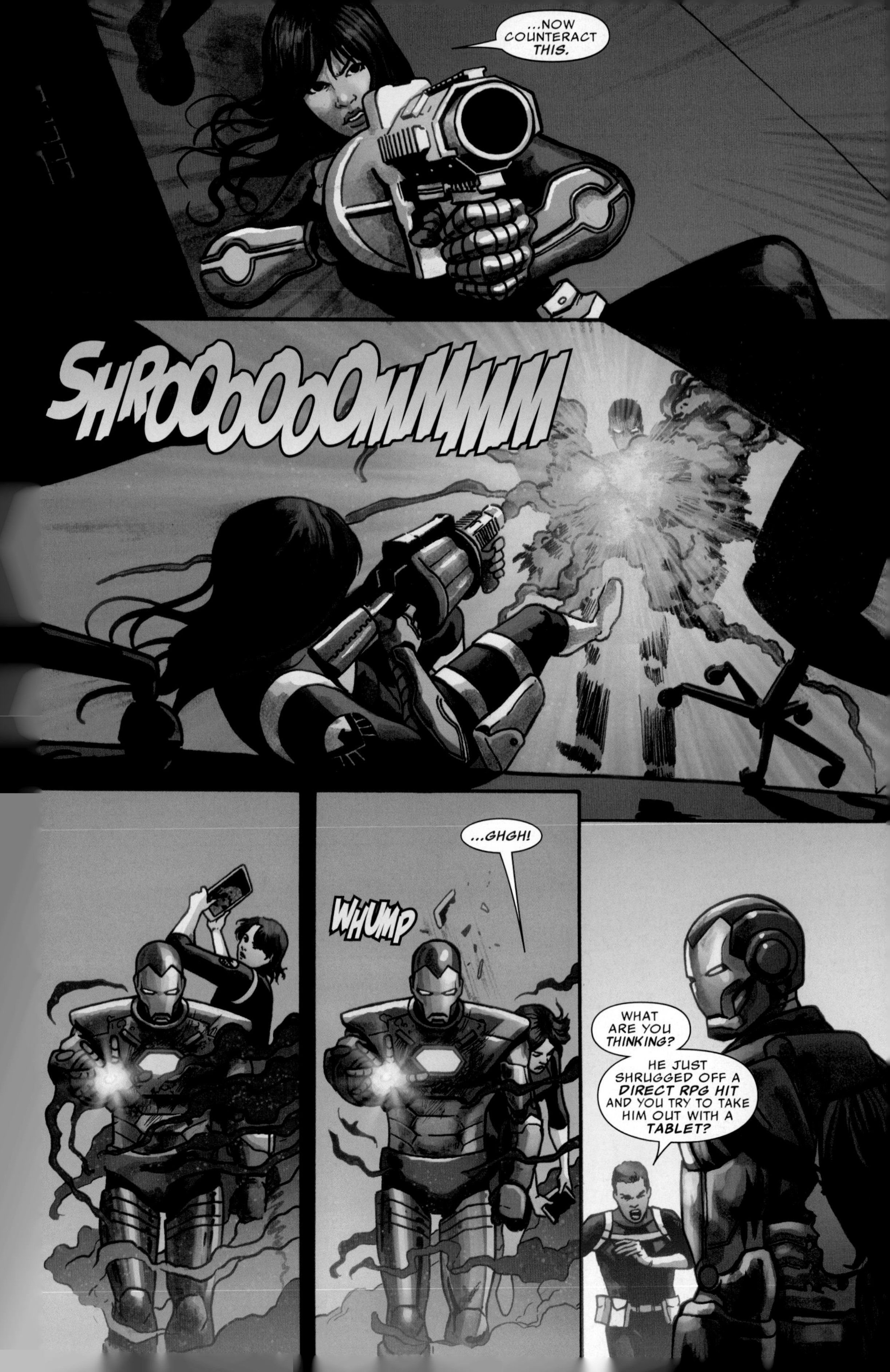
...NOW COUNTERACT THIS.
SHROOOOOOOMMMMM
...GHGH!
WHUMP
WHAT ARE YOU THINKING?
HE JUST SHRUGGED OFF A DIRECT RPG HIT AND YOU TRY TO TAKE HIM OUT WITH A TABLET?

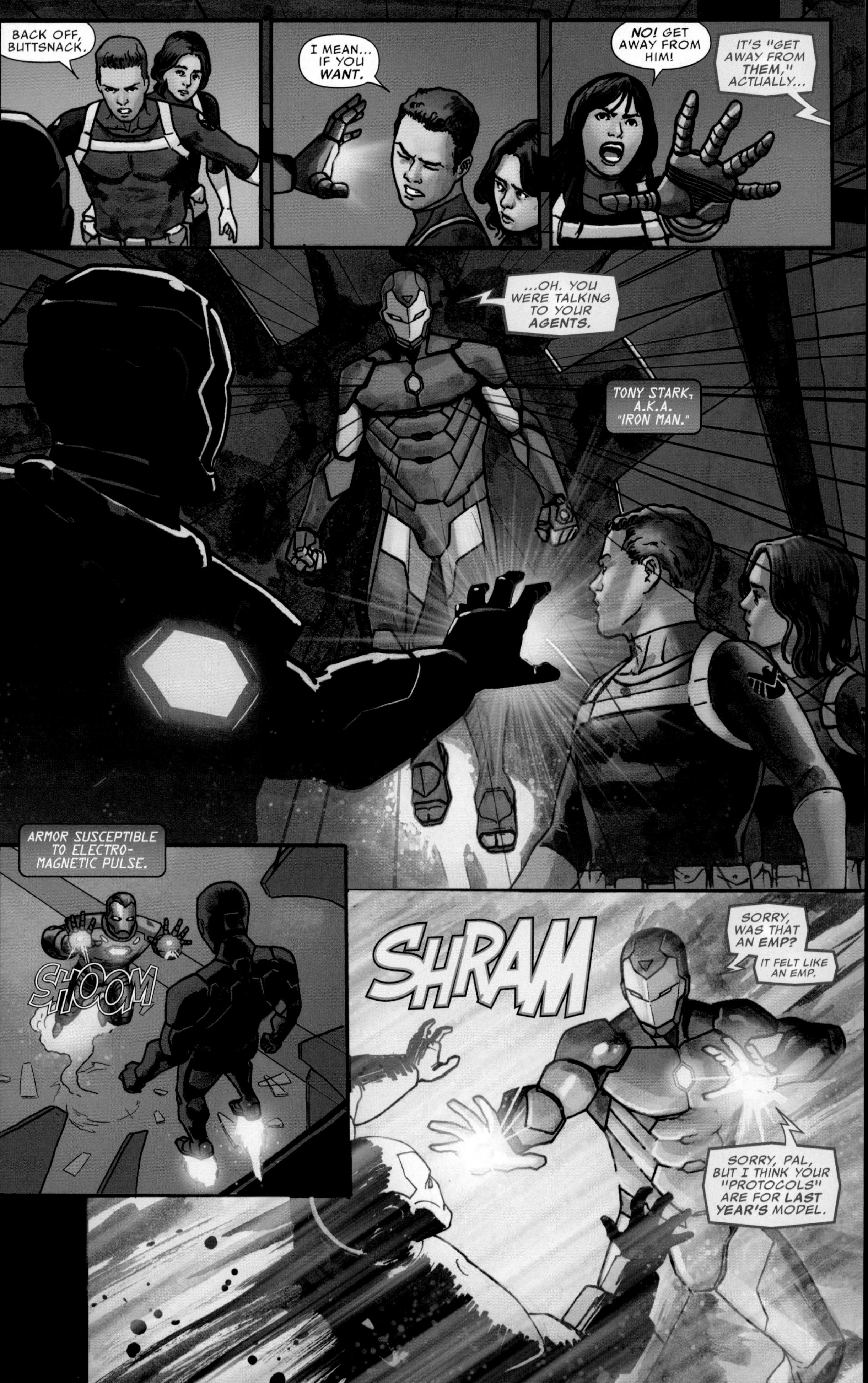

BACK OFF, BUTTSNACK.
I MEAN... IF YOU WANT.
NO! GET AWAY FROM HIM!
IT'S "GET AWAY FROM THEM," ACTUALLY...
...OH. YOU WERE TALKING TO YOUR AGENTS.
TONY STARK, A.K.A. "IRON MAN."
ARMOR SUSCEPTIBLE TO ELECTRO-MAGNETIC PULSE.
SHOOM
SHRAM
SORRY, WAS THAT AN EMP?
IT FELT LIKE AN EMP.
SORRY, PAL, BUT I THINK YOUR "PROTOCOLS" ARE FOR LAST YEAR'S MODEL.

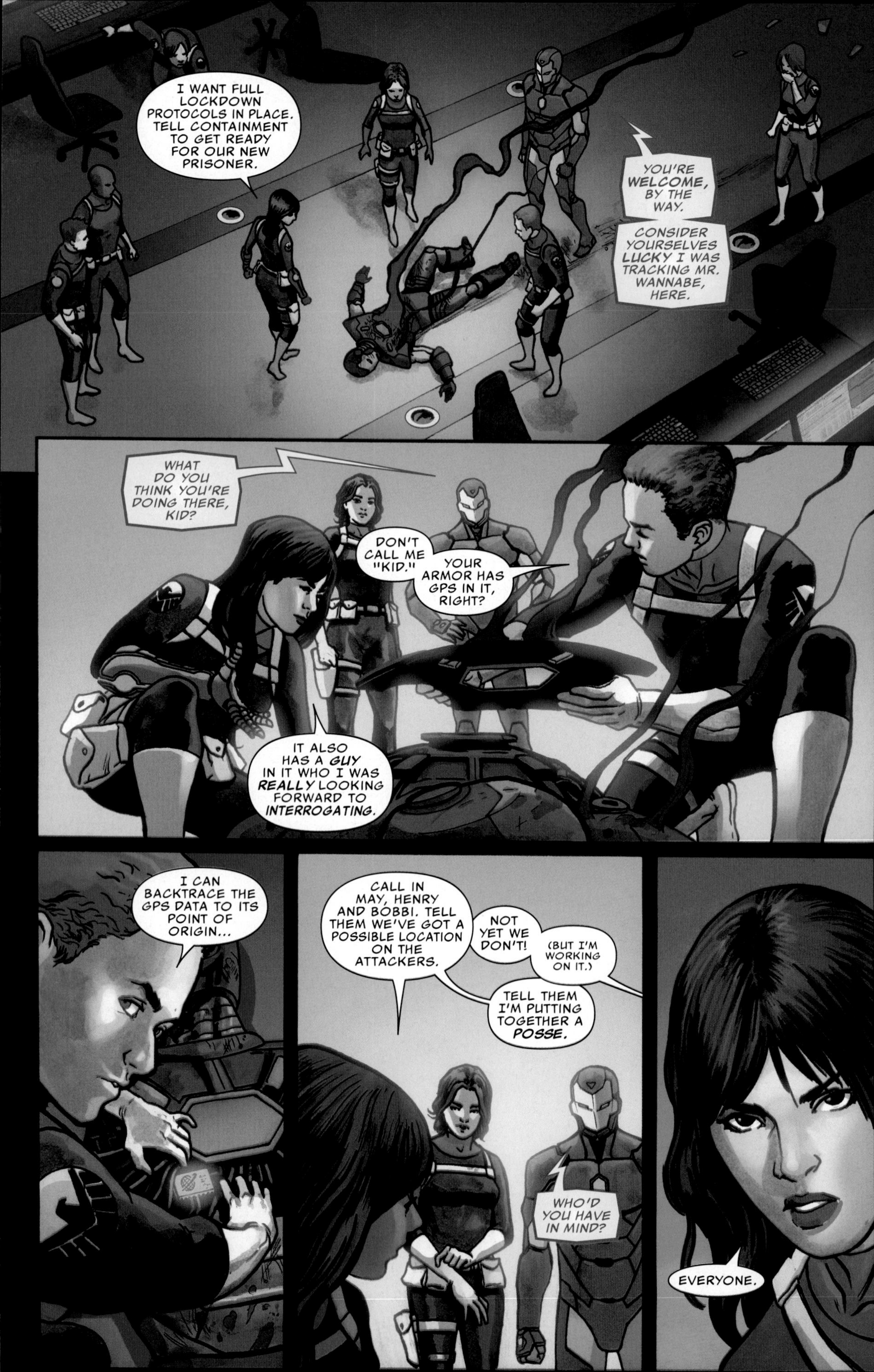
I WANT FULL LOCKDOWN PROTOCOLS IN PLACE. TELL CONTAINMENT TO GET READY FOR OUR NEW PRISONER.
YOU'RE WELCOME, BY THE WAY.
CONSIDER YOURSELVES LUCKY I WAS TRACKING MR. WANNABE, HERE.
WHAT DO YOU THINK YOU'RE DOING THERE, KID?
DON'T CALL ME "KID."
YOUR ARMOR HAS GPS IN IT, RIGHT?
IT ALSO HAS A GUY IN IT WHO I WAS REALLY LOOKING FORWARD TO INTERROGATING.
I CAN BACKTRACE THE GPS DATA TO ITS POINT OF ORIGIN...
CALL IN MAY, HENRY AND BOBBI. TELL THEM WE'VE GOT A POSSIBLE LOCATION ON THE ATTACKERS.
NOT YET WE DON'T!
(BUT I'M WORKING ON IT.)
TELL THEM I'M PUTTING TOGETHER A POSSE.
WHO'D YOU HAVE IN MIND?
EVERYONE.

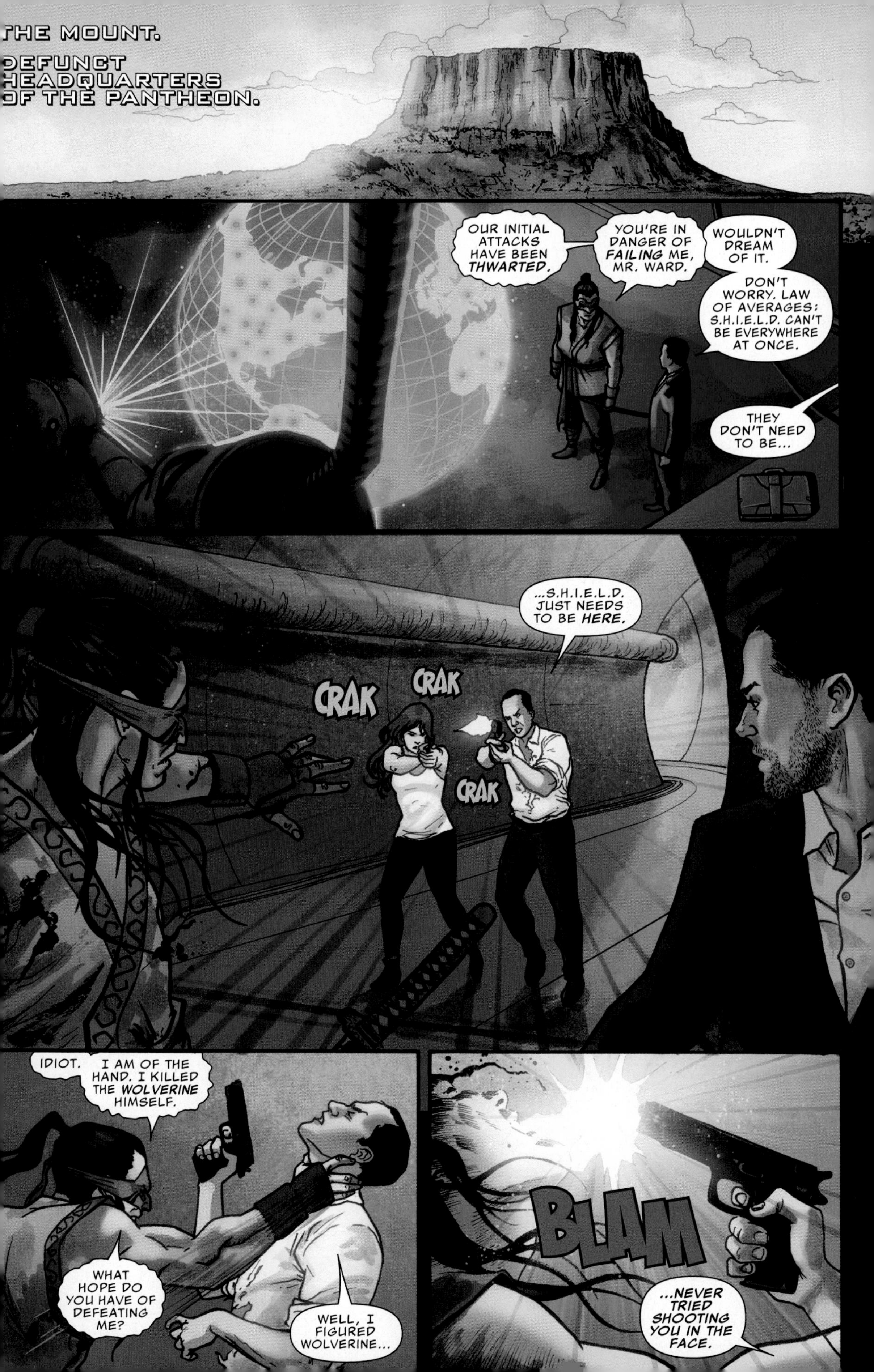
THE MOUNT.
DEFUNCT HEADQUARTERS OF THE PANTHEON.
OUR INITIAL ATTACKS HAVE BEEN THWARTED.
YOU'RE IN DANGER OF FAILING ME, MR. WARD.
WOULDN'T DREAM OF IT.
DON'T WORRY. LAW OF AVERAGES: S.H.I.E.L.D. CAN'T BE EVERYWHERE AT ONCE.
THEY DON'T NEED TO BE...
...S.H.I.E.L.D. JUST NEEDS TO BE HERE.
CRAK
CRAK
CRAK
IDIOT.
I AM OF THE HAND. I KILLED THE WOLVERINE HIMSELF.
WHAT HOPE DO YOU HAVE OF DEFEATING ME?
WELL, I FIGURED WOLVERINE...
BLAM
...NEVER TRIED SHOOTING YOU IN THE FACE.

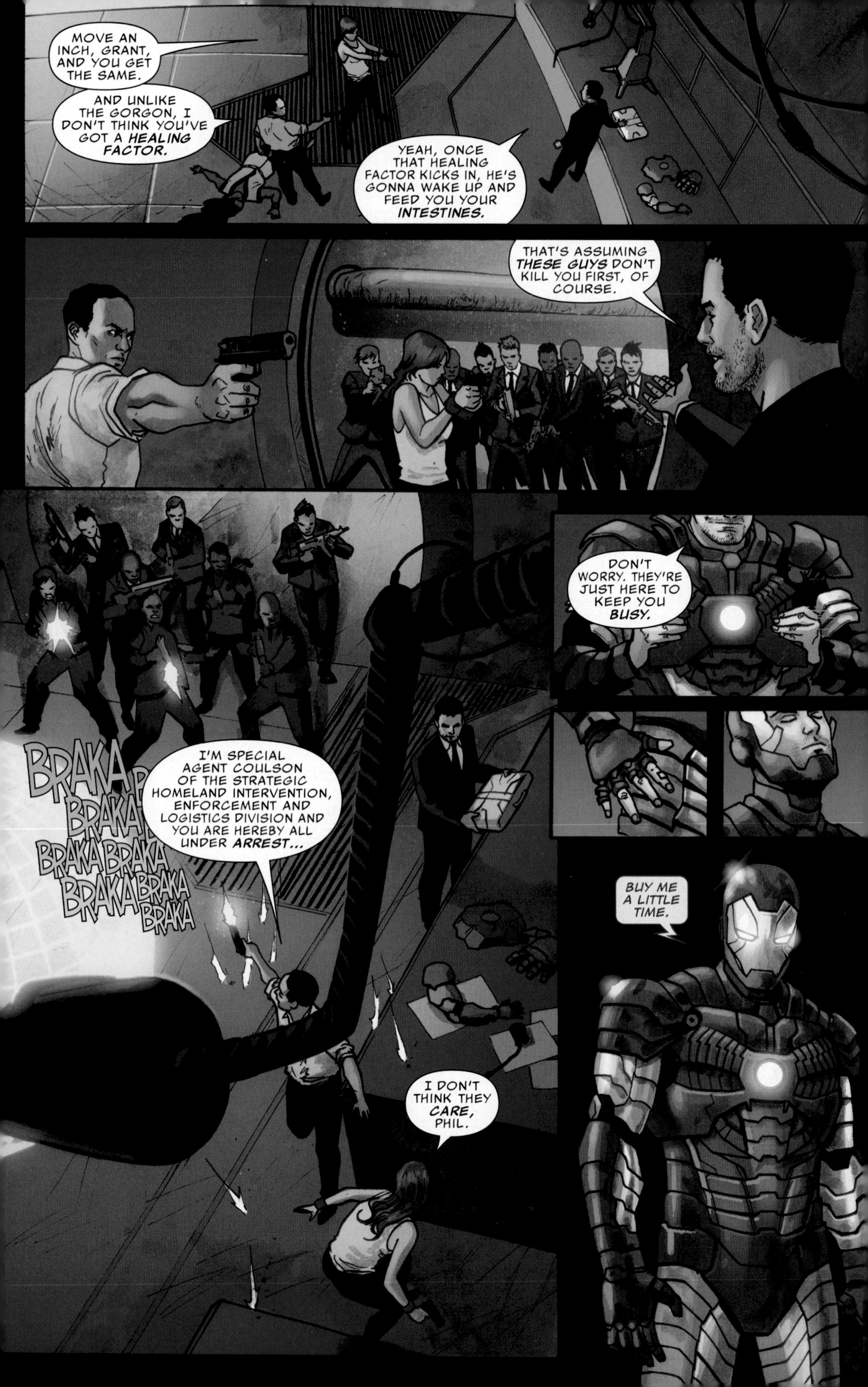
MOVE AN INCH, GRANT, AND YOU GET THE SAME.
AND UNLIKE THE GORGON, I DON'T THINK YOU'VE GOT A HEALING FACTOR.
YEAH, ONCE THAT HEALING FACTOR KICKS IN, HE'S GONNA WAKE UP AND FEED YOU YOUR INTESTINES.
THAT'S ASSUMING THESE GUYS DON'T KILL YOU FIRST, OF COURSE.
DON'T WORRY. THEY'RE JUST HERE TO KEEP YOU BUSY.
BRAKA BRAKA BRAKA BRAKA BRAKA BRAKA BRAKA
I'M SPECIAL AGENT COULSON OF THE STRATEGIC HOMELAND INTERVENTION, ENFORCEMENT AND LOGISTICS DIVISION AND YOU ARE HEREBY ALL UNDER ARREST...
I DON'T THINK THEY CARE, PHIL.
BUY ME A LITTLE TIME.

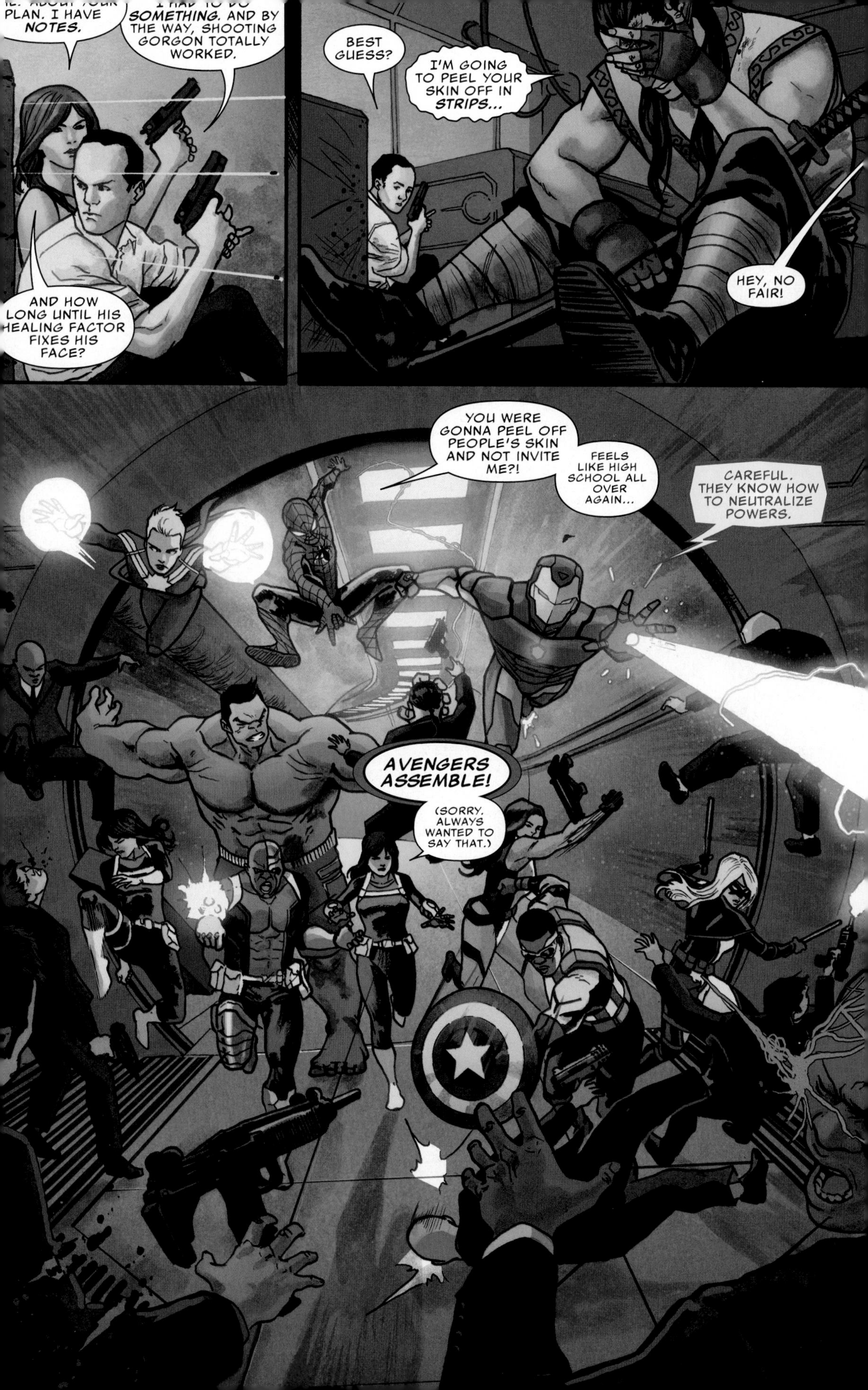
...ABOUT YOUR PLAN. I HAVE NOTES.
I HAD TO DO SOMETHING. AND BY THE WAY, SHOOTING GORGON TOTALLY WORKED.
AND HOW LONG UNTIL HIS HEALING FACTOR FIXES HIS FACE?
BEST GUESS?
I'M GOING TO PEEL YOUR SKIN OFF IN STRIPS...
HEY, NO FAIR!
YOU WERE GONNA PEEL OFF PEOPLE'S SKIN AND NOT INVITE ME?!
FEELS LIKE HIGH SCHOOL ALL OVER AGAIN...
CAREFUL. THEY KNOW HOW TO NEUTRALIZE POWERS.
AVENGERS ASSEMBLE!
(SORRY. ALWAYS WANTED TO SAY THAT.)

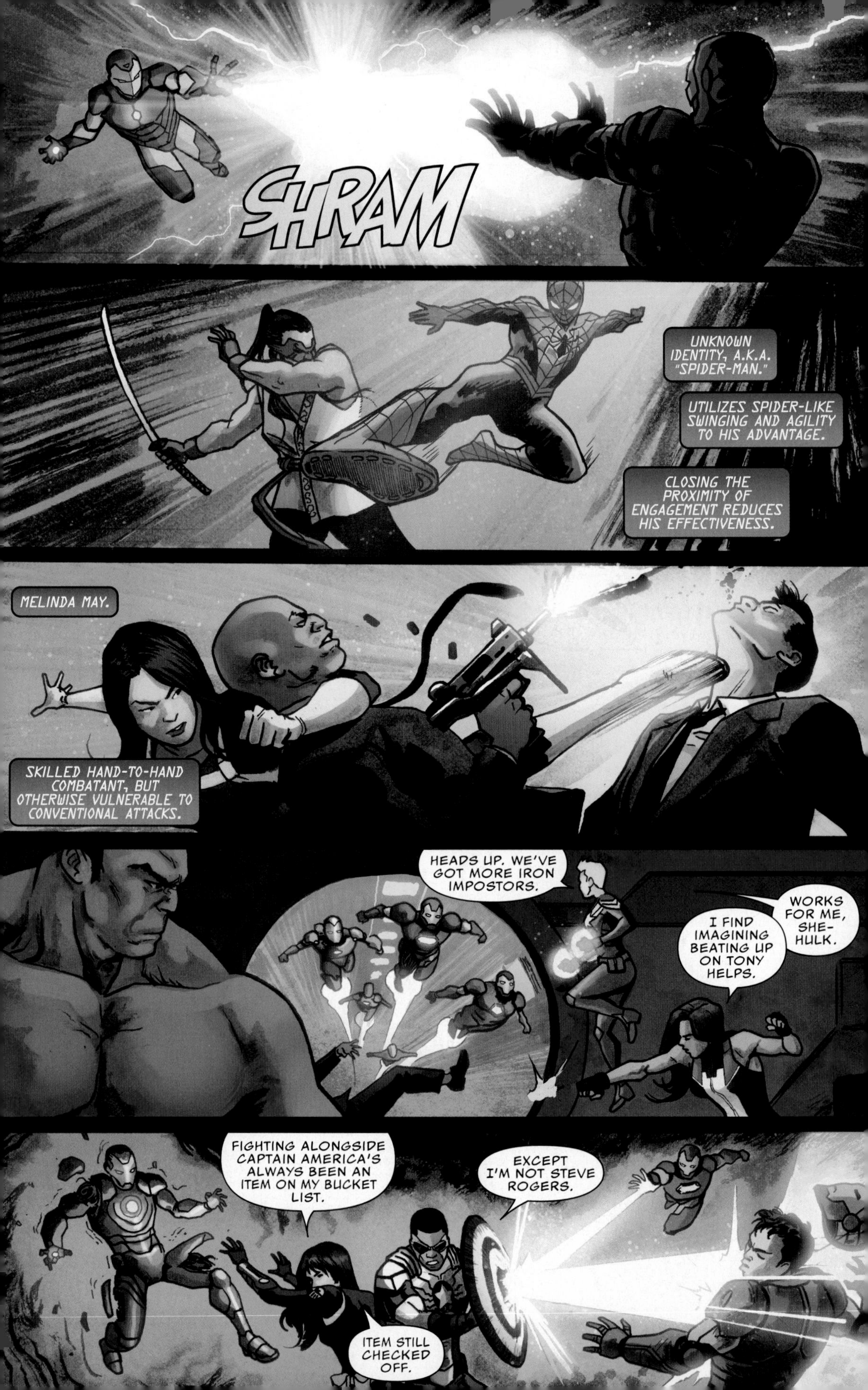
SHRAM
UNKNOWN IDENTITY, A.K.A. "SPIDER-MAN."
UTILIZES SPIDER-LIKE SWINGING AND AGILITY TO HIS ADVANTAGE.
CLOSING THE PROXIMITY OF ENGAGEMENT REDUCES HIS EFFECTIVENESS.
MELINDA MAY.
SKILLED HAND-TO-HAND COMBATANT, BUT OTHERWISE VULNERABLE TO CONVENTIONAL ATTACKS.
HEADS UP. WE'VE GOT MORE IRON IMPOSTORS.
I FIND IMAGINING BEATING UP ON TONY HELPS.
WORKS FOR ME, SHE-HULK.
FIGHTING ALONGSIDE CAPTAIN AMERICA'S ALWAYS BEEN AN ITEM ON MY BUCKET LIST.
EXCEPT I'M NOT STEVE ROGERS.
ITEM STILL CHECKED OFF.

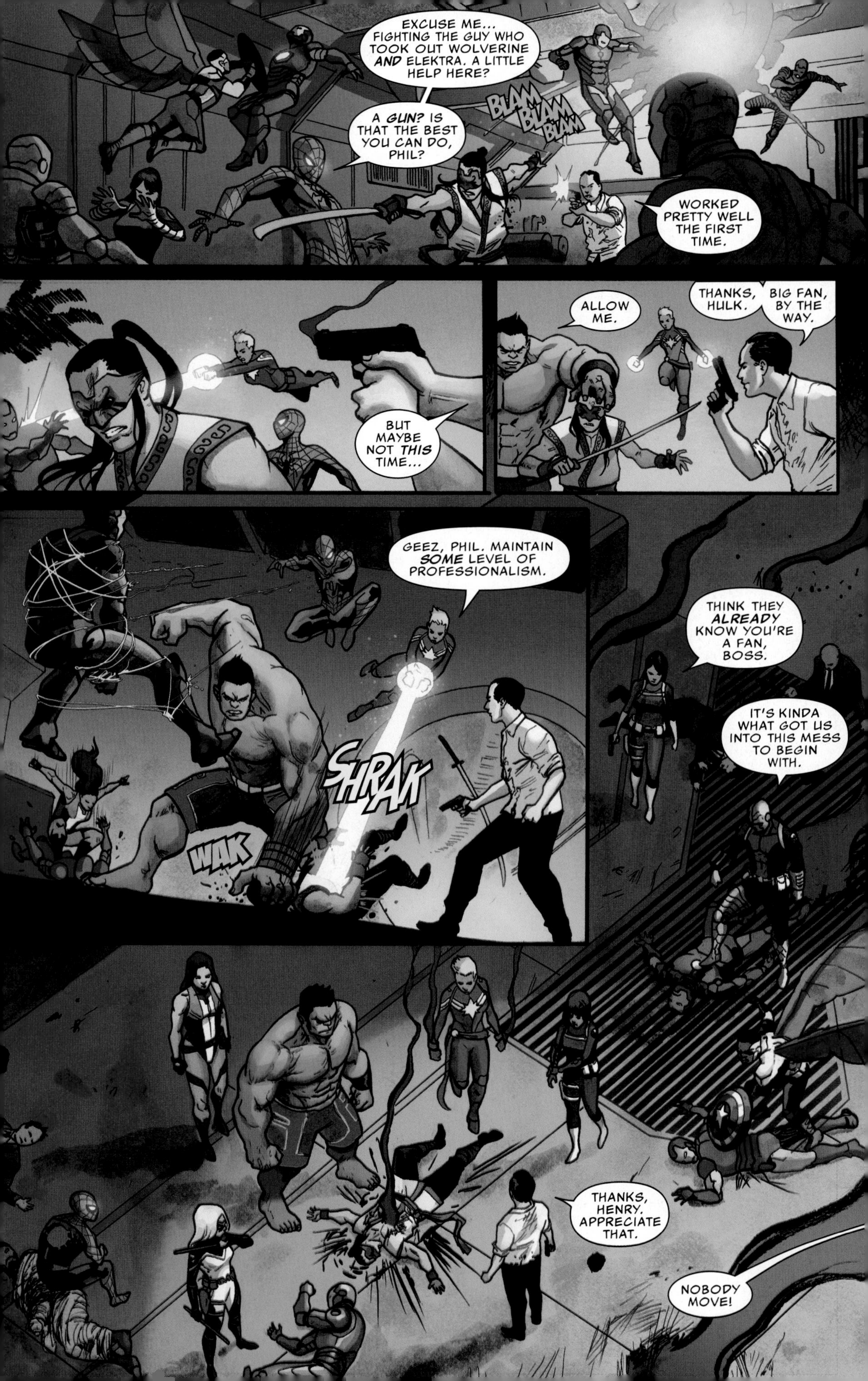
EXCUSE ME... FIGHTING THE GUY WHO TOOK OUT WOLVERINE AND ELEKTRA. A LITTLE HELP HERE?
A GUN? IS THAT THE BEST YOU CAN DO, PHIL?
BLAM BLAM BLAM
WORKED PRETTY WELL THE FIRST TIME.
BUT MAYBE NOT THIS TIME...
ALLOW ME.
THANKS, HULK.
BIG FAN, BY THE WAY.
GEEZ, PHIL. MAINTAIN SOME LEVEL OF PROFESSIONALISM.
SHRAK
WAK
THINK THEY ALREADY KNOW YOU'RE A FAN, BOSS.
IT'S KINDA WHAT GOT US INTO THIS MESS TO BEGIN WITH.
THANKS, HENRY. APPRECIATE THAT.
NOBODY MOVE!

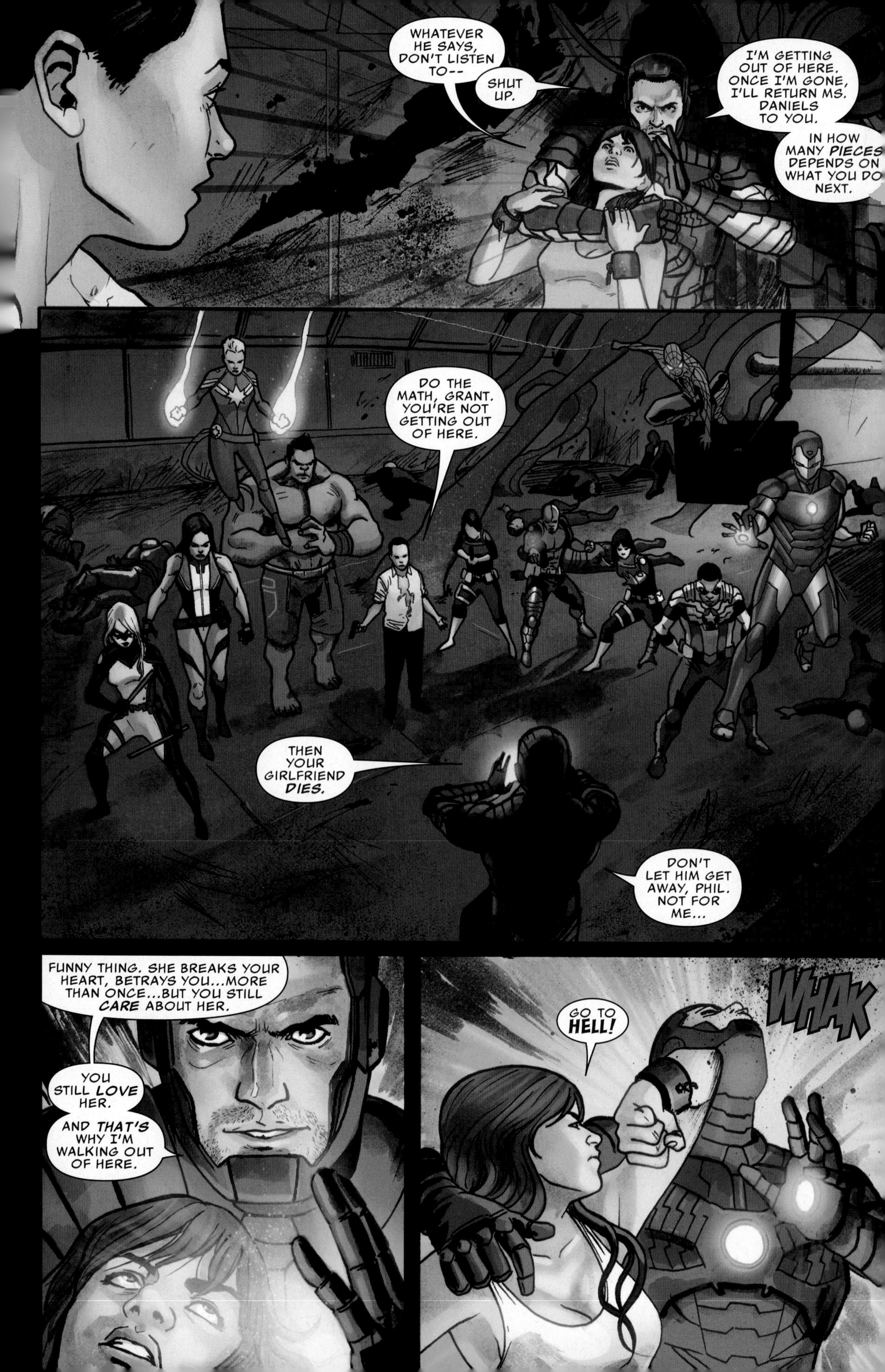
WHATEVER HE SAYS, DON'T LISTEN TO--
SHUT UP.
I'M GETTING OUT OF HERE. ONCE I'M GONE, I'LL RETURN MS. DANIELS TO YOU.
IN HOW MANY PIECES DEPENDS ON WHAT YOU DO NEXT.
DO THE MATH, GRANT. YOU'RE NOT GETTING OUT OF HERE.
THEN YOUR GIRLFRIEND DIES.
DON'T LET HIM GET AWAY, PHIL. NOT FOR ME...
FUNNY THING. SHE BREAKS YOUR HEART, BETRAYS YOU...MORE THAN ONCE...BUT YOU STILL CARE ABOUT HER.
YOU STILL LOVE HER.
AND THAT'S WHY I'M WALKING OUT OF HERE.
GO TO HELL!
WHAK

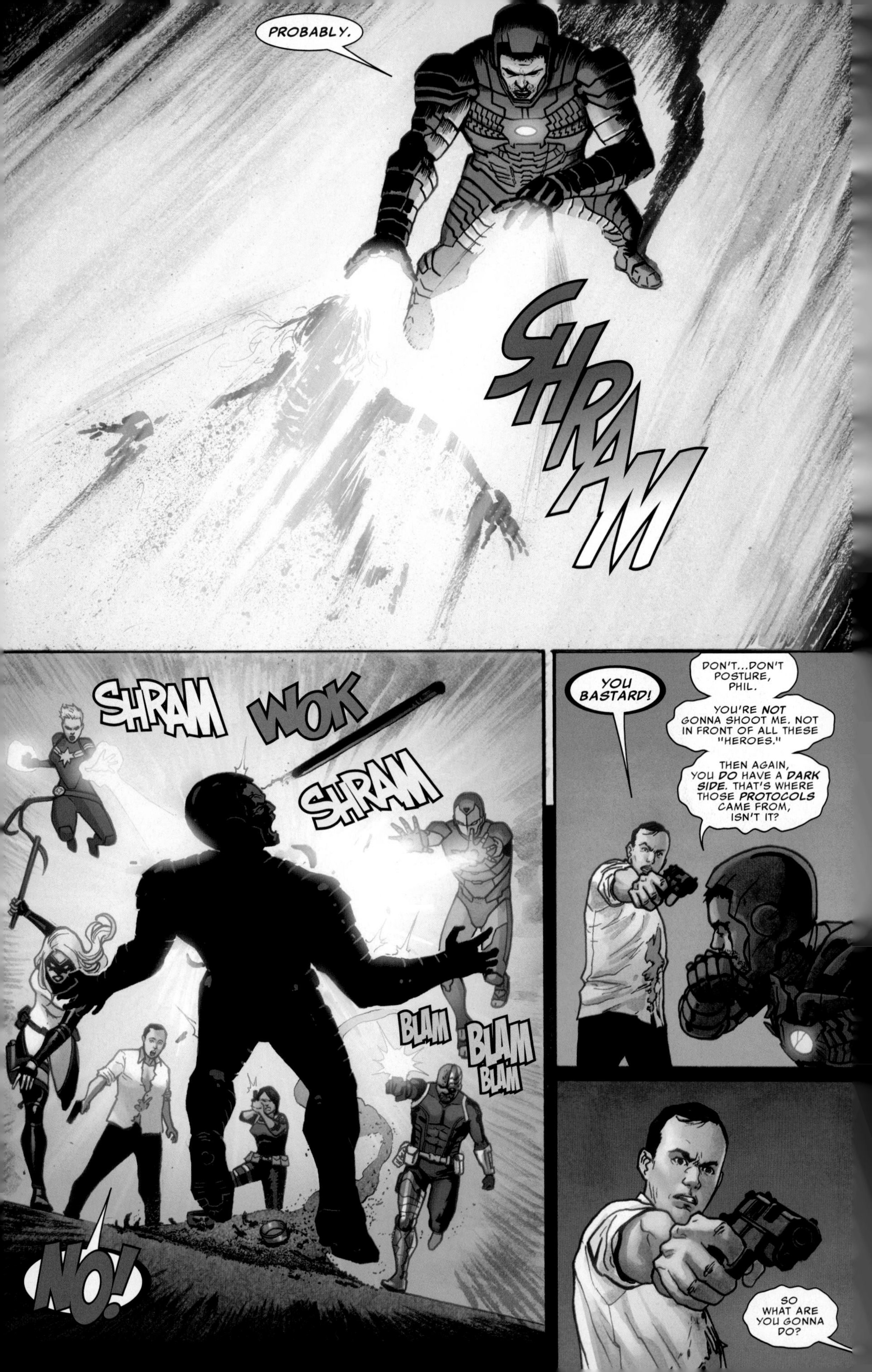
PROBABLY.
SHRAM
SHRAM
WOK
SHRAM
BLAM
BLAM
BLAM
NO!
YOU BASTARD!
DON'T...DON'T POSTURE, PHIL.
YOU'RE NOT GONNA SHOOT ME. NOT IN FRONT OF ALL THESE "HEROES."
THEN AGAIN, YOU DO HAVE A DARK SIDE. THAT'S WHERE THOSE PROTOCOLS CAME FROM, ISN'T IT?
SO WHAT ARE YOU GONNA DO?

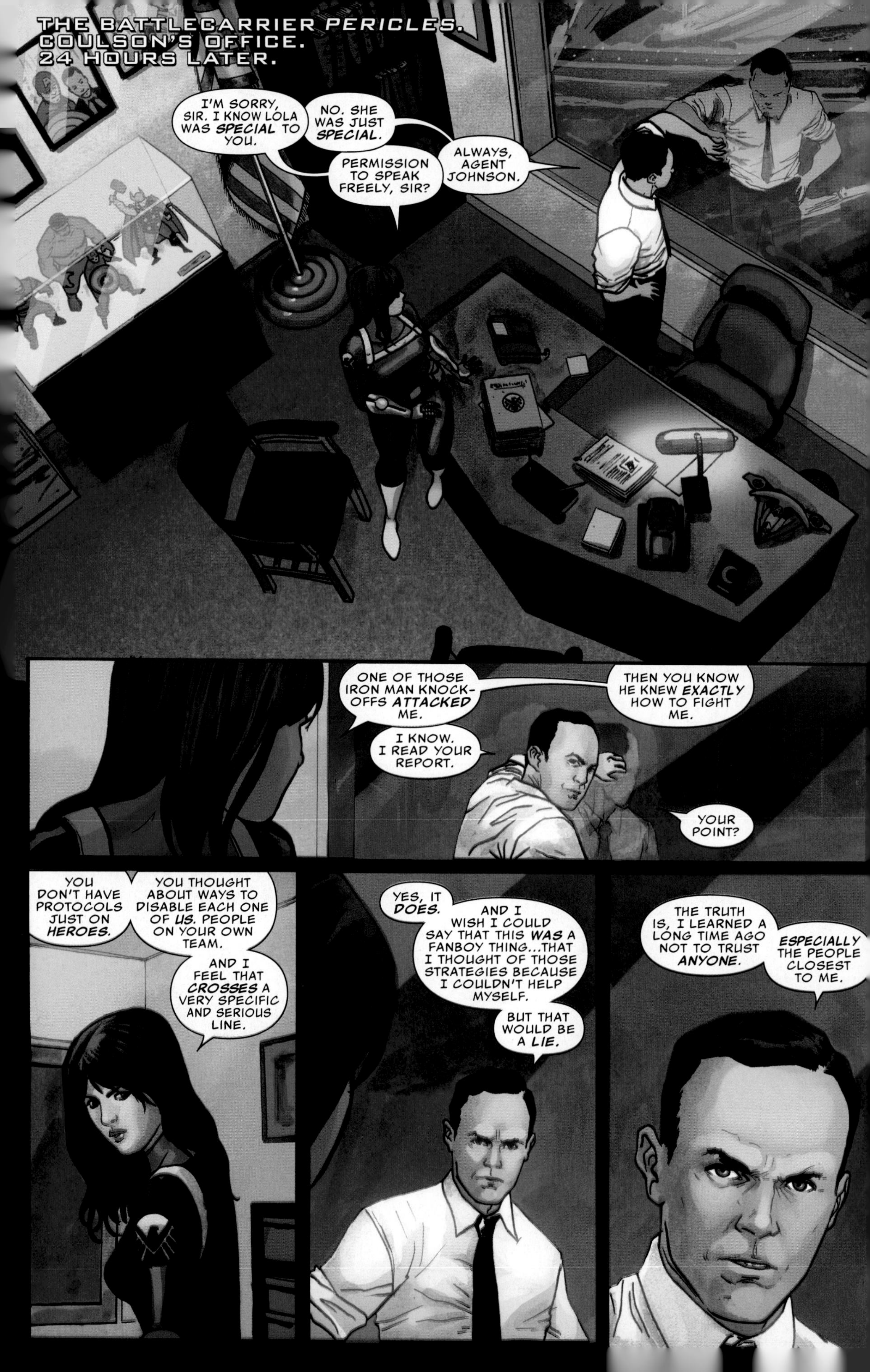
THE BATTLECARRIER PERICLES. COULSON'S OFFICE. 24 HOURS LATER.
I'M SORRY, SIR. I KNOW LOLA WAS SPECIAL TO YOU.
NO. SHE WAS JUST SPECIAL.
PERMISSION TO SPEAK FREELY, SIR?
ALWAYS, AGENT JOHNSON.
ONE OF THOSE IRON MAN KNOCK-OFFS ATTACKED ME.
I KNOW. I READ YOUR REPORT.
THEN YOU KNOW HE KNEW EXACTLY HOW TO FIGHT ME.
YOUR POINT?
YOU DON'T HAVE PROTOCOLS JUST ON HEROES.
YOU THOUGHT ABOUT WAYS TO DISABLE EACH ONE OF US. PEOPLE ON YOUR OWN TEAM.
AND I FEEL THAT CROSSES A VERY SPECIFIC AND SERIOUS LINE.
YES, IT DOES.
AND I WISH I COULD SAY THAT THIS WAS A FANBOY THING...THAT I THOUGHT OF THOSE STRATEGIES BECAUSE I COULDN'T HELP MYSELF.
BUT THAT WOULD BE A LIE.
THE TRUTH IS, I LEARNED A LONG TIME AGO NOT TO TRUST ANYONE.
ESPECIALLY THE PEOPLE CLOSEST TO ME.

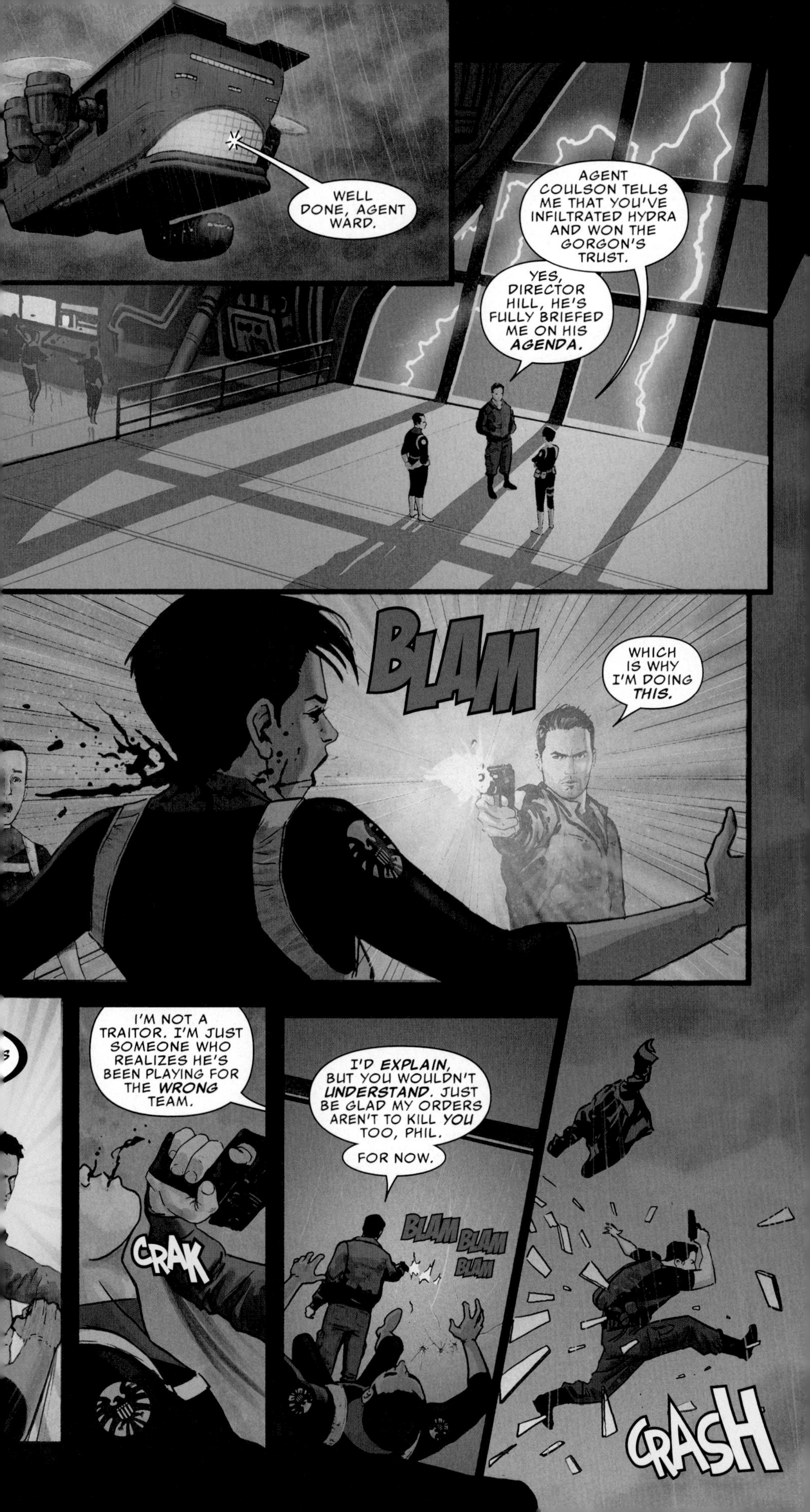

WELL DONE, AGENT WARD.
AGENT COULSON TELLS ME THAT YOU'VE INFILTRATED HYDRA AND WON THE GORGON'S TRUST.
YES, DIRECTOR HILL, HE'S FULLY BRIEFED ME ON HIS AGENDA.
BLAM
WHICH IS WHY I'M DOING THIS.
I'M NOT A TRAITOR. I'M JUST SOMEONE WHO REALIZES HE'S BEEN PLAYING FOR THE WRONG TEAM.
CRAK
I'D EXPLAIN, BUT YOU WOULDN'T UNDERSTAND. JUST BE GLAD MY ORDERS AREN'T TO KILL YOU TOO, PHIL.
FOR NOW.
BLAM BLAM BLAM
CRASH

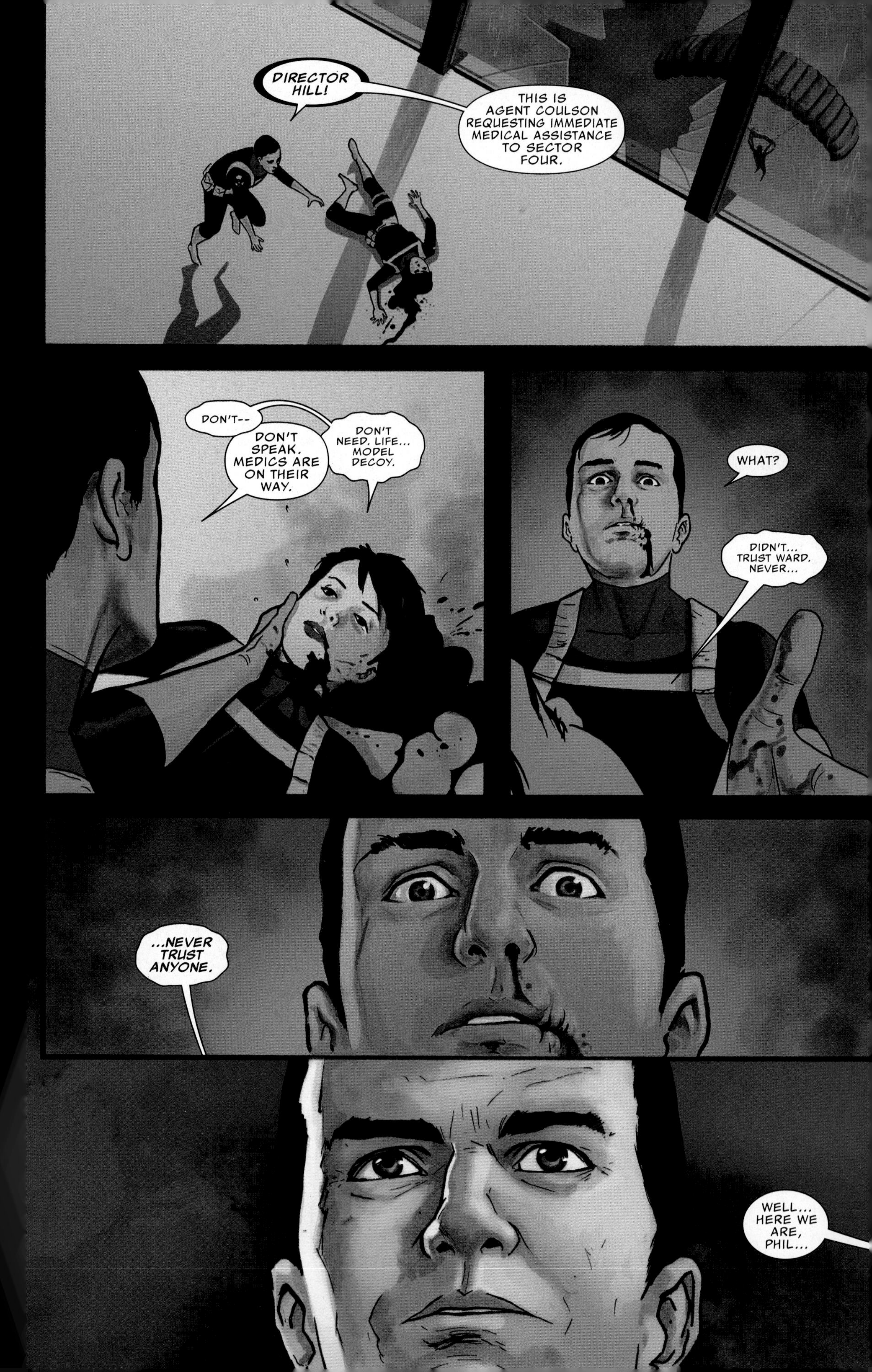
DIRECTOR HILL!
THIS IS AGENT COULSON REQUESTING IMMEDIATE MEDICAL ASSISTANCE TO SECTOR FOUR.
DON'T--
DON'T SPEAK. MEDICS ARE ON THEIR WAY.
DON'T NEED. LIFE... MODEL DECOY.
WHAT?
DIDN'T... TRUST WARD. NEVER...
...NEVER TRUST ANYONE.
WELL... HERE WE ARE, PHIL...

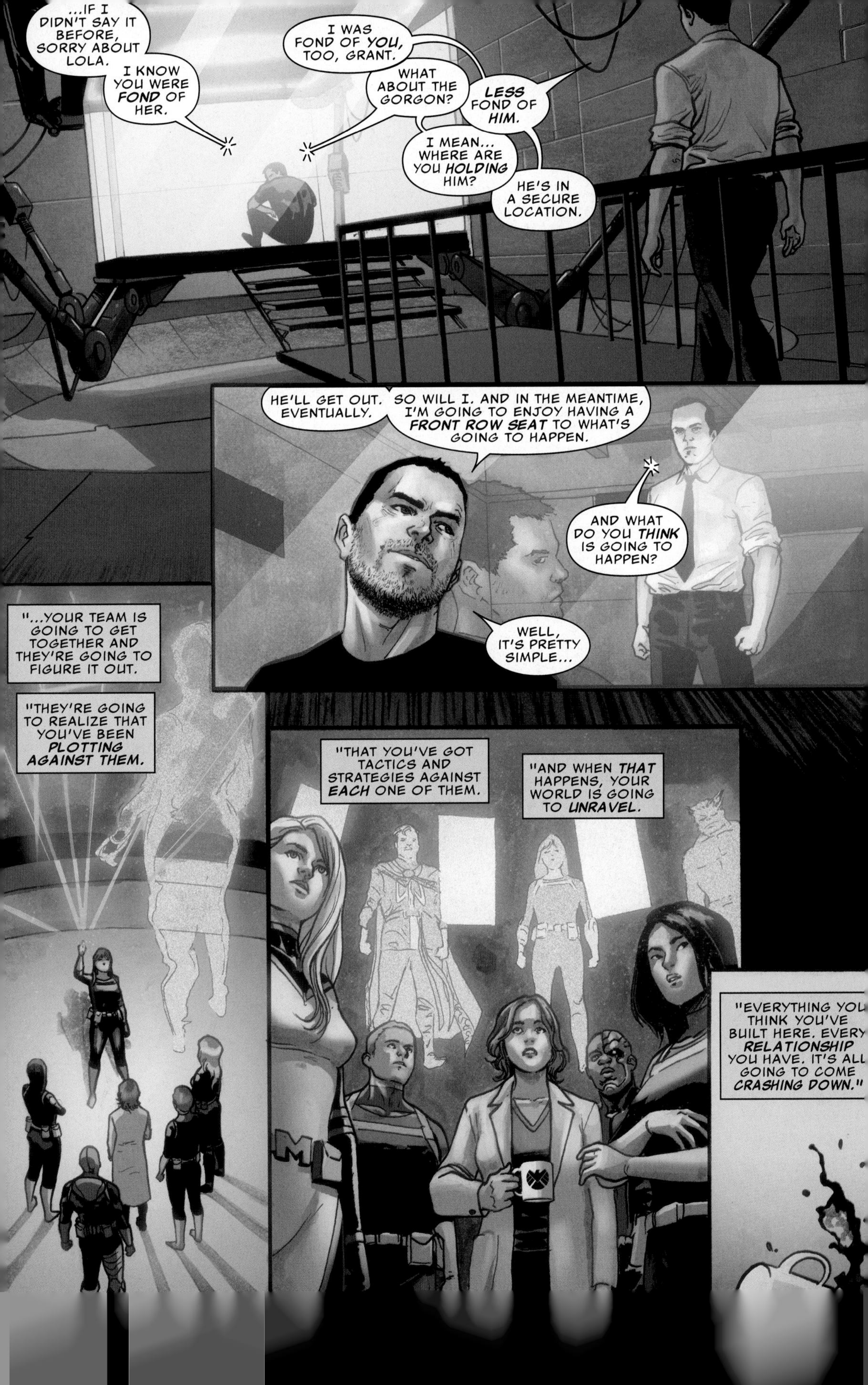
...IF I DIDN'T SAY IT BEFORE, SORRY ABOUT LOLA.
I KNOW YOU WERE FOND OF HER.
I WAS FOND OF YOU, TOO, GRANT.
LESS FOND OF HIM.
WHAT ABOUT THE GORGON?
I MEAN... WHERE ARE YOU HOLDING HIM?
HE'S IN A SECURE LOCATION.
HE'LL GET OUT. EVENTUALLY.
SO WILL I. AND IN THE MEANTIME, I'M GOING TO ENJOY HAVING A FRONT ROW SEAT TO WHAT'S GOING TO HAPPEN.
AND WHAT DO YOU THINK IS GOING TO HAPPEN?
WELL, IT'S PRETTY SIMPLE...
"...YOUR TEAM IS GOING TO GET TOGETHER AND THEY'RE GOING TO FIGURE IT OUT.
"THEY'RE GOING TO REALIZE THAT YOU'VE BEEN PLOTTING AGAINST THEM.
"THAT YOU'VE GOT TACTICS AND STRATEGIES AGAINST EACH ONE OF THEM.
"AND WHEN THAT HAPPENS, YOUR WORLD IS GOING TO UNRAVEL.
"EVERYTHING YOU THINK YOU'VE BUILT HERE. EVERY RELATIONSHIP YOU HAVE. IT'S ALL GOING TO COME CRASHING DOWN."

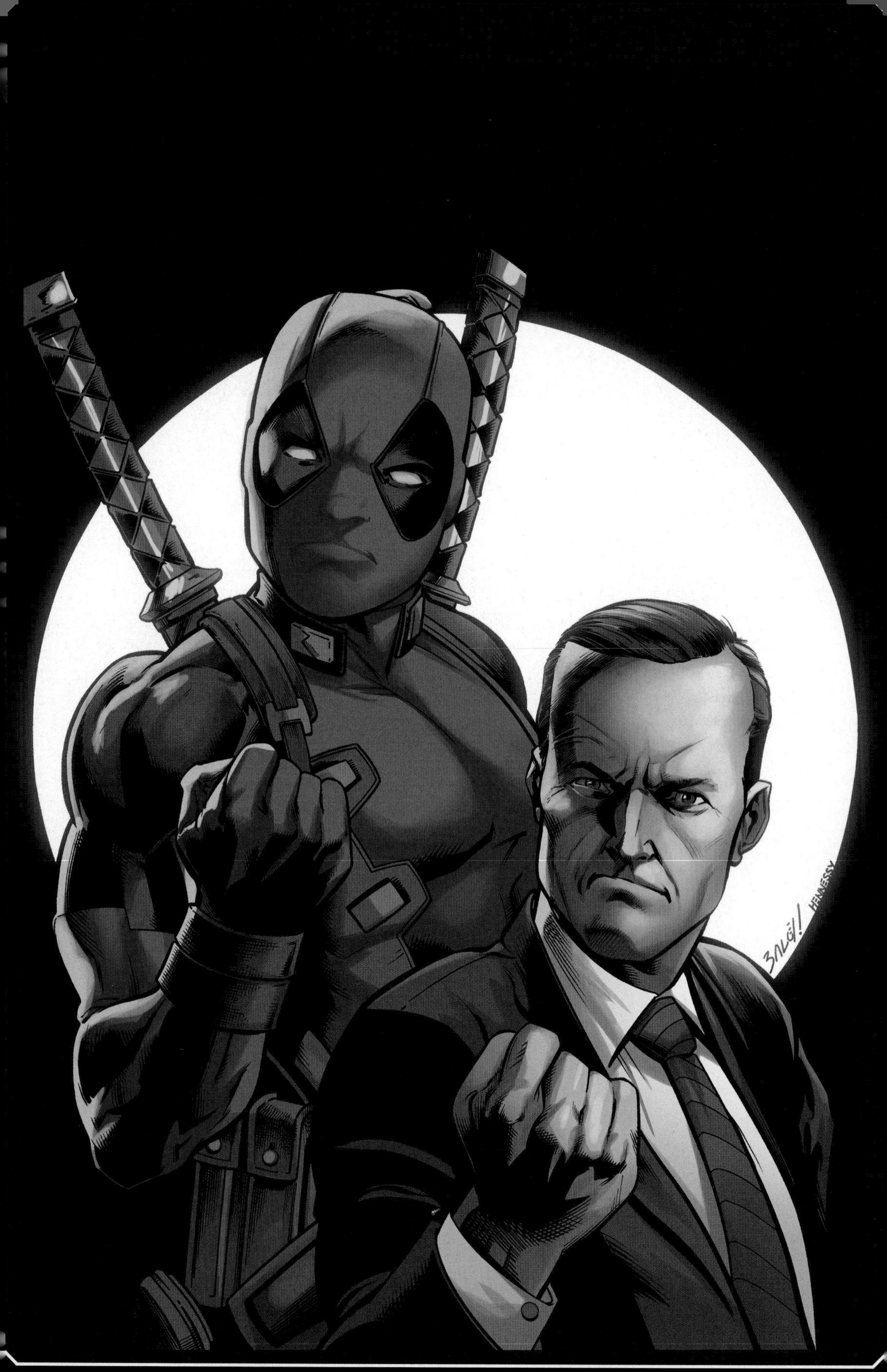

1 DEADPOOL VARIANT COVER FILE BY:
MARK BAGLEY, DREW HENNESSY & FRANK MARTIN

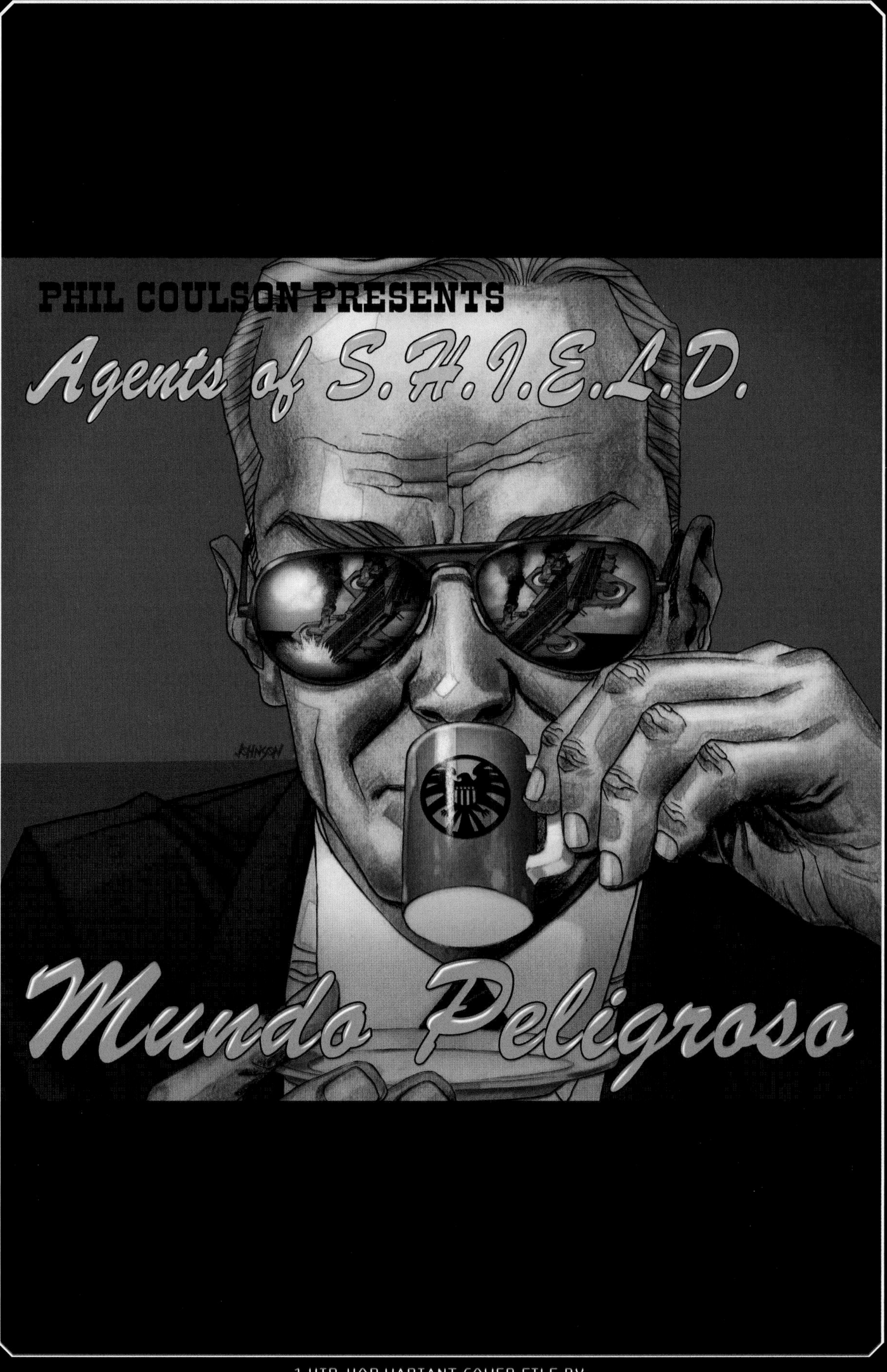
PHIL COULSON PRESENTS
Agents of S.H.I.E.L.D.
JOHNSON
Mundo Peligroso

1 HIP-HOP VARIANT COVER FILE BY:
DAVE JOHNSON

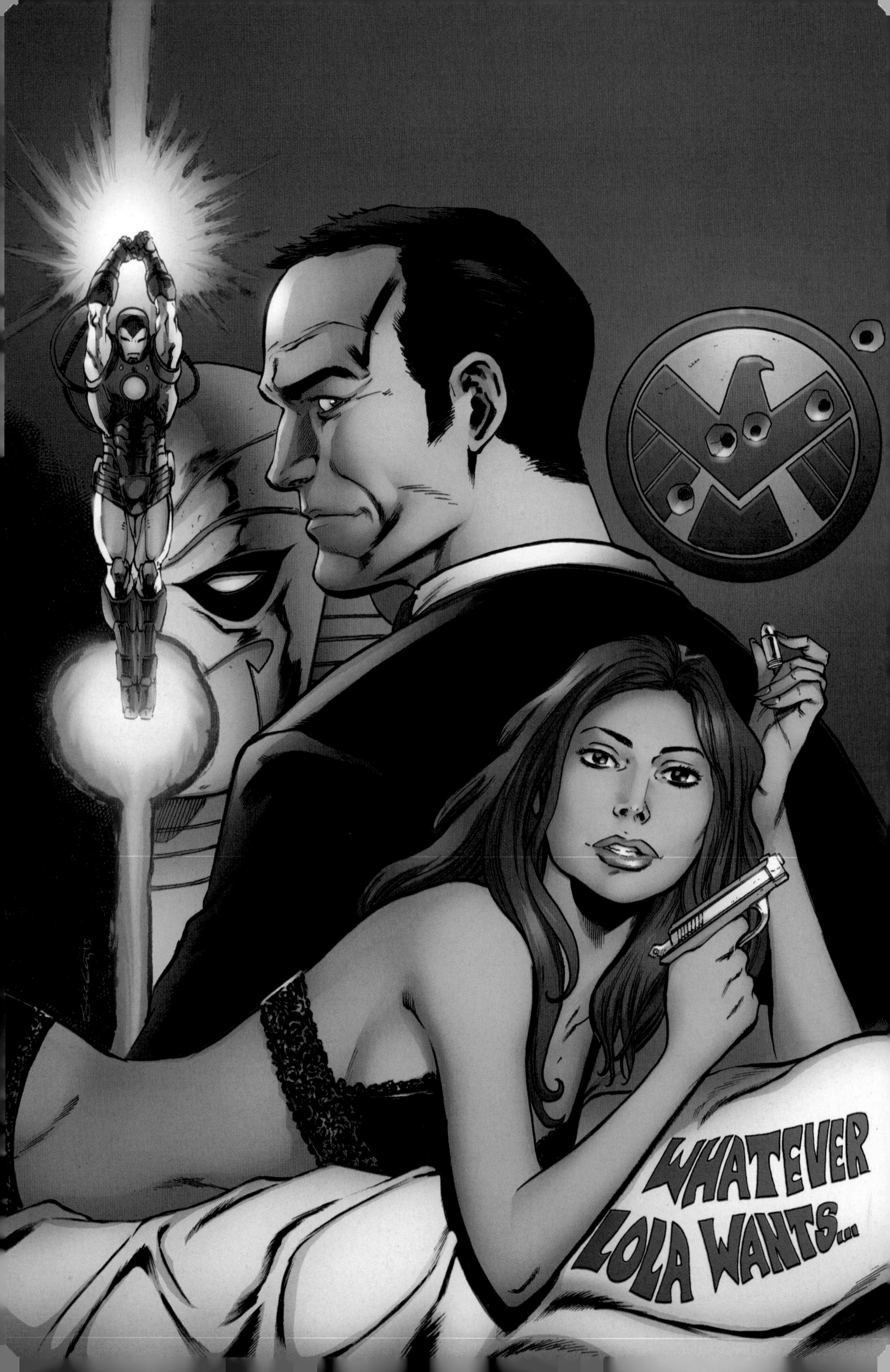
WHATEVER
LOLA WANTS...

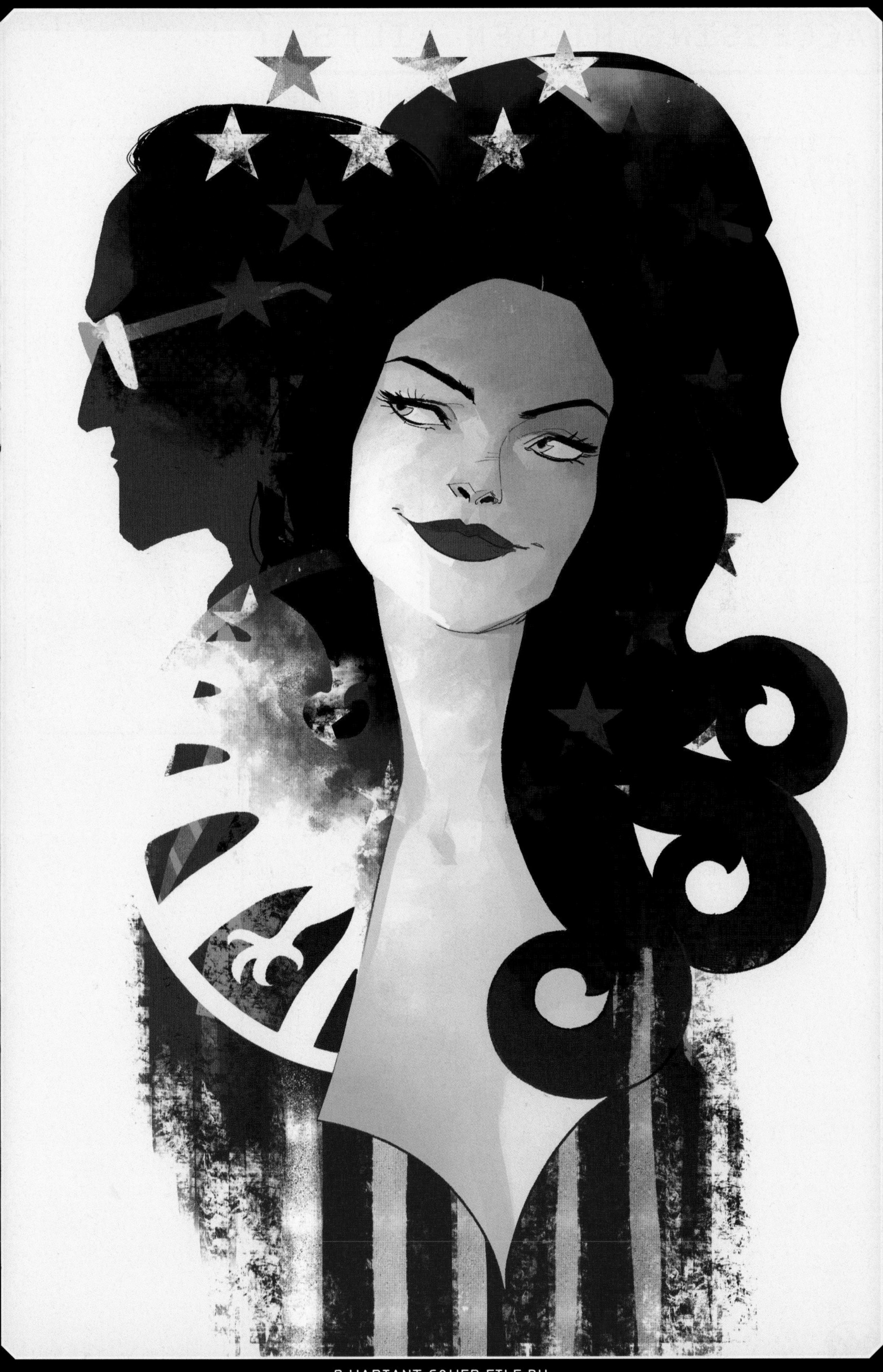

3 VARIANT COVER FILE BY:
OTTO SCHMIDT

ACCESSING HIDDEN FILES...

ISSUE 2 COVER SKETCHES BY **MIKE NORTON**

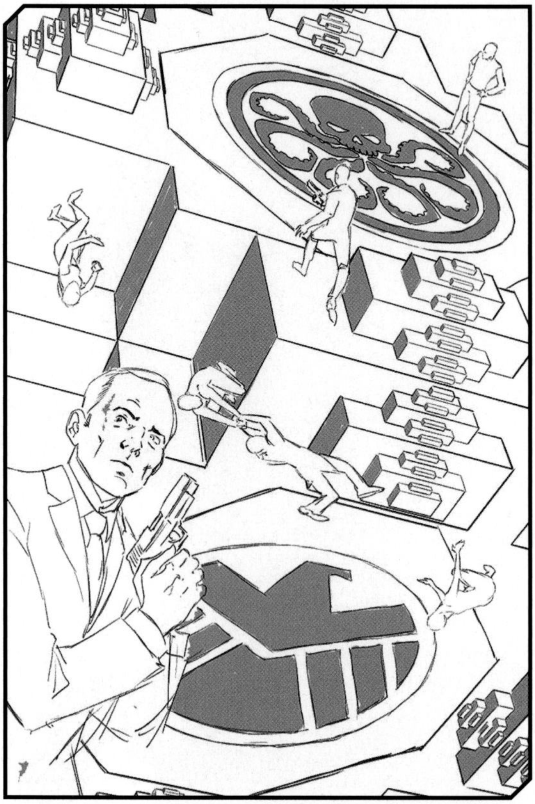

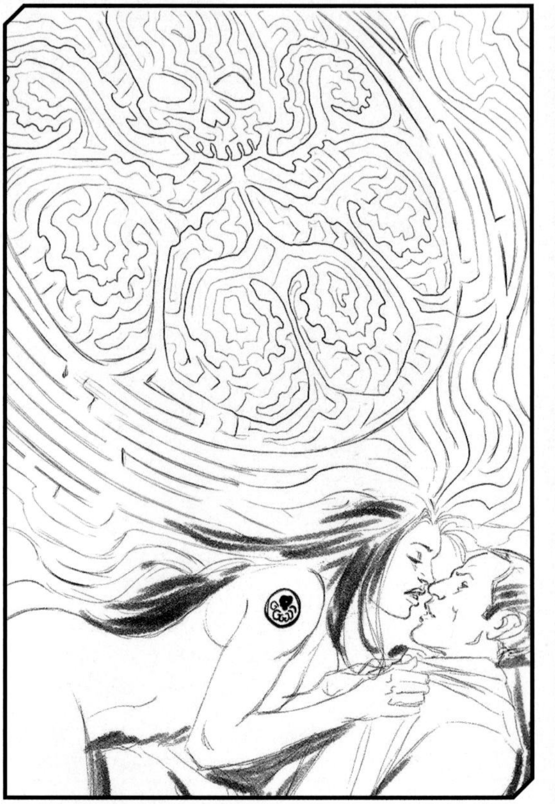

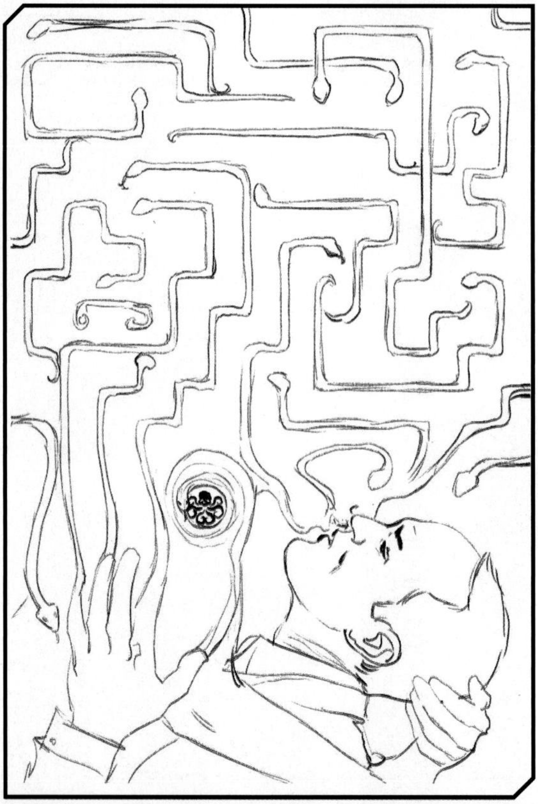

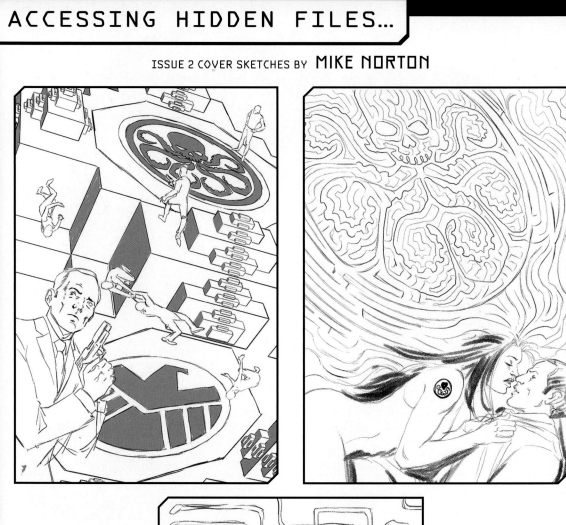

ISSUE 3 COVER SKETCHES BY **MIKE NORTON**

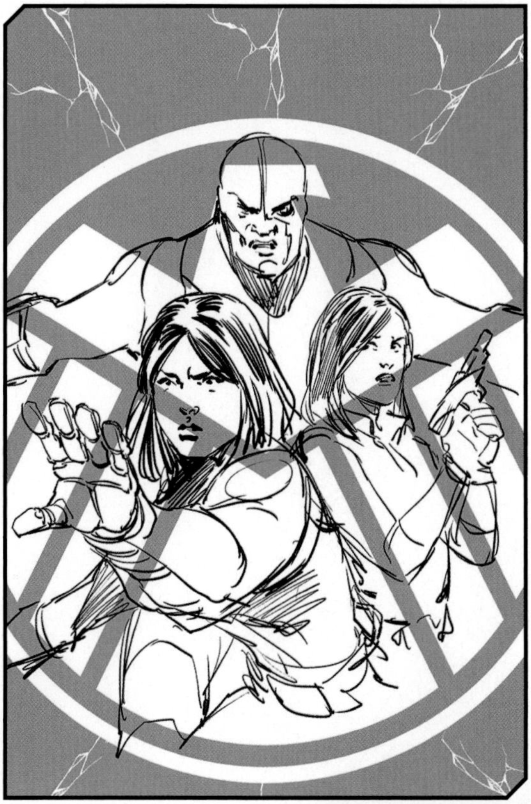

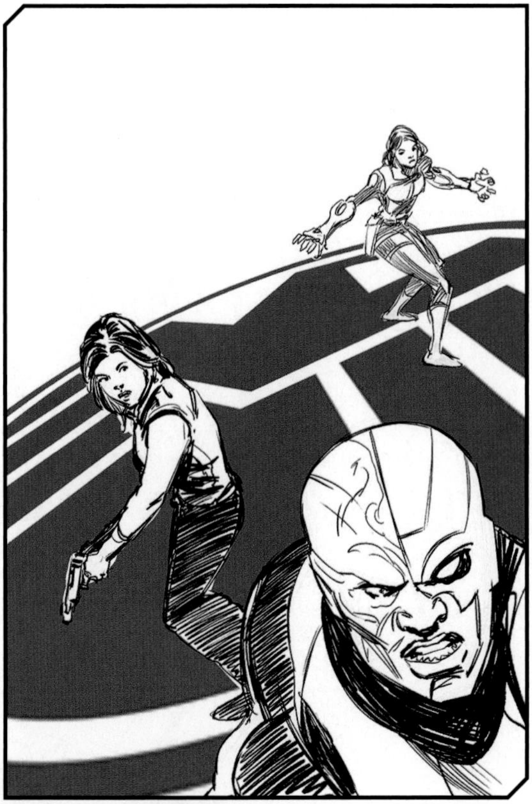

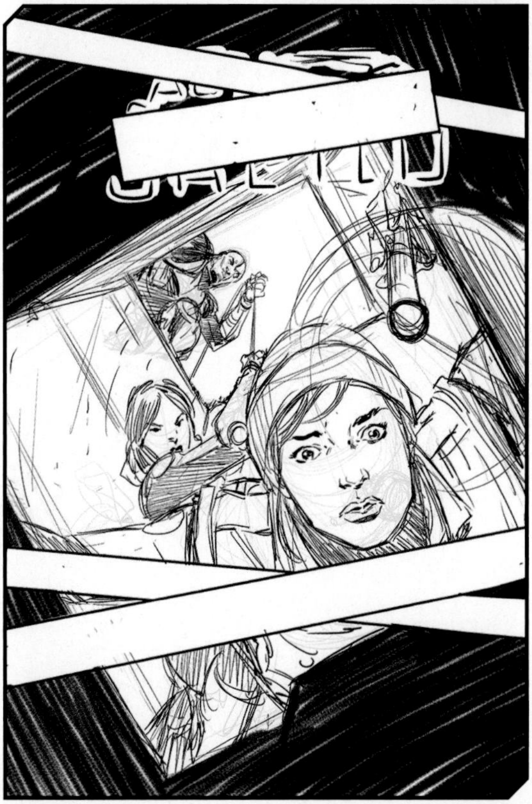

MOCKINGBIRD CHARACTER DESIGN BY **GIUSEPPE CAMUNCOLI**

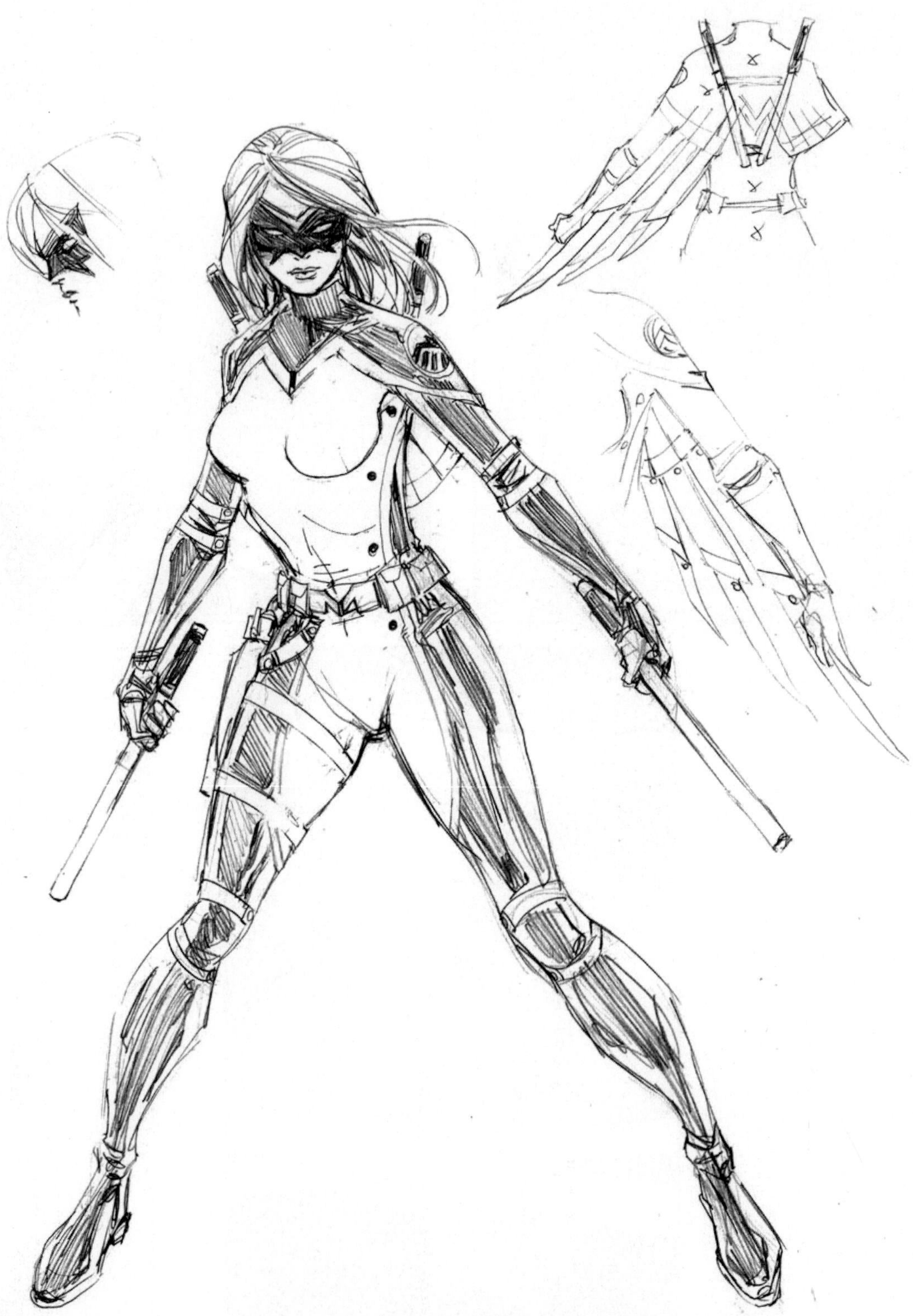